The Air Pilot's **Manual**

Volume 5

Instrument Flying

Radio Navigation Aids

Instrument Procedures

Night Flying

IMC Rating

Night Qualification

Trevor Thom

Airlife England

Copyright © 1989, 1997 Aviation Theory Centre

ISBN 1 84037 160 9

First edition published 1989
Reprinted with revisions 1990, 1991, 1992 and 1994
This second revised edition published 1997
Reprinted 1998
Third edition 1999

Origination by Bookworks Ltd, Ireland.

Printed in England by Livesey Ltd, Shrewsbury, England.

A Technical Aviation Publication Ltd title published
under licence by

Airlife Publishing Ltd
101 Longden Road, Shrewsbury SY3 9EB, Shropshire England
Email: airlife@airlifebooks.com
Website: www.airlifebooks.com

The Air Pilot's **Manual**

Volume 5

Contents

Editorial Team

Trevor Thom
A former Boeing 757 and 767 Captain with a European airline, Trevor has also flown the Airbus A320, Boeing 727, McDonnell Douglas DC-9 and Fokker F-27. He has been active in the International Federation of Airline Pilots' Associations (IFALPA), based in London, and was a member of the IFALPA Aeroplane Design and Operations Group. He also served as IFALPA representative to the Society of Automotive Engineers (SAE) S7 Flight-Deck Design Committee, a body which makes recommendations to the aviation industry, especially the manufacturers. Prior to his airline career Trevor was a Lecturer in Mathematics and Physics, and an Aviation Ground Instructor and Flying Instructor. He is a double degree graduate from the University of Melbourne and also holds a Diploma of Education.

Peter Godwin
Head of Training at Bonus Aviation, Cranfield (formerly Leavesden Flight Centre), Peter has amassed over 14,000 instructional flying hours as a fixed-wing and helicopter instructor. As a member of the CAA Panel of Examiners, he is a CAA Authorised Examiner (AE), Instrument Rating and Class Rating Examiner, Fellow of the Royal Institute of Navigation (FRIN), and is currently training flying instructors and applicants for the Commercial Pilot's Licence and Instrument Rating. Previously he was Chief Pilot for an air charter company and Chief Instructor for the Cabair group of companies based at Denham and Elstree. Peter has been Vice Chairman and subsequently Chairman of the Flight Training Committee on behalf of the General Aviation Manufacturers' and Traders' Association (GAMTA) since 1992.

Graeme Carne
Graeme is a BAe 146 Captain with a dynamic and growing UK regional airline. He has been a Training Captain on the Shorts 360 and flew a King Air 200 for a private company. He learned to fly in Australia and has an extensive background as a flying instructor in the UK. He has also been involved in the introduction of JAR OPS procedures to his airline.

John Fenton
A Flying Instructor for over 20 years, John was joint proprietor and assistant CFI of Yorkshire Flying Services at Leeds/Bradford, was a PPL examiner, and received the Bronze Medal from the Royal Aero Club for his achievements and contributions to air rallying. John made considerable contributions to the field of flying instruction in this country and pioneered the use of audio tapes for training.

Edward Pape
Director of MSF Aviation, Manchester and Portugal, and a former Chief Flying Instructor of the Lancashire Aero Club, Ed has amassed over 5,000 instructional flying hours and is dedicated to private pilot training.

Robert Johnson

Bob produced the first edition of this manual. His aviation experience includes flying a Cessna Citation II-SP executive jet, a DC-3 (Dakota) and light aircraft as Chief Pilot for an international university based in Switzerland, and seven years on Fokker F27, Lockheed Electra and McDonnell Douglas DC-9 airliners. Prior to this he was an Air Taxi Pilot and also gained technical experience as a draughtsman on airborne mineral survey work in Australia.

Warren Yeates

Warren has been involved with editing, indexing, desktop publishing and printing Trevor Thom manuals since 1988 for UK, US and Australian markets. He currently runs a publishing services company in Ireland.

Acknowledgements

The Civil Aviation Authority, British Airways/Aerad, Captain Horace Galop (British Airways Flying College, Prestwick), Captain R. W. K. Snell (CAA Flight Examiner [ret.]), Jeppesen & Co. GmbH, Allied Signal (Bendix/King Radio Corp.), Narco Avionics, Airtour International; Bill Bennett, Bill Constable, Robyn Hind, Rick James, David Langford, Robert Lawson, Ian Suren (ex-ICAO, Montreal), and the many other instructors and students whose comments have helped to improve this manual.

Introduction

A ir travel becomes much more reliable when aeroplane operations are not restricted by poor weather or by darkness. This
can be achieved with a suitably equipped aeroplane and a pilot
skilled in instrument flying.

■ *Figure 1* **Flying on instruments**

The instrument-qualified pilot and the instrument-equipped
aeroplane must be able to cope with restricted visibility, because
when you are flying in cloud, mist, smog, rain or snow, the natural
horizon and ground features are difficult, or even impossible, to
see.

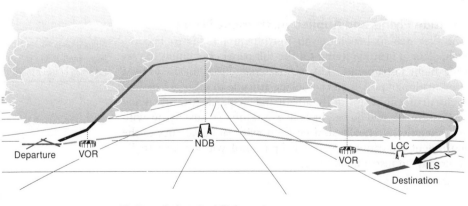

■ *Figure 2* **A typical flight on instruments**

You must learn to trust what you see on the instruments. We generally use our vision to orientate ourselves with our surroundings, supported by other bodily senses (such as feel and balance) which can sense gravity. However, even with our eyes closed, we can usually manage to sit, stand and walk on steady ground without losing control. This becomes much more difficult on the tray of an accelerating or turning truck, or even in an accelerating lift (elevator).

In an aeroplane, which can accelerate in three dimensions, the task becomes almost impossible – unless you have the use of your eyes. The eyes must gather information from the external ground features, including the horizon, or, in poor visibility, gather substitute information from the instruments. A pilot's eyes are very important. The starting point in instrument training is using the eyes to derive information from the instruments in the cockpit.

■ Figure 3 **The eyes, and the instruments**

Attitude Flying, and Applied Instrument Flying

The first step in becoming an instrument pilot is to become competent at attitude flying on the full panel containing the six basic flight instruments. The term *attitude flying* means using a combination of **power** and aeroplane **attitude** to achieve a desired **performance** in terms of flightpath and airspeed. Attitude flying on instruments will be taught as an extension of visual flying, with your attention gradually shifting from external visual cues to the instrument indications in the cockpit, until you are able to fly accurately on instruments alone.

Attitude flying on instruments is an extension of visual flying.

Partial (or limited) panel attitude instrument flying will be introduced fairly early in your training. For the limited panel exercises, the main control instrument, the *attitude indicator*, is assumed to have malfunctioned.

The *heading indicator* (direction indicator), often powered from the same source as the attitude indicator, may also be unavailable. Limited panel training will probably be practised concurrently with full panel training, so that the exercise does not assume an importance out of proportion to its difficulty. You will perform the same basic flight manoeuvres, but on a reduced number of instruments. The limited panel exercise will increase your instrument flying competence, as well as your confidence.

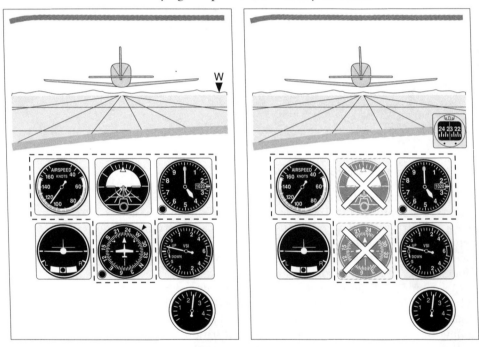

■ Figure 4 **The full panel (left) and partial panel (right)**

Unusual flight attitudes should never occur inadvertently! But practice in recovering from them will increase both your confidence and your overall proficiency. This exercise will be practised on a full panel, and also on a limited panel.

After you have achieved a satisfactory standard in attitude flying, both on a full panel and on a partial panel, your instrument flying skills will then be applied to en route flights using radio navigation aids and radar.

Procedural instrument flying (getting from one place to another) is based mainly on knowing where the aeroplane is in relation to a particular radio ground transmitter (orientation), and then accurately tracking TO or FROM the ground station. **Tracking** is simply attitude flying, plus a wind correction angle to allow for drift. Typical radio aids used are the ADF, VOR, DME and ILS, as well as ground-based radar. In many ways, en route navigation is easier using the radio navigation instruments than it is by visual means. It is also more precise.

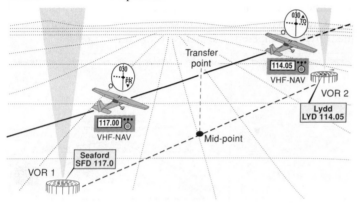

■ Figure 5 **En route tracking on instruments**

Having navigated the aeroplane on instruments to a destination, a visual approach and landing may be made if suitable conditions exist. If instrument conditions exist, then an **instrument approach** can be made. The option is there to make an instrument approach in visual conditions also, but this will probably add some minutes to the overall flight time.

Only published instrument approach procedures may be followed, with charts commonly used in the UK available from *Aerad* or *Jeppesen*. An instrument approach usually involves positioning the aeroplane over (or near) a ground station, and then using precise attitude flying to descend along the published flightpath at a suitable airspeed.

If visual conditions are encountered on the instrument approach before a predetermined minimum height (or **decision height**) is reached, then the aeroplane can be manoeuvred for a landing. If, however, visual conditions are not met before decision height for the approach, a **missed approach** should be carried out. The options are to climb away and manoeuvre for another approach, or to divert to another aerodrome.

■ Figure 6 **(opposite) Plan and profile of a precision instrument approach (Aerad chart for Luton ILS/DME Rwy 08)**

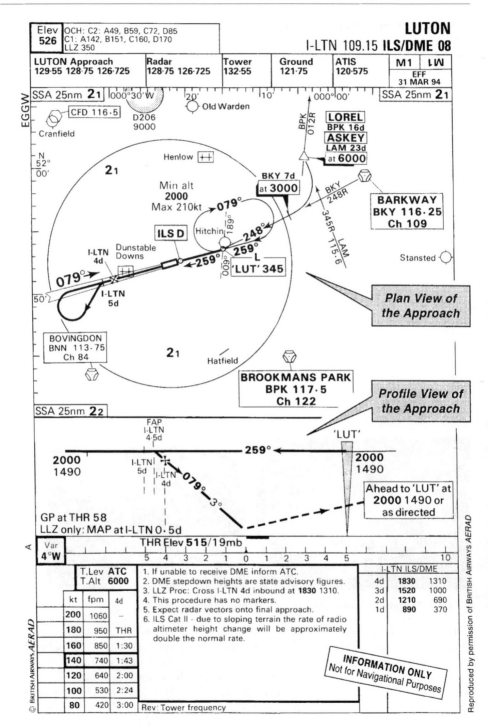

The Aeroplane, and the Ground Trainer

The **simulator** or **ground trainer** is a valuable training aid for practising both attitude flying and instrument procedures. It allows certain manoeuvres (for instance, climbing turns at 5,000 ft) to be practised without having to pre-flight check an actual aeroplane, then taxi out, wait in the queue, take off and climb for ten minutes. It is not dependent on weather – strong crosswinds on the runway making take-off impossible will not stop your practice. It allows easy conversation between the student and instructor without the distractions of engine noise or radio calls. Time can be 'frozen', while the instructor discusses some fine point before the exercise continues.

Manoeuvres can be repeated without delay and without interruption. Instrument procedures (such as an ILS approach to busy Manchester International Airport) can be practised repetitively in the simulator – a situation probably not possible in the aeroplane because of the heavy commercial traffic in the area. Procedures at aerodromes about to be visited in the aeroplane can be practised beforehand – very useful when about to proceed into unfamiliar territory.

The fact that most ground trainers do not move, and experience only the 1g gravity force, is not really a disadvantage for instrument training, since one of its aims is to develop the ability to interpret the instruments using your eyes, and to disregard the other senses. The ground trainer is also less expensive to operate than an aeroplane. This, and the many other advantages, make it an extremely valuable aid. But, it is still not an aeroplane.

■ *Figure 7* **The ground trainer (left) and aeroplane cockpit (right)**

Instrument flying in the aeroplane is the real thing! It is very important psychologically that you feel confident about your instrument flying ability in an actual aeroplane, so in-flight training is important. There will be more noise, more distractions, more duties and different sensations in the aeroplane. You will experience g-forces resulting from manoeuvring, and turbulence, which may mislead your senses. Despite the differences, however, the ground trainer can be used very successfully to prepare you for the real thing. And it will save you money. Practise in it often to improve your instrument skills. Time in the real aeroplane can then be used more efficiently.

Attitude Instrument Flying

Power plus attitude equals performance.

The **performance** of an aeroplane in terms of **flightpath** and **airspeed** is determined by a combination of the **power** set and the **attitude** selected. Aeroplane attitude has two aspects – pitch and bank. **Pitch attitude** is the angle between the longitudinal axis of the aircraft and the horizontal. **Bank angle** (or bank attitude) is the angle between the lateral axis of the aeroplane and the horizontal.

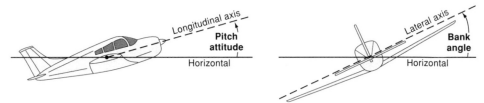

■ *Figure 8* **Pitch attitude (left) and bank angle (right)**

For a given aeroplane weight and configuration, a particular attitude combined with a particular power setting will always result in a similar flightpath through the air, be it a straight and level flightpath, a climb, a descent or a turn. Any change of power and/or of attitude will result in a change of flightpath and/or airspeed.

The pilot selects pitch attitude using the elevator. In visual conditions, you refer to the external natural horizon. At any time (in cloud, at night or in visual conditions) you can select a specific pitch attitude with reference to the **attitude indicator (AI)** on the instrument panel. In visual flight, the pitch attitude can be estimated from the position of the natural horizon in the windscreen. In instrument flight, pitch attitude is selected with reference to the AI, using the position of the *centre dot* of the wing bars relative to the *artificial horizon line*. The centre dot represents the nose of the aeroplane.

The pilot selects bank angle (bank attitude) using the ailerons. In visual conditions, you refer to the angle made by the external natural horizon in the windscreen. On instruments, you select bank angle on the attitude indicator, either by estimating the angle between the wing bars of the miniature aeroplane and the artificial horizon line, or from the *sky pointer* position on a graduated scale at the top of the AI.

■ *Figure 9* **Low pitch attitude, and wings level**

■ *Figure 10* **Level pitch attitude, and right bank**

Most of your attention during flight, irrespective of whether you are flying visually or on instruments, is concerned with achieving and holding a suitable attitude. A very important skill to develop when flying on instruments, therefore, is to check the attitude indicator every few seconds. Other tasks must, of course, be performed, and there are other instruments to look at as well, but the eyes should always return fairly quickly to the AI.

Check the attitude indicator every few seconds.

To achieve the desired **performance** (in terms of flightpath and airspeed), you must not only place the aeroplane in a suitable **attitude** with the flight controls, you must also apply suitable **power** with the throttle. Just because the aeroplane has a high pitch attitude does not mean that it will climb – it requires climb power as well as climb attitude to do this. With less power, it may not climb at all. *Attitude flying* is the name given to this skill – controlling the aeroplane's flightpath and airspeed with changes in attitude and power. The techniques used in attitude flying are the same visually or on instruments.

Pitch Attitude

The pitch attitude is the geometric relationship between the longitudinal axis of the aeroplane and the horizontal. **Pitch attitude** refers to the aeroplane's inclination to the horizontal, and not to where it is going. The **angle of attack,** however, is the angle between the wing chord and the relative airflow. The angle of attack, therefore, is closely related to flightpath. Pitch attitude and angle of attack are different, but they are related in the sense that, if the pitch attitude is raised, then the angle of attack is increased. Conversely, if the pitch attitude is lowered, then the angle of attack is decreased.

*Pitch attitude is **not** angle of attack.*

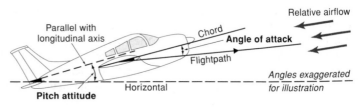

■ *Figure 11* **Pitch attitude and angle of attack are not the same**

An Aeroplane Flies Identically, In or Out of Cloud

The principles of flight do not change when an aeroplane enters cloud. The aeroplane will fly identically, and be controlled in the same way. The only difference is that the pilot loses reference to external visual clues, and must derive substitute information from the instrument panel.

When flying visually, you derive a lot of information from the instruments. The exact altitude, for instance, cannot be determined from external features – you must look at the altimeter. Similarly, the precise heading is found on the heading indicator or the magnetic compass, and not by reference to external features. The precise airspeed can only be determined from the airspeed indicator. To set a precise power, you must look (briefly) at the power indicator.

Balance, or coordination, in turns as well as in straight and level flight, is maintained precisely with reference to the balance ball, in both visual and instrument flight. The main change, when switching to instrument flying, is to transfer attention from the natural horizon outside the cockpit to the artificial horizon line of the AI in the cockpit.

IMC-rated or instrument-rated pilots are no different from other pilots, except that they have acquired more knowledge, and can derive more information from the instrument panel. An altimeter, for instance, can tell you more than just the current altitude – it also says something about the rate of change of height, and if the selected pitch attitude is correct for height to be maintained. Similarly, the heading indicator can provide heading information, but it also can tell you if the wings are banked – if the heading is changing and the balance ball is centred, then the wings are banked.

The skill of instrument interpretation (deriving all sorts of information from various instruments) will develop quickly during your instrument training. It is not difficult – it just takes practice. The aeroplane will fly the same on instruments as when you are flying visually, and you will control it in the usual way. The information required to do this is available – on the instrument panel.

During instrument training, most manoeuvres will be performed initially in *visual conditions,* where the AI indications can be related to the appearance of the natural horizon in the windscreen. After a satisfactory standard of visual flying is demonstrated, practice will occur in *simulated instrument conditions* – probably achieved by your instructor restricting your view of the outside world with a screen or hood.

His view will remain unobstructed so that he can act as *safety pilot,* keep a lookout for other aircraft, and monitor the position of the aeroplane. You will concentrate on attitude flying using the instruments, interpreting their indications, and then responding with the controls. You should then be able to cope with actual instrument conditions.

A good understanding of each manoeuvre, and the ability to put it into practice in visual conditions, will speed up your instrument training. Volume 1 of *The Air Pilot's Manual* contains detailed briefings for each visual manoeuvre, if you happen to be a little rusty.

Scanning the Instruments

Scanning the instruments with your eyes, interpreting their indications, and applying this information is a vital skill to develop if you are to become a good instrument pilot.

Power is selected with the throttle, and can be checked (if required) on the power indicator. Pitch attitude and bank angle are selected using the control column, with frequent reference to the attitude indicator. With correct power and attitude set, the aeroplane will perform as expected. The attitude indicator and the power indicator, because they are used when controlling the aeroplane, are known as the **control instruments.**

The actual performance of the aeroplane, once its power and attitude have been set, can be cross-checked on what are known as the **performance instruments** – the altimeter for height, the airspeed indicator for airspeed, the heading indicator for direction, and so on.

A valuable instrument, important in its own right, is the clock or **stopwatch**. Time is extremely important in instrument flying. The stopwatch is used in holding patterns (e.g. 1-minute or 2-minute holding patterns), in timed turns (e.g. a 180° change of heading at rate 1, which is a change of heading at 3°/sec, will take 60 seconds), and it is also used to measure time after passing certain ground beacons during instrument approaches (e.g. knowing the groundspeed of the aeroplane, it is possible to determine the time it will take to travel a further known distance).

Another group of instruments on the panel contains the **radio navigation instruments,** which indicate the position of the aeroplane relative to selected radio navigation facilities. These radio navaids will be considered in detail later in your training, but the main ones are:

- **the automatic direction finder (ADF),** which has a needle that points at an NDB ground station;
- **the distance measuring equipment (DME),** which indicates the slant distance in nautical miles to the selected DME ground station; and
- **the VHF omni range (VOR)** cockpit display, which indicates the aeroplane's position relative to a selected track.

Figure 12 shows a typical instrument panel.

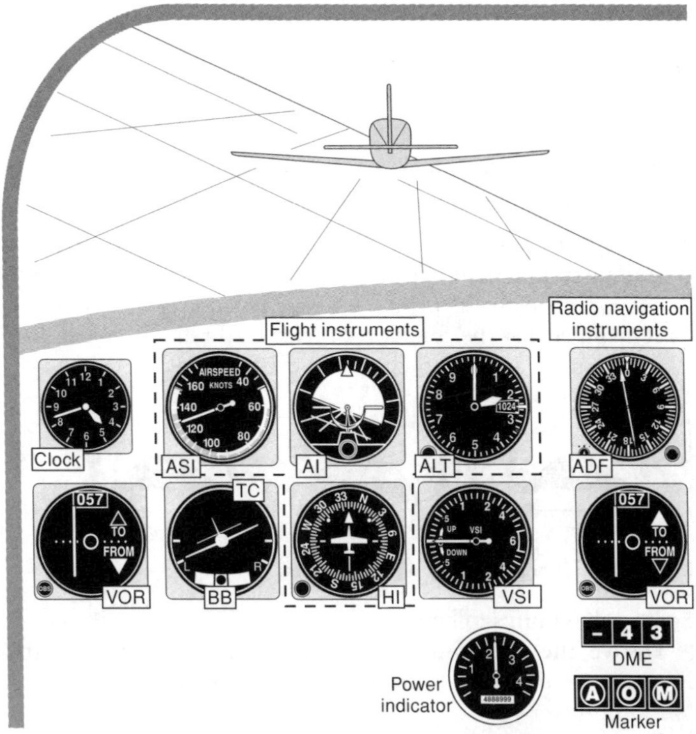

■ *Figure 12* **A typical instrument panel**

Your main scan is across six basic instruments:
•ASI •AI •ALT
•TC •HI •VSI

Scanning is an art that will develop naturally during your training, especially once you know what to look for. The main scan to develop initially is that of the six basic flight instruments – concentrating on the AI, and radiating out to the others as required. Chapter 1 covers instrument scanning in detail. Then, as you move on to en route instrument flying, the radio navigation instruments will be introduced.

Controlling the Aeroplane

During instrument flight, the aeroplane is flown using the normal controls according to the 'picture' displayed on the instrument panel. From this picture, you will, with practice, know what control movements (elevator, aileron, rudder and throttle) are required, either to maintain the picture as it is, or to change it.

When manoeuvring the aeroplane, a suitable **control sequence** to follow (the same as in visual flight) is:

1. **Visualise** the desired new flightpath and airspeed.

2. **Select the attitude** and the **power** required to achieve the desired performance by moving the controls, and then **checking** when the aeroplane has achieved the estimated attitude on the AI.

3. **Hold the attitude** on the AI, allowing the aeroplane to settle down into its new performance, and allowing the instruments that experience some lag to catch up.

4. **Make small adjustments** to attitude and power until the actual performance equals the desired performance.

5. **Trim** (which is essential, if you are to achieve accurate and comfortable instrument flight). Heavy loads can be trimmed off earlier in the sequence to assist in control, if desired, but remember that the function of trim is to relieve control loads on the pilot, and *not* to change aircraft attitude.

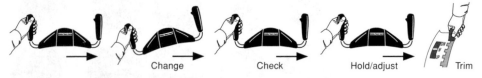

Change   Check   Hold/adjust   Trim

■ *Figure 13* **Change–check–hold–adjust–trim**

Some helpful hints follow.

☐ **Derive the required information** from the relevant instrument, e.g. direction from the heading indicator, altitude from the altimeter.

☐ **Do not be distracted** from a scan of the flight instruments for more than a few seconds at a time, even though other duties must be attended to, such as checklists, radio calls and navigation tasks.

☐ **Relax.** (Easier said than done at the beginning, but it will come with experience.)

☐ **Respond to deviations** from the desired flightpath and/or airspeed. Use the AI as a control instrument, with power as required. For instance, if you are 50 ft low on altitude, then raise the pitch attitude on the AI slightly and climb back up to height. Do not accept steady deviations – it is just as easy to fly at 3,000 ft as it is to fly at 2,950 ft. A lot of instrument flying is in the mind and, in a sense, it is a test of character as well as of flying ability. Be as accurate as you can!

☐ **Do not over-control.** Avoid large, fast or jerky control movements, which will probably result in continuous corrections, over-corrections and re-corrections. This can occur if attitude is changed without reference to the AI, or it might be caused by the aeroplane being out of trim, or possibly by a pilot who is fatigued or tense.

Sensory Illusions

Sensory illusions can lead you astray.

Most people live in a 1-g situation with their feet on the ground. However, some variations to this do occur in everyday life, for instance when driving a car. Accelerating a car, hard braking, or turning on a flat bend will all produce g-forces on the body different to the 1g force of gravity alone. Passengers with their eyes shut could perhaps detect this by bodily feel or with their sense of balance.

A right turn on a flat road, for instance, could be detected by the feeling of being thrown to the left – but it might be more difficult to detect if the curve was perfectly banked for the speed. A straight road sloping to the left (and causing the passenger to lean to the left) might give him the false impression that the car is turning right, even though it is in fact not turning at all. The position-sensing systems of the body, using nerves all over the body to transmit messages of feel and pressure to the brain, can be 'fooled' in this and other ways.

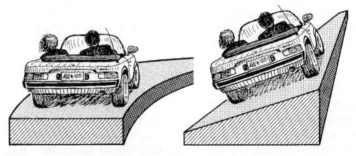

■ *Figure 14* **Turning right – or simply leaning?**

The organs within the inner ear, used for balance and to detect acceleration, can also be fooled, as in a car travelling around a banked curve. The sensing system interprets the g-force holding the occupants firmly and comfortably in the seats in a banked turn as a vertical force, which it is not. The inner ear organs also have other limitations, one being that a constant velocity is not detected (another train passing our train – is it moving, or are we?), nor is a very gradual change in velocity. False impressions of motion can also be caused by unusual g-forces, for instance by rapid head motion, or by lowering the head.

More complicated illusions can occur in an aeroplane, which, of course, has the ability to move and accelerate in three dimensions. Pulling up into a steep climb, for instance, holds a pilot tightly in his seat, which is exactly the same feeling as in a steep turn. With his eyes shut, it is difficult to say which manoeuvre it is.

Another example is: decelerating while in a turn to the left may give a false impression of a turn to the right. Be aware that your senses of balance and bodily feel can lead you astray in an aeroplane, especially with rapidly changing g-forces in manoeuvres such as this. The one sense that can resolve most of these illusions is sight. If the car passenger could see out, or if the pilot had reference to the natural horizon and landmarks, then the confusion would be easily dispelled.

The senses of balance and bodily feel can be misleading; trust your eyes and what the instruments tell you.

Unfortunately, in instrument flight you do not have reference to ground features, but you can still use your sense of sight to scan the instruments, and obtain substitute information. Therefore, an important instruction to the budding instrument pilot is "Believe your eyes and what the instruments tell you".

An instrument pilot must learn to believe the instruments.

It is good airmanship to avoid any situation in flight or prior to flight that will affect your vision. While in cloud at night, for instance, turn off the strobe light if it is bothering you. It could induce vertigo, a sense of dizziness or of whirling around, if enough of its flashing light is reflected into the cockpit. If flying in dark conditions with electrical storms in the vicinity, turn the cockpit lights up bright to minimise the effects of nearby lightning flashes. If expecting to fly out of cloud tops and into bright sunlight, have your sunglasses handy. Protect your sight!

While sight is the most important sense, and must be protected, also avoid anything that will effect your balance or position-sensing systems. Avoid alcohol, drugs (including smoking in the cockpit) and medication. Do not fly when ill or suffering with an upper respiratory infection (e.g. a cold). Do not fly when tired or fatigued. Do not fly with a cabin altitude higher than 10,000 ft amsl without using oxygen. Avoid sudden head movements, and avoid lowering your head. Looking for a dropped pen on the cockpit floor can have a strange effect on your balance.

Despite all these *don'ts,* there is one very important *do – do trust what your eyes tell you from the instruments.*

The Ratings and their Privileges

Information regarding requirements and privileges of the UK IMC Rating, and the Night Rating, is included as Appendices to this manual. Detailed information on these ratings and the full Instrument Rating is available in CAA publication CAP 53.

■ *Figure 15* **Typical light aircraft instrument panel**

Good, clear knowledge minimises flight training hours.

Section **One**

Instrument Flying
Techniques

Instrument Scanning

The *performance* of an aeroplane is determined by the *power* set and the *attitude* selected. In visual flying conditions, the external natural horizon is used as a reference when selecting pitch attitude and bank angle. The power indicator in the cockpit is only referred to occasionally, for instance when setting a particular power for cruise or for climb.

In instrument conditions, when the natural horizon cannot be seen, pitch attitude and bank angle information is still available to the pilot in the cockpit from the **attitude indicator (AI)**. Relatively large pitch attitude changes against the natural horizon are reproduced in miniature on the attitude indicator.

In straight and level flight, the wings of the index aeroplane should appear against the artificial horizon line, while in a climb they should appear one or two *bar widths* above it.

In a turn, the wing bars of the index aeroplane will bank along with the real aeroplane, while the artificial horizon line remains horizontal. The centre dot of the index aeroplane represents the aeroplane's nose position against the horizon.

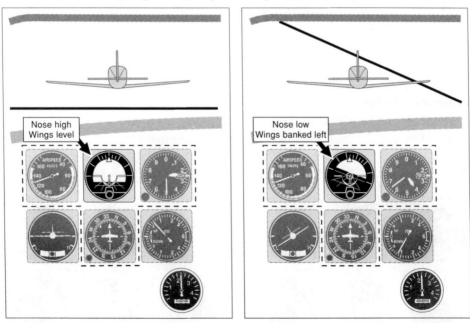

■ *Figure 1-1* **The attitude indicator (AI) is the master instrument for pitch attitude and bank angle**

Simple Scans

BALANCE (COORDINATION). The AI, while it shows pitch attitude and bank angle directly, does *not* indicate balance or yaw. Balance information can be obtained simply by moving the eyes from the AI diagonally down to the left to the **balance indicator,** to check that the balance ball is indeed being centred with rudder pressure. The eyes should then return to the AI.

HEADING. Directional information can be obtained from the **heading indicator (HI)** or from the magnetic compass. From the AI, the eyes can be moved straight down to the HI to absorb heading information, before returning to the AI. Each eye movement to obtain particular information is very simple, starting at the AI and radiating out to the relevant instrument, before returning again to the AI.

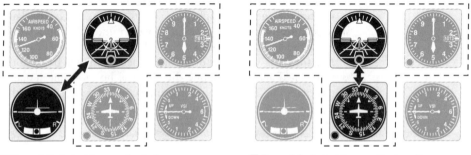

■ Figure 1-2 **A simple scan for balance**　　　■ Figure 1-3 **A simple scan for heading**

AIRSPEED. Airspeed information is also very important, and this is easily checked by moving the eyes left from the AI to the **airspeed indicator (ASI),** before returning them to the AI.

ALTITUDE. The **altimeter** is the only means of determining the precise altitude of the aeroplane, in visual as well as in instrument conditions. To obtain altitude information, the eyes can move from the AI towards the right where the altimeter is located, before moving back to the AI.

■ Figure 1-4 **A simple scan for airspeed**　　　■ Figure 1-5 **A simple scan for altitude**

VERTICAL SPEED. The rate of change of altitude, either as a rate of climb or a rate of descent in feet per minute, can be monitored on the **vertical speed indicator (VSI)** by moving the eyes from the AI diagonally down to the right to the VSI, before returning them to the AI. The VSI, since it is often used in conjunction with the altimeter, is located directly beneath it on most instrument panels.

TURNING. A turn is entered using the AI to establish bank angle and the balance indicator to confirm balance. Additional information on the turning rate is available from the **turn coordinator.** The normal rate of turn in instrument flying is 3°/second, known as rate 1, and this is marked on the turn coordinator (or turn indicator).

■ *Figure 1-6* **A simple scan for vertical speed information**   ■ *Figure 1-7* **A simple scan for turn rate**

With these **six basic flight instruments,** plus the **power indicator,** it is possible to fly the aeroplane very accurately and comfortably without any external visual reference, provided they are scanned efficiently, and you control the aeroplane adequately in response to the information that you derive from them.

Control and Performance

Power plus attitude equals performance.

The attitude selected on the AI and the power set on the power indicator determines the *performance* of the aeroplane, hence these two instruments are known as the **control instruments.** The AI is located centrally on the instrument panel directly in front of the pilot, so that any changes in attitude can be readily seen. Because continual reference to the power indicator is not required, it is situated slightly away from the main group of flight instruments, easy to scan occasionally, but not in the main field of view.

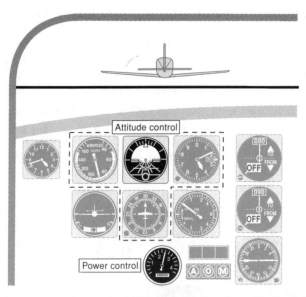

■ *Figure 1-8* **Use the control instruments to select attitude and power**

The other flight instruments are **performance instruments** that display how the aeroplane is performing (as a result of the power and attitude selected) in terms of:
☐ **altitude,** on the altimeter and VSI;
☐ **direction,** on the HI and turn coordinator; and
☐ **airspeed,** on the ASI.

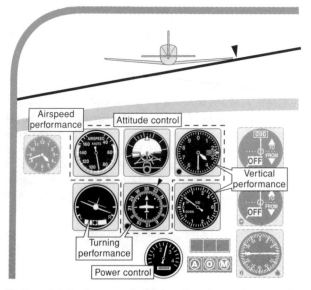

■ *Figure 1-9* **Performance is displayed on the performance instruments**

Changes in **pitch attitude** are shown directly on the AI, and are reflected on the altimeter, VSI and ASI. Changes in **bank angle** are shown directly on the AI, and are reflected on the turn coordinator and the heading indicator. The *quality* of flight is shown by the balance ball.

■ Figure 1-10 **The pitch instruments**   ■ Figure 1-11 **The bank instruments**

The Selective Radial Scan

The attitude indicator is the master flight instrument.

Of the six main flight instruments, the **attitude indicator** is the master instrument. It will be the one most frequently referred to (at least once every few seconds in most stages of flight). The eyes can be directed selectively towards the other instruments to derive relevant information from them as required, before returning to the AI. This eye movement radiating out and back to selected instruments is commonly known as the **selective radial scan**.

For instance, when climbing with full power selected, the estimated climb pitch attitude is held on the attitude indicator, but with reference to the airspeed indicator to confirm that the selected pitch attitude is correct. If the ASI indicates an airspeed that is too low, then lower the pitch attitude on the AI (say by a half-bar width or one-bar width), allow a few seconds for the airspeed to settle, and then check the ASI again.

Correct pitch attitude in the climb is checked on the airspeed indicator.

The key instrument in confirming that the correct attitude has been selected on the AI during the climb is the airspeed indicator. Because it determines what pitch attitude changes should be made on the AI during the climb, the ASI is the primary performance guide to pitch attitude in the climb.

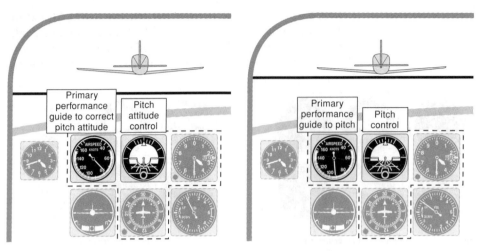

■ Figure 1-12 **The ASI is the primary instrument in the climb to confirm correct pitch attitude**

Approaching the desired cruise altitude, however, more attention should be paid to the altimeter to ensure that, as pitch attitude is lowered on the AI, the aeroplane levels off right on the desired altitude. Once cruising, any minor deviations from altitude detected on the altimeter can be corrected with small changes in pitch attitude. Because now it is the altimeter which determines what pitch attitude changes on the AI are required to maintain level flight, the altimeter is the primary performance guide to pitch attitude in the cruise.

Correct pitch attitude when cruising is checked on the altimeter.

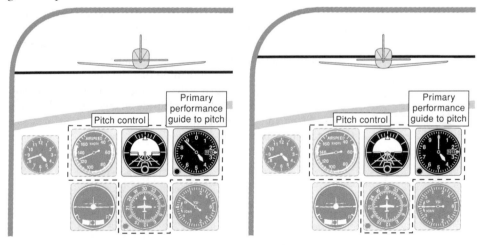

■ Figure 1-13 **The altimeter is the primary instrument in the cruise to confirm correct pitch attitude**

If climb power is still set after the aeroplane has been levelled off at cruise altitude, the aeroplane will accelerate, shown by an increasing airspeed on the ASI. At the desired speed, the power should be reduced to a suitable value.

Correct power when cruising is checked on the airspeed indicator.

While it is usual simply to set cruise power and then accept the resulting airspeed, it is possible to achieve a precise airspeed by adjusting the power. Because the ASI indications will then determine what power changes should be made during level flight, the airspeed indicator is the primary performance guide to power requirements in the cruise.

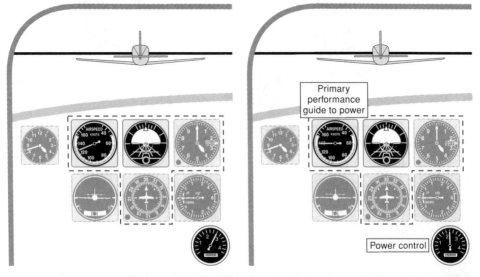

■ *Figure 1-14* **The ASI is the primary instrument in the cruise to confirm correct power**

Check wings level on the heading indicator.

Heading is maintained with reference to the HI, and any deviations corrected with gentle coordinated turns. Because the indications on the HI will determine what minor corrections to bank angle should be made on the AI during straight flight, the heading indicator is the primary performance guide to zero bank angle in maintaining a constant heading.

Keep the ball centred.

The balance ball should be centred to keep the aeroplane in balance, avoiding any slip or skid, i.e. to provide coordinated straight flight.

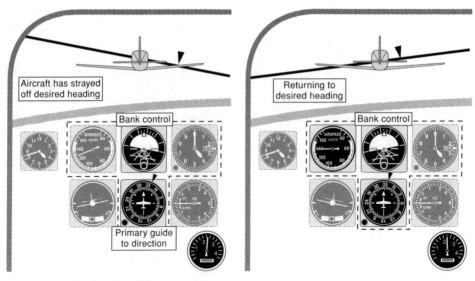

■ *Figure 1-15* **The heading indicator is the primary instrument in straight flight to confirm wings level**

The 'Basic T' Scan

A basic scan suitable for straight and level flight (where altitude, direction and airspeed need to be monitored) is centred on the AI, and radiates out and back, following the 'basic T' pattern on the panel, to the relevant performance instrument:

☐ **the HI to confirm heading** (and correct with small turns of the AI);

☐ **the altimeter to confirm altitude** (and correct with pitch changes on the AI);

☐ **the ASI to confirm airspeed** (and, if desired, correct with power changes).

■ *Figure 1-16* **The 'basic T' scan in cruise flight**

If cruise power is set and then left alone with the resulting airspeed being accepted (as is often the case in a normal cruise), then scanning the ASI need not be as frequent, and the scan can concentrate on the AI, HI and altimeter. Also, once established and well-trimmed on the cruise, the aeroplane will tend to hold height because of its longitudinal stability, making it less essential to scan the altimeter continually compared to when the aeroplane is out of trim. The aeroplane may not be as stable laterally as it is longitudinally, however, so the HI should be scanned quite frequently to ensure that heading is maintained.

Visual pilots are used to scanning the altimeter regularly, since it is the only means of accurately holding height, but they may not be used to scanning the HI quite so frequently as is necessary in instrument conditions. This skill will have to be developed.

What about the other Flight Instruments?

In smooth air, the VSI will show a trend away from cruising altitude often before it is apparent on the altimeter, and can be used to indicate that a minor pitch attitude correction is required if altitude is to be maintained. The VSI provides supporting pitch information to that provided by the altimeter, although it is of less value in turbulence, which causes the VSI needle to fluctuate.

If the wings are held level on the AI, and heading is being maintained on the HI, then it is almost certain that the aeroplane is in balance with the balance ball centred. Normally, the balance indicator does not have to be scanned as frequently as some of the other instruments, but it should be referred to occasionally, especially if heading is changing while the wings are level, or if the 'seat of your pants' tells you that the aeroplane is skidding or slipping.

The turn coordinator will show a wings-level indication during straight flight, and provides supporting information regarding bank to that provided by the HI during straight flight.

Choice of Scan Pattern

Use a logical scan for each manoeuvre.

Starting with your eyes focused on the AI, scan the performance instruments that provide the information required. Certain information will be obtained from different instruments, depending on the manoeuvre. Primary pitch information (to confirm whether or not the pitch attitude selected on the AI is correct) is obtained from the altimeter during cruise flight, but from the ASI during climbs and descents. There is no need to memorise particular scan patterns, since they will develop naturally as your training progresses.

Keep your eyes moving, and continually return to the attitude indicator.

Do not allow the radial scan to break down. Avoid fixation on any one instrument, since this will certainly cause a breakdown in the radial scan and result in deviations from the desired flightpath and/or airspeed. Fixation on the HI, for instance, can lead to heading being maintained perfectly, but in the meantime altitude and airspeed may go out of control – tendencies which would have been detected (and corrected for) if the altimeter, VSI and ASI had been scanned. Keep the eyes moving, and continually return to the AI.

Occasionally, the eyes will have to be directed away from the main flight instruments for a short period, for instance when checking the power indicator during or following a power change, or when periodically checking the oil temperature and pressure gauges, fuel gauges, the ammeter, or the suction gauge, or when referring to instrument approach charts, filling in the flight log, or tuning radios. Do not neglect the radial scan for more than a few seconds at a time, even though other necessary tasks have to be performed.

Avoid omission of any relevant instrument. After rolling out of a turn, check the HI to ensure that the desired heading is being achieved and maintained. The wings might be level and the aeroplane flying straight, but on the wrong heading.

Use available resources. With correct power set and the correct attitude selected on the AI, it is possible to hold altitude at least approximately using only the AI and the power indicator but, if precision is required, then the altimeter must be included in the scan as the primary reference for altitude. Furthermore, do not forget that supporting instruments can provide additional information to back up primary instruments. Altitude is indicated directly on the altimeter, but any tendency to depart from that altitude may first be indicated on the VSI (especially in smooth air), which makes it a very valuable supporting instrument to the altimeter.

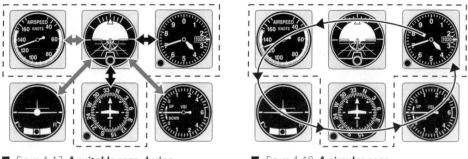

■ *Figure 1-17* **A suitable scan during straight and level flight**   ■ *Figure 1-18* **A circular scan**

Other Scans

It is necessary on some occasions to have a fast scan, such as on final for an instrument approach. On other occasions, however, the scan can be more relaxed, for instance when cruising with the autopilot engaged. It may then be suitable just to have a fairly relaxed **circular scan**.

If you are performing other tasks while flying a constant heading, such as map reading, then a very simple scan to make sure things do not get out of hand is a **vertical scan** from the AI down to the heading indicator and back again.

If at any time, you suspect an **instrument failure,** then a very efficient means of establishing what instrument or system has failed is to commence an **inverted-V scan,** centred on the AI and radiating to the turn coordinator and the VSI.

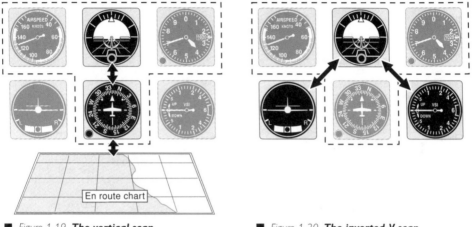

■ Figure 1-19 **The vertical scan**   ■ Figure 1-20 **The inverted-V scan**

Each of these instruments normally has a different power source – the vacuum system for the AI, the electrical system for the turn coordinator, and the static system for the VSI – so a false indication on one should not be reflected on the others. Confirmation of attitude and flightpath can then be achieved using the other instruments.

With practice, you will develop scans to suit every situation.

Performance Table

To help you adjust to a new aeroplane type, we have included a type performance table on the following page. You can fill in this table as you become familiar with the power settings and attitudes required to achieve the desired performance in the various phases of flight.

Attitude can be shown on the AI by inserting a horizon line. The table allows for aircraft with retractable landing gear – if yours has a fixed undercarriage, then just pencil the wheels in on the chart, and only fill in the power settings and attitudes that you need. Knowing the numbers simplifies the game.

PERFORMANCE TABLE

	Configuration		Power	Attitude	Performance	V-speeds
	Flaps	Gear	MP rpm		Airspeed VSI	
Take-off	...........°	down				
	...........°	up				
Climb	...........°	up				$V_{S1} =$ .... (stall speed, clean) $V_X =$ .... (best angle) $V_Y =$ .... (best rate)
Cruise						$V_A =$ .... (manoeuvring speed) $V_{NO} =$ .... (normal maximum) $V_{NE} =$ .... (never exceed)
Cruise descent (500 ft/min)						
Slow-speed cruise **1.** Clean						
2. Flaps extended	...........°	up				$V_{FE} =$ .... (flaps extended)
3. Flaps and landing gear extended	...........°	down				$V_{LO} =$ .... (landing gear operation) $V_{SO} =$ .... (landing flaps and landing gear extended)

The Instruments

The first impression most people have of an aeroplane cockpit is just how many instruments there are. Yet, when you analyse the instrument panels of even the largest jet transport aeroplanes, the instrumentation is not all that complicated. In fact, the basic instruments in large passenger aircraft are very similar to those in the smallest training aeroplane.

The flight instruments, which provide a pilot with vital flight information such as attitude, airspeed, altitude and direction, fall into two basic categories:

- those that use variations in **static and/or ram air pressure,** such as the airspeed indicator, the altimeter and the vertical speed indicator; and
- those that use the properties of **gyroscopic inertia,** such as the attitude indicator, the heading indicator and the turn coordinator.

We will consider each flight instrument individually, as well as the systems which might affect them, such as the pitot-static system for the pressure instruments and the vacuum system for the gyroscopic instruments.

We look first at the attitude indicator and the power indicator, since they are used as control instruments by the pilot to set flight *attitude* and *power.* It is power and attitude that determine the *performance* of the aeroplane, which can be measured on the other flight instruments.

The Attitude Indicator (AI)

The attitude indicator is the only instrument that gives a direct and immediate picture of pitch attitude and bank angle. Its main features are an artificial horizon line that remains horizontal as the aeroplane banks and pitches about it, and an index aeroplane that is fixed to the case of the instrument and moves with the aeroplane.

The AI is the master instrument in the cockpit, providing a clear visual representation of the aeroplane's movement in two planes (pitching and rolling). However, since the AI does not have any 'landmarks' on its artificial horizon line, it does not provide any information in the yawing plane.

Pitch attitude is indicated on the AI by the relative positions of the index aeroplane and the artificial horizon line. Ideally, they will be perfectly aligned when the aeroplane is in the level attitude, with the central dot in the wing bars directly over the horizon line. When the aeroplane is pitched up into the climbing attitude, the index aeroplane moves with it and appears above the horizon line. This is achieved within the instrument, not by the index aeroplane moving up, but by the horizon line moving down. Conversely, when the aeroplane is pitched down into the descent attitude, the horizon line will appear above the index aeroplane.

■ *Figure 2-1* **Typical attitude indicators**

Small horizontal lines marked above and below the artificial horizon line indicate the number of degrees of pitch up or pitch down but, generally, there is no need to use these. Most pilots alter pitch in terms of bar width, one bar width being the thickness of the wing bar and the central dot on the index aeroplane (or of the horizon line, if it is thicker). The central dot is easier to use when setting pitch attitude against the horizon line during a banked turn, since the wing bars will, of course, be at an angle to the horizon.

Bank angle is displayed both by the **bank pointer** against degree markings at the top of the AI, and by the angle between the wing bar of the index aeroplane and the artificial horizon line. Some instruments have converging lines on the earth part of the background to enhance the picture and assist in estimating the bank angle. Bank pointer displays vary in design, but are easy to interpret.

How it Works

The basis of the AI is a self-erecting gyroscope with a vertical spin axis. It may be driven either electrically or by an airflow induced over vanes on the edge of the gyroscope by suction. The gyroscope is connected to the artificial horizon line. Once it is spinning fast enough, and the spin axis has stabilised vertically, the gyroscope acts to holds the horizon line of the AI horizontal. Because the spin axis is vertical and the gyroscope spins in the horizontal plane, the AI cannot provide a reference in the yawing plane, but only in pitch and roll.

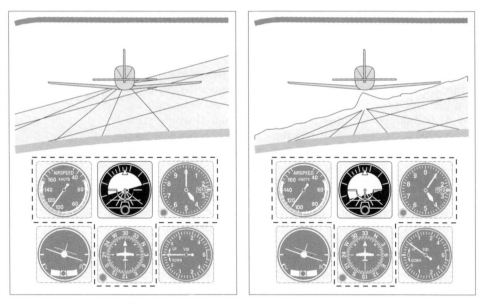

■ Figure 2-2 **The AI provides pitch and bank information only**

If the spin axis of the gyroscope moves off the vertical for some reason, the AI's internal self-erecting mechanism, which senses gravity, will realign it at a rate of approximately 3° per minute. The AI should work perfectly in steady 1g conditions, when the artificial horizon line should be exactly horizontal.

Faults

The attitude indicator, even though it is an exceptionally good instrument, is not perfect. Its power source can fail, and it does have some small gyroscopic precession errors induced during rapid speed changes and turns (but they are generally small and easily coped with). Any tendency to follow a slightly incorrect artificial horizon bar will be detected by scanning the other instruments, and corrective action can be taken to maintain height and/or direction.

If the power source fails, then the AI may become unusable. An electrically driven AI should then show a red warning flag, but the vacuum-driven AI may just gradually run down and give a false indication without a warning flag. For this reason, the suction gauge should be periodically checked for a vacuum of approximately 4.5"Hg (especially since the HI may also be vacuum-driven).

Any acceleration (such as a rapid speed change or a turn) will exert additional g-forces on the aeroplane. Everything within it, including the pilot and the AI's self-erecting mechanism, will sense a false 'gravity' force, which may cause the gyroscope's spin axis to move off the vertical briefly, resulting in a slightly incorrect artificial horizon line.

During a rapid acceleration, the horizon line will move down and, if the pilot follows it, the aeroplane will have a lower pitch attitude than desired. Conversely, during a deceleration, the horizon line will move up, causing a false pitch-down indication, i.e. the AI will display a greater pitch-down attitude than the aeroplane actually has. You will detect these small pitch errors in your scan of the vertical performance instruments, and either maintain height in level flight using the altimeter and VSI, or maintain airspeed in a climb or descent using the ASI.

Skids, sideslips and turns exert additional forces that may cause the artificial horizon line to move off the horizontal briefly, resulting in a small error in bank display. You will detect this in your scan of the other instruments, and can maintain heading and wings level with reference to the HI in straight flight, or maintain a particular turn rate during a heading change with reference to the turn coordinator. The small bank error in the AI will be greatest following a turn of 180° (possibly up to 5° of bank error), and will cancel itself out at the completion of 360°.

These precession errors correct themselves fairly quickly and can, in general, be disregarded in light aircraft, which do not have high rates of acceleration and deceleration. A good scan will ensure that errors in the AI do not affect the accuracy of instrument flying, with the pilot able to hold height, heading or airspeed quite accurately with reference to the other instruments.

Some types of AI have a gyroscope which will topple when the aeroplane is in extreme attitudes well beyond normal flight attitudes (typically in excess of 60° of pitch and 100° of roll). This will temporarily render the AI useless. Some gyroscopes can be caged, and then uncaged once the aeroplane is back in straight and level flight.

Some newer types of AI can tolerate any aircraft attitude (360° of pitch and/or roll) without the gyroscope toppling. If the self-erecting mechanism is unable to cope with large errors, then this may also make the AI unusable. If the AI becomes unusable for any reason, accurate instrument flight is still attainable, although more difficult using the other instruments. Chapter 7, *Instrument Flight on a Limited Panel*, discusses this in detail.

Pre-Flight Checks of the Attitude Indicator

After engine start-up, and allowing the AI gyroscope time to stabilise (which may take several minutes), the AI should be checked for serviceability. There should be no electrical warning flag visible for an electrically driven gyroscope, and no unusual or irregular mechanical noise as the gyroscope winds up. Adequate suction should be indicated for a vacuum-driven gyroscope. The artificial horizon line should appear horizontal, and the index aeroplane should be checked to ensure that it is aligned with the artificial horizon line when the aeroplane is on level ground.

While taxiing to the take-off position, the AI can be observed as the aeroplane makes right and left turns (which will be in the yawing plane only), to check that the artificial horizon bar does not move appreciably. Significant bank or pitch errors could indicate something wrong within the gyroscopic system. (While not recommended, the AI pitch error caused by rapid deceleration can be demonstrated during a straight taxi by applying the brakes, which will cause a false pitch-down indication as the horizon bar moves up.)

The Power Indicator(s)

Different engine and propeller types require different power instruments. For this reason, the power indicator in the cockpit will be referred to as just that, whereas in a specific aeroplane it may be a tachometer, in another a manifold pressure gauge, and in a jet an EPR gauge.

In an aeroplane with a fixed-pitch propeller (most basic trainers), the power instrument is a tachometer, which measures engine rpm. Moving the throttle forward increases power by increasing engine rpm, displayed by the tachometer needle moving clockwise.

More advanced aeroplanes have a constant speed unit (CSU) propeller whose rpm can be set to a constant value with a pitch lever or pitch knob placed beside the throttle. With rpm set, a power increase made by advancing the throttle is shown in the cockpit as an increase in manifold pressure (MP) on the manifold pressure gauge, which is now the main power indicator.

A power increase on a jet engine made by advancing the throttle may be shown on an engine pressure ratio (EPR) gauge, which may be the main power indicator to the jet pilot. There are a variety of instruments that can perform this function.

From the point of view of instrument flying, it does not matter what sort of aeroplane is being flown and what sort of power instruments it has, but what does matter is that the pilot has a power indicator in the cockpit to refer to when power changes are being made. For this reason, we will use a non-specific type of indicator in the illustrations, mainly to show power increases or decreases. Endorsement training on the aeroplane that you are flying will include knowledge of its particular power indicators and engine/propeller controls.

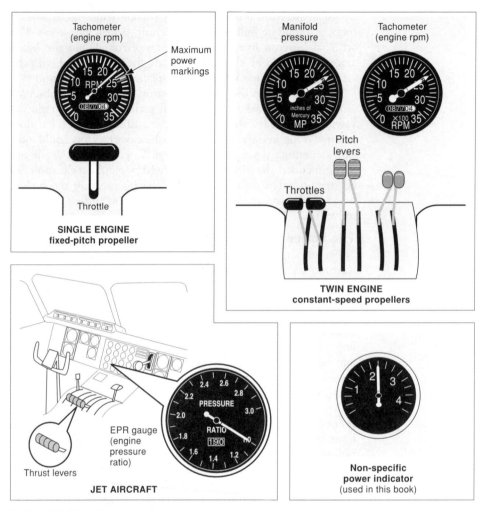

■ Figure 2-3 **Typical power indicators**

The Airspeed Indicator

We know that the airspeed indicator (ASI) displays indicated airspeed (IAS). IAS is related to dynamic pressure, which is the difference between total (or ram air) pressure and static pressure. This is determined within the airspeed indicator by having a diaphragm with total pressure (from the pitot tube) being fed onto one side of it, and static pressure (from the static vent) being fed onto the other side of it, as shown in Figure 2-4.

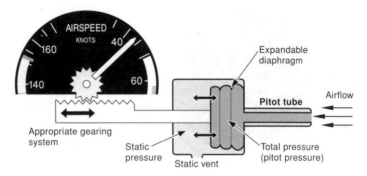

■ *Figure 2-4* **The airspeed indicator (ASI) measures dynamic pressure**

As airspeed increases, dynamic pressure increases, but static pressure remains the same. The difference between the total pressure or ram air pressure (measured by the pitot tube) and the static pressure (measured by the static vent or static line) gives us a measure of dynamic pressure, which is related to indicated airspeed. This difference between the total and static pressures causes the diaphragm to reposition itself, and the pointer to indicate a higher airspeed.

Colour Coding on the Airspeed Indicator

To assist the pilot, ASIs in modern aircraft have speed ranges and specific speeds marked according to a conventional colour code.

GREEN ARC denotes the normal operating speed range, from V_{S1} (stall speed at maximum gross weight, flaps up, wings level), up to V_{NO} (normal operating limit speed or maximum structural cruising speed), which should not be exceeded except in smooth air. Operations at an IAS in the green arc should be safe in all conditions, including turbulence.

YELLOW ARC denotes the caution range, which extends from V_{NO} (normal operating limit speed) up to V_{NE} (the never-exceed speed). The aircraft should be operated at indicated airspeeds in the caution range only in smooth air.

WHITE ARC denotes the flap operating range, from V_{S0} (stall speed at maximum gross weight in the landing configuration – full flap, landing gear down, wings level, power-off), up to V_{FE} (maximum flaps extended speed).

RED RADIAL LINE denotes V_{NE}, the never-exceed speed.

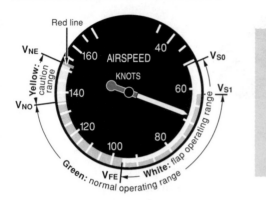

V_{S0}	Stall speed at max. weight, landing gear down, flaps down, power off
V_{S1}	Stall speed at max. weight, landing gear up (if retractable), flaps up, power off
V_{FE}	Maximum speed, flaps extended
V_{NO}	Maximum structural cruising speed (for normal operations)
V_{NE}	Never-exceed speed (max. speed, all ops.)

■ Figure 2-5 **Indicated airspeed is what we read on the ASI**

NOTE

1. The ASI in a twin-engined aeroplane will usually be marked with a blue radial line to denote best single-engine rate of climb speed, V_{YSE}.

2. All ASI markings refer to indicated airspeed (IAS) and not true airspeed (TAS). Where weight is a factor in determining the limit speed (e.g. stall speeds) the value marked is for the maximum take-off weight (MTOW) situation in all cases.

3. Some limiting speeds are not marked on the ASI, but should be known by the pilot. They can be found in the Flight Manual and the Pilot's Operating Handbook.

   V_{LO} is the maximum landing gear operating speed, for raising or lowering the landing gear. V_{LE} is the maximum landing gear extended speed, which for some aeroplanes exceeds V_{LO} (since structural strength may be increased once the gear is down and locked in place).

   Manoeuvring speed V_A should not be exceeded in turbulence, to avoid excessive g-loading on the aeroplane structure.

   V_X is best-angle climb speed.

   V_Y is best-rate climb speed.

TAS Indication

Some airspeed indicators, as well as showing IAS, can also show TAS. These ASIs have a manually rotatable scale known as a temperature/altitude correction scale, which allows the pilot to read TAS as well as IAS. It indicates speeds up to approximately 200 knots TAS. Above 200 knots, compressibility has to be allowed for.

   Setting the temperature/altitude scale on the airspeed indicator performs exactly the same function as setting the same scale on the navigation computer.

Since for performance purposes (take-off, landing and stalling speeds), it is IAS that is important, and not TAS, some TAS scales do not extend into the low speed range.

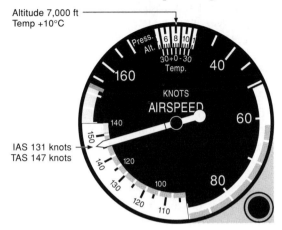

■ *Figure 2-6* **IAS/TAS indicator**

Errors in the Airspeed Indicator
Small errors will occur in each airspeed indicator. Errors due to imperfections in manufacture and maintenance are known as instrument error. Errors due to the position of the pitot tube and static vent are known as position error. If the indicated airspeed is corrected for these errors, the result is calibrated airspeed (CAS). A correction table to convert IAS to CAS appears in the Pilot's Operating Handbook.

At high speeds, above about 200 kt IAS, the air tends to compress in front of the pitot tube, thereby causing the airspeed indicator to overread. If CAS is corrected for compressibility error the result is equivalent airspeed (EAS). EAS will always be less than CAS.

High-Speed Flight
For high-speed flight at high altitude, the most appropriate speed instrument is the Machmeter, which displays the Mach number – the true airspeed of the aeroplane as a fraction of the TAS of the *local* speed of sound. Mach 0.78 means that the aeroplane is flying at 78% of the speed of sound.

The Heading Indicator (HI)
Although it does not automatically sense magnetic heading, the heading indicator can indicate magnetic heading once it has been aligned with the magnetic compass. The HI will be either electrically driven or vacuum-driven, and its power source in many aeroplanes is the same as that for the AI.

The modern HI cockpit display is a vertical compass rose of 360° that can rotate around a model aeroplane fixed in the centre of the dial with its nose pointing up. Typically, the rose is labelled every 30° with a number or letter, with large markings every 10° and smaller markings every intermediate 5°. The compass rose can be rotated using a slaving knob until the direction determined from the magnetic compass appears at the top of the dial. As heading changes, the compass rose rotates until the new heading is at the top of the dial, either under a fixed marker or at the nose of the model aeroplane.

There may be further fixed markings relative to the nose of the aeroplane at the 45°, 90° and 180° positions. The reciprocal to the heading can be read off the bottom of the dial. The abeam bearings can be read off the 90° markings. Mental arithmetic calculations are not necessary. To turn left 45°, for instance, simply note the direction at the 45° left marking, and perform a banked turn to the left until it appears at the top of the dial. The modern HI is an easy instrument to interpret because, in a left turn, for instance, the model aeroplane appears to move left relative to the compass rose. (In actual fact, it is the compass rose that rotates to the right.)

■ Figure 2-7 **Typical modern heading indicators (direction indicators)**

The HI is a non-magnetic instrument. It contains a gyroscope with a lateral horizontal spin axis, which provides the HI card with short-term directional stability. The gyro-stabilised HI is not subject to the problems which the magnetic compass experiences as a result of magnetic dip (turning and acceleration errors), nor does it oscillate in rough air. It is a much easier instrument to use than the compass in the short term, especially in turns and in turbulence, although the magnetic compass remains the fundamental reference source for magnetic direction.

Older directional gyros do not have a compass rose, but rather a circular strip card that can rotate, with heading shown under a lubber line. In fact, it is not the card that rotates; it is the aeroplane changing heading that moves around the card, similar to the magnetic compass. It is a more difficult presentation to interpret than the modern HI, since only 30° either side of heading is shown and, if the aeroplane turns left, the lubber line moves to the right relative to the card. For instance, in the situation shown below, to take up a heading of 110°M from a heading of 120°, the aeroplane should turn left.

■ *Figure 2-8* **An older directional gyro**

Errors of the Heading Indicator

The HI will gradually drift off direction due to internal mechanical reasons (such as friction and gimbal effect), and also because of apparent drift resulting from the earth's rotation. As the earth rotates about its axis at 15° per hour, the direction in space from a point on the earth's surface to north continually changes. This effect increases towards the poles, and is zero on the equator. The aeroplane can compound this effect as it flies across the face of the earth. Realigning the HI periodically with the magnetic compass solves the problem.

Older HIs have internal limits that may cause them to lose their direction-holding ability if bank angle or pitch attitude exceeds 55°. Newer types will not topple, even in extreme attitudes.

For several reasons, therefore, the HI must be periodically realigned with the magnetic compass, which is unaffected by the rotation of the earth and always points, at least within a few degrees, towards magnetic north during steady straight and level flight. Remember that a small correction may have to be made to the magnetic compass to allow for deviation due to extraneous magnetic fields in the aeroplane. The correction required is found on the deviation card displayed in the aeroplane. If not allowed for, the the compass deviation error will be transferred to the HI.

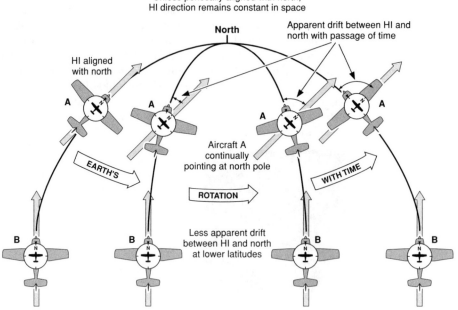

■ *Figure 2-9* **The HI will gradually drift off direction**

The HI should be checked at least every 15 minutes, and reset to the correct heading with reference to the magnetic compass (and deviation card) during steady straight and level flight. For the HI to be acceptable in normal operations, this correction should not exceed 3° in 15 minutes.

Complete failure of the HI makes life a little more difficult, as then you must scan right across to the magnetic compass (with its turning and acceleration errors) for heading information. Since the AI and HI often share the same power source, loss of one may mean the loss of the other. See Chapter 7, *Instrument Flight on a Limited Panel.*

Pre-flight Checks of the HI

After start-up, the electrical or vacuum power source should be checked to ensure that the gyroscope will reach operating speed. Once up to speed, the HI should be aligned with the magnetic compass using the slaving knob. The HI can then help in orientation on the ground – for instance, in which direction the take-off will be.

While taxiing, the HI should be checked for correct functioning, "Turning right, heading increases – turning left, heading decreases".

At the holding point, just prior to take-off, the HI should again be checked against the magnetic compass (but not while turning or accelerating), and it can be used to verify that the correct runway is about to be used.

The Remote Indicating Compass

A remote indicating compass combines the functions of the magnetic compass and the heading indicator. It employs a magnetic sensor, called a magnetic flux detector (or flux valve), which is positioned well away from other magnetic influences in the airframe, usually in a wingtip. The sensor detects magnetic direction and sends electrical signals to the heading indicator to automatically align it with the current magnetic heading of the aeroplane. This process is known as slaving. It eliminates the need for the pilot to manually periodically align the heading indicator, which now becomes known as a remote indicating compass.

However, there is usually a small slaving knob on the instrument to allow the pilot to manually align the compass card quickly if the indicated heading is grossly in error. A small slaving annunciator is usually provided to assist manual alignment and allow the pilot to check that normal automatic slaving is occurring. This is indicated by small regular oscillations of the slaving needle.

The Horizontal Situation Indicator (HSI)

The horizontal situation indicator is a slaved heading indicator (a remote indicating compass) with superimposed VOR/ILS navigation indications.

When fitted, the HSI occupies the same position on the instrument panel as a heading indicator, directly below the attitude indicator.

■ Figure 2-10 **A typical horizontal situation indicator**

The Altimeter

The altimeter is an aneroid barometer that measures static pressure and relates it to height in the atmosphere. The lower the pressure, the greater the height. It is a vital instrument if altitude is to be accurately maintained. It is also vital in determining height above the aerodrome during an instrument approach to land in cloud or poor visibility. An aeroplane, unlike a car, must be navigated in three dimensions. The altimeter is the most important instrument for vertical navigation.

The altimeter relates the static pressure at the aeroplane's level to a height in the International Standard Atmosphere (ISA), a theoretical 'average' atmosphere which acts as a measuring stick. The main purpose of the ISA is to calibrate altimeters but, unfortunately for altimeters, the real atmosphere can differ significantly from the standard atmosphere.

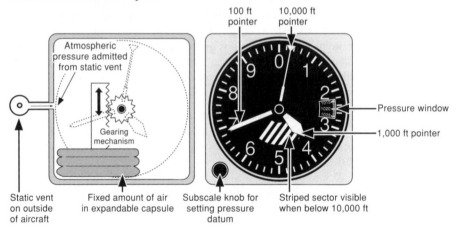

■ Figure 2-11 **The altimeter is a pressure-sensitive instrument**

Since pressure varies from place'to place, and from time to time, the altimeter has a small subscale that allows the pilot to select the pressure level from which height will be measured. Subscale settings that will be used in a typical flight are:

- ☐ **Aerodrome QNH** for circuit operations, to provide altitude (height above mean sea level – amsl);
- ☐ **Aerodrome QFE** for circuit operations, to provide height above aerodrome level (aal);
- ☐ **Regional QNH** for en route cruise at or below the transition altitude (usually 3,000 ft amsl in the UK, but higher in places);
- ☐ **Standard pressure** 1013.2 mb for cruising at flight levels above the transition altitude.

The only place a pilot can really check the accuracy of an altimeter is on the aerodrome. With Aerodrome QFE set in the subscale, the altimeter should read zero. (Conversely, on the ground with the altimeter reading zero, the current QFE should appear in the subscale.) With Aerodrome QNH set in the subscale, the altimeter should read aerodrome elevation (or vice versa). Accuracy should be within ±50 ft (±2 mb approximately, since 1 mb is equivalent to 30 ft in height). If the aerodrome is not on reasonably flat ground, then allow for the fact that aerodrome elevation is measured at the highest point on an operating runway, which may be at a slightly different height amsl to an aeroplane elsewhere on the aerodrome.

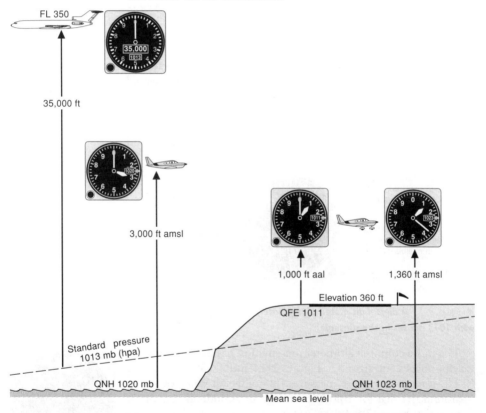

■ *Figure 2-12* **The altimeter measures height above the pressure level set in the subscale**

How the Altimeter Works

The altimeter contains a sealed, but expandable, capsule that is surrounded by the current static pressure. As the aeroplane climbs and static pressure decreases, the sealed capsule is able to expand.

Through a linkage, it drives a pointer around the altimeter scale to indicate height above the pressure level already selected in the subscale. There may be a short lag in time, however, before changes in height are registered on the altimeter.

Different Altimeter Presentations

You must interpret the altimeter reading correctly since it provides absolutely vital information. Lives have been lost in the past because pilots (even professional pilots) have misread the altimeter by 10,000 ft. Learn how to read it accurately right from the start!

The most easily understood altimeter presentation is a simple digital readout of height, supported by a single pointer indicating 100s of feet.

It will make one complete revolution of the dial for every 1,000 ft gain or loss of altitude. The digital readout displays the actual altitude. The pointer does not indicate the complete altitude, but only the last three digits of it (e.g. at 15,200 ft it would indicate 200). It is very useful to an instrument pilot, because it gives a better picture of any tendency to depart from a height than does a set of changing digits. Trends of 20 or 50 ft either side of the precise altitude are more easily spotted on the pointer and corrected with an attitude change on the AI.

Outer graduated scale
Marked in hundreds, with 20-foot sub-graduations

Pressure window
Indicates pressure setting in millibars (hPa)

Knob
Used to wind in altimeter setting

Rotating pointer
Indicates 1,000 ft for each revolution

Rotating drum
Indicates altitude in feet

■ *Figure 2-13* **A digital altimeter, plus pointer, indicating 29,100 feet, with 1013 mb set in the subscale**

The more common altimeter presentation has three pointers of varying shapes and sizes (see Figures 2-14 and 2-15).

☐ The long thick pointer measures 100s of feet. It will move once around the dial for 10,000 ft change in altitude. If it is on 7, then that means 7 × 100 = 700 ft.

☐ The short wide pointer measures 1,000s of feet. It will move once around the dial for a change of 10,000 ft. If it is on 4 (or just past it), then that means 4,000 ft. To reinforce to pilots that the aeroplane is below 10,000 ft, a striped sector remains visible, gradually becoming smaller as 10,000 ft is approached.

■ *Figure 2-14*
Conventional altimeter display

☐ The pointer with a stubby base and a long fine pointer measures 10,000s of feet. If it is on 1 (or just past it), then that means 10,000 ft. This pointer is particularly easy to misread.

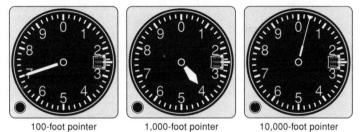

| 100-foot pointer | 1,000-foot pointer | 10,000-foot pointer |

■ *Figure 2-15* **The three pointers on a conventional altimeter**

Pre-Flight Checks

During the walk-around, the pilot should check that the static vent is clear (since a blocked static vent will affect the altimeter, the VSI and the ASI). To check altimeter readings, the subscale can be set to QFE (when the altimeter should read approximately zero), or to QNH (when it should read aerodrome elevation).

Density Error

The altimeter is calibrated to read the height above the pressure level selected in the subscale as if the characteristics of the real atmosphere (temperature, pressure, density) were identical to the International Standard Atmosphere. They rarely are, which means that the altimeter reading will not match the true altitude precisely.

A string dropped to sea level would be a different length to the altimeter's indicated altitude. Usually, this is not significant, since all aeroplanes in the one area will have their altimeters affected identically, and so vertical separation will not be degraded. Aeroplanes always cruise at *indicated* altitude (what appears on the altimeter), and not on *true* altitude.

While density error is of little significance in normal operations, an interesting point may occur later in your training on precision instrument approaches. In very warm air, the density will be less than standard. Climbing a true 1,000 feet, the altimeter will sense less than 1,000 ft difference in density in the thinner air, and the altimeter will under-read. The aeroplane is actually at 3,100 ft, but the altimeter only indicates 3,000 ft. In air colder than ISA, the reverse is the case: the altimeter will indicate higher than the aeroplane actually is.

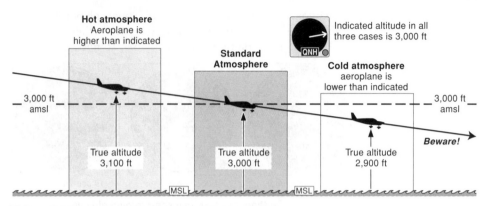

■ *Figure 2-16* **Indicated altitude may not be true altitude**

When carrying out an instrument approach to a runway by following an ILS glideslope, you will check height as you pass the outer marker (either amsl on QNH, or aal on QFE). You might notice a small difference between the indicated altitude on the altimeter compared to the height published on the instrument approach charts. The actual height is fixed but, even if the aeroplane is exactly on slope, the altimeter reading may be a little different to the published value. In warm air, it will read a little lower; in cold air, it will read a little higher.

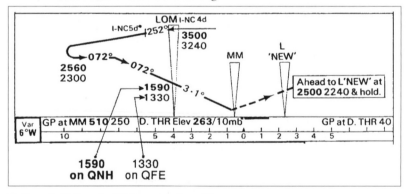

■ *Figure 2-17* **A typical ILS approach profile**

The Vertical Speed Indicator

The VSI provides a readout of the rate of change of altitude. If the aeroplane climbs steadily through 250 ft in 30 seconds, then the VSI should read 500 ft/min. Its dial is usually marked in 100s of feet either side of a zero marking, with 500 ft/min UP or DOWN clearly labelled.

The VSI, as well as being useful in climbs and descents, is a very useful instrument when trying to achieve precise level flight. In smooth air, it will show any trend to move away from an altitude very quickly. It will respond faster to an altitude change than the altimeter, and allow a pitch attitude correction to be made on the AI almost before the altimeter has registered a change in height. In rough air, however, the VSI pointer fluctuates, making it a less valuable instrument.

With large and sudden attitude changes, the VSI may briefly show a reversed reading because of disturbed airflow near the static vent, with some lag before a steady rate of climb or descent is indicated. In such a case, allow the indication to settle before using its information.

The main value of the VSI is the support it gives to the altimeter when maintaining height, and the rate of climb or descent it displays during climbs and descents.

How the VSI Works

The VSI has an expandable capsule connected to the static line so that it contains the actual static pressure. The VSI instrument case containing the capsule is also connected to the static line, but through a metered leak. As the aeroplane changes altitude, the static pressure within the capsule changes immediately, but the metered leak causes the pressure change surrounding the capsule to be more gradual.

On a climb, the pressure in the capsule changes instantaneously to the now lower static pressure. The case that surrounds the capsule, however, contains the original higher pressure which takes some time to change. The effect is to compress the capsule, driving a pointer around the dial to indicate a rate of climb.

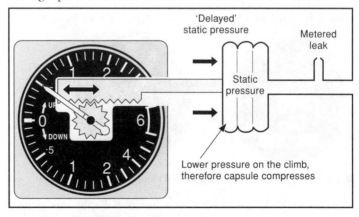

■ *Figure 2-18* **The VSI compares actual static pressure in the capsule with 'delayed' static pressure in the case**

The changed pressure gradually leaks into the instrument case. If the aeroplane continues to climb, the pressure within the instrument case never quite catches up with the external static pressure within the capsule, so the VSI continues to indicate a rate of climb. Once the aeroplane levels off, the two pressures do gradually equalise, and the VSI reads zero.

The VSI is good as a trend instrument ("Am I going up?" or "Am I going down?"), as well as a rate instrument ("How fast an I going up or down?"). Whereas the trend is obvious almost immediately in smooth air, the precise rate will take a few seconds to settle down. In rough air, it may take longer.

Pre-Flight Checks

Like all static pressure instruments, the VSI requires a static vent and line that is not blocked. The VSI should also indicate approximately zero while the aeroplane is on the ground (and not climbing). Indication errors may exist in some VSIs, in which case allowances will have to be made for this in flight. For instance, if it indicates 100 ft/min UP while on the ground, then this may have to be the 'zero' position in flight. But, be sure to check its indication against the altimeter when cruising.

The Turn Coordinator, and the Turn Indicator

The turn coordinator is an advanced modification of an earlier instrument, the turn indicator. They are both rate gyroscopes, where the rotating mass has freedom to move about two of its three axes and is designed to show movement of the aircraft about the third axis. The gyroscope in the turn indicator or turn coordinator will not topple in extreme attitudes, making for a very reliable instrument. It may be driven electrically or by suction.

■ Figure 2-19 **The turn coordinator (left) and turn indicator (right)**

The turn indicator has a lateral horizontal spin axis (with a vertical spinning gyro) attached to a gimbal. The gimbal axis is fixed and aligned with the aeroplane's longitudinal axis. The turn indicator is designed to show motion about the normal axis, the *rate of turn* in the yawing plane.

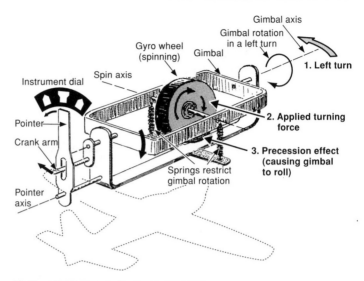

■ *Figure 2-20* **Turn indicator mechanism**

Any turning motion of the aircraft is mechanically transmitted to the spin axis, and exerts a force on the spinning mass of the gyroscope. In Figure 2-20, the force exerted on the gyro by a left turn is translated 90° by the gyroscopic precession effect, causing the gyro and its spin axis to tilt. This tilting is opposed by a spring – the greater the turning force, the greater the tilt. The tilt is transmitted to a pointer which moves on the turn indicator dial, usually calibrated to show rate 1 turns left or right. Some instruments, however, have their dials calibrated to turns other than rate 1, a point which must be established before relying on the instrument.

The turn coordinator is a very clever development of the same principle. The gimbal axis is angled up at about 30° to the aeroplane's longitudinal axis, which makes the gyro sensitive not only to turning about the normal axis, but also to banking about the longitudinal axis (see Figure 2-21). Since a turn is commenced by banking the aeroplane, the turn coordinator will react to roll, even before the aeroplane actually starts turning.

The turn coordinator presentation is usually a set of wings pivoted in the centre of the instrument, the wings moving to indicate the direction of bank. Calibrations around the edge of the instrument show rate 1 turns. Note that the wings are pivoted in the centre and so will not move up or down to indicate pitch attitude. Many turn coordinators are labelled "NO PITCH INFORMATION". The "2 MIN" label refers to a rate 1 turn taking 2 minutes to achieve a heading change of 360°.

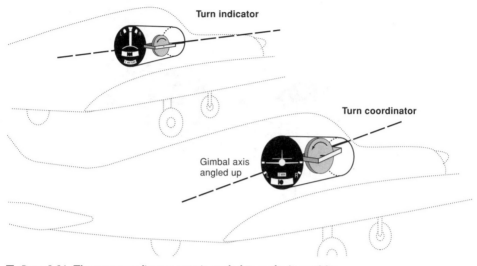

■ *Figure 2-21* **The turn coordinator gyro is angled to make it sensitive to banking as well as turning**

A significant advantage of the turn coordinator is that it can be used easily to keep the wings level in straight flight if the attitude indicator has failed. The wings of the turn coordinator will react first to roll, and then to yaw.

Pre-Flight Checks of the Turn Coordinator (and Balance Indicator)

During the taxi, a very simple check is to turn the aircraft and observe the indications "Turning left (on the turn coordinator) – skidding right" (on the balance indicator), followed by "Turning right – skidding left".

Any doubts about calibration can be checked with a timed rate 1 turn in flight.

The Balance Indicator

The balance indicator (or balance ball) is a simple and useful mechanical device that indicates the direction of the g-forces, i.e. the combined effect of the earth's gravity force and any turning force. It does not require a power source.

The balance indicator is usually incorporated into the instrument face of the turn coordinator (or turn indicator). It is simply a small ball, free to move like a pendulum bob, except that it moves in a curved cylinder filled with damping fluid. In straight flight, it should appear at the lowest point in the curved cylinder (like a pendulum bob hanging straight down), and the aeroplane is then said to be in balance. If there is any slip or skid, the ball will move to one side in the same way as a pendulum bob would swing out. In such cases, you would feel a force pushing you in or out of the turn, usually through the 'seat of your pants'. If the ball is out to the right, apply right rudder pressure to centralise it.

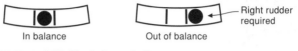

In balance   Out of balance

■ Figure 2-22 **The balance indicator**

In a balanced turn, you will feel no sideways forces, nor will the balance ball, which should remain centralised. Any sideways force (either a slip in towards the turn or a skid out) will be shown by the balance indicator (and felt in the seat of your pants). This can be counteracted with same-side rudder pressure to centralise the ball.

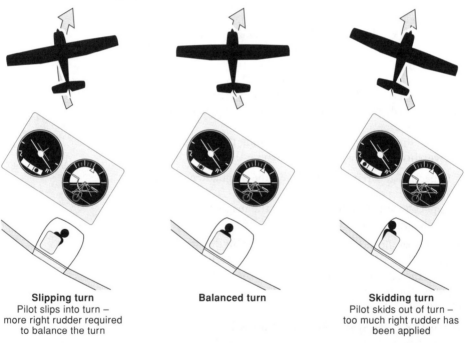

Slipping turn
Pilot slips into turn –
more right rudder required
to balance the turn

Balanced turn

Skidding turn
Pilot skids out of turn –
too much right rudder has
been applied

■ Figure 2-23 **Keep the aeroplane in balance with rudder pressure**

The Magnetic Compass

The magnetic compass is the primary source of directional information in the cockpit. In steady flight, it aligns itself with magnetic north so that the aeroplane's magnetic heading appears under the *lubber line*. Small errors in this reading due to other known magnetic fields in the aeroplane can be allowed for by the pilot by using information on the deviation card.

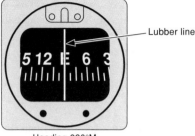

Heading 090°M

■ *Figure 2-24* **Magnetic compass**

Compass Errors

The magnetic compass does, however, experience dip errors when the aeroplane is turning (especially through N or S), and when accelerating (especially on E or W). The easiest approach for a pilot is to align the gyroscopic heading indicator (which is not subject to these errors) with the magnetic compass during steady straight flight periodically, and then use it as a short-term guide to magnetic direction, rather than the compass.

If, however, the HI is unserviceable and the magnetic compass has to be used, certain allowances for these dip errors need to be made. They are:

☐ **Undershoot** the heading when turning through north.

☐ **Overshoot** the heading when turning through south.

☐ Expect an apparent turn north on the magnetic compass when accelerating on east or west.

☐ Expect an apparent turn south on the magnetic compass when decelerating on east or west.

NOTE These allowances apply to dip errors in the northern hemisphere. They are greatest towards the North Pole, decrease towards the equator, and are reversed in the southern hemisphere. More on the magnetic compass and its errors appears in Vol. 4 of *The Air Pilot's Manual*.

Pre-Flight Checks of the Magnetic Compass

Check that the magnetic compass is mounted securely, and that the bowl is full of fluid and without bubbles. Its reading can be checked against a known heading, at least approximately. Ensure that no magnetic materials are stored near it, as these could introduce large errors. During the taxi, the card can be checked for free movement during a turn.

Straight and Level Flight

Flying *straight* means maintaining a constant heading, which can be achieved by holding the wings level with the ailerons and keeping the aeroplane in balance with the ball centred using rudder pressure.

Flying *level* means maintaining a constant height, which can be achieved by holding the correct pitch attitude for the power set.

Straight and level flying is very important, since most flights contain a cruise segment which is often quite long. Accurate straight and level flying is important for aerodynamic efficiency, fuel efficiency and comfort, and is one sign of a good pilot.

The Control Instruments

The control instruments for straight and level flight, as for all flight, are:

☐ **the attitude indicator;** and
☐ **the power indicator.**

With reference to these control instruments, you can use the controls (the control column for pitch and bank attitude, the throttle for power) to select straight and level flight at the desired height and airspeed. The AI gives a direct and instantaneous picture of the aeroplane's pitch attitude and bank angle, and the power indicator gives a direct reading of power.

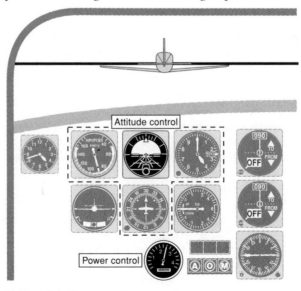

■ Figure 3-1 **The control instruments**

The Performance Instruments

VERTICAL PERFORMANCE of the aeroplane is indicated primarily on:

☐ the altimeter;
☐ the vertical speed indicator (VSI); and, to a lesser extent,
☐ the airspeed indicator (ASI).

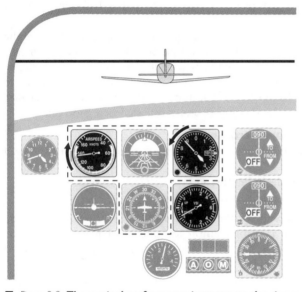

■ *Figure 3-2* **The vertical performance instruments showing a
gradual loss of height**

The altimeter indicates height directly. The VSI indicates any trend away from that height. The ASI indicates airspeed, but can also provide information indirectly regarding pitch attitude and height. For instance, an increasing airspeed at a constant power setting means a lower pitch attitude and, in straight and level flight, possibly a loss of height.

For the altimeter reading to be meaningful, you must have the appropriate pressure setting in the subscale, since this will be the pressure level from which the altimeter measures height. The subscale is generally set to:

☐ **Regional QNH** for en route cruise at or below the transition altitude;
☐ **Standard pressure** 1013.2 mb for en route cruise above the transition altitude; and
☐ **either Aerodrome QNH or QFE** for circuit operations.

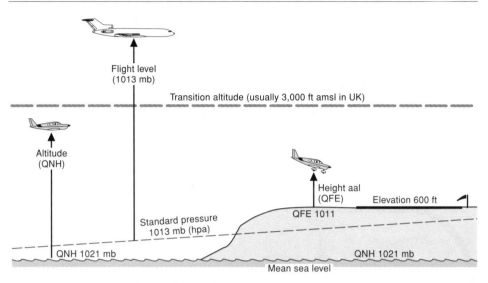

Flight level
(1013 mb)

Transition altitude (usually 3,000 ft amsl in UK)

Altitude
(QNH)

Height aal
(QFE)   Elevation 600 ft

QFE 1011

Standard pressure
1013 mb (hpa)

QNH 1021 mb   QNH 1021 mb

Mean sea level

■ *Figure 3-3* **Set the altimeter subscale correctly**

HORIZONTAL PERFORMANCE, in directional terms, is indicated primarily on:
- the heading indicator (HI); and
- the turn coordinator (TC) and balance ball.

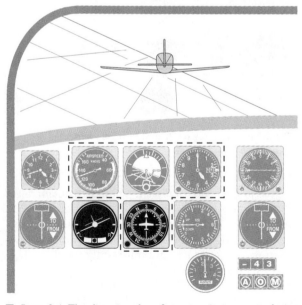

■ *Figure 3-4* **The directional performance instruments during
a left turn towards north**

The HI gives a direct reading of magnetic direction provided it has been correctly aligned with the magnetic compass during steady flight. It also gives an indirect indication of bank (because, if the heading is changing in coordinated flight, then the wings are banked), plus an indirect indication of rate of turn (by comparing the heading change with the time taken).

The turn coordinator (or the older style turn indicator, also known as the 'bat and ball') indicates the rate of turn. The balance ball is important since coordinated flight is almost always desirable to avoid any sideslip or skid through the air.

Horizontal performance in terms of airspeed is indicated on the airspeed indicator.

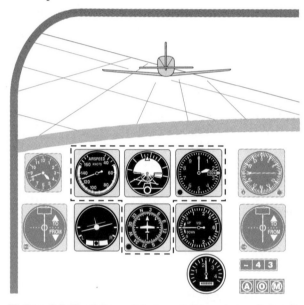

■ Figure 3-5 **The full panel during a left turn to regain heading 360°M at altitude 2,000 ft and 130 kt**

Keep the Aeroplane in Trim

When properly trimmed, the aeroplane should maintain level flight with little or no assistance from you. If not properly trimmed, level flight is much more difficult to maintain, and you are likely to become fatigued and tense on the controls. Instrument flying requires a light touch, and this is only possible when the aeroplane is well trimmed and you are relaxed.

Remember that trim is used *only* to relieve steady control pressure, and *not* to change aeroplane attitude. Significant trim changes in straight and level flight will generally only be required when you make significant changes in airspeed, or changes in configuration, for instance by lowering flap.

The natural stability designed into the aeroplane will help it to maintain pitch attitude in rough air as well as smooth air, even though there may be some significant deviations from altitude as a result of turbulence. You can correct for altitude deviations with smooth elevator control, but should avoid constant re-trimming in turbulence.

Stay Relaxed

A relaxed pilot with a fast instrument scan and a light touch on the controls will be a good instrument pilot.

If at any time you feel tense on the controls, a good relaxation technique is to first ensure that the aeroplane is in trim, and then (provided conditions are not turbulent), release all pressure on the elevator control for just a moment or two. Flex your fingers, before replacing them on the control column. The thumb and first two fingers will be more than sufficient for adequate control; a full hand grip may lead to lack of sensitive control and to further tenseness. Being in trim is vital!

Pitch Attitude and Cruise Speed

Different cruise speeds require different pitch attitudes. The pitch attitude established on the attitude indicator will vary for different cruise speeds.

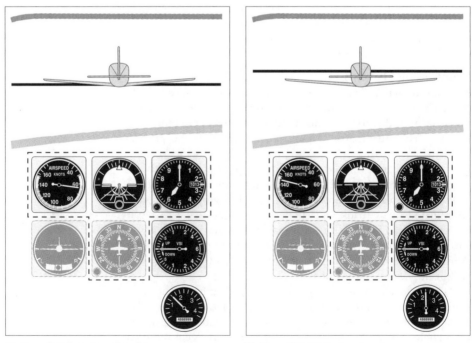

■ Figure 3-6 **Low-speed cruise**   ■ Figure 3-7 **High-speed cruise**

For instance, the pitch attitude required for low-speed cruise will be *higher* than that for normal cruise, in order to generate sufficient lift at the lower speed to balance the weight. This is summarised in the lift formula ($L = C_L \times \frac{1}{2} rho V^2 \times S$), which tells us that lift produced (L) is a function of the angle of attack (C_L) and the indicated airspeed (related to $\frac{1}{2} rho V^2$). A high angle of attack at a low airspeed is capable of producing the same lift as a low angle of attack at a high airspeed.

The VSI and the altimeter will confirm if the pitch attitude selected on the AI is correct to maintain height with that power set. If not, do something about it! The power required will differ with each airspeed, but more of this later.

Also, compared to when it is light, a heavily laden aeroplane will require a greater lift force to support the greater weight, and so will require a higher angle of attack at a given cruise speed, hence a higher pitch attitude in the cruise. You may not notice this directly, but reference to the VSI and altimeter will ensure that the correct pitch attitude is selected no matter what the weight is. What may be noticeable, however, is the higher power required to maintain airspeed because of the higher drag.

When establishing straight and level flight, use the control instruments, namely the power indicator (throttle) and the AI (control column), to set the expected power and pitch attitude. Fine tuning to accurately hold height, confirmed on the altimeter and VSI, is achieved by making minor corrections to this pitch attitude with the elevator.

Maintaining Heading

Keeping the wings level and the ball centred will ensure that the desired heading is maintained. The heading can be monitored on the **heading indicator,** with any tendency to turn being indicated on the **turn coordinator** (Figure 3-9). The HI is the primary performance instrument used to maintain a constant heading. Remember that it should be realigned periodically with the magnetic compass (every 10 or 15 minutes while in steady flight).

If the aeroplane is allowed to drift off heading, then small coordinated turns (bank and rudder) should be made to regain heading (Figure 3-10). With a reasonable scan rate, you will always have the aeroplane within a few degrees of the desired heading. Aim for perfection as an instrument pilot, and at least remain within the heading limits of ±5°.

As a guide, when correcting for small heading errors, limit the bank angle to the number of degrees to be turned or even less. For instance, a heading change of 5° can be comfortably made with a bank angle of 5° or less. If a significant heading change is required, however, do not exceed the bank required for a rate 1 turn (at

120 kt this will be approximately $^{120}\!/_{10}$ + 7 = 12 + 7 =19° bank angle). Approaching the desired heading, level the wings with aileron and balance with rudder pressure to maintain coordinated flight.

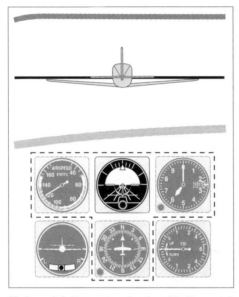

■ Figure 3-8 **Keep wings level and ball centred to achieve straight flight**

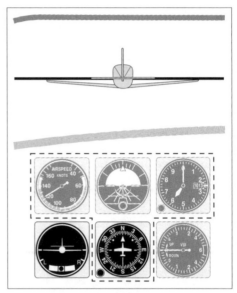

■ Figure 3-9 **Monitor HI and TC for heading performance**

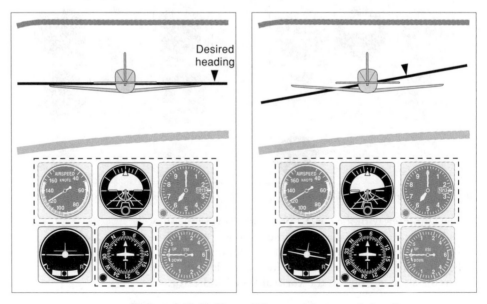

■ Figure 3-10 **Making a slight turn right to regain heading**

Maintaining Height

Perfectly level flight is almost impossible to achieve in real life. Level flight, in practice, actually consists of a series of very small climbs and descents as the aeroplane moves off altitude and is brought back to it again by the pilot. Once again, aim for perfection, and certainly do not allow the aeroplane to deviate from the desired altitude by more than ±100 ft in smooth air; turbulence of course will make this accuracy more difficult to achieve, in which case do the best you can.

You *control* straight and level flight by setting the correct pitch attitude on the attitude indicator and the correct cruise power on the power indicator, and then *monitor* vertical performance on:
- ☐ the altimeter;
- ☐ the vertical speed indicator; and, to a lesser extent
- ☐ the airspeed indicator.

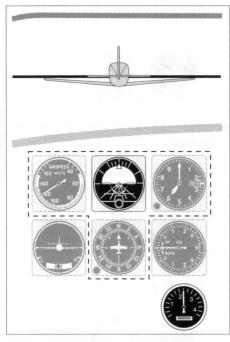

■ *Figure 3-11* **Set power and attitude**

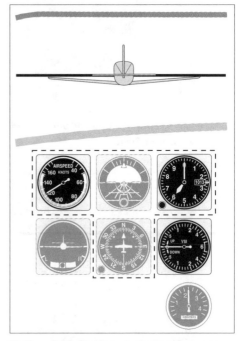

■ *Figure 3-12* **Monitor vertical performance**

The **altimeter,** with the correct pressure setting in the subscale, is used to ensure that the correct altitude is indeed being flown. It will indicate deviations from this altitude but, in smooth air, the earliest sign of a tendency to deviate from altitude will be shown, not on the altimeter, but on the **vertical speed indicator.**

In smooth air, an altitude deviation will be shown first on the VSI.

Often, a slight correction to pitch attitude can be made on the
AI in response to a *trend* on the VSI before any significant deviation is registered on the altimeter. A large VSI indication may
mean a large pitch attitude correction is required. A VSI reading
of 600 ft/min down might suggest an initial pitch correction of
one bar width up, whereas a VSI reading of only 150 ft/min might
suggest that one half bar width correction is adequate.

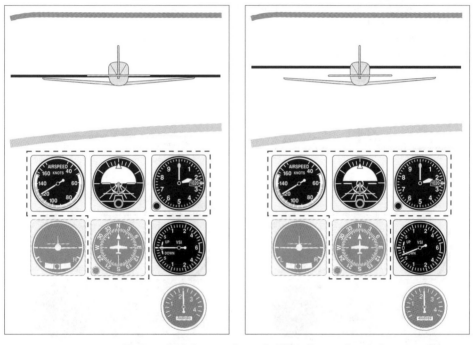

■ *Figure 3-13* **In smooth air, the VSI indicates the pitch error well in
advance of the altimeter**

In rough air, the VSI reading unfortunately will fluctuate
considerably, making it of less value to the pilot. In this situation,
the altimeter becomes the best guide to any tendency to deviate
from altitude.

The **airspeed indicator** also provides valuable information
regarding level flight. If cruise power is set, and the airspeed
gradually increases, then the pitch attitude is too low and the
aeroplane will be gradually descending. This will be indicated on
the VSI and altimeter. Raise the pitch attitude to return to the
desired altitude.

Small Deviations from Altitude

In stable cruise, a small climb will usually be accompanied by a small loss of airspeed. For a gain in altitude of less than 100 ft, you need only make a slight adjustment to pitch attitude, say by lowering it a half bar width on the attitude indicator, to regain altitude (and airspeed).

Once the aeroplane is at or near altitude, the pitch attitude can be raised slightly to maintain level flight. No power alterations should be required during these small corrections to height. Minor adjustments to altitude using elevator alone can be thought of as gentle *zooms* and *dives*.

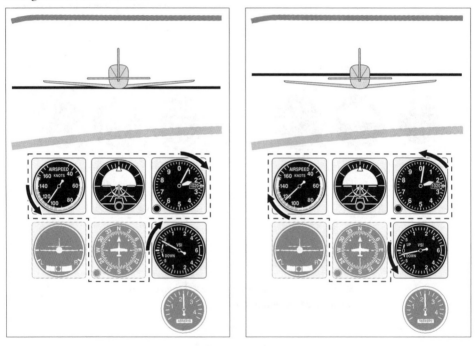

■ *Figure 3-14* **Make a small pitch correction for an altitude deviation of less than 100 ft high**

Conversely, a small descent in a stable cruise will usually be accompanied by a slight gain in airspeed. A deviation of 100 ft or less beneath the desired altitude can be corrected by a slight adjustment to pitch attitude, say by raising it one half bar width on the attitude indicator to regain altitude (and airspeed). Once at or near altitude, the pitch attitude can then be lowered slightly to maintain level flight. No power alterations should be required.

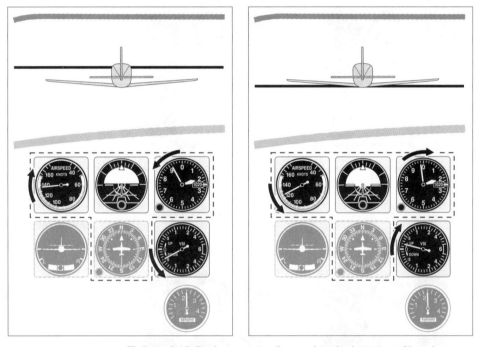

■ *Figure 3-15* **Pitch correction for an altitude deviation of less than 100 ft low**

Larger Deviations from Altitude

Correcting a large deviation from altitude (say in excess of 100 ft) will require an **attitude change** and possibly a **power change** as well.

Even if the altitude is changing rapidly, the correction made to pitch attitude by the pilot should still be smooth, with light control pressures, and can be thought of in two stages: one to stop the movement of the altimeter needle and reduce the VSI indication to zero, and a further pitch correction to return the aeroplane towards the desired altitude. The *total* pitch correction required may only be one or two bar widths on the AI.

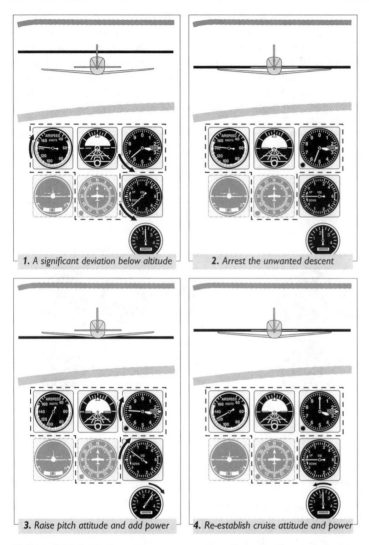

1. A significant deviation below altitude
2. Arrest the unwanted descent
3. Raise pitch attitude and add power
4. Re-establish cruise attitude and power

■ Figure 3-16 **Attitude and power corrections for a significant deviation below altitude**

Following a large deviation below altitude, a significant climb back to the desired altitude of 100 ft or more will probably require increased power for the period of the climb if airspeed is to be maintained. Once back on height at the desired airspeed, cruise power can be reset to maintain that airspeed.

Conversely, a significant descent to regain the desired altitude will require a lower pitch attitude, and a temporary reduction in power to avoid an unwanted airspeed increase. Once back on height with the correct pitch attitude set and at the desired airspeed, cruise power can be reset to maintain that airspeed.

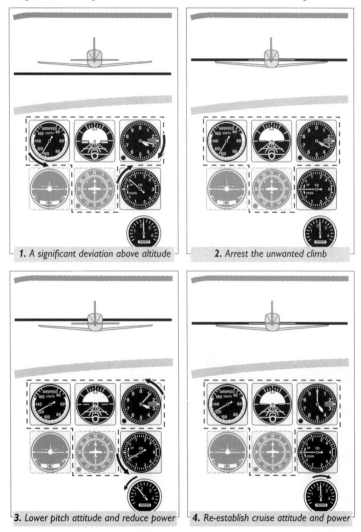

1. A significant deviation above altitude

2. Arrest the unwanted climb

3. Lower pitch attitude and reduce power

4. Re-establish cruise attitude and power

■ Figure 3-17 **Attitude and power corrections for a significant deviation above altitude**

Energy Transfer in Straight and Level Flight

Maintaining both a steady height and a steady airspeed can be thought of in terms of energy management. An aeroplane in flight has **kinetic energy** in the form of airspeed and **potential energy** in the form of height. It is possible to convert between these two forms of energy either by *zooming* to a greater height and converting airspeed to height, or by *diving* and converting height to airspeed. Additional energy, if required, can be supplied to the aeroplane by adding power with the throttle.

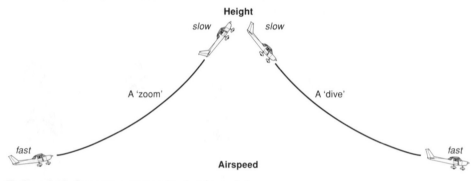

■ *Figure 3-18* **Converting airspeed to height, and vice versa**

If, for instance, the aeroplane is below the desired altitude with the airspeed well in excess of that desired, you can convert the excess airspeed to altitude without the use of additional power. If there is no excess airspeed, however, then additional engine power will be required to maintain airspeed. Conversely, excess height can be lost by lowering the pitch attitude with elevator and either accepting an airspeed increase or reducing power with the throttle to maintain airspeed.

Scanning the vertical performance instruments will tell you what to do. As in all flight, the performance of the aeroplane depends on a combination of both attitude and power but, in straight and level flight, it is easiest to think in terms of controlling:

- ☐ **height** with elevator (pitch attitude); and
- ☐ **airspeed** with throttle (power).

Possible deviations and remedies are shown below.

■ *Figure 3-19* **Possible deviations and remedies**

Recovering from Slightly Unusual Attitudes

It is possible, even probable, that early during instrument training you will find the aeroplane in some slightly unusual attitudes.

The remedies are quite straightforward:

☐ If the aeroplane is banked, level the wings on the AI with the ailerons.

☐ If the nose is too high or too low, ease it into the correct attitude on the AI with elevator.

☐ If the airspeed is excessively high or low, or if large alterations to height are required, some adjustment of power may be necessary.

■ *Figure 3-20* **Nose high and turning left.**
Lower pitch attitude and level the wings.

■ *Figure 3-21* **Nose low and turning left.**
Level the wings and raise the pitch attitude.

Coping with a Faulty Attitude Indicator

The attitude indicator is the master instrument for the pilot and, if it is not functioning correctly, your task is made that much harder. There are situations where it may fail totally, and others where its indications are not perfectly correct, but are still usable.

Re-setting the Index Aeroplane

A symbol of the real aeroplane appears as an **index aeroplane,** or model aeroplane, in the centre of the attitude indicator. Its position can be adjusted, when required, using a small adjustment knob. The index aeroplane should be positioned so that, during normal cruise flight, it will appear in line with the horizon bar. You should always check this on the ground with the aeroplane in a level attitude before every instrument flight.

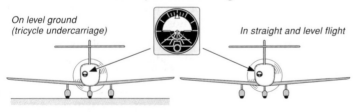

On level ground
(tricycle undercarriage)

In straight and level flight

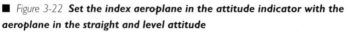

■ *Figure 3-22* **Set the index aeroplane in the attitude indicator with the aeroplane in the straight and level attitude**

If the pre-flight check of the AI shows that the model aeroplane is not properly aligned, then it should be adjusted immediately. If, for some reason, it requires resetting in flight, establish straight and level flight (monitored on the other instruments), and then reset the index aeroplane against the artificial horizon. After resetting, the AI will give its normal indications in all attitudes.

Coping with a Faulty Wings-Level Indication

Occasionally you will see an AI that gives a faulty wings-level indication, due to either a lopsided index aeroplane or an artificial horizon line that is not perfectly horizontal. It may also be due to small gyroscopic precession errors following strenuous manoeuvres, but these will correct themselves and only be short-lived.

The clue that the AI is not indicating bank correctly is that, with the wings held level according to the AI and with the balance ball centred, the heading indicator shows a gradually changing heading and the turn coordinator shows a turn.

To cope with a suspected faulty wings-level indication on the attitude indicator, you should;

☐ **keep the aeroplane in balance** with rudder pressure (ball centred);

☐ **hold the desired heading** with reference to the heading indicator; and

☐ **accept** the slightly erroneous lopsided AI indication.

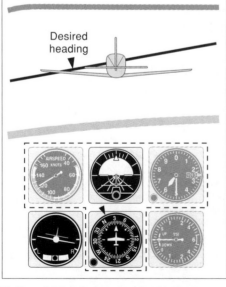

■ *Figure 3-23* **A faulty wings-level indication on the AI**

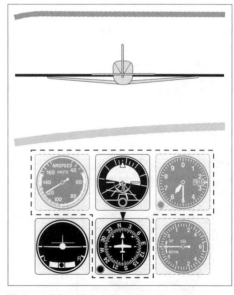

■ *Figure 3-24* **Maintaining heading with a faulty AI**

Failure of the Attitude Indicator

A complete failure of the attitude indicator is possible, although unlikely, since it is generally very reliable. For instance, a vacuum pump failure to a vacuum-driven AI, or an electrical failure to an electrically driven AI, or even an internal gyroscopic failure, will make the AI unusable as the gyroscope runs down.

Any failure of the AI prior to flight should be detected during the pre-flight checks of the instruments while the aeroplane is still on the ground. The rare event of the AI failing in flight, causing you to fly on instruments without reference to the most important one of all, is considered in Chapter 7, *Instrument Flight on a Limited Panel*.

Changing Airspeed in Straight and Level Flight

Normal cruise involves setting cruise power, holding cruise altitude, and accepting the airspeed that is achieved, which should be close to the figure published in the Pilot's Operating Handbook.

On occasions, however, there is a need to fly at other than normal cruise airspeed. This will require a different pitch attitude and a different power setting. To slow the aeroplane down, throttle back and gradually raise the pitch attitude to maintain height; to increase airspeed, advance the throttle, and gradually lower the pitch attitude to maintain height.

Once the desired airspeed is reached, adjust the power to maintain it. The precise power required for steady flight will depend on the amount of total drag, which on the cruise varies with angle of attack and airspeed. High power will be required for:

☐ **high-speed cruise** (when total drag is high mainly due to parasite drag); and

☐ **low-speed cruise** (when total drag is high mainly due to induced drag).

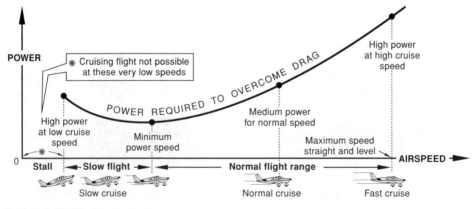

■ *Figure 3-25* **The power curve**

The ASI is the primary performance guide to power requirements during level flight

Medium power will be required for normal cruise. The ASI will confirm whether or not correct power is set. If not, do something about it.

Practising airspeed changes on the cruise is excellent instrument flying practice since pitch, bank, balance and power changes must all be coordinated to maintain constant height and heading. When the pilot changes power, a single-engined propeller-driven aeroplane will tend to move around all three axes of movement. If the propeller rotates clockwise as seen from the cockpit, which is the usual case, adding power will cause the nose to pitch up and yaw left, with a tendency for the aeroplane to bank left.

The pilot, of course, can counteract this by applying forward elevator pressure to avoid the nose pitching up, with right rudder and aileron pressure to overcome the tendency to yaw and roll left. The converse applies when reducing power – hold the nose up and apply left rudder pressure. Refer to the AI to keep the wings level and hold the pitch attitude, and refer to the balance indicator to remain in balance.

Some hints on changing cruise speed follow. The AI gives a direct picture of pitch and bank attitudes. The balance ball gives a direct indication of balance. Useful performance instruments are the altimeter and VSI to ensure that height is being maintained, and the heading indicator to ensure that heading is being maintained. The airspeed indicator will indicate the power requirements. If too slow, add more power; if too fast, reduce power.

The **scan rate** of the flight instruments during the power change needs to be reasonably smart to counteract the pitch/yaw effects smoothly and accurately. For this reason, it is good to develop the skill of judging power changes by throttle movement and engine sound, rather than only by observation of the power indicator. This will allow concentration on the flight instruments until after the power change has been made, at which time a quick glance at the power indicator for fine adjustment will suffice.

If you memorise the approximate power settings necessary to maintain the various cruise speeds, then power handling and airspeed changes become simpler to manage.

Small airspeed changes (say a few knots either way) can generally be handled by a single small power change, and then allowing the aeroplane to gradually slow down or accelerate to the desired speed. Large airspeed changes, however, are most efficiently achieved within a few seconds by **underpowering** on the initial power change for a speed decrease, or **overpowering** on the initial power change for a speed increase. This allows more rapid deceleration or acceleration to the desired speed, at which time the necessary power to maintain that airspeed is set.

The degree of over- or underpowering will depend on how quickly you want to reach the desired speed (typically 200 to 300 rpm, or 3–4″ MP), and also on engine limitations (which must not be exceeded). Once the desired airspeed is achieved and suitable power is set, the ASI will indicate if further fine adjustment of power to maintain airspeed is required. In level flight, the ASI is the primary guide to power requirements.

To Increase Speed in Level Flight

A small airspeed increase, 5 kt for instance, may be achieved by a small power increase that allows the airspeed to gradually increase by the desired amount. To achieve a large airspeed increase without delay, however, excess power should be applied to accelerate the aeroplane quickly, and then adjusted when the desired airspeed is reached. This can be thought of as *overpowering* on the initial power change, a typical amount being 200–300 rpm (or 3–4″ MP for CSUs).

☐ **Increase power** with the throttle (*overpower* for large speed increases). Hold forward pressure to maintain height, referring to the VSI and altimeter; balance with rudder pressure referring to the balance ball; keep wings level with aileron and check HI for heading. See Figure 3-26.

☐ **Lower the pitch attitude** slightly on the AI to maintain height (VSI and altimeter), and allow airspeed to increase to the desired value (ASI).

☐ **At or approaching** the desired airspeed, adjust the power to maintain it (ASI).

☐ **Hold the pitch attitude** (AI) using elevator, and trim off the elevator pressure.

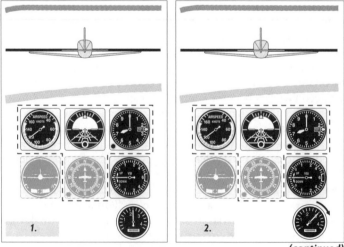

(continued)

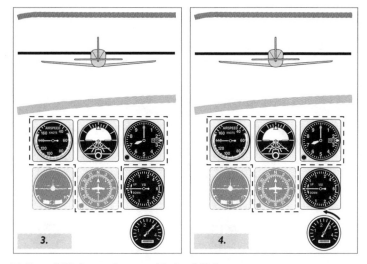

■ *Figure 3-26* **Increasing speed in level flight**

To Decrease Speed in Level Flight

A small speed decrease can be achieved with a single small power change, but a large speed decrease without delay is best achieved with *underpowering*. Once the aeroplane has decelerated to the desired airspeed, power can be increased to maintain it.

☐ **Decrease power** with the throttle (*underpower* for large speed decreases). Hold backward pressure to maintain height referring to the VSI and altimeter; balance with rudder pressure referring to the balance ball; keep wings level with aileron and check HI for heading. See Figure 3-27.

☐ **Raise the pitch attitude** slightly on the AI to maintain height (VSI and altimeter), and allow airspeed to decrease to the desired value (ASI).

☐ **At or approaching** the desired airspeed, adjust the power to maintain it (ASI).

☐ **Hold the pitch attitude** (AI), and trim.

Once approximate level flight is achieved:

☐ **the height** can be accurately maintained with elevator; and
☐ **the airspeed** can be accurately maintained with power.

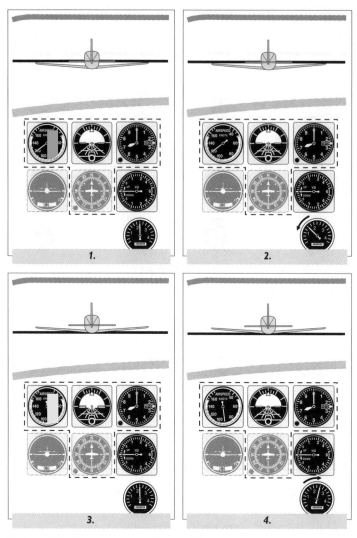

■ *Figure 3-27* **Decreasing speed in level flight**

Changing Configuration in Level Flight

On occasions it is necessary to change the configuration of the aeroplane while maintaining level flight, for instance when lowering some flap or lowering the undercarriage while manoeuvring prior to landing. Before making any changes in configuration, you must ensure that airframe limitations are satisfied. For instance, the airspeed must be less than V_{FE} before flaps are lowered, and below V_{LE} in a retractable undercarriage aeroplane before the landing gear is extended.

Lowering the flaps or landing gear in most aeroplanes will cause an increase in total drag and therefore a tendency to lose airspeed, as well as a pitch change. With familiarity, you will be prepared to counteract these tendencies smoothly and comfortably. Unwanted pitch changes can be counteracted using elevator pressure, with reference to the attitude indicator, altimeter and VSI. Airspeed control is achieved using the throttle, with reference to the airspeed indicator, additional power being required to counteract the increased drag if airspeed is to be maintained. If, however, a further airspeed reduction is required, application of additional power can be delayed.

Lowering Flap

To maintain height and airspeed as flap is lowered:

☐ **Ensure IAS** is at or below V_{FE} with reference to the ASI;

☐ **Lower the flaps,** maintaining height with elevator pressure (monitoring the VSI and altimeter), and maintaining airspeed with power (monitoring the ASI). A lower pitch attitude and higher power can be expected.

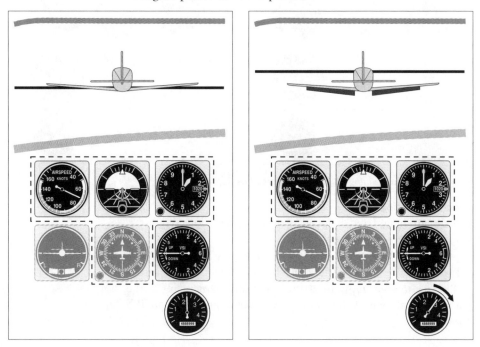

■ *Figure 3-28* **Maintaining height and airspeed as flap is lowered**

Raising Flap

To maintain height and airspeed as flap is raised:

☐ **Ensure IAS** is at or below V_{FE};

☐ **Raise the flaps,** maintaining height with elevator back pressure, and airspeed with reduced power. If an airspeed increase is desired, then the power can be adjusted, if necessary, to achieve this.

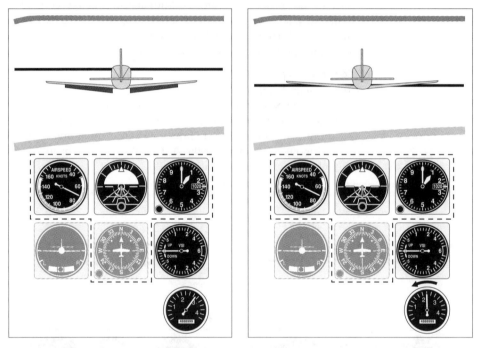

■ *Figure 3-29* **Maintaining height and airspeed as flap is raised**

Lowering Landing Gear

To maintain height and airspeed as landing gear is lowered:

☐ **Ensure IAS** is at or below V_{LE};

☐ **Lower the undercarriage,** maintaining height with elevator pressure, and airspeed with additional power.

This manoeuvre typically is used in instrument flying as the aeroplane is flown level towards the descent point for an ILS approach.

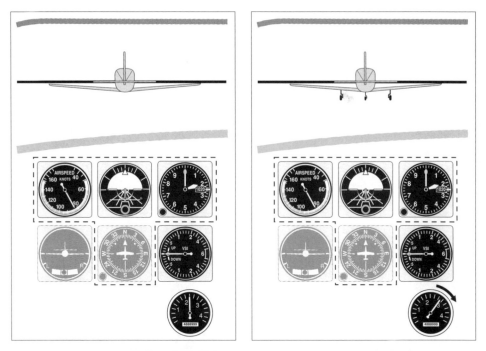

■ *Figure 3-30* **Maintaining height and airspeed as the landing gear**
is lowered

Raising Landing Gear

To maintain height and airspeed as landing gear is raised:

☐ **Ensure IAS** is at or below V_{LE};

☐ **Raise the undercarriage,** maintaining height with elevator
pressure, and airspeed with power.

Usually the undercarriage is raised during the initial climb-out
after take-off, although there are occasions when it may be
required to raise the gear from the extended position at other
times, for instance when manoeuvring in level flight and deciding
to discontinue an approach to land.

The Straight Climb and Descent

With the correct power and attitude set, the aeroplane should achieve the desired performance, which in this case is a straight climb. The **control instruments** for the climb are the same as for all manoeuvres:
- **the power indicator,** used to set power with the throttle; and
- **the attitude indicator,** used to set pitch attitude with the elevator (typically one or two bar widths above the cruise position).

The Straight Climb

To Enter a Climb
As in visual flight, the procedure for entering the climb on instruments is P–A–T: power–attitude–trim.
- **Set climb power** using the throttle (with the mixture RICH if necessary).
- **Select the climb attitude** with reference to the attitude indicator using elevator.
- **Trim.**

In the typical single-engined propeller-driven aeroplane there will be a tendency for the nose to pitch up and yaw left as power is applied. To ensure that heading is maintained, the wings are kept level on the AI with aileron, and the balance ball kept centred with rudder pressure.

Hold the attitude and allow the airspeed to settle on the ASI, then make fine adjustments to the attitude with elevator to achieve the desired climbing speed precisely, and finally trim off any steady control pressure. It is a good idea to make a coarse trim adjustment initially, followed by a finer trim adjustment as the precise climb speed is achieved and maintained.

Once established in the climb, the climbing performance of the aeroplane, or its **vertical performance,** is monitored on:
- the altimeter;
- the vertical speed indicator; and
- the airspeed indicator.

With a smooth transition from level flight to a climb, the VSI will show an upward trend, and then the altimeter reading will start to increase. The VSI will eventually indicate a rate appropriate to the stabilised climb airspeed and pitch attitude for the power set.

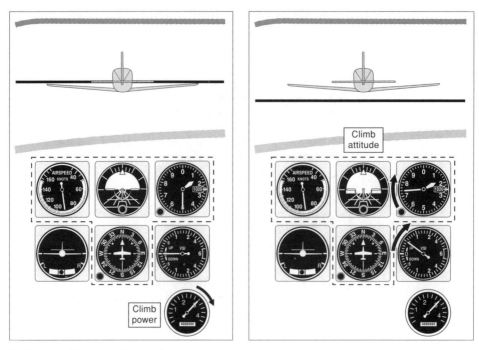

■ Figure 4-1 **Enter the climb with power, attitude and trim**

Maintaining the Climb

Keeping the wings level with aileron and the ball centred with
rudder pressure will ensure that heading is maintained, which can
be verified on the heading indicator. With climb power set (often
full power in light aircraft), you achieve the desired climbing
airspeed precisely with slight adjustments to pitch attitude on the
AI using elevator.

> *The airspeed indicator is the primary performance instrument in the climb*
> *to ensure that pitch attitude is correct.*

■ Figure 4-2 **Make minor pitch attitude adjustments to maintain**
climbing airspeed

Once established in the climb, any fine adjustments to pitch
attitude should be confined to just one quarter or one half bar

width on the AI. If the climbing airspeed is correct, then the pitch attitude is correct. If the airspeed is low, then the pitch attitude is too high and should be lowered slightly. Conversely, if the airspeed is too high, then the pitch attitude should be raised slightly. Once the airspeed has settled to its new value, any steady control pressure can be trimmed off.

Heading is maintained by keeping the wings level on the AI and the balance ball centred, and direction can be monitored on the HI. Small heading corrections can be made with gentle coordinated turns.

Clearing turns (that are made in visual flight every 500 ft or so to look for other aircraft) are meaningless in cloud and nil visibility but, if you happen to be in visual conditions (which is often the case during an instrument flight), clearing turns may be made. During training, your instructor will probably restrict your outside vision to simulate instrument conditions, but he will require clearing turns to be made periodically for him to adequately perform his function as safety pilot.

Engine temperatures and pressures should be checked periodically during the climb, since the engine is working hard and the cooling airflow is less, but do not be distracted from your scan of the flight instruments for more than a few seconds at a time.

As the desired cruising altitude is approached, the altimeter should be increasingly brought into the scan, and its subscale checked to ensure that the correct subscale setting (Regional QNH, 1013, Aerodrome QNH or QFE) is wound in.

Levelling Off from the Climb

Raise the pitch attitude and reduce the rate of climb to capture the desired altitude.

As for visual flight, the procedure for levelling off from a climb on instruments is A-P-T: attitude-power-trim. As the desired altitude is approached, the focus for changes in pitch attitude shifts from the airspeed indicator to the altimeter – the aim being to lower the pitch attitude to capture the desired altitude. Levelling off should be commenced before actually reaching the altitude, a suitable lead-in height being "10% of the rate of climb", which at RoC 500 ft/min would be 50 ft before reaching the desired altitude.

Commencing at the lead-in height, gradually lower the pitch attitude towards the level flight position on the AI. The VSI will show a gradually reducing climb rate, and movement of the altimeter needle will slow down. The aim is to reduce the rate of climb to zero just as the desired altitude is captured.

Normally, climb power is retained after levelling off to allow the aeroplane to accelerate to the cruise speed. Once at the desired airspeed, reduce to cruise power, holding the desired pitch attitude with elevator, and trim.

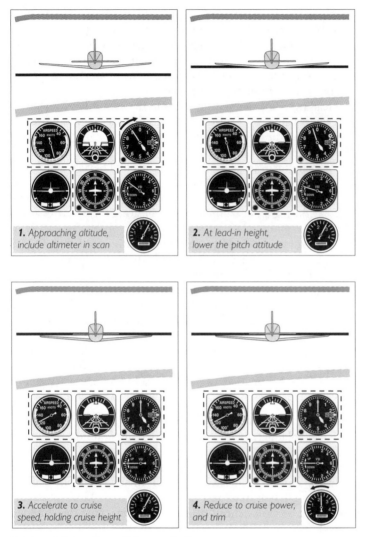

1. Approaching altitude, include altimeter in scan

2. At lead-in height, lower the pitch attitude

3. Accelerate to cruise speed, holding cruise height

4. Reduce to cruise power, and trim

■ Figure 4-3 **Levelling off from a climb**

Heading is monitored on the HI, and will remain constant if the wings are kept level and the balance ball centred. Heading corrections can be made using shallow coordinated turns. Minor adjustments to pitch attitude using the elevator will be required to maintain the exact height. If a particular cruise airspeed is desired, then power adjustments may also be required.

Climbing at Different Airspeeds

With climb power set, climbing airspeed is selected with pitch attitude on the AI, a higher pitch attitude resulting in a lower

airspeed. Different climb airspeeds are used to achieve different objectives, for instance:
- **the best angle of climb** airspeed (V_X) to clear obstacles;
- **the best rate of climb** airspeed (V_Y) to gain height as quickly as possible;
- **the cruise-climb** airspeed, sacrificing rate of climb for a higher airspeed, often used to provide faster journeys, better aeroplane control because of the increased airflow over the control surfaces, better engine cooling, and a more comfortable (lower) aeroplane attitude.

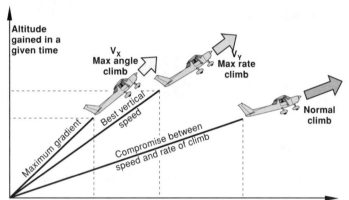

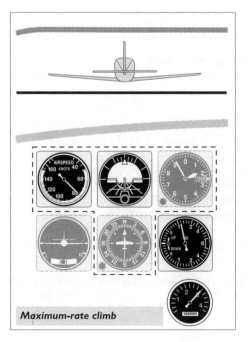

Maximum-rate climb

(continued)

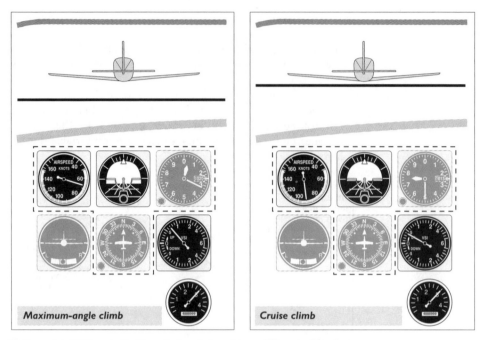

Maximum-angle climb

Cruise climb

■ *Figure 4-4* **Different climbing airspeeds to achieve different objectives**

The precise values of V_X and V_Y appear in the Pilot's Operating Handbook. To achieve the desired airspeed, simply adjust the pitch attitude on the AI, the airspeed indicator being the primary performance instrument to verify that pitch attitude is correct.

Variations on Entering the Climb

The technique used to enter the climb from level flight will depend on the level airspeed and the desired climb speed. If the same airspeed is to be used both cruising and climbing, then simultaneously apply power and gently raise the pitch attitude to maintain the airspeed and then, once settled into the climb, trim off any steady pressure.

If, however, the climb airspeed is to be less than the cruising airspeed (which is generally the case), then you can either:

☐ **apply power** and raise the pitch attitude, allow the airspeed to wash off to climb speed, and then make pitch adjustments to maintain the desired climb speed (the usual P–A–T); or

☐ **raise the pitch attitude** and allow the speed to wash-off before applying power to maintain the desired climb speed (A–P–T).

In general, the order P–A–T is acceptable, but some instructors prefer the second method.

Climbing at a Particular Rate

Controlling the rate of climb to a specific value in most light aircraft is not generally required, because of their moderate performance capabilities even at full power. High-powered aeroplanes, however, may occasionally be required to climb at a particular rate.

The airspeed in a climb is controlled by small alterations in pitch attitude using elevator, with the airspeed indicator as the primary performance instrument for climb speed. You have a measure of **rate of climb** from either:

☐ the **vertical speed indicator (VSI)**; or
☐ the **clock and the altimeter combined.**

500 ft/min rate of climb indicated on the VSI

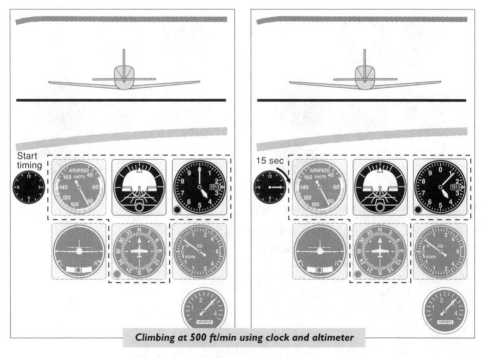

Climbing at 500 ft/min using clock and altimeter

■ *Figure 4-5* **Monitoring rate of climb**

The VSI, after it has stabilised, is normally the primary performance instrument for rate of climb but, if turbulence causes the VSI to fluctuate, then you can either estimate the average reading of the VSI, or use the clock and altimeter to time the climb. In Figure 4-5, the aeroplane has climbed 125 ft in 15 seconds (¼ minute), a rate of 500 ft/min.

Power can be adjusted until the desired rate of climb is achieved precisely, accompanied by minor adjustments of pitch attitude on the AI to hold airspeed. For instance, in Figure 4-6, a decrease in power to reduce the rate of climb from 900 ft/min to 500 ft/min will require a slight lowering of the pitch attitude to maintain a constant airspeed of 80 kt.

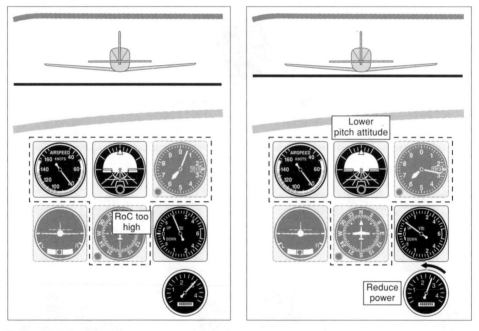

■ Figure 4-6 **Establishing a precise rate of climb**

Conversely, the rate of climb can be increased at a constant airspeed by adding power and raising the pitch attitude. If, however, maximum power is already being used (often the case in light aircraft), the only way of improving rate of climb is to fly closer to V_Y, the best rate of climb airspeed.

Be warned that raising the pitch attitude too high, and reducing the airspeed to *below* V_Y, will lead to a poorer rate of climb.

In an extreme case, the aeroplane may simply 'stagger' along in a nose-high attitude with a poor rate of climb (if any), facing the possibility of a stall, and with the risk of poor engine cooling because of the high power and reduced cooling airflow.

| Climbing into Cloud after Take-Off

The actual take-off ground run and lift-off will be made with external visual reference to the runway and its surroundings. Once airborne and climbing away from the ground, however, it is possible that visual reference to ground objects and to the natural horizon will be lost. This will occur if the aeroplane enters cloud, but it may also occur in conditions of poor visibility (e.g. mist, haze, smog, rain, snow or dust), or at night.

> *Between take-off and loss of external reference, you must transfer your attention to the instruments.*

The importance of the instrument checks made prior to take-off is obvious, since these may now suddenly become the only source of attitude and performance information.

When instrument conditions are expected to be entered shortly after becoming airborne, carry out a visual take-off and stabilise the aeroplane in the climb-out, with climb power and climb attitude set, and with the aeroplane in trim for the climb speed. In other words, make a normal visual take-off. Then, *prior* to entering cloud or otherwise losing visual reference, transfer your attention from external references to the instrument panel.

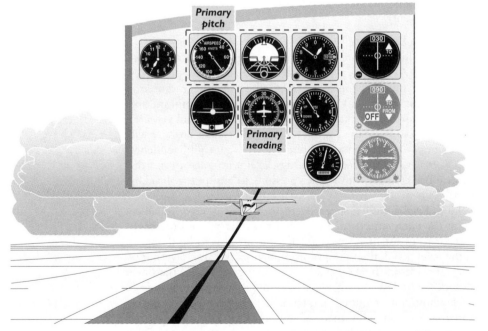

■ *Figure 4-7* **Transfer your attention to the instrument panel shortly after take-off**

- ☐ **Maintain pitch attitude** and wings level on the AI, with the ball centred.
- ☐ **Hold airspeed** on the ASI with small pitch changes on the AI.
- ☐ **Keep in trim.**
- ☐ **Maintain heading** on the HI with small coordinated turns.
- ☐ **Monitor climbing** performance on the altimeter and VSI.

Transferring attention to the flight instruments shortly after lift-off when established in the climb-out is especially important at night, when there is little ground lighting or when low cloud might be encountered unexpectedly. See Chapter 25.

The Straight Descent

With the correct power and attitude set, the aeroplane should achieve the desired performance, which in this case is a straight descent. The **control instruments** for the descent are the same as for all manoeuvres:
- ☐ **the power indicator,** used to set or remove power with the throttle;
- ☐ **the attitude indicator,** used to set pitch attitude with the elevator (slightly below the horizon bar for a powered descent, and typically one or two widths below the horizon bar for a glide descent).

To Enter a Descent
As in visual flight, the procedure for entering a descent on instruments is P-A-T: power-attitude-trim. Reduce the power by moving the mixture control to RICH (fully in), the carburettor control to HOT (fully out) if the power reduction is significant, and smoothly move the throttle out until the desired descent power is set. Back-pressure on the control column and rudder pressure will be required to counteract the "pitch down/yaw right" tendency as power is reduced. Keep the wings level with aileron, and the balance ball centred with rudder pressure, to ensure that heading is maintained.

Hold height until airspeed decreases to that desired, and then lower the pitch attitude one or two bar widths beneath the horizon bar to maintain airspeed. (If descent speed is to be the same as the level speed, then the power reduction and the lowering of pitch attitude on the AI should be simultaneous.) Hold the pitch attitude and allow the airspeed to settle, then make any minor pitch adjustments required, and trim. It is a good idea to make an initial coarse trim adjustment after the power and attitude have been selected, followed by a finer trim adjustment once the precise airspeed is achieved and maintained.

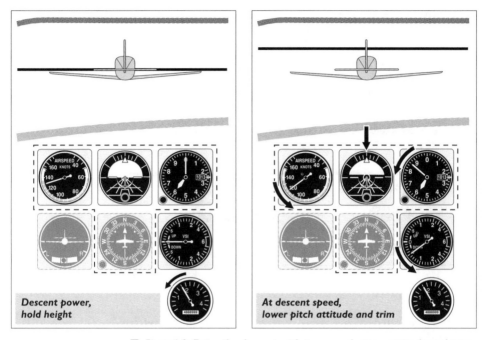

■ Figure 4-8 **Enter the descent with power reduction, attitude and trim**

Descent performance, or **vertical performance,** is monitored on:
☐ **the altimeter;**
☐ **the vertical speed indicator; and**
☐ **the airspeed indicator.**

With a smooth transition from level flight to a descent, the VSI will show a downward trend, and then the altimeter reading will start to decrease. The VSI will eventually indicate a rate appropriate to the stabilised descent airspeed and pitch attitude for the power set.

■ Figure 4-9 **Monitoring descent performance**

Maintaining the Descent

Keeping the wings level with aileron and the ball centred with rudder pressure will ensure that heading is maintained, which can be verified on the heading indicator. With descent power set (often throttle fully closed), you achieve the precise descent airspeed desired with slight adjustments to pitch attitude on the AI using elevator.

> *The airspeed indicator is the primary performance instrument in the descent (as in the climb) to verify that pitch attitude is correct.*

Airspeed low	Airspeed high
Lower the pitch attitude	**Raise the pitch attitude**

■ *Figure 4-10* **Make minor pitch attitude adjustments to maintain descent airspeed**

Once established in the descent, any fine adjustments to pitch attitude should be confined to just one quarter or one half bar widths. If the descent airspeed is correct, the pitch attitude is correct. If the airspeed is low, the pitch attitude is too high and should be lowered slightly. Conversely, if the airspeed is too high, the pitch attitude should be raised slightly. Once the airspeed has settled to its new value, any steady control pressure can be trimmed off.

If the power is kept constant, a pitch attitude change is the only way of achieving a change in airspeed, and this will be accompanied by a change in the rate of descent. If a precise rate of descent is required, as well as a precise airspeed, then a combination of power and attitude is used (see page 79).

In a prolonged descent with low power, thought should be given to clearing the engine every 1,000 ft or so by applying 50% power for a few seconds. This will keep the engine and oil warm, avoid carbon fouling on the spark plugs, and ensure that the carburettor heat is still supplying warm air. Be prepared to counteract the pitch/yaw tendencies as the power is changed.

As the desired altitude or flight level is approached, the altimeter should be increasingly brought into the scan, and the subscale checked for correct pressure setting (Regional QNH, 1013, Aerodrome QNH or QFE).

Levelling Off from a Descent

Raise the pitch attitude to capture the desired altitude.

The procedure for levelling off from a descent is P–A–T: power-attitude-trim. As the desired altitude is approached, the focus for changes in pitch attitude shifts from the airspeed indicator to the altimeter, the aim being to raise the pitch attitude to capture the desired altitude, and to use power to achieve the desired cruise speed. A suitable lead-in height is "10% of the rate of descent", which at RoD 400 ft/min would be 40 ft before reaching the desired altitude.

Commencing at the lead-in height, smoothly apply cruise power (carburettor heat COLD), and gradually raise the pitch attitude towards the level flight position on the AI, keeping the aeroplane in balance with rudder pressure. The VSI will show a gradually decreasing descent rate, and movement of the altimeter needle will slow down. The aim is to reduce the rate of descent to zero just as the desired altitude is captured. A fairly quick scan rate will help to make this a smooth and comfortable manoeuvre. Once established in level flight at the desired airspeed, trim off any steady pressures.

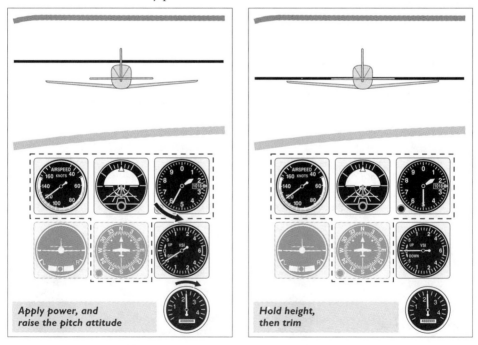

Apply power, and raise the pitch attitude

Hold height, then trim

■ Figure 4-11 **Levelling off from a descent**

Heading is monitored on the HI, and will remain constant if the wings are kept level and the balance ball centred. Heading corrections can be made using shallow coordinated turns. Minor adjustments to pitch attitude using the elevator will be required to maintain height. If a particular cruise airspeed is desired, then power adjustments may also be required.

If the cruise airspeed is significantly greater than the descent airspeed, then power can be added a little earlier than usual, say 100 ft before reaching the desired altitude, and the aeroplane can commence accelerating to be at or near the higher cruise speed just as levelling out is completed.

Climbing Away from a Descent

This is a very important instrument manoeuvre, since it is used when you elect to go around from a missed approach to land, as well as at any other time you wish to go directly from a descent into a climb. The procedure is still P–A–T: power-attitude-trim, except that it is climb power and climb attitude that are selected, and the change in control pressures and trim will be much greater than in previous manoeuvres.

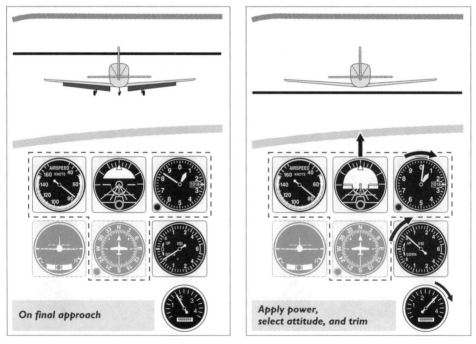

On final approach

Apply power, select attitude, and trim

■ Figure 4-12 **Climbing away from a descent**

A greater pitch/yaw tendency can be expected with the large power increase in the go–around, and this must be counteracted.

In a genuine go-around, full power will probably be used (with carburettor heat COLD and mixture RICH). Once established in the climb, it is acceptable to make a coarse trim adjustment, and then fine tune the trim as the aeroplane settles down in the climb.

For a go-around off final approach (perhaps because unexpected cloud has been encountered at a low level) then, associated with the application of climb power and the selection of a suitable pitch attitude, you may also have to think about retracting the undercarriage and raising the flaps.

Descending at a Particular Rate

Airspeed in the descent at constant power is controlled with small pitch attitude changes, using the ASI as the primary performance instrument. Rate of descent is shown directly on the VSI, or can be determined from the clock and altimeter.

The desired **airspeed** and **rate of descent** can be achieved by using a combination of **power** and **attitude.** Again, it is the interplay of power and attitude that determines the performance of the aeroplane. If the rate of descent is too great, it can be reduced by raising the pitch attitude and increasing power to maintain the same airspeed. Retrimming to relieve steady control pressures will be necessary once the aeroplane has settled into the new descent.

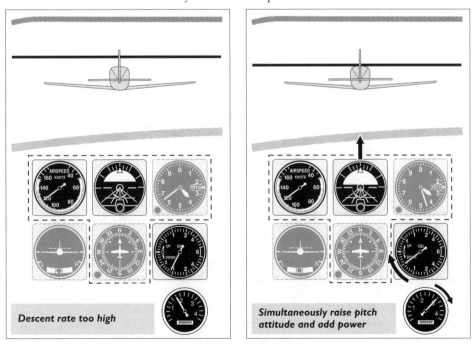

Descent rate too high

Simultaneously raise pitch attitude and add power

■ Figure 4-13 **Reducing the rate of descent**

Conversely, the rate of descent can be increased by simultaneously lowering the pitch attitude and reducing power to maintain the same airspeed.

If you cannot reduce power because the throttle is already fully closed, then the rate of descent can be increased by other means:

- ☐ **by lowering the pitch attitude** and accepting a higher airspeed; or
- ☐ **by increasing drag,** which can be achieved by lowering flaps, lowering the landing gear, or deploying spoilers if fitted.

The Precision Approach

While the precision approach will be fully covered in the latter stages of your instrument training, it is appropriate to introduce it here.

The precision approach is a very precise instrument descent towards the touchdown zone on a runway. If the runway is not sighted by a certain minimum altitude, then a go-around is made; if the runway is sighted and the aeroplane is in a position to be landed, then a landing may be made.

The most common precision approach in instrument flying is achieved using the electronic **instrument landing system** (ILS) that provides:

- ☐ **guidance in azimuth** (left or right of the extended runway centreline); and
- ☐ **approach slope guidance** (referred to as the **glideslope** even though the aeroplane will not in fact be gliding, but in a powered descent).

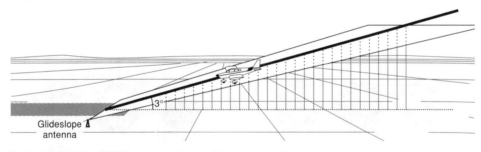

■ *Figure 4-14* **The glideslope onto the touchdown zone of a runway**

The ILS glideslope is an inclined surface, typically 3° or 1:20 to the horizontal, that intersects the runway in the touchdown zone, usually about 300 metres in from the threshold. It is generally intercepted 2,000 ft or 3,000 ft above aerodrome level, some 7 to 10 nm from the aerodrome and in line with the runway. The position of the glideslope relative to the aeroplane is displayed in the cockpit on an instrument associated with the VHF-NAV radio.

Hold the glideslope with
elevator. Hold airspeed
with power.

Maintaining the glideslope at the desired airspeed during an instrument approach is one of the major tasks of an instrument pilot, but this task is very similar to maintaining straight and level cruise flight. In both cases, you are trying to direct the aeroplane along a particular surface (horizontal for level flight, sloping for the approach) while maintaining a particular airspeed. The easiest control technique in both cases is:

☐ **hold the glideslope** (or height) with elevator;
☐ **hold the airspeed** with throttle.

As always, **power** and **attitude** (controlled by throttle and elevator respectively) determine the **performance** of the aeroplane. Often a change in one will necessitate a change in the other, but it is still easier to separate the functions in your own mind as stated above – maintain glideslope with attitude and airspeed with power.

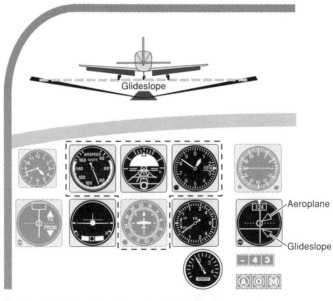

■ Figure 4-15 **An accurate approach to land**

Turning

The aim of a turn is to change heading. This is achieved by banking the aeroplane and tilting the lift force produced by the wings. The horizontal component of the tilted lift force (known as the centripetal force) pulls the aeroplane into the turn.

If height is to be maintained, the vertical component of the tilted lift force must be increased to equal the weight. This is achieved with back pressure on the control column to increase the angle of attack (raise the pitch attitude), thereby increasing the lift generated by the wings.

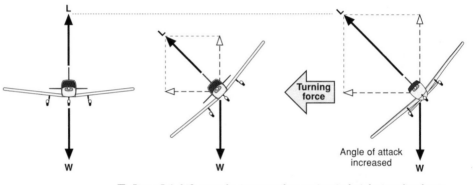

■ *Figure 5-1* **Lift must be increased to maintain height in a level turn**

A consequence of the increased lift is increased induced drag. The aeroplane will therefore slow down unless power is applied. In a medium turn, the loss of a few knots is usually acceptable, and additional power is not normally applied. The airspeed loss is regained fairly quickly once the aeroplane is returned to straight and level flight.

Bank Angle and Rate of Turn

The standard rate of turn in instrument flying is **rate 1,** with the heading of the aeroplane changing at **3° per second.** At rate 1, it will therefore take 30 seconds to turn through a heading change of 90°, 1 minute to turn through 180°, and 2 minutes to turn through 360°.

Rate of turn is a function of airspeed and bank angle, and so a higher airspeed requires a greater bank angle to achieve the same rate of turn. A very quick method of estimating the bank angle required for a rate 1 turn is *airspeed*/10 + 7. For instance, at an airspeed of 80 kt, the bank angle for a rate 1 turn is 80/10 + 7 = 8 + 7 = 15° bank angle, whereas at 150 kt it is 22°.

If you prefer, you can simply drop the last numeral of the airspeed and then add 7. For instance, at 125 kt, bank angle required for a rate 1 turn is 12 + 7 = 19°.

It is permissible to use a turn in excess of rate 1, but it is strongly advised not to exceed a bank angle of 25° in instrument conditions (although your instructor may use steep turns during your training to give you practice in coordination of eyes, hands and feet).

Do not exceed a bank angle of 25° in normal instrument flight.

Be in Trim before Commencing the Turn

A turn is usually commenced from straight flight. It can be flown more accurately if the aeroplane, prior to being banked, is exactly on height, on speed, and in trim. There is no need to retrim during the turn, since it will only be a transient manoeuvre and the aeroplane will most likely be returned to straight flight fairly quickly.

In Visual Conditions, Keep a Good Lookout

A good lookout is essential in visual flight but, in cloud with zero visibility, there is little point. However, a surprising amount of a typical instrument flight will occur in visual conditions, and a good lookout then shows good airmanship. During training, the instructor will act as safety pilot and maintain a good lookout for you.

Roll-In and Roll-Out Rate

All instrument flying should be smooth and unhurried. Turns should be entered at a comfortable rate with coordinated aileron and rudder pressure, with time allowed to check the attitude indicator for bank angle and the balance ball for balance. As training progresses, and the rate of scanning and interpreting the instruments increases, roll-in and roll-out of turns can occur at a faster rate if desired. Strive to achieve a constant rate of roll-in and roll-out for all turns, which will make it easier to judge when to commence the roll-out onto a precise heading.

Part (i)
The Medium Level Turn

Rolling into a Medium Turn

Note the position of the index aeroplane on the attitude indicator in steady straight and level flight before entering the turn, and then roll into the turn at a comfortable roll rate with coordinated aileron and rudder pressure. At the desired bank angle, the roll–in can be stopped by neutralising the ailerons and keeping the ball centred with rudder pressure, and then holding a steady bank angle.

> **Apply back pressure to prevent height loss.**

Early in the roll in, the pitch attitude can remain the same as before entry but, as the bank angle increases, a height loss will be seen on the VSI and altimeter unless the pitch attitude is raised slightly with back pressure. The VSI is the best guide in smooth air for correct pitch attitude in the level turn, since it will show a tendency to depart from height before the altimeter registers any change. In rough air, however, the VSI fluctuates and is of less value, and the altimeter then becomes the primary guide to correct pitch attitude.

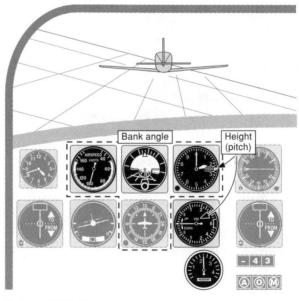

■ *Figure 5-2* **Rolling into a level turn**

Maintaining a Medium Level Turn

Bank angle and pitch attitude are maintained on the AI, which is a control instrument, and the ball is kept centred. The **bank pointer** on the AI will give an accurate indication of the bank angle, in degrees.

Maintain bank angle and pitch attitude on the AI.

Turning performance can be confirmed on the turn coordinator, which is graduated to indicate a rate 1 turn of 3°/sec. Small bank angle corrections, when required, can be made on the AI using aileron. There is generally no need to check the heading indicator until well established in the turn and approaching the desired heading (which at rate 1 will be 30 seconds away for a 90° change of heading).

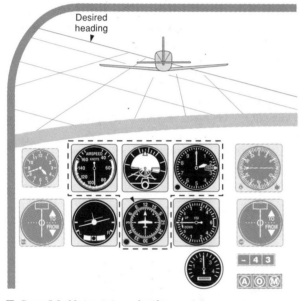

■ *Figure 5-3 Maintaining a level turn on instruments*

Confirm **vertical performance** on the VSI and altimeter, making any small pitch corrections on the AI using elevator. In general, slight back pressure will be required, increasing as the bank angle becomes steeper.

Confirm **balance** with the balance ball, and keep it centred with rudder pressure. Confirm **airspeed** with the airspeed indicator and be prepared for a loss of several knots. If a constant airspeed is required, then increase power slightly.

It is difficult to hold bank angle, height and balance perfectly, but a good instrument pilot will notice trends very quickly and act to correct them. Aim for perfection, and at least stay well within the limits of ±5° bank angle and ±100 ft of altitude during the turn. Remember that the **performance instruments** (VSI, altimeter, turn coordinator) may indicate a need for change, but these changes should be made with reference to the **control instruments.** In particular, use the attitude indicator for any pitch attitude or bank angle changes. The throttle can be used for airspeed control in the level turn, if required.

Rolling Out of a Level Turn

Begin the roll-out a few degrees before the desired heading. A suitable lead is by one half of the bank angle. For example, if the bank angle in the turn is 20°, commence roll-out 10° before reaching the desired heading. Aim to level the wings just as the desired heading is reached.

Roll out of the turn at a comfortable roll rate with coordinated aileron and rudder pressure. The **attitude indicator** is monitored for control of the bank angle during the early part of the roll-out, and the **heading indicator** monitored to check that the desired heading is achieved.

Vertical performance is confirmed on the VSI and altimeter, with small pitch adjustments on the AI to maintain height. The back pressure applied on entering the turn can now be released, and the pitch attitude lowered slightly.

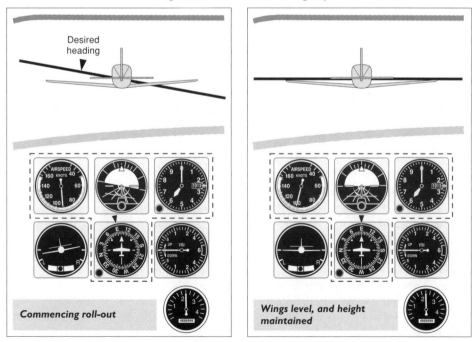

■ Figure 5-4 **Rolling out of a turn**

After the roll-out, your instrument scan should revert to the normal straight and level scan:

☐ **use the AI** to set the pitch attitude and hold the wings level;
☐ **keep the balance ball** centred; and confirm:
☐ **vertical performance** on the VSI and altimeter (hold height with elevator);
☐ **directional performance** on the heading indicator and turn coordinator (adjust heading with gentle coordinated turns if necessary); and
☐ **monitor airspeed** on the ASI (controlling with power if necessary).

The few knots of airspeed that were lost in the turn will gradually return. If additional power was applied in the turn to maintain airspeed, it should be removed in the roll-out to avoid an unwanted airspeed increase.

Instrument Turns onto a Specific Heading

Turns onto a particular heading can be achieved using:

☐ the heading indicator;
☐ **timed turns,** with the clock and turn coordinator, knowing that rate 1 is 3°/second; or
☐ the magnetic compass.

The primary source of direction information in the aeroplane is the magnetic compass, but it is an awkward instrument to use, especially when the aeroplane is turning and causing it to read incorrectly. Since directional information is very important in a turn, pilots are provided with a more stable instrument, the **heading indicator (HI),** driven by a gyroscope and not subject to turning errors. The HI occupies a position within the main area of the instrument panel where it can easily be scanned, whereas the magnetic compass is well away, generally somewhere above the cockpit coaming panel near the windscreen – not out of sight, but certainly outside the primary scanning area.

Using the Heading Indicator

Unlike the magnetic compass, the HI does *not* automatically align itself with magnetic north. For its reading to be meaningful, ensure that the HI is realigned with the magnetic compass during steady straight and level flight every 10 or 15 minutes.

Ensure that the HI is correctly aligned with the magnetic compass.

Before commencing a turn, the HI can be used to decide whether to turn left or right onto the new heading. Usually, the turn is made in the shorter direction, but not always. In a *teardrop turn* carried out in certain instrument manoeuvres, the turn is made in the longer direction and exceeds 180°.

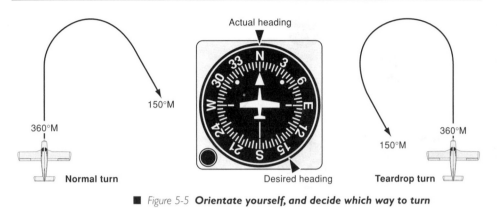

Actual heading

150°M

360°M

360°M

150°M

Normal turn

Desired heading

Teardrop turn

■ *Figure 5-5* ***Orientate yourself, and decide which way to turn***

Anticipate the heading by half the bank angle.

Having decided which way to turn, the HI need not be scanned until the aeroplane is approaching the desired heading. The roll-out should be commenced a few degrees before the desired heading is reached. Anticipate the heading by half the bank angle. For instance, if the bank angle is 20°, commence rolling out 10° before the required heading is reached – the roll-out for a right turn onto 150°M commencing as the HI passes through 140°. Aim to level the wings just as the desired heading is reached.

Settle into normal straight flight, checking direction on the HI and height on the VSI and altimeter. Hold the desired heading accurately by making small coordinated turns as needed. Aim for perfection, and certainly stay within the limits of ±5° of heading.

Timed Turns using the Turn Coordinator and Clock

Timed turns are very useful in instrument flying. It is good habit to develop the skill of estimating time to turn, as explained at the beginning of the chapter. Rate 1 is 3° per second, so a 45° turn at rate 1 will take 15 seconds. A rate 1 turn is achieved at a particular bank angle dependent on airspeed (airspeed/10 + 7, i.e. 16° bank angle at 90 kt), and can be monitored on the turn coordinator (or turn indicator).

A 15° change of heading at rate 1 will therefore require 15/3 = 5 seconds (or a little longer allowing for roll-in and roll-out), 30° will take 10 seconds, 45° will take 15 seconds, 90° will take 30 seconds, 180° will take 1 minute, and 360° will take 2 minutes. By establishing a rate 1 turn on the turn coordinator and measuring the time on a clock, very accurate turns can be made without reference to the HI or magnetic compass.

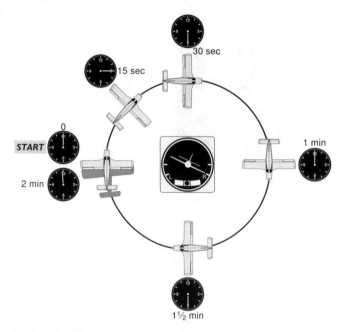

■ *Figure 5-6 **Timed turns with the clock and turn coordinator can be
very accurate***

It is usual to use rate 1 turns in instrument flying but, especially
if the heading change required is only small, rate ½ on the turn
coordinator could be used. Then the heading would change at
only 1.5°/sec, and a 12° heading change would take 8 seconds.

To carry out a rate 1 timed turn:

1. Calculate heading change and divide by 3 (e.g. a right turn
   from 340°M onto 100°M is 120° change at 3°/sec = 120/3 sec
   = 40 sec);

2. Start the stopwatch or note the reading of the second hand (say
   against 12, 3, 6 or 9 to make it easier), and roll into the turn
   with the coordinated use of aileron and rudder, achieving the
   estimated bank angle for a rate 1 turn.

3. Confirm turning performance is rate 1 on the turn coordinator, and make slight adjustments to bank angle on the AI if
   required. Confirm vertical performance on the VSI and altimeter.

4. Commence the roll-out when the second hand reaches the
   calculated number of seconds. If the roll-in and roll-out rates
   are approximately the same, they will compensate each other,
   and will not require consideration.

5. At the end of the timed turn, with the wings level and the balance ball centred, check heading on the heading indicator, or on the magnetic compass once it settles down. Make minor adjustments to heading with gentle coordinated turns.

Calibration of the Turn Coordinator

The accuracy of the turn coordinator can be checked by banking the aeroplane until the turn coordinator indicates rate 1 precisely, and then timing the rate of actual heading change using the heading indicator and clock. In 10 seconds, if the turn is exactly at rate 1, the heading should change by 30°. If the aeroplane only turns through 27° in this time, then you know that the turn coordinator is over-reading in that direction, and must increase bank until the turn coordinator is indicating slightly more than rate 1 for a rate 1 turn to occur.

Conversely, if the heading changes say 34° in the 10 seconds, you must decrease bank until the turn coordinator indicates slightly less than rate 1 for a rate 1 turn to occur. You can make allowances for any known peculiarities of your turn coordinator.

Using the Magnetic Compass

Turning using the compass is the least preferred method of making accurate turns, since it suffers considerable indication errors in a turn. It can, however, be used to achieve at least an approximate heading, which can then be checked once the compass has settled down in steady straight flight and its oscillations have ceased.

The construction of the magnetic compass is such that, when an aeroplane is turning (especially through north or south), the compass will give false indications of magnetic heading. To allow for magnetic compass errors in the northern hemisphere, observe the following:

1. When turning onto northerly headings, roll out when the magnetic compass indicates approximately 30° *before* the desired heading (undershoot on north).

2. When turning onto southerly headings, roll out when the magnetic compass indicates approximately 30° *past* the desired heading (overshoot on south).

These allowances should be reduced when turning onto headings well removed from north and south (in fact when turning onto east or west no allowance at all need be made).

NOTE In the southern hemisphere, these allowances must be reversed (overshoot on north, and undershoot on south).

Part (ii)
Climbing Turns

The technique for flying a climbing turn is the same as for a level turn, except that airspeed (rather than height) is maintained.

Rolling into a Climbing Turn

Note the position of the index aeroplane relative to the horizon on the AI, and then roll into the turn with coordinated aileron and rudder until the estimated bank angle is reached. Monitor the ASI, and be prepared to lower the pitch attitude slightly to maintain a constant climbing airspeed. There will be a natural tendency for the aeroplane to drop its nose when it is banked, so (even though the pitch attitude in the climbing turn is slightly lower than when the wings are level) slight back pressure may have to be applied to prevent the nose dropping too far.

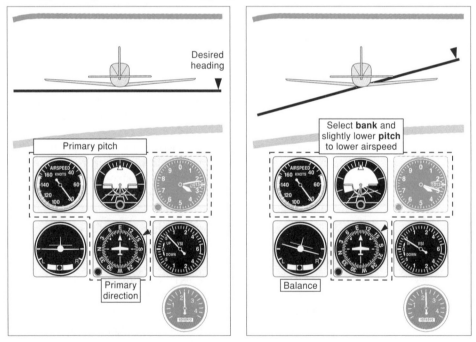

■ Figure 5-7 **Entering a climbing turn**

Maintaining a Climbing Turn

The AI is used to maintain bank and pitch attitude, with the balance ball kept centred with rudder pressure. Airspeed is monitored on the ASI and, if the airspeed is slightly lower than desired, the pitch attitude should be lowered slightly on the AI. The ASI is the primary indicator in the climb that correct pitch attitude is being held.

The **vertical performance** will be less than in the straight climb, indicated by a reduced rate of climb on the VSI, and slower movement of the altimeter needle.

The **turning performance** can be monitored on the turn coordinator, with the bank angle being altered with reference to the AI to achieve the desired rate of turn. The balance ball is kept centred with rudder pressure. The heading indicator should be brought increasingly into the scan as the desired heading is approached.

Rolling out of a Climbing Turn

As the desired heading on the HI is approached, roll off bank with coordinated aileron and rudder, aiming to level the wings on the AI just as heading is reached. Monitor airspeed on the ASI, and select a slightly higher pitch attitude on the AI to maintain climbing airspeed.

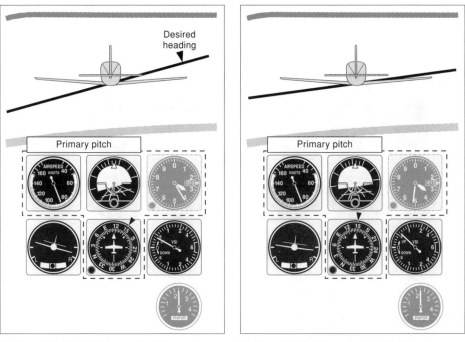

■ *Figure 5-8* **Maintaining a climbing turn**   ■ *Figure 5-9* **Rolling out of a climbing turn**

Part (iii)
Descending Turns

The technique for flying a descending turn is the same as for a level turn, except that airspeed (rather than height) is maintained. This makes the ASI an important performance guide to the correct pitch attitude.

Rolling into a Descending Turn

Note the position of the index aeroplane relative to the horizon on the AI, and then roll into the turn with coordinated aileron and rudder until the estimated bank angle is reached. Monitor the ASI and be prepared to lower the pitch attitude slightly to maintain a constant descent airspeed. There will be a natural tendency for the aeroplane to drop its nose when it is banked, so (even though the pitch attitude in the descending turn is slightly lower than when the wings are level), slight back pressure may have to be applied to stop the nose dropping too far.

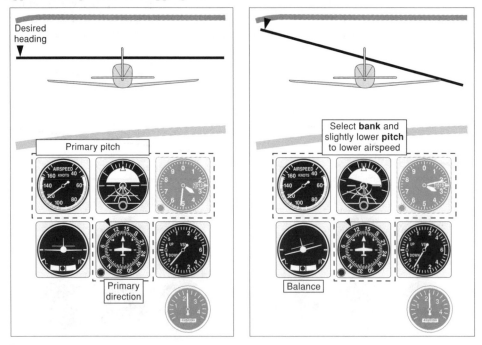

■ Figure 5-10 *Entering a descending turn*

Maintaining a Descending Turn

The AI is used to maintain bank angle and pitch attitude, with the balance ball kept centred with rudder pressure. Airspeed is monitored on the ASI and, if the airspeed is slightly lower than desired, the pitch attitude should be lowered on the AI. If the airspeed is slightly high, then the pitch attitude should be raised.

The ASI is the primary indicator that correct pitch attitude is being maintained in the descent.

The **vertical performance** of the aeroplane can be monitored on the VSI and altimeter. An increased rate of descent in a descending turn is to be expected but, if desired, this can be reduced by the addition of power and the selection of a slightly higher pitch attitude.

The **turning performance** can be monitored on the turn coordinator, with the bank angle being altered with reference to the AI to achieve the desired rate of turn. The balance ball is kept centred with rudder pressure. The heading indicator should be brought increasingly into the scan as the desired heading is approached.

Rolling out of a Descending Turn

As the desired heading on the HI is approached, roll off bank with coordinated aileron and rudder, aiming to level the wings on the AI just as heading is reached. Monitor airspeed on the ASI, and select a slightly higher pitch attitude on the AI to maintain descent airspeed.

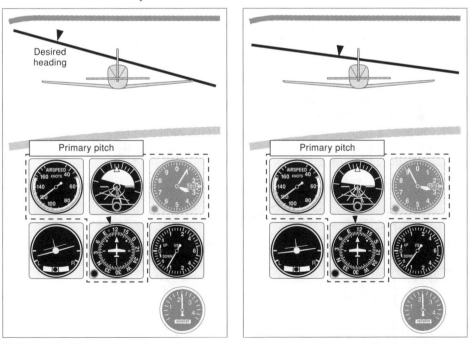

■ *Figure 5-11* **Maintaining a descending turn**   ■ *Figure 5-12* **Rolling out of a descending turn**

Part (iv)
Steep Turns

Rate 1 is the typical instrument flying turn but, on occasions, turns up to 25° bank angle may be used when required. Any turn steeper than this in instrument flying may be considered a **steep turn.**

It is poor airmanship to exceed a 25° bank angle in normal operations, since the required coordination of hands, eyes and feet makes accurate flying more difficult. The end result, if it gets out of hand, could be a spiral dive.

Steep turns under instrument conditions with an instructor on board, however, can be good practice in:
- improving basic flying skills;
- speeding up the scan rate; and
- recovering from flight attitudes neither usual, nor desirable, in normal instrument flight (see Chapter 6, *Unusual Attitudes*).

The Steep Level Turn

Tilting the lift force as the aeroplane banks will reduce its vertical component. Back pressure on the control column is therefore required to increase the angle of attack of the wings and increase the magnitude of the lift force so that its vertical component will still balance the weight and avoid a loss of height (monitored on the VSI and altimeter).

The load factor (lift/weight) increases significantly in a steep turn – two consequences being a greater g-loading on the aeroplane and pilot, and a higher stalling speed.

The increased angle of attack in a steep turn means not only increased lift, but also greatly increased drag. Airspeed will decrease significantly unless additional power is applied (monitored on the ASI).

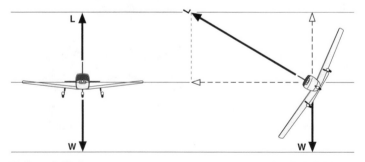

■ *Figure 5-13* **A steep turn requires increased lift to maintain height**

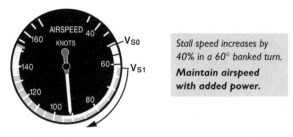

Stall speed increases by
40% in a 60° banked turn.

**Maintain airspeed
with added power.**

■ *Figure 5-14* **Increase power to maintain airspeed in a steep turn**

PRIOR TO ENTERING A STEEP LEVEL TURN

Achieve straight and level flight at the desired height and airspeed,
and be in trim. Note the heading on the heading indicator, and
decide which way you will turn and onto what heading. Ask the
safety pilot to check outside for other aircraft.

Rolling into a Steep Level Turn

Roll into the steep turn with coordinated aileron and rudder, the
same as you would for a medium turn, except that, as the bank
angle increases through 30°:

☐ progressively increase back pressure to raise the pitch attitude
on the AI to maintain height;

☐ progressively add power to maintain airspeed.

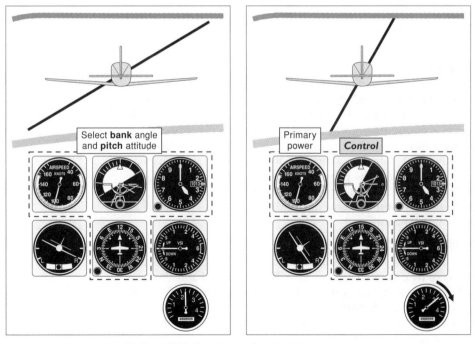

■ *Figure 5-15* **Entering and maintaining a steep turn**

Maintaining a Steep Level Turn

Increase your instrument scan rate as the turn steepens, to cope
with all of the variables. The secret of an accurate steep level turn
on instruments is to:
- have a good scan;
- hold the correct bank angle and pitch attitude on the attitude
  indicator; and
- maintain airspeed with power.

Bank Angle and Balance

Control of the bank angle and balance is achieved with coordinated use of aileron and rudder, with reference to the attitude
indicator and the balance ball. The turn coordinator is of little
use, since the steep turn will be well in excess of rate 1, but it is
still useful as an indication of the direction of the turn, left or
right. The desired bank angle is held on the AI.

> Hold bank angle on the attitude indicator.

Pitch Control

Pitch control is more difficult to achieve than bank control,
because of the considerably increased back pressure required (and
also, for some people, the slightly unpleasant g-forces that increase
as back pressure is applied). The pitch attitude is higher in the
steep turn than in level flight. Vertical performance can be monitored on the VSI and altimeter to ensure that height is being
maintained. The primary performance indicator that the pitch
attitude held on the AI is correct is the altimeter, supported by the
VSI.

> The altimeter is the primary performance indicator for pitch attitude.

Airspeed

Airspeed control is achieved with the throttle. If insufficient additional power is applied, then airspeed can diminish quite rapidly.
The power should be increased progressively as the bank angle
steepens during the roll-in, and you should imagine that there is
a direct link from the airspeed indicator to your hand on the
throttle – any hint of an airspeed loss requiring an immediate
increase in power. The primary performance indicator for power
in level flight (including turns) is the ASI. There is no need to
monitor the power indicator directly unless there is a possibility of
exceeding limitations.

> The ASI is the primary performance indicator for power in level flight.

Height

Loss of height will result if insufficient back pressure is applied as
the steep turn is entered, the nose will drop, the VSI and altimeter
will indicate a rapid loss of height, and the ASI will indicate an
increasing airspeed. Simply increasing back pressure at a steep
bank angle when the nose has dropped will only tighten the turn
without raising the nose.

The recommended technique if **height is lost** is:
- [ ] reduce bank angle with aileron;
- [ ] raise pitch attitude with elevator (back pressure); and
- [ ] re-apply bank.

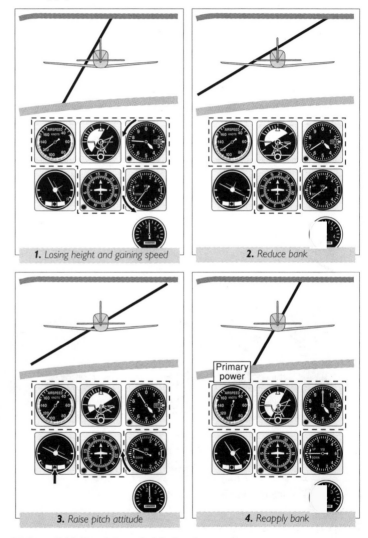

1. *Losing height and gaining speed*

2. *Reduce bank*

3. *Raise pitch attitude*

4. *Reapply bank*

■ Figure 5-16 **Regaining a height loss in a steep turn**

If height is being gained:
- [ ] relax some of the back pressure, and lower the pitch attitude slightly; and/or
- [ ] steepen the bank angle slightly.

Extreme cases of nose-high or nose-low attitudes are considered in Chapter 6. They can result from a poorly flown steep turn, especially under instrument conditions, and especially when you have a slow scan rate or are not prepared to exert your authority over the aeroplane and make it do exactly what you want.

Rolling Out of the Steep Level Turn

If the aim is to roll out onto a particular heading, then approximately 30° lead should be allowed because of the high rate of turn. Roll out of the steep turn using coordinated aileron and rudder. Gradually release the back pressure on the control column and lower the pitch attitude on the AI to maintain height (as monitored on the VSI and altimeter). Gradually reduce power to maintain the desired airspeed (as monitored on the ASI).

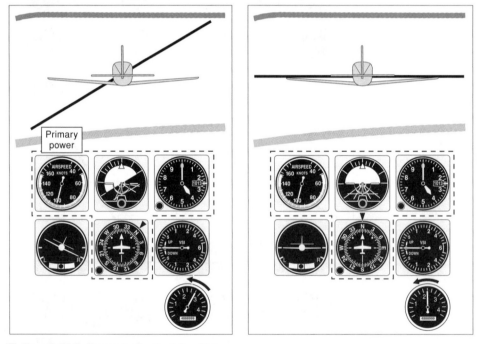

■ Figure 5-17 **Rolling out of a steep level turn**

Steep Descending Turns

The steep descending turn is never flown in normal instrument flight operations, but it may be used during your training (with your flying instructor on board as safety pilot) as a practice manoeuvre to improve coordination. Note that there is no steep climbing turn, since this is beyond the performance capability of most training aircraft, and a useful rate of climb could not be maintained.

It is usual to allow airspeed to increase in a steep descending turn in order to maintain an adequate safety margin over the stalling speed (which increases during a turn). Typical speed increases, controlled by use of the elevator, are:

☐ 10 kt for a 45° bank in a steep descending turn; and

☐ 20 kt for a 60° bank in a steep descending turn.

Rolling into a Steep Descending Turn

From a steady descent, roll on bank with coordinated aileron and rudder. Keep the balance ball centred with whatever rudder pressure is required; in a gliding turn, there will be more rudder pressure required one way compared to the other because of the lack of a slipstream.

Lower the pitch attitude slightly on the AI, using elevator to maintain the desired nose position to achieve the higher airspeed. The nose will tend to drop in a descending turn and so, even though the pitch attitude on the attitude indicator will be lower to achieve a higher airspeed, some back pressure on the control column will be needed to stop the nose dropping too far.

Maintaining a Steep Descending Turn

Increase your scan rate as the turn steepens to cope with all the variables. Hold the desired pitch attitude and bank angle with reference to the AI, and monitor the ASI closely. Control bank angle with coordinated use of aileron and rudder. Control pitch attitude on the AI with elevator to achieve the desired airspeed. The ASI is the primary indicator that pitch attitude is correct.

If the pitch attitude is too low and the airspeed becomes excessive:

☐ reduce the bank angle on the AI using ailerons;

☐ raise the pitch attitude on the AI with elevator to reduce airspeed on the ASI; and

☐ re-apply the bank.

If the bank angle is not reduced, then simply applying back pressure may only serve to tighten the turn without decreasing airspeed, and the g-loading may increase beyond acceptable limits. A spiral dive can result if pitch attitude, bank angle and airspeed are not kept within acceptable limits.

The rate of descent in a steep descending turn will increase significantly, not only because of the lower pitch attitude for the higher airspeed, but also because of the tilting of the lift force reduces its vertical component. If desired, the rate of descent can be controlled with power, and monitored on the VSI and altimeter. Increasing power, and raising the pitch attitude to maintain airspeed, will result in a reduced rate of descent.

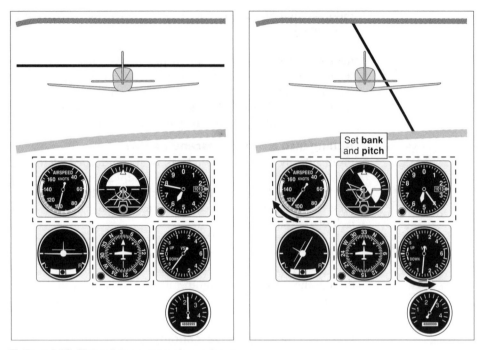

■ Figure 5-18 **Maintaining a steep descending turn**

Rolling out of a Steep Descending Turn

With reference to the attitude indicator, roll off bank with coordinated aileron and rudder, and select the slightly higher pitch
attitude with elevator required for the straight descent. Monitor
the ASI and adjust pitch attitude on the AI to achieve the desired
airspeed. The ASI is the primary guide to a correct pitch attitude.
If the aim is to roll out onto a particular heading, then approximately 30° lead should be allowed because of the rapid rate of
turn.

A steep descending turn that is not monitored carefully can
result in a spiral dive, an unusual attitude best avoided. How to
recover from a spiral dive is described on page 107.

Unusual Attitudes

An **unusual attitude** in instrument flying is any attitude not normally used during flight solely on instruments, including:

☐ bank angles in excess of 30°;

☐ nose-high attitudes with a decreasing airspeed; and

☐ nose-low attitudes with an increasing airspeed.

An unusual attitude may result from some external influence such as turbulence, or it can be induced by pilot error. For instance, if you become disoriented or confused (Where am I? Which way is up?), or become preoccupied with other cockpit duties (such as radio calls, or the study of charts) at the expense of an adequate scan rate, or if you over-react or under-react on the controls, interpret the instruments incorrectly, or follow an instrument that has (unknown to you) failed, then the aeroplane may enter an unusual attitude.

Whatever the cause of the unusual attitude, the immediate problem is to recognise exactly what the aeroplane is actually doing, and to return it safely to normal acceptable flight (generally straight and level flight). Analysis at a later stage as to what led to the event should avoid a recurrence.

In unusual attitudes, the physiological sensations may be disconcerting, but do not allow these to influence either the recognition of the attitude, or the subsequent recovery action.

Recognising an Unusual Attitude

Increase your scan rate to determine the actual attitude and/or if any instrument has malfunctioned.

If you notice any unusual instrument indication or rate of change not expected in the normal gentle instrument flight manoeuvres, or if you experience unexpected g-forces or air noise, assume that the aeroplane could be in (or about to enter) an unusual attitude. Increase the scan rate to determine the attitude and/or if any instrument has malfunctioned.

If all instruments are functioning normally, then an **excessive bank angle** will be indicated directly on the AI, supported by an excessive rate of turn on the turn coordinator, and a rapidly turning HI. Which way the wings are banked can be determined from the AI, supported by the turn coordinator. (Be aware that some attitude indicators can topple and become unusable when the aeroplane is in an extreme attitude. This is discussed shortly.)

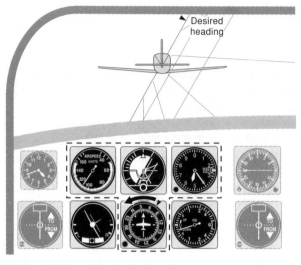

■ Figure 6-1 **An excessive bank angle**

A **nose-low attitude** will be indicated by a low pitch attitude on the AI, supported by descent indications on the altimeter and VSI, and an increasing airspeed on the ASI. An excessive bank angle will often lead to a nose-low attitude as well, since the nose tends to drop naturally when the wings are banked. The result could be a spiral dive – a most undesirable unusual attitude that, uncorrected, can result in tragedy.

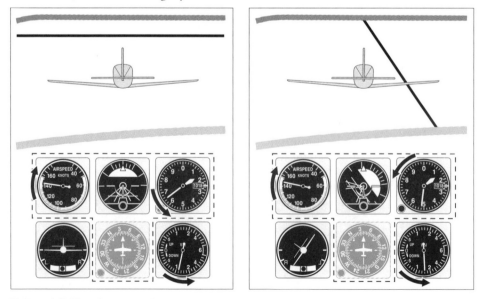

■ Figure 6-2 **Nose-low unusual attitudes**

If all the instruments are functioning correctly, a **nose-high attitude** will be indicated by a high pitch attitude on the AI, supported by climb indications on the altimeter and VSI, and a decreasing airspeed on the ASI. In an extreme nose-up attitude, however, a stall could result, with the VSI and altimeter indicating a descent, and the ASI a low airspeed.

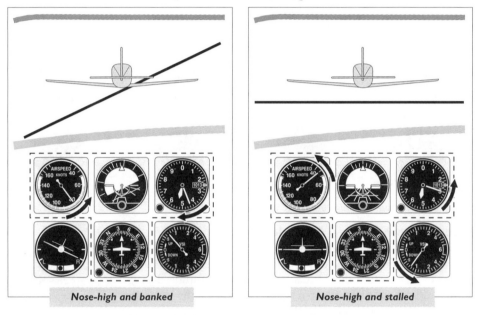

| Nose-high and banked | Nose-high and stalled |

■ *Figure 6-3* **Nose-high unusual attitudes**

If any instrument has failed, then a **cross-check** of the others should enable you to isolate it and disregard its indications. For instance, if limits are exceeded the AI could topple and become unusable, which can happen in some aircraft as a result of the unusual attitude. Similarly, a suction failure in some aircraft can lead to both the AI and HI becoming unusable. (This situation is considered in Chapter 7, *Instrument Flight on a Limited Panel*.) In such a case:

☐ nose-high or nose-low information can be derived from the ASI, altimeter and VSI; and

☐ bank information can be derived from the turn coordinator.

In recognising an unusual attitude, the key points to establish are:

1. Is the aeroplane nose-high or nose-low?

2. Is it banked?

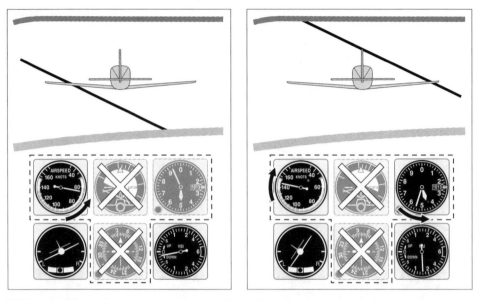

■ *Figure 6-4* **Unusual attitudes indicated by a limited panel**

Recovery from Unusual Attitudes

It is easy for inexperienced pilots to over-react to an unusual attitude with rapid and excessive control movements, since they do not expect to find themselves in an unusual attitude during normal instrument flight. Over-reaction can worsen the situation and, possibly, overstress the airframe.

Having recognised the unusual attitude for what it is, do not over-react.

One purpose of instrument training, therefore, is to place the aeroplane into unusual attitudes on purpose and to develop recovery techniques that allow the pilot, having recognised the nature of the unusual attitude, to return the aeroplane to normal flight calmly, quickly and safely.

Each unusual attitude, and the recovery should be practised:
☐ in fully visual conditions with external references;
☐ on a full panel of instruments; and then
☐ on a limited panel of instruments.

It is possible that some AIs may topple during an unusual attitude and become unusable. You may suddenly have to revert to limited panel techniques quite unexpectedly. For this reason, we have included limited panel recovery techniques in this chapter for ease of reference after your training has been completed. During your training, however, your flying instructor may prefer to consider the full panel techniques alone at this stage, and then return to the limited panel later.

Nose-Low Attitudes with Increasing Airspeed

If the pitch attitude is too low, the airspeed will start to increase. In an extreme situation, the aeroplane may end up in a steep dive, either straight or spiral. If not corrected, the aeroplane may exceed V_{NE} (the never-exceed speed shown on the ASI as a red line), possibly suffering excessive airframe stress in the dive and, if not handled correctly, in the recovery.

Reduce power.

To reduce the rate at which the airspeed is increasing, and to avoid unnecessary loss of height, reduce the power with the throttle, even closing it completely if necessary. As well as reducing the thrust as an accelerating force, this will increase drag as a result of the now windmilling propeller, further reducing the tendency for airspeed to increase.

Level the wings.

A steep bank angle and nose-low attitude may develop into a **spiral dive**. If the control column is simply pulled back to raise the nose while the aeroplane is still steeply banked, then the spiral dive will be tightened without the descent being stopped. Therefore, it is most important to level the wings using the AI and the turn coordinator, changing a banked or spiral dive into a straight dive, before raising the pitch attitude to ease the aeroplane out of the dive.

Smoothly raise the pitch attitude to ease the aeroplane out of the dive.

Throttling back and rolling the wings level can be done simultaneously, with the aeroplane being kept in balance with rudder pressure. Once the wings are level, the aeroplane will be in a straight dive. Then, to ease the aeroplane out of the straight dive, smoothly raise the pitch attitude through the level flight position on the AI. See Figure 6-5.

There is a danger of overstressing the airframe at high airspeeds with large and sudden elevator control movements, hence the instruction to 'ease' the aeroplane out of the dive with firm elevator pressure rather than with sudden and large movements of elevator control. (See the V-n diagram in Vol. 4 of *The Air Pilot's Manual*.)

On reaching the level flight attitude, the airspeed will 'check' (stop increasing), and the altimeter will move from a descent indication to a level (or even climbing) indication. The VSI initially may be erratic and unusable due to the large change in attitude (possibly showing a reversed reading), although it will settle down fairly quickly to a steady and usable reading once the recovery is complete.

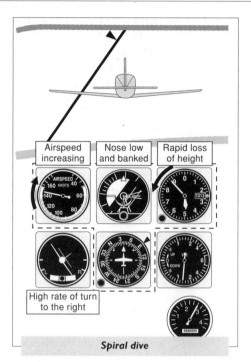

Airspeed increasing

Nose low and banked

Rapid loss of height

High rate of turn to the right

Spiral dive

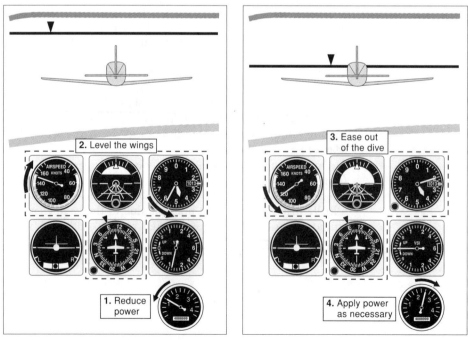

2. Level the wings

1. Reduce power

3. Ease out of the dive

4. Apply power as necessary

■ *Figure 6-5* **Regaining normal flight from a spiral dive – full panel**

After taking initial recovery action, increase your instrument scan rate to ensure that there is no over-controlling, which is a possibility, since the control pressures at the start of the recovery (when the airspeed is high) may be quite heavy.

To regain lost height after recovering from a spiral dive or a straight dive, apply power, raise the pitch attitude to the climbing attitude and commence a normal climb.

Once in steady straight flight, the heading indicator should be checked to ensure that it is aligned with the magnetic compass.

NOTES

1. The airspeed will continue to increase until the aircraft passes through the level flight attitude, when it will 'check' (stop increasing).

Always level the wings before easing out of the dive.

2. Unless the wings are fairly level when you raise the pitch attitude with back pressure, the turn indicator will show an exaggerated turn rate, and the spiral will tighten. This is undesirable.

3. With the fairly large initial pitch-up control movement to achieve the level flight attitude, the VSI may *initially* show a reverse indication, i.e. an initial increase in the rate of descent, even though the opposite is in fact occurring. Excessive attitude corrections can cause VSI indication reversal, so this instrument should be disregarded in the first few seconds following a large pitch change.

LIMITED PANEL. On a limited panel, with no usable information available from the AI, the indication of a nose-low attitude will be an increasing airspeed on the ASI, with secondary information from the altimeter and VSI showing a high and possibly increasing rate of descent, and with bank angle (if any) indicated on the turn coordinator.

The recovery manoeuvre is the same for visual and instrument flight – both full and limited panel, the only difference being the instruments available to provide information (Figure 6-6).

To recover from a nose-low/high-airspeed attitude on a limited panel:
- **reduce power;**
- **level the wings** (using the turn coordinator on a limited panel);
- **ease out of the dive** (level pitch attitude indicated on the limited panel when the airspeed checks, and the altimeter stabilises).

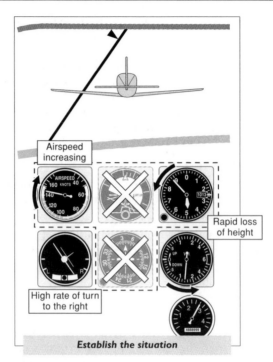

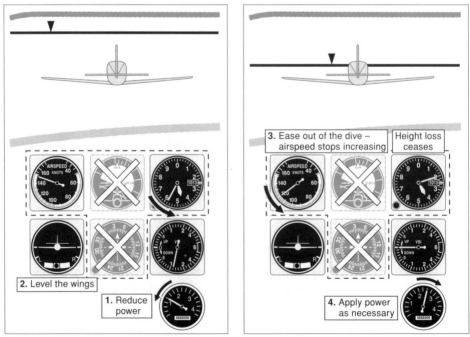

■ Figure 6-6 **Recovery from nose-low and high airspeed – limited panel**

Nose-High Attitudes with Decreasing Airspeed

If the pitch attitude is too high, the airspeed will start to decrease. A high pitch attitude will be shown on the AI, with the ASI indicating a decreasing airspeed, and the altimeter and VSI showing a climb (depending on the power used). Whether the wings are level or not will be shown on the AI and the turn coordinator.

In an extreme situation the aeroplane may stall, either wings-level or with a wing drop, and the altimeter and VSI will show a descent. The nose attitude may be high to begin with, but may drop, depending on the aeroplane. Never allow the aeroplane to inadvertently approach a stall. Initiate recovery action well before a stall starts to occur.

Simultaneously: increase power; level the wings; lower the pitch attitude.

The recovery manoeuvre when the aeroplane is in a nose-high/airspeed decreasing attitude, but not in or near a stalling condition, is to simultaneously increase power, roll the wings level on the AI with coordinated use of aileron and rudder, and lower the pitch attitude gently to regain level flight. Which wing (if any) is low is indicated by the AI and the turn coordinator.

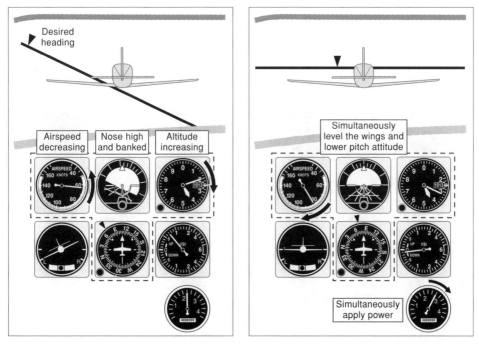

■ *Figure 6-7* **Regaining normal flight using the full panel**

The level flight attitude, when it has been achieved, will be shown directly on the AI. It will also be indicated by the fact that the airspeed change is 'checked' (stops decreasing). The altimeter reading will also stabilise. Following a large pitch attitude change, the VSI may be erratic, and even show a reversed reading, so it should be disregarded initially.

Having regained normal steady straight flight following recovery from an unusual attitude, you should check the heading indicator against the magnetic compass, to ensure that it is aligned.

LIMITED PANEL. Using a limited panel with no usable information available from the AI, a nose-high attitude will be indicated by:
- ☐ a decreasing airspeed on the ASI, with supporting information from the altimeter and VSI; and with
- ☐ bank angle (if any) indicated on the turn coordinator.

Recovery is the same, with the level pitch attitude being indicated on the ASI when the airspeed is checked and stops decreasing, and the altimeter stabilises. The wings-level bank attitude is achieved when the wings are level on the turn coordinator.

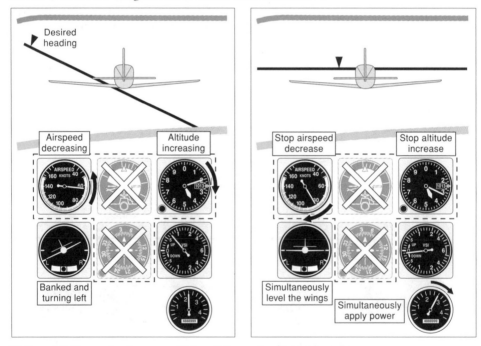

■ *Figure 6-8* **Recovering from nose-high and decreasing airspeed on the limited panel**

Nose High, and Approaching the Stall

A nose-high/airspeed decreasing situation can result ultimately in a stall. In this situation, it should be possible to regain normal flight, with a maximum altitude loss of 50 ft or less.

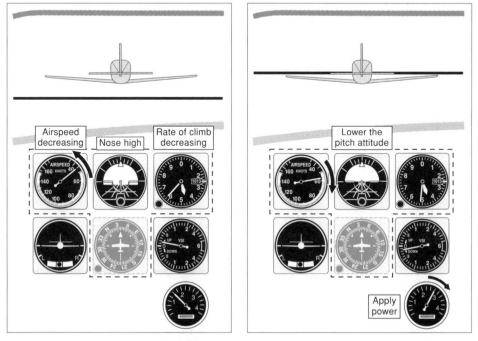

■ Figure 6-9 **Recovering from the incipient stall**

There is little danger of overstressing the airframe at low airspeeds with large elevator control movements, because the aeroplane will stall before any load limits are reached. (See the V-n diagram in Vol. 4 of *The Air Pilot's Manual*.)

However, if the recovery from a nose-high attitude is not followed through correctly and the aeroplane placed into a normal flight condition, a nose-low attitude could develop, resulting in either a straight or spiral dive with rapidly increasing airspeed. Recovery from a 'nose-low/airspeed increasing' situation (as previously discussed) will then be required.

LIMITED PANEL. Using a limited panel, with no usable information available from the AI, the indication of a nose-high attitude approaching the stall will be a decreasing airspeed on the ASI, with secondary information from the altimeter and VSI (which may show a decreasing rate of climb or even a descent). Any departure from wings level will be indicated by deflections on the turn coordinator.

The recovery procedure is similar. Simultaneously:

☐ **lower the nose** to the level pitch attitude (or lower if necessary – with the level pitch attitude on a limited panel being indicated when the airspeed checks and stops decreasing, and the altimeter stabilises); and

☐ **apply full power.**

☐ **Prevent further yaw** with rudder and, once certain flying speed is achieved on the ASI, level the wings on the turn coordinator with coordinated aileron and rudder.

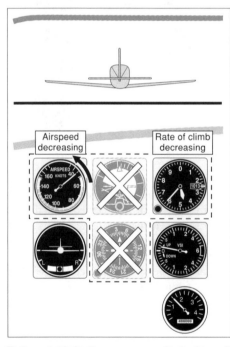 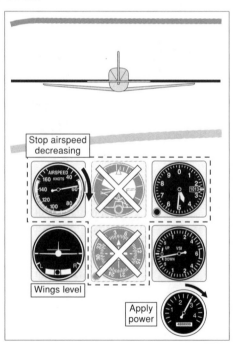

■ Figure 6-10 **Stall recovery on a limited panel**

Instrument Flight on a Limited Panel

For the exercises on the limited (or partial) panel, one or more of the flight instruments is assumed to have failed. It is possible to cope with this situation quite comfortably because, even though there is less information available, the aeroplane will fly exactly the same and respond in exactly the same way to any pilot inputs.

Cross-Check Available Instruments

If any instrument has failed, then a cross-check of the other instruments should enable you to isolate it and disregard its indications. The AI is the master instrument, and its loss is perhaps the most difficult to cope with. The AI could be lost as a result of its power source failing (electrical or suction), or its gyroscope could topple and become unusable during an extreme unusual attitude.

Suction Failure

In many aircraft, both the AI and HI are powered by suction. Their gyroscopes are driven by an airflow induced through them by the vacuum system. A suction failure could lead to the loss of both of these instruments. This is the common limited panel situation (unusable attitude indicator and heading indicator). In such a case, the aircraft is controlled by reference to the **performance instruments**:

1. Nose-high or nose-low information can be derived from the ASI, altimeter and VSI.

2. Bank information can be derived from the turn coordinator, and heading information from the magnetic compass.

3. Balance, as always, is shown by the simple balance ball that never suffers a power failure.

Electrical Failure

An electrical failure may make electrically driven instruments unusable. This could include the attitude indicator, the heading indicator and the turn coordinator. An electrical failure could also make the pitot heater unavailable, leading to icing problems with the pitot-static system unless the pilot avoids icing conditions.

Electrical failure will make the radios unusable unless there is an emergency source of power available (e.g. the battery). Instrument navigation without VHF-NAV or the ADF is difficult. Radar assistance may be requested, but this requires the VHF-COM to be working.

Following an electrical failure, check that the master switch is
ON, and check any circuit breakers or fuses for the particular item.
Do not interrupt your scan of the operating flight instruments for
more than a few seconds at a time. If an electrically powered
instrument has indeed failed and cannot be restored, then cross-
checking the other instruments will help to cover its loss.

Pitot Tube Blockage
A damaged or iced-up pitot tube will affect the airspeed indicator,
but the use of electric pitot heat in icing conditions will generally
prevent the occurrence of icing problems in the pitot-static
system. A more serious situation is a pitot cover that has not been
removed prior to flight. As well as probably being impossible to
remedy in flight, it indicates that the pilot has been derelict in the
pre-flight check.

Pre-flight checks of the pitot tube are very important. Remove
the pitot cover, and check the pitot tube for damage and block-
ages, possibly by insects.

If the ASI is unusable, then all is not lost. Selecting a suitable
attitude on the AI and suitable power on the power indicator
should result in the desired performance, even though airspeed
information is not available.

Static Vent Blockage
A damaged or blocked static system will affect the airspeed indicator, the altimeter and the VSI. If totally blocked, a constant static
pressure may be trapped in the system. The altimeter indication
will not alter and the VSI will remain on zero as the aeroplane
changes height. In cloud or at night, this could be very dangerous.
The ASI will indicate an incorrect airspeed. The indicated
airspeed is a measure of *dynamic pressure = pitot (total) pressure −
static pressure.* Therefore, as the aeroplane climbs, the too-high
static pressure trapped will cause the ASI to read too low. The
danger on the climb is to follow the false ASI reading and speed
up, possibly exceeding V_{NE}.

Conversely, on descent the trapped static pressure will be too
low, causing the ASI to read too fast. The danger on descent is to
follow the false ASI indication and slow down, possibly to the
point of stalling.

A blocked static system may be tackled by switching to the
alternate static source that most aircraft have and, hopefully, the
affected instruments will become usable again.

As a last resort if both normal and static sources are unusable (a
most unlikely event), the instrument glass of the VSI could be
broken to admit cabin static pressure into the whole static system.
Cabin pressure in an unpressurised aircraft is slightly lower than
the external static pressure because of the venturi effect caused by

the aeroplane's motion through the air. This slightly lower static pressure would cause the altimeter to read 50 to 100 ft too high, and the ASI to read 5 kt or so too high.

Adapt to Suit the Situation

Whatever instrument fails, you should be able to cope, using whatever resources remain, and adapting control of the aircraft to suit the situation. For instance, without the aid of the attitude indicator, the effects of inertia appear to be more marked than usual. Therefore, when using only a limited panel, you must develop the ability to make smooth and gentle changes using the 'change – check – hold – adjust – trim' technique, using the instruments that are available, and avoiding chasing the needles.

Hold a new attitude and allow the instruments to stabilise before making further changes.

Because the immediate and direct presentation of attitude changes on the attitude indicator is missing on a limited panel, and because performance instruments like the ASI, altimeter and VSI suffer some lag, it is even more important to hold any new attitude and allow time for the performance instruments to stabilise, before making further adjustments.

Therefore, in a limited panel situation, reduce the rate and extent of control movements compared to when operating on a full panel. The lag in readings will be less severe, and there will be less tendency to overreact by chasing the needles. Small control movements should be made, then checked and held while the performance instruments catch up with the change and settle into their correct readings. Then, fine tune with further adjustments if necessary, before trimming off any steady control pressures.

The scan for each manoeuvre when using a limited panel will need to be modified to increase reference to the now more-important instruments, and to bypass the unusable instruments. This is easier to do than it sounds. Simply look at the instrument that will give you the information you want. If it is bank angle you want, and the AI is not usable, then refer to the turn coordinator. It will not tell you bank angle directly, but it will tell you if the aeroplane is turning and, if it is, which way and at what rate. From this information, you can gain some idea of bank angle.

Interpreting Pitch Attitude on a Limited Panel

The **attitude indicator** is a control instrument. It is the best guide to pitch attitude, since it gives a direct and immediate picture of the attitude of the aeroplane relative to the (artificial) horizon. However, for practice in flying on a limited panel, it may not be available. If the attitude indicator is indeed unusable, then the pilot can determine the pitch attitude of the aeroplane using the three air pressure instruments which derive their information from the pitot-static system. They are the airspeed indicator, the altimeter and the vertical speed indicator.

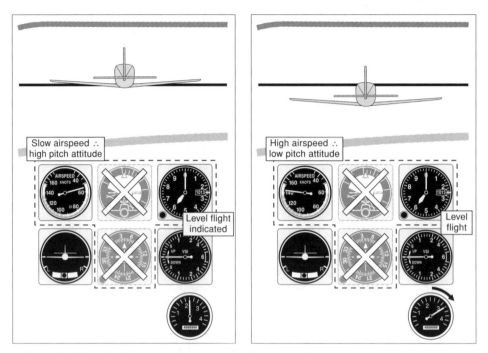

■ *Figure 7-1* **Using the pitot-static instruments to determine pitch attitude (without the attitude indicator)**

The **altimeter** not only indicates height, but also can provide pitch attitude information. If height is remaining constant, then the pitch attitude is correct for level flight at that power setting, whereas increasing or decreasing height would indicate a pitch attitude that is too high or too low.

The **airspeed indicator,** as well as indicating airspeed, can also provide pitch attitude information. If the ASI shows that the desired airspeed is being maintained, then the pitch attitude for the power set is correct. If it indicates an increasing airspeed, or an airspeed that is too high, then the pitch attitude is too low for the power set. Conversely, if the ASI indicates a decreasing airspeed, or an airspeed that is too low, then the pitch attitude is too high for the power being used.

Used in conjunction with the altimeter, the ASI is an extremely valuable guide to pitch attitude, but remember that, because of its inertia, an aeroplane will take some time to change speed and, therefore, the ASI indication must have settled before it can confidently be regarded as an accurate indication of pitch attitude. In other words, hold any new attitude for a few seconds to allow the airspeed and the ASI to settle.

The **vertical speed indicator** not only indicates the rate of climb or descent, but also can provide pitch attitude information. If the VSI indication remains approximately zero, then the pitch attitude is correct for level flight at that power, whereas a significant and sustained departure from zero would indicate a pitch attitude that is either too high or too low for level flight. In a climb or descent, a steady and fairly constant VSI reading can be used to support information on pitch attitude from the other performance instruments. Remember that large or sudden changes in pitch attitude may cause the VSI to initially give reverse indications – another reason for avoiding dramatic attitude changes when flying on a limited panel.

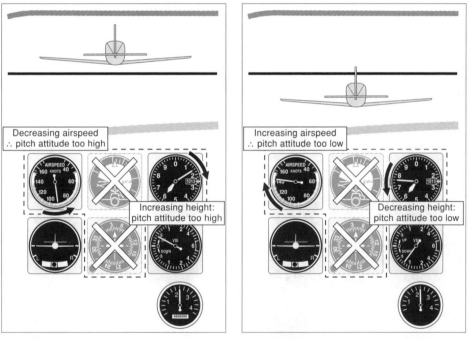

■ Figure 7-2 **Pitch attitude too high**   ■ Figure 7-3 **Pitch attitude too low**

Interpreting Bank Attitude on a Limited Panel

The attitude indicator is the best guide to bank attitude, since it gives a direct picture of the attitude of the aeroplane relative to the (artificial) horizon. However, for practice in flying on a limited panel, it may not be available. If the attitude indicator is indeed unusable, then you can determine bank attitude from the turn coordinator and balance ball, and the heading indicator (if it is working) or the magnetic compass.

For the purpose of this exercise, the heading indicator is assumed to be unusable (say because the suction has failed to both it and the attitude indicator). If, in a real situation, the HI is working, then use it.

> If the aeroplane is in balanced flight (balance ball centred), any indication of turning will mean that the aeroplane is banked.

A steady zero reading on the turn coordinator, with the balance ball centred, will mean that the wings are level. If the turn coordinator reading is not zero and the ball is centred, then the direction and rate of turn will be indicated. In most instrument flying, the normal rate of turn is rate 1, which is a change of heading at 3°/second.

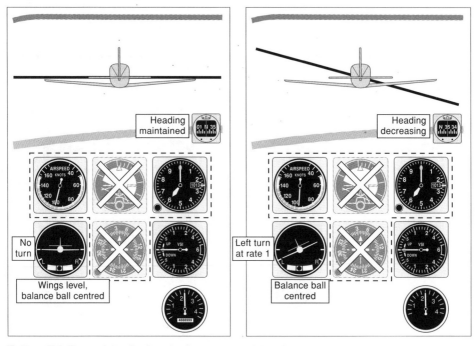

■ Figure 7-4 **Determining bank attitude on a limited panel**

While most modern aircraft are fitted with a turn coordinator, there are some still fitted with a turn indicator. The modern turn coordinator is a superior instrument in that, as well as indicating *rate of turn* as does the turn indicator, the turn coordinator also shows *rate of bank* because its gyroscope is mounted slightly angled. It will respond immediately an aeroplane banks, even before the aeroplane actually starts turning. It is therefore an easier instrument to use when trying to keep the wings level.

> *Remember that, even though it has symbolic wings to indicate banking and turning, the turn coordinator does not give pitch information.*

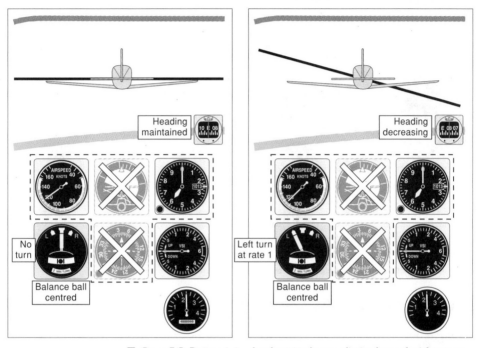

■ *Figure 7-5* **Determining bank attitude on a limited panel with a turn indicator**

If, for some reason, the turn coordinator or turn indicator is not working, then bank information can be derived from the heading indicator or magnetic compass.

> *If the heading is constant and the balance ball centred, the wings are level.*

If the heading is changing at 3°/sec (i.e. 15° heading change in 5 seconds) and the ball is centred, then the wings are banked sufficiently to give a rate 1 turn (bank angle = airspeed/10 + 7).

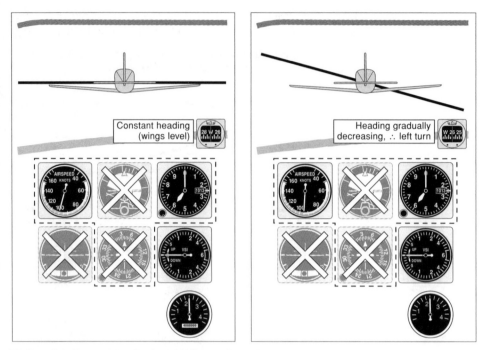

■ *Figure 7-6* **Determining bank attitude on a limited panel**

Straight and Level Flight on a Limited Panel

Setting cruise power and placing the aeroplane in the cruise attitude will provide cruise performance, with the aeroplane in straight and level flight.

To achieve straight and level flight at a particular altitude on a limited panel without the use of the AI:

- ☐ **set cruise power** on the power indicator;
- ☐ **hold the wings level** with reference to the turn coordinator, with the balance ball centred; and
- ☐ **adjust the pitch attitude** with reference to the altimeter and VSI; and then
- ☐ **trim.**

To maintain straight and level flight at the chosen altitude, once it has been achieved:

Heading

Maintain heading by keeping the wings level using the turn coordinator, and the ball centred. Heading can be checked on the heading indicator if it is working, otherwise on the magnetic compass.

Any corrections to heading should be made with gentle coordinated turns (rate ½ on the turn coordinator, which is 1.5°/sec, should be more than adequate). The heading indicator, if usable, will indicate heading directly but, if the magnetic compass is used, then some allowance will be needed to undershoot on northerly headings and overshoot on southerly headings.

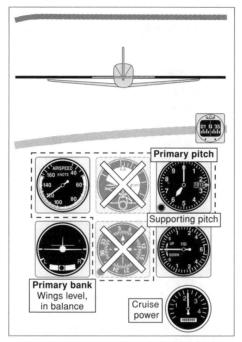

■ *Figure 7-7* **Achieving straight and level flight on a limited panel**

Altitude

Any tendency to drift off altitude due to a slightly incorrect pitch attitude will first be shown on the VSI, and minor adjustments with the elevator can be made almost before any change is registered on the altimeter. In turbulent conditions, however, the VSI will tend to fluctuate, in which case the altimeter will be the more useful instrument. Aim to stay right on altitude. Minor deviations of less than 100 ft can generally be corrected with very small pitch alterations; any deviation in excess of 100 ft may also require a small power change as well as an attitude change. Keep in trim to make the task easier.

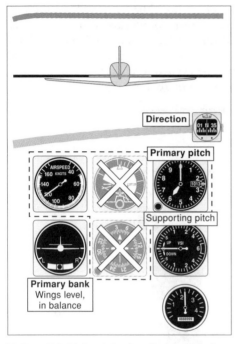

■ *Figure 7-8* **Maintaining heading and height**

Airspeed

Airspeed is normally just accepted on the cruise, once cruise power has been set. If, however, precise airspeed control is desired, then this can be achieved with power. Once cruise speed is achieved, ensure that the aeroplane is in trim.

To change airspeed in straight and level flight, a coordinated change of both power and pitch attitude will be required. Greater precision using only a limited panel of instruments can be achieved if these changes are gradual and smooth.

HIGHER AIRSPEED. A higher speed will require more power and a lower pitch attitude. Remember that a power increase will cause a *pitch up/yaw left* tendency in most aircraft, and this should be resisted with gentle control pressures. Therefore, as power is slowly increased with the throttle to achieve a speed increase, monitor the VSI (backed up by the altimeter) to determine the small increases in forward pressure required on the control column to maintain height, and keep the ball centred with a slight increase in (right) rudder pressure.

Refer to the turn coordinator to ensure that the wings are kept level, so that heading is maintained. Power adjustment may be required to maintain the desired airspeed. Once stabilised at the desired speed, retrim the aircraft. The heading indicator (if available) or the magnetic compass (once it has settled down) can be checked to verify heading.

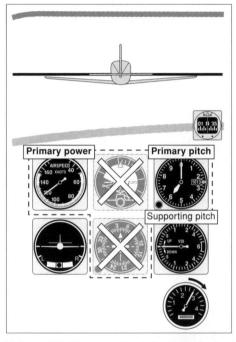

■ Figure 7-9 **Changing airspeed on a limited panel**

LOWER AIRSPEED. A lower airspeed will require less power and a higher pitch attitude. The power reduction will cause a *pitch down/yaw right* tendency, which the pilot should be ready to counteract. Any tendency to lose altitude can be monitored on the VSI, and corrected with elevator. The turn coordinator and balance ball can be used to monitor any tendency to drift off heading. Once the desired lower airspeed is achieved, minor power adjustments with the throttle may be required. The aeroplane should then be retrimmed.

Climbing on a Limited Panel

Entering a Climb

The procedure to enter a climb using only a partial instrument panel is the same as with a full panel: P-A-T, power-attitude-trim. Smoothly apply climb power (mixture RICH if necessary), keeping the wings level on the turn coordinator and the ball centred to maintain heading, and raise the pitch attitude slightly. There will be a pitch-up tendency as power is applied, so probably only a slight back pressure on the control column will be required.

Hold the new pitch attitude until the **airspeed indicator** stabilises. The VSI will show a climb and, once you are familiar with the particular aeroplane, this will provide useful backup information to the ASI regarding correct pitch attitude. An initial trim adjustment will assist in maintaining the new attitude. Once the airspeed has settled, minor adjustments can be made with the elevator to fine tune the airspeed, and then the aeroplane can be trimmed precisely to maintain the desired climbing speed.

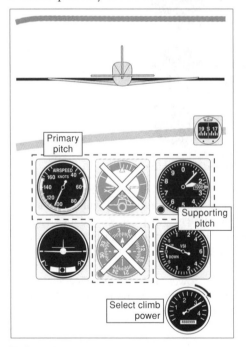

■ Figure 7-10 **Entering a climb on a limited panel**

Maintaining a Climb

To maintain a straight climb on a limited panel, hold the pitch attitude with reference to the **ASI,** which is the primary indicator of correct pitch attitude during the climb. Maintain heading by keeping the wings level on the **turn coordinator** and the **balance ball** centred. Heading can be checked on the **heading indicator** or **magnetic compass.**

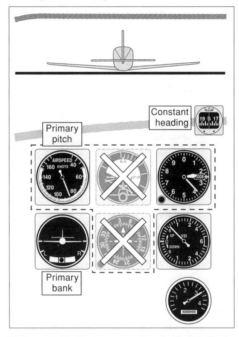

■ *Figure 7-11* **Maintaining the climb on a limited panel**

It is good airmanship to periodically check engine temperatures and pressures on the climb, since the engine is working hard and the cooling airflow is less, but this should not take more than one or two seconds and should not distract you from your main scan of the flight instruments. Being in trim will make life easier.

Levelling Off from a Climb

To level off at a particular height, it is important that the altimeter has the correct setting in its subscale (Regional QNH, 1013, or Aerodrome QNH or QFE, as the case may be). The **altimeter** should be increasingly brought into the scan as the desired height is approached, and the focus for pitch control shifted to it from the ASI. Levelling off should be commenced smoothly before the desired height is actually reached, a suitable lead-in being 10% of the rate of climb (say 40 ft before the height for a rate of climb of 400 ft/min).

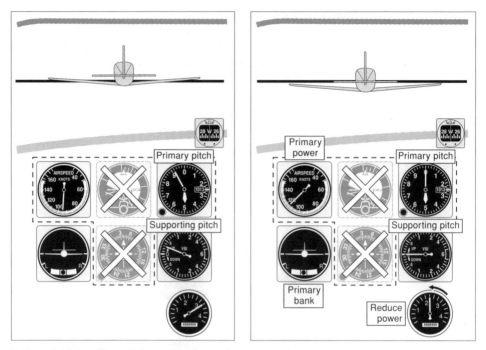

■ *Figure 7-12* **Levelling off from a climb on a limited panel**

The procedure to level off is A-P-T, attitude-power-trim. Gradually lower the pitch attitude towards the level flight position, noting a decreasing climb rate on the VSI, and capture the desired altitude with reference to the altimeter. Keep the wings level and the ball centred to maintain heading. Once the airspeed has increased to the desired cruising value on the ASI, smoothly reduce power, and then trim the aircraft.

Once the aeroplane is stabilised, the scan becomes that for normal straight and level flight, although particular attention should be paid to the ASI in the early stages to ensure that adequate power is set to maintain the desired airspeed.

Descending on a Limited Panel

Entering a Descent

A descent will require less power and a lower pitch attitude than for level flight. To enter a descent, the procedure is P-A-T, power-attitude-trim. Smoothly reduce the power (mixture control RICH, carburettor heat HOT if necessary) with the throttle. Hold the wings level and the ball centred to maintain heading, and hold the pitch attitude with slight back pressure until the desired descent airspeed on the **ASI** is almost reached in level flight, at which time the nose can be gently lowered slightly to maintain airspeed.

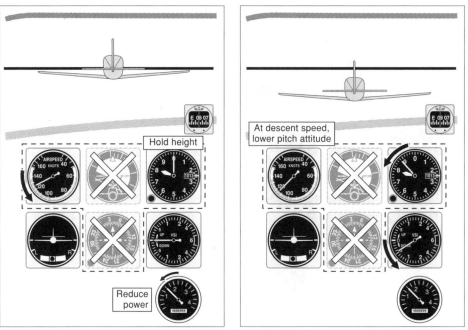

■ *Figure 7-13* **Entering a descent**

If the descent airspeed is to be the same as the level airspeed, then the pitch attitude should be lowered simultaneously with the power reduction. Remember that there will be a natural tendency for the nose to drop and yaw as power is reduced.

The **VSI** can be used to monitor any vertical tendencies. An initial coarse trim adjustment as soon as the descent attitude is adopted is acceptable to remove most steady control pressures, followed by fine adjustments to the pitch attitude to maintain the desired airspeed and a final fine trim adjustment.

Maintaining a Descent

To maintain the descent on a limited panel:

☐ **maintain heading** with wings level on the turn coordinator and the balance ball centred, checking heading against the heading indicator or the magnetic compass;

☐ **maintain airspeed** with gentle changes in pitch attitude, using the ASI and VSI – if a particular rate of descent is required, then coordinated use of power and attitude can be used to achieve it, with the airspeed being monitored on the ASI, and the rate of descent being monitored on the VSI.

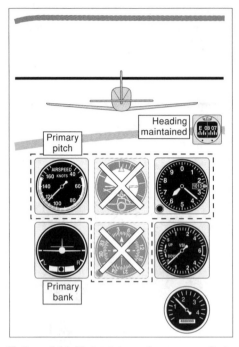

■ *Figure 7-14* **Maintaining a descent on a limited panel**

In a prolonged descent with low power, consider clearing the engine every 1,000 ft or so by applying 50% power for a few seconds to keep the engine and oil warm, to avoid carbon fouling of the spark plugs and to keep warm air available for carburettor heat.

Applying the extra power, and then removing it, should not distract you from scanning the flight instruments for more than a few seconds. Be prepared to counteract pitch/yaw tendencies as the power is changed.

Levelling Off from a Descent

To level off from a descent at a particular height, it is important that the altimeter has the correct setting in its subscale. As the desired height is approached, the focus for pitch attitude control should shift from the ASI to the altimeter, and the levelling off manoeuvre commenced before the height is actually reached (a suitable lead-in being 10% of the rate of descent).

The procedure to level off from a descent is P–A–T, power-attitude-trim. Smoothly increase power to the cruise setting and raise the pitch attitude, noting that the VSI shows a reducing rate of descent, and aim to capture the desired height precisely on the altimeter. Trim the aeroplane. Revert to the normal straight and level scan, checking the altimeter for height, and initially checking the ASI to ensure that the desired airspeed is indeed being maintained.

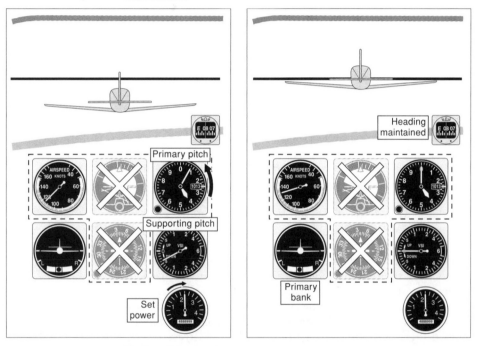

■ Figure 7-15 **Levelling off from a descent on a limited panel**

Entering a Climb from a Descent

Entering a climb from a descent, such as in a go-around, is a more demanding manoeuvre on a limited panel than on a full panel, since a large and fairly rapid power increase, accompanied by a higher pitch attitude, will be required. The large pitch attitude change may cause the VSI to give a reversed reading initially, so it must be disregarded until its reading has stabilised. Practising a go-around on a limited panel is, perhaps, an exercise for the more advanced student.

Turning on a Limited Panel

To turn onto a specific heading, the best instruments to use for directional guidance are (in order):

☐ **the heading indicator;**

☐ **the clock** (for timed turns – rate 1 being 3°/sec); or

☐ **the magnetic compass** (with its turning and acceleration errors).

If the **heading indicator** is used, then it must first have been aligned with the magnetic compass while in steady straight and level flight.

If the HI is not usable, then a timed turn with **clock** and **turn coordinator** is the preferred method. This method can be quite accurate. Once established in straight flight on the new heading, the magnetic compass will settle down and allow the heading to be checked.

If, however, the **magnetic compass** has to be used during the turn, then the roll-out should occur *before* any desired northerly heading is indicated on the compass (by about 30° in a rate 1 turn) and *after* any desired southerly heading is indicated. No allowances need be made when using the magnetic compass to turn onto easterly or westerly headings, and lesser corrections are required for intermediate headings.

Prior to commencing a turn, ensure that you are comfortable in straight and level flight, exactly on height, on speed, and in trim. Check the heading indicator (if available) or the magnetic compass for the present heading, establish which way to turn, left or right, to take up the new heading, and what rate of turn, will be used. Rate 1 is suitable for significant heading changes, but just a few degrees of heading change can be achieved satisfactorily at rate ½. Calculating time to turn, even if using the HI or compass, provides a very convenient backup. The ASI, altimeter and VSI should all be fairly steady before rolling into a level turn using a limited panel.

Entering a Level Turn

To enter a level turn, note the time in seconds on the **clock** (or start the stopwatch), roll on bank in the desired direction using coordinated aileron and rudder until the **turn coordinator** shows rate 1, at which point the ailerons should be neutralised to stop further banking, and the **balance ball** kept centred with rudder pressure. Height can be maintained by counteracting any trend on the **VSI** with elevator, which will probably require a slight back pressure. In turbulent conditions, the altimeter may be more useful than the VSI which could be fluctuating. Neutralising the ailerons will hold the bank angle fairly constant, but minor corrections will have to be made continually to maintain rate 1 on the turn coordinator.

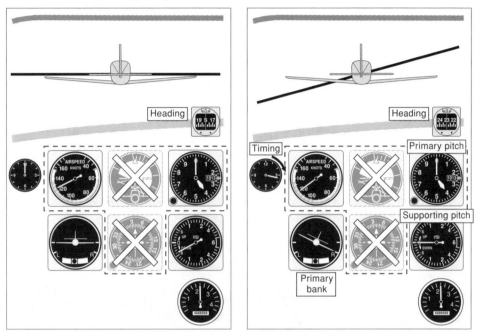

■ Figure 7-16 **Entering and maintaining a level turn on a limited panel**

Maintaining a Level Turn

To maintain a level turn, hold rate 1 on the **turn coordinator** using the ailerons, and keep the ball centred with rudder pressure. Hold height on the **altimeter,** by noticing trends on the **VSI** and counteracting with elevator. The altimeter will confirm that the precise height is being maintained. The ASI will show the expected loss of several knots, which is acceptable, unless a constant airspeed is desired, in which case the addition of some power is required. It is not usual to trim in the turn, since it is a transient manoeuvre and straight flight will soon be resumed. As the desired heading is approached, bring the heading indicator (HI, clock or compass) increasingly into the scan.

Rolling Out of a Level Turn

To roll out of a level turn, anticipate the desired heading by some degrees and roll off bank with coordinated aileron and rudder until the **turn coordinator** shows wings level. Hold height using the **VSI** and **altimeter,** smoothly relaxing any back pressure held during the turn. Allow the magnetic compass to settle down in steady straight flight, then check it for heading and make any necessary adjustments with small coordinated turns.

Climbing Turn on a Limited Panel

The climbing turn is normally entered from a straight climb, and is more easily achieved if the aeroplane is first well established and trimmed in the straight climb. Climb airspeed should be maintained in the climbing turn, therefore the primary performance guide to pitch attitude is the ASI.

To enter a climbing turn, roll on bank with coordinated aileron and rudder until the desired rate of turn is indicated on the **turn coordinator.** Adjust the pitch attitude with reference to the **ASI.** It will be slightly lower than in the straight climb.

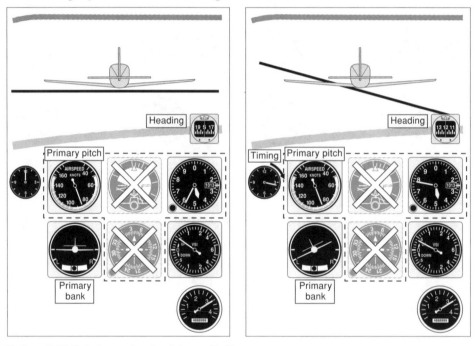

■ *Figure 7-17* **Entering and maintaining a climbing turn**

Maintain the climbing turn with reference to the **turn coordinator** and the **ASI,** and bring the heading indicator (HI, clock or magnetic compass) into the scan as the desired heading is approached.

Roll out of the climbing turn into a straight climb with coordinated aileron and rudder, achieving wings level with the **turn coordinator,** balance ball centred, and maintaining climb airspeed with reference to the **ASI.**

Descending Turn on a Limited Panel

The descending turn is normally entered from a straight descent, and is more easily achieved if the aeroplane is well established and trimmed in the straight descent. Descent airspeed should be maintained in the descending turn, therefore the primary performance guide to pitch attitude is the ASI.

To enter a descending turn, roll on bank with coordinated aileron and rudder until the desired rate of turn is indicated on the turn coordinator. Adjust the pitch attitude with reference to the ASI. Pitch attitude in a descending turn will be slightly lower than in the straight descent.

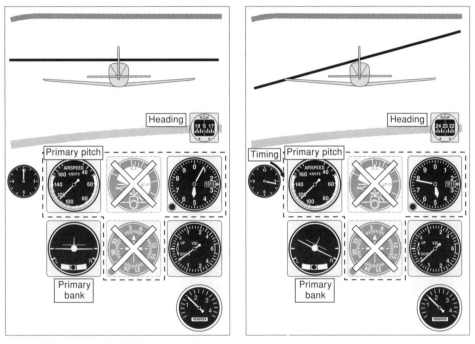

■ *Figure 7-18* ***Entering and maintaining a descending turn using a limited panel***

To maintain the descending turn, hold bank angle with reference to the **turn coordinator,** and hold pitch attitude with reference to the **ASI.** Bring the heading indicator (HI, clock or magnetic compass) into the scan as the desired heading is approached.

Roll out of the descending turn into a straight descent with coordinated aileron and rudder, achieving wings level with the **turn coordinator,** balance ball centred, and maintaining descent airspeed with reference to the **ASI.**

Now complete the exercises on **Section 1, Instrument Flying.**
(Exercises and Answers are at the back of the book).

Section **Two**

Radio Navigation Aids

Introduction to Radio Navigation Aids

Having achieved a high standard in attitude flying using the flight instruments, it is now time to apply this ability to cross-country navigation on instruments.

It is, in fact, possible to fly cross-country using attitude flying only, without referring to any radio navigation instrument in the cockpit, simply by following instructions passed to you by a radar controller.

Instructions such as "Turn onto heading three four zero, and descend now to eight hundred feet," can be followed, even to the point of a cloudbreak for a straight-in landing on a particular runway.

Radar is the first of the radio navigation aids, or *radio navaids,* that we consider in this section, since it does not involve a great deal of understanding before you can benefit from it. As well as explaining how radar can be of use to you, we also discuss the basic theory of its operation, along with the transponder in the aircraft.

It is possible that your instructor may follow an order of study different to that presented here. If so, simply bypass the other chapters and proceed to the one desired. Each chapter is self-contained, and reading earlier chapters is not necessary to understand the content of a later one.

VHF direction finding (VDF), which, like radar, does not require additional instrumentation in the cockpit, may also be used for cross-country flying. By requesting ATC to provide you with a magnetic bearing to the station, known as a QDM, which can be determined at some aerodromes by detecting the direction from which your VHF radio communications are received, a track to or from the station can be flown. The procedure used is a little more complicated than simply steering radar headings, so we have left it until the end of this section.

Radio navigation aids covered that do require cockpit instruments include:

☐ the **non-directional beacon (NDB)** and **automatic direction finder (ADF)** combination. The ADF has various cockpit presentations, such as the relative bearing indicator (RBI) and radio magnetic indicator (RMI).

☐ the **VHF omni range (VOR);**

☐ **distance-measuring equipment (DME);** and

☐ the **instrument landing system (ILS).**

We also introduce some rapidly developing RNAV (area navigation) systems – pseudo-VOR/DMEs, LORAN-C and GPS.

It may sound a little complicated at this stage, but careful consideration of each of these radio navigation aids one at a time will make it easy for you. There is a certain amount of jargon associated with instrument flying, but it will not take long before you are familiar with all the terms.

The main function of this section of the manual is for you to understand how the aids work, and how to use them, especially for tracking to or from a ground station.

Section Three considers the slightly more advanced aspects of instrument flying, such as:

- **instrument departures;**
- **instrument holding;**
- **instrument approaches to land;** and
- **visual manoeuvring** at the end of a successful instrument approach.

These depend to a large extent on the lessons learned in Section Two. A good instrument approach, for instance, consists mainly of accurate attitude flying and accurate tracking.

Radar

Most air traffic control in busy airspace occurs in a *radar environment*. This means that the air traffic controller has a radar map of the area showing the position of the various aircraft within it, bringing enormous advantages, such as:

▣ A significant reduction in the amount of air–ground communication. For instance, there is no need for pilots to transmit regular position reports.

▣ The ability to handle an increased number of aeroplanes in the same airspace, with reduced, but still safe, separation distances.

▣ The ability to fix an aircraft's geographic position.

▣ The ability to *radar vector* an aeroplane along various tracks by passing headings to steer to the pilot.

▣ The ability to feed aeroplanes onto final approach to land, either to the commencement of an instrument approach such as an ILS (instrument landing system) or until the pilot becomes 'visual', without the need for excessive manoeuvring, and with more than one aeroplane on the approach at any one time.

This use of radar is known as **surveillance radar.** Surveillance radar, although extensively used in air traffic control, is not confined to controlled airspace. Wide areas of the UK have radar coverage, and you may, even if operating in uncontrolled airspace, take advantage of services such as the Lower Airspace Radar Advisory Service (LARS).

Most aeroplanes are now fitted with a secondary surveillance radar **transponder,** which transmits a unique signal in response to a radar signal from the ground, thereby allowing the radar controller to identify a particular aeroplane on a radar screen. You are probably familiar with the operation of the transponder – if not, it is considered in detail towards the end of this chapter. The name *transponder* is derived from *transmitter/responder.*

■ *Figure 9-1* **A typical SSR transponder**

At certain aerodromes, the surveillance radar controller can provide tracking guidance and height information down final approach in what is called a surveillance radar approach (SRA). This is a common approach for an IMC-rated pilot.

A completely different set of ground-based equipment available at only a small number of aerodromes, known as **precision approach radar** (PAR), enables a radar controller to provide to a pilot extremely accurate approach guidance to land on a particular runway. PAR voice guidance is given in both *azimuth* (horizontal navigation) and *slope* (vertical navigation). The PAR is a rare approach for an IMC-rated pilot. PAR is *not* available at civil airfields, but is readily available at selected military airfields.

In this chapter, we first consider radar vectoring, and then look at a surveillance radar approach. There is no need for you to understand the theory of radar to be able to fly according to instructions from a radar controller, although towards the end of this chapter the theory of radio (including radar) is considered.

Radar Vectoring

Radar vectoring is when a radar controller passes a heading to steer to a pilot with an instruction such as:

Charlie Delta
Steer heading two five zero

Bear in mind that the radar controller is trying to get you to achieve a particular track over the ground and, because he does not know precisely what the wind at your level is and the amount of drift that it is causing, he will occasionally request a modification to your heading while radar vectoring your aeroplane.

No radio navigation instruments are required in the aeroplane for it to be radar vectored, but radio communication is necessary. The pilot concentrates on attitude flying (maintaining the desired heading, altitude and airspeed), while the radar controller concentrates on the aeroplane achieving the desired track over the ground. This is not to say that you should not be very aware of where your track is taking you, especially if high terrain is in the vicinity, and you should always maintain a picture of where the aeroplane is with respect to the aerodrome. This is essential in case of radio communication failure.

The termination of radar vectoring is indicated by the phrase:

Resume own navigation

Radar vectoring is a very useful procedure in busy terminal areas where an aeroplane may be vectored quite efficiently onto final approach to land. Radar vectoring by the controller may cease once the aeroplane is established on a visual approach or on an instrument approach such as an ILS (instrument landing system), or it may continue down a surveillance radar approach (SRA).

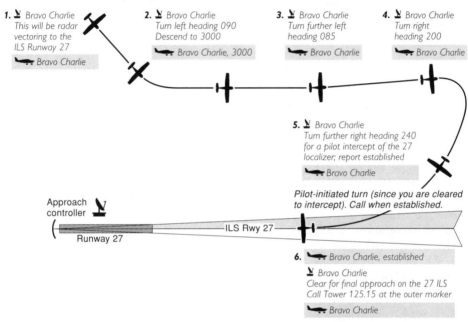

■ Figure 9-2 **Radar vectoring in the vicinity of an aerodrome**

Surveillance Radar Approach (SRA)

A surveillance radar approach is carried out by the pilot under guidance from the radar controller on the VHF–COM radio who passes:

☐ horizontal navigation (tracking) instructions in the form of turns to make and headings to steer; and

☐ vertical navigation (descent) instructions in the form of range to touchdown and desired height at that range.

A 3° glideslope is approximately 300 ft/min.

The usual instrument approach slope is 3° to the horizontal, a slope of 1 in 20. (The 1 in 60 rule is useful here, 3° being approximately equal to 3 in 60, 1 in 20.)

To achieve a 3° descent, for each 1 nm (approximately 6,000 ft) travelled horizontally, an aeroplane must descend ¹⁄₂₀ of this, 300 ft. Therefore a 3° slope is approximately 300 ft/nm.

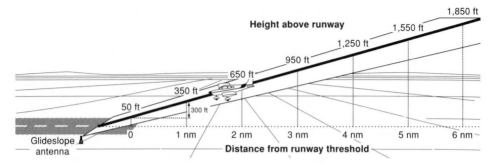

Height above runway

■ *Figure 9-3* **The usual instrument approach slope is 3°**

Since the landing aeroplane should pass 50 ft above the runway threshold, it is quite simple to develop a *height/distance* profile. Working backwards from 50 ft above the runway threshold, the aeroplane should pass through a *window* 300 ft higher for each 1 nm further back from the runway.

The figures shown above are what the pilot would aim to achieve with QFE set in the altimeter subscale.

On a surveillance radar approach, the controller will radar vector the aeroplane onto final and advise the pilot:

☐ when to commence a 3° descent;
☐ the appropriate height for the aeroplane's distance from touchdown; and
☐ what heading to steer if the aeroplane diverges from the approach track.

Phrases used will be similar to:

Range 5 miles – height should be 1550

Track guidance will be given in a form such as:

Turn right five degrees – heading one eight five

How to Initiate a 3° Descent

There is no instrument in the cockpit that indicates descent in terms of feet/nm; such an instrument would make it easy to set a descent of 300 ft/nm to give a 3° approach slope. What you do have, however, is a vertical speed indicator that measures the rate of descent in ft/min, and an airspeed indicator that measures indicated airspeed in knots (nm/hr).

The approach slope is measured in *ground nautical miles* (and not air nautical miles), so estimating the groundspeed, taking into account the wind strength, will increase the accuracy of an estimate of the desired descent rate.

☐ With a groundspeed of 60 kt, an aeroplane will travel 1 nm in 1 minute, and to achieve a slope of 300 ft/nm would require a descent rate of 300 ft/min.

☐ With a groundspeed of 120 kt, an aeroplane will travel 2 nm in 1 minute, and to achieve a slope of 300 ft/nm would require a descent rate of 600 ft/min.

☐ With a groundspeed of 90 kt, an aeroplane will travel 1.5 nm in 1 minute, and to achieve a slope of 300 ft/nm would require a descent rate of 450 ft/min.

EXAMPLE 1 An aeroplane has an approach speed of TAS 75 kt. To achieve a 3° slope of 300 ft/nm, the required rate of descent is:

☐ in nil wind, TAS 75 kt, GS 75 kt, 375 ft/min;

☐ in 15 kt headwind, TAS 75 kt, GS 60 kt, 300 ft/min;

☐ in 30 kt headwind, TAS 75 kt, GS 45 kt, 225 ft/min;

☐ in 15 kt tailwind, TAS 75 kt, GS 90 kt, 450 ft/min; in this case, however, be wary of continuing the approach in case the tailwind limitation for landing is exceeded.

Perhaps an easier means of quickly determining an approximate descent rate to achieve a 3° slope is:

Rate of descent (ft/min) for a 3° approach slope
= 5 × groundspeed (kt)

EXAMPLE 2 At GS 80 kt, required RoD = 5 × 80 = 400 ft/min.

Surveillance radar approach (SRA) guidance may be given to a distance of 2 nm (approximately 650 ft above the runway elevation), or, if the ground equipment is satisfactory and the radar controller has only one aircraft on approach, to ½ nm, where the height above the runway should be approximately 200 ft. The minimum for an IMC-rated pilot, however, is much higher than this, 600 ft aal at least. (See Chapter 22.)

For SRAs that terminate at 2 nm, calls will be given each 1 nm; for SRAs that terminate at ½ nm, calls will be given at each ½ nm.

Other Information Passed to the Pilot

1. Prior to the commencement of the SRA, the radar controller will pass the Aerodrome QFE to the pilot which, when set in the altimeter subscale, will cause the altimeter to read height above aerodrome elevation. Threshold QFE may alternatively be given, which would cause the altimeter to read height above threshold elevation. Height information, such as an instruction to descend to the intermediate approach height, or as included in the 'range/height' calls down final approach, will then refer to height above the airport or runway threshold.

NOTE If the pilot requests it, Aerodrome QNH will be passed. QNH set in the subscale will cause the altimeter to read altitude (height above mean sea level) rather than above runway elevation, and the radar controller will have to modify his calls to be altitudes rather than heights. For instance, at an aerodrome of elevation 700 ft, the call:

☐ "Range three miles; height should be nine five zero" – based on QFE, will become:
☐ "Range three miles; altitude should be one six five zero" – based on QNH.

2. The obstacle clearance height (OCH) will also be passed as a height above the aerodrome or threshold elevation (i.e. based on QFE), and the pilot will be reminded to check his minimum descent height (MDH).

> *Golf Delta Sierra*
> *This will be a surveillance radar approach*
> *Terminating at one half mile from ...*
> *Obstacle clearance height ... feet*
> *Check your minima*

As mentioned above, calculating your own particular minima (height and visibility) is discussed in Chapter 22; however, the surveillance radar approach minimum height must not be less than 600 ft aal for an IMC-rated pilot. Obstacles in the vicinity may require it to be higher. Required visibility is at least 1,800 metres. Further information on SRA minima is found in the UK AIP AD 2, and on radar approach procedure charts.

How Radar Works

> *The remainder of this chapter discusses the theory of radio waves and of radar. It is not essential knowledge but it will help your understanding of radio, radar and radio navigation aids.*

Radio uses the ability to transmit electromagnetic energy, in the form of radio waves, from one place to another. Radio has played a pivotal part in the development of aviation, and radar is an important type of radio system.

Waves of electromagnetic energy emanating from a radio transmitter can carry information, such as speech, music and Morse code, out into the surrounding environment. Radio receivers tuned to the *same* frequency can detect and use these signals, often at long distances from the transmitter.

Common uses for radio in aviation are:
☐ air–ground voice communication; and
☐ radio navigation (the ADF/NDB combination, VOR and ILS).

■ *Figure 9-4* **Radio is the transmission of electromagnetic energy and the reception of it at a distant location**

The Reflection of Radio Waves

Electromagnetic radiation can be reflected from certain surfaces. Light waves, for instance, will be reflected by the metallic coating on a mirror. Similarly, radio waves of certain frequencies will be reflected from metallic and other surfaces, with some of the radio energy returning to the point from which it was transmitted as a return echo. Other surfaces and objects, such as wood, may not cause reflection of the radio waves, which will simply pass through like X-rays pass through a body.

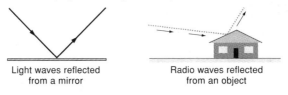

Light waves reflected
from a mirror

Radio waves reflected
from an object

■ *Figure 9-5* **Radio waves, like light waves, can be reflected**

Radar

Detection of the reflected radio waves at the point from where they were originally transmitted is known as radar. The principle of radar has been known since the mid-1930s, and was used with devastating effect during World War II (1939–45) to detect objects such as aeroplanes and measure their range. Indeed, the name *radar* was devised from *radio detection and ranging*.

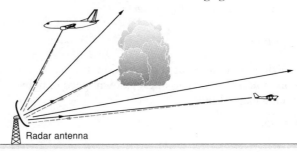

Radar antenna

■ *Figure 9-6* **Radar is the transmission of electromagnetic radio energy and the detection of some of the reflected energy back at the point of transmission**

The combined transmitter-receiver used in radar is usually a parabolic dish that is very efficient both in transmitting radio energy in a particular direction and then receiving the reflected radio energy from the same direction. The best results are obtained with ultra-high frequency radio energy. The whole sky can be scanned systematically if desired, simply by slowly rotating the radar dish.

■ Figure 9-7 **A typical radar antenna**

The Relationship of Time and Distance

All electromagnetic energy travels at the speed of light, 300,000 kilometres per second (162,000 nautical miles per second), the equivalent of almost eight journeys around the world in one second. Some common forms of electromagnetic energy are light, radio waves, X-rays, ultra-violet radiation and infra-red radiation.

By measuring the elapsed **time** between the transmission of a bundle or *pulse* of radio energy and the reception back at the source of its reflected echo, it is a simple mathematical calculation (knowing velocity) to determine the **distance** or *range* of the object causing the echo.

Radar converts an *elapsed time* to a *distance*.

$$\frac{distance}{time} = speed$$

Multiplying both sides of this equation by *time* gives an expression for *distance* in terms of the known speed of light and the measured elapsed time.

$$distance = speed \times time$$

During the elapsed time between transmission of the pulse and reception of its reflection (measured electronically at the radar site), the distance between the radar site and the object will of course have been travelled twice – once out and once back – so the elapsed time needs to be halved, and this is also done electronically.

The speed of light, being so great, means that the times involved are extremely short. This allows a stream of pulses to be transmitted, with only short time intervals between the pulses when no transmission occurs, to allow for reception of any echo. As a matter of interest, the time taken for a radar pulse to travel to and from a reflector 20 nm away (a total of 40 nm) is 0.000250 seconds, or 250 millionths of a second.

$$40 \text{ nm } (2 \times 20) \text{ at } \textit{speed of light } 162,000 \text{ nm/sec} = \frac{40}{162,000} \text{ sec}$$

$$= 0.000250 \text{ sec}$$

☐ If the measured elapsed time interval is 250 millionths of a second, then the object is 20 nm distant.

☐ If the measured elapsed time interval is 750 millionths of a second, then the object is 60 nm distant.

☐ If the measured elapsed time interval is 125 millionths of a second, then the object is 10 nm distant.

☐ If the measured elapsed time interval is 12.5 millionths of a second then the object is 1 nm distant. A time interval of 12.5 millionths of a second (or microseconds) can be thought of as a **radar mile.**

At what Range can Radar Detect Targets?

Radar uses ultra-high frequency (UHF) transmissions, which are basically *line of sight,* and so propagation will be interrupted by buildings, high terrain and the curvature of the earth. These will cause **radar shadows,** and objects in these shadow areas may not be detected.

Bearing in mind the curvature of the earth, the higher an aeroplane is flying, the greater the distance at which it can be detected by radar. An approximate maximum distance in nautical miles is given by the relationship:

$$\textit{Radar range} = \sqrt{1.5 \times \textit{height agl in feet}} \text{ (nm)}$$

NOTE $\sqrt{1.5 \ \textit{height}}$ is the same as $1.22 \sqrt{\textit{height}}$, which some people prefer. It is a similar expression, since the square root of 1.5 is 1.22.

EXAMPLE 3 At 5,000 ft agl over flat terrain with no obstruction, an aeroplane will be detected up to approximately 87 nm away.

$$Radar\ range\ =\ \sqrt{1.5\ \text{ht in feet}} \qquad ^{or} \qquad =\ 1.22\ \sqrt{\text{ht in feet}}$$

$$=\ \sqrt{1.5 \times 5{,}000\ \text{ft}} \qquad\qquad =\ 1.22\ \sqrt{5{,}000\ \text{ft}}$$

$$=\ \sqrt{7{,}500\ \text{ft}} \qquad\qquad\qquad =\ 1.22\ \times 71\ \text{nm}$$

$$=\ \sqrt{87\ \text{nm}} \qquad\qquad\qquad =\ \sqrt{87\ \text{nm}}$$

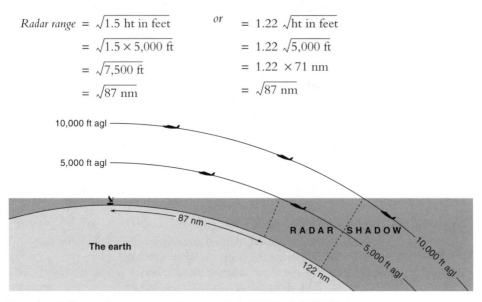

■ *Figure 9-8* **Radar detection range for aircraft at 5,000 and 10,000 ft**

EXAMPLE 4 At 10,000 ft agl over flat terrain with no obstructions, an aeroplane will be detected up to approximately 120 nm.

$$Radar\ range\ =\ \sqrt{1.5\ \text{ht in ft}} \qquad ^{or} \qquad =\ 1.22\ \sqrt{\text{ht in ft}}$$

$$=\ \sqrt{1.5 \times 10{,}000\ \text{ft}} \qquad\qquad =\ 1.22\ \sqrt{10{,}000\ \text{ft}}$$

$$=\ \sqrt{15{,}000\ \text{ft}} \qquad\qquad\qquad =\ 1.22\ \times 100\ \text{nm}$$

$$=\ \sqrt{122\ \text{nm}} \qquad\qquad\qquad =\ \sqrt{122\ \text{nm}}$$

NOTE These are expected ranges under ideal conditions; in reality, the range of a radar may be significantly less than this, and it may experience *blind spots* and *radar shadows*.

Radar range may be increased if the radar antenna is sited at a high elevation, both to raise it above nearby obstacles that would cause shadows, and to allow it to 'see' further around the curvature of the earth. Hence radar dishes are to be seen on the tops of hills and buildings. The range at which an aeroplane can now be detected by a radar sited well above a uniform surface is given approximately by:

$$Radar\ range\ =\ \sqrt{1.5\ height\ of\ radar\ dish}\ +\ \sqrt{1.5\ height\ of\ aircraft}$$

or

$$Radar\ range\ =\ 1.22\ \sqrt{height\ of\ radar\ dish}\ +\ 1.22\ \sqrt{height\ of\ aircraft}$$

EXAMPLE 5 At 5,000 ft agl over flat terrain with no obstructions, an aeroplane will be detected up to approximately 99 nm if the radar dish is elevated 100 ft above a uniform surface.

$$Radar\ range\ =\ \sqrt{1.5 \times 100}\ +\ \sqrt{1.5 \times 5,000}\ \text{ft}$$

$$=\ (\sqrt{150}\ +\ \sqrt{7,500})$$

$$=\ (12 + 87)\ \text{nm}$$

$$=\ 99\ \text{nm}$$

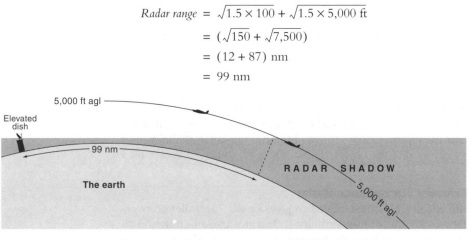

■ Figure 9-9 **Radar range is increased if the radar dish is elevated**

If the radar dish can be elevated 400 ft, then its range will increase by:

$$\sqrt{1.5 \times 400}\ =\ 24\ \text{nm}$$

Another technical design feature (apart from the positioning of the radar dish) that determines the range of a radar is the interval existing between pulse transmissions to allow the transmitter to act as a receiver. The greater the time interval, the greater the range from which echoes can be received. Greater time intervals between pulses means that fewer per second may be transmitted, which is referred to as a lower **pulse repetition rate** (PRR).

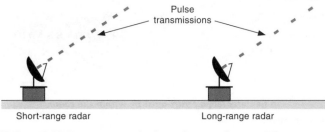

■ Figure 9-10 **Long-range radar has a lower pulse repetition rate**

Radar that makes use of reflected radio energy is known as **primary radar,** and it is used for a number of purposes in aviation, including:

☐ **surveillance radar** to provide an overview of a whole area, and used in surveillance radar approaches (SRA) for azimuth and height guidance on final approach to land; and

☐ **precision approach radar** (PAR) for extremely accurate azimuth and slope guidance on final approach to land.

Direction by Radar

If the direction from which the reflected signal comes can be determined, as well as its range, then the **position** of the object can be pinpointed. This is achieved by slowly rotating the radar dish, a typical rate being two revolutions per minute, during which time it will have fired out many millions of pulses in its radar beam and received almost instantaneously any reflected returns. The angle of the radar antenna compared to north at the time the return echo is received indicates the horizontal direction (or *azimuth*) of the object. These *returns* are displayed as *blips* on a screen.

Primary Surveillance Radar

Surveillance radar is designed to give a radar controller an overview of his area of responsibility. It does not transmit pulses in all directions simultaneously, but rather as a beam, which is slowly rotated. For an aeroplane to be detected, the beam must be directed roughly towards it. If the radar controller has his radar tilted up, then it may miss lower aircraft at a distance; conversely, nearby high aeroplanes may not be detected if the tilt is down.

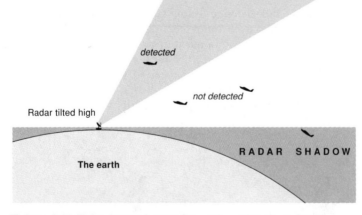

■ *Figure 9-11* **To be detected, aircraft must be within the radar transmitter's beam**

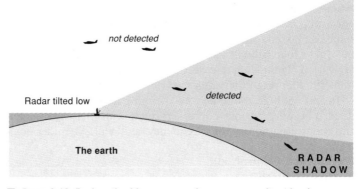

■ *Figure 9-12* ***Radar tilted low cannot detect targets directly above***

The Radar Screen

Most radar screens are simply cathode ray tubes (CRT) that resemble circular television screens. Using the same principle as television, a beam of electrons is directed onto the fluorescent coating of the CRT to provide a radar picture. Radar controllers generally have circular displays showing the position of the radar antenna in the centre, with range marks to aid in estimating distance. The radar screen is also known as a **plan position indicator (PPI)**.

The actual radar dish may be located away from the position of the radar controller, possibly on a nearby hill or tower. As the radar antenna rotates slowly, the small electron beam in the controller's CRT also rotates, leaving a faint line or trace on the screen in a direction aligned with the direction of the antenna at that moment. Any radar return signal appears as a *blip* or *paint* at the appropriate spot on the screen.

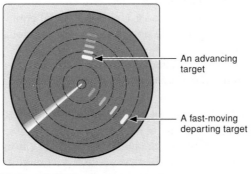

■ *Figure 9-13* ***A radar screen***

An indication of north on the screen allows the controller to estimate the direction of the target, and the range marks assist in estimating its distance. The *paint* of the target remains visible for some seconds after the small trace line has moved on, and will still be visible (but fading) as its next *paint* occurs in the following revolution. This fading trail of blips allows the controller to determine the motion of the target in terms of direction and speed.

In areas of high traffic density, the radar responsibility may be divided between various controllers, each with their own screen and radio communications frequency, and will go under such names as:

☐ **Approach Control;** and
☐ **Zone Control.**

Other markings besides the range circles may be superimposed on the screen as a video map to indicate the location of nearby controlled airspace, aerodromes, radio navigation aids such as VORs and NDBs, Restricted Areas, etc.

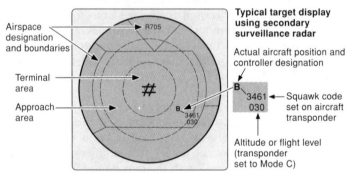

■ *Figure 9-14* **A typical ATC radar screen**

Some Disadvantages of Primary Radar

While a big advantage of primary radar is that no special equipment is required in an aeroplane, it does have some operational disadvantages, including:

☐ **clutter** from precipitation and high ground;
☐ **uneven returns** from different aircraft; and
☐ **blind spots.**

The radio energy in the reflected signal received at the radar dish may be quite small, depending on the strength of the original transmission, how good a reflector the target is, its distance from the radar antenna, and so on. A radar that is sensitive enough to pick up weak returns from targets may also pick up returns from terrain and precipitation, leading to *ground clutter* and *weather clutter* on the screen. During periods of heavy rain, primary radar may be significantly degraded.

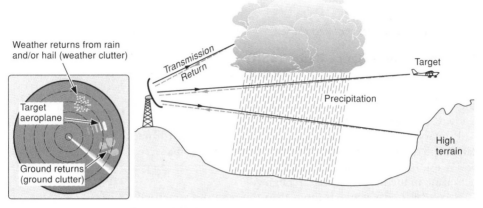

■ *Figure 9-15* **Primary surveillance radar is subject to clutter**

Some radars incorporate an electronic sifting device known as a **moving target indicator** (MTI) that only allows signals from moving targets to be shown on the screen, in an attempt to eliminate clutter from stationary objects.

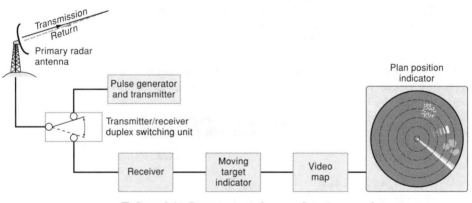

■ *Figure 9-16* **Diagrammatic layout of a primary radar system**

With primary radar only, it is often difficult for the radar controller to distinguish between various signals, and he may have to request one aeroplane to carry out a manoeuvre such as a turn to distinguish its radar blip from that of another aeroplane. A typical request could be:

> *Golf Sierra Delta*
> *For identification*
> *Turn left thirty degrees*
> *Heading zero six zero*

Once the controller observes this turn on the screen:

> *Golf Delta Sierra*
> *Identified one two miles northwest of Exeter*

Secondary Surveillance Radar (SSR)

Secondary surveillance radar removes most of the limitations of primary radar simply by adding energy to the return pulse from the aeroplane, using a device carried on board the aeroplane known as a **transponder.**

Primary radar detects radar energy passively reflected from a target and displays it as a blip, or fading series of blips, on a screen; this is a similar process to a searchlight operator at night seeing an aeroplane in the beam of the searchlight.

Secondary radar is much more than this, and the target is far from passive. It is as if each time the searchlight strikes the target, the target is triggered to light itself up very brightly in response, and not just passively reflect some of the energy transmitted from the ground site. Secondary radar is really two radar sets talking to each other.

Because only a small amount of energy transmitted from the ground is required to act as a trigger for the airborne SSR transponder, the secondary radar ground transmitter and antenna system can be quite small (unlike the large primary radar dish and powerful transmitter in a system which depend on reflected echoes proportional to the original power of transmission). A long and narrow secondary surveillance radar antenna can often be seen above the large primary radar dish.

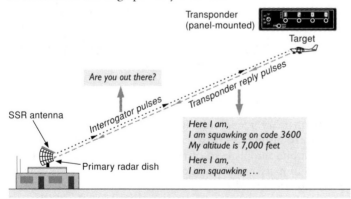

■ *Figure 9-17* **SSR is two radars talking to each other**

The SSR ground equipment consists of:
- [ ] **an interrogator** that provides a coded signal asking a transponder to respond;

☐ a highly directional rotating radar **antenna** that transmits the coded interrogation signal, then receives any responding signals, and passes them back to the interrogator; and

☐ **a decoder,** which accepts the signals from the interrogator, decodes them and displays them on the radar screen.

The SSR aircraft equipment consists of a transponder carried in the individual aeroplane.

The originating signal transmitted from the ground station triggers an automatic response from the aeroplane's transponder. It transmits a strong answering coded signal which is then received at the ground station. This response signal is much, much stronger than the simple reflected signal used in primary radar. Even a very weak signal received in the aircraft will trigger a strong response from the transponder.

The secondary responding pulse from the aeroplane's transponder can carry coding that distinguishes the aeroplane from all others on the radar screen. Depending on the code selected in the transponder by the pilot, it can also carry additional information, such as:

☐ the identity of the aeroplane;

☐ its altitude; and

☐ any abnormal situation such as radio failure, distress, emergency, etc.

A significant advantage is that SSR is not degraded to the same extent as primary radar by weather or ground clutter, it presents targets of the same size and intensity to the controller, it allows the controller to select specific displays, and the system has minimal blind spots.

Unfortunately, not all aircraft are fitted with transponders, yet they may be flying in the same airspace. For this reason, both primary and secondary surveillance radar information will be presented to a radar controller on the one screen.

SSR Symbols on the Radar Screen

We recommend that you visit a radar control centre to see the system in action from the air traffic controller's point of view. Understanding his task and how it interacts with yours as pilot-in-command will lead to greater professionalism.

Sometimes ATC need to distinguish a particular aeroplane from others in its vicinity. This situation may arise with a number of aircraft holding in the one area, or with a light aircraft that is having navigational difficulties and has requested assistance. ATC will then assign a code (such as 1700 or 4000) to this particular aircraft.

Technological advances are being made and already many aero-planes and some SSRs are equipped for altitude reporting and the like. For instance, some aircraft squawk specific codes, e.g. code 3916 applies to only one particular aeroplane, and on certain advanced SSR screens this will show up as that aeroplane, with a read-out of its altitude and groundspeed. Under less sophisticated radar coverage, the older SSR screens will show this only as belonging to the 3000 family, i.e. as a large circle.

All of these symbols are continually shown on the screen as a result of the coding selected on the aircraft transponder, except for the large *squawk* triangle which appears on the radar screen for 15 to 20 seconds only when a pilot presses the IDENT button.

"Squawk ident" is often requested by ATC when they want positive identification of an aeroplane on their screen. For this reason you should only press the IDENT button on your trans-ponder when specifically requested to do so by ATC.

Using the Transponder in the Cockpit

Usually the transponder is warmed up in the STANDBY position during the taxi, the code to be used (a four-figure number) selected, and then switched ON just prior to take-off.

Even though transponders produced by various manufacturers vary slightly in design, they are operated in basically the same manner. As a responsible pilot, you will become familiar with your particular transponder.

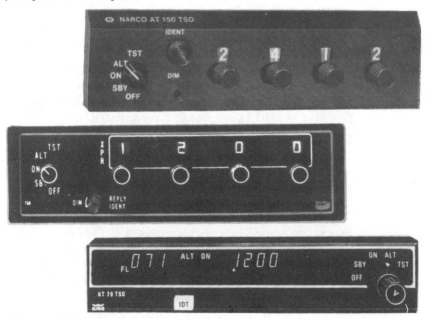

■ *Figure 9-18* **Transponders from various manufacturers**

The Function Selector Knob

The function selector knob enables you to select the transponder to one of its various operation modes, e.g. OFF, ON, STANDBY, ALT. Typical transponder modes include:

OFF: switches the transponder off.

STANDBY: warmed up, and ready for immediate use. This is the normal position until you are ready for take-off, when you would select ALT or ON (if transponder is to be used in flight).

ON: transmits the selected code in Mode A (aircraft identification mode) at the normal power level.

ALT: (altitude) may be used if the altitude-reporting capability (known as mode C) is installed in your aircraft. This is a special **encoding altimeter** which feeds your altitude to the transponder for transmission on to the ATC radar screen. (If not installed, the transponder still transmits in Mode A, i.e. aircraft identification without altitude reporting.)

TST: tests that the transponder is operating correctly and if so, illuminates the reply monitor light. It causes the transponder to generate a self-interrogating signal to check its operation.

Code Selection

Knobs are provided for you to select the appropriate squawk code for your transponder, and the selected code is prominently displayed in digital form.

An important procedure to follow when selecting and altering codes is to avoid passing through vital codes (such as 7700 for emergencies, 7600 for radio failure) when the transponder is switched ON. This can be avoided by selecting STANDBY while the code is being changed. Your flying instructor will explain further.

The Reply-Monitor Light

The reply light will flash to indicate that the transponder is replying to an interrogation pulse from a ground station.

The reply-monitor light will glow steadily when you:
- press the TEST button or move the function switch to the TEST position (depending on the design of your particular transponder) to indicate correct functioning; or
- transmit an IDENT pulse.

The IDENT Switch or Button

When the IDENT button is pressed by the pilot on request from the radar controller to SQUAWK IDENT, a special pulse is transmitted with your transponder's reply to the interrogating ground station. This causes a special symbol to appear for a few seconds on the radar screen around the return from your aircraft's transponder, thus allowing positive identification by the radar controller.

NOTE Your particular transponder may have minor variations to that described above, but will certainly be fundamentally the same. It may for instance have a separate mode selector to select Mode A (position reporting) or Mode C (position and altitude reporting). These variations are easily understood.

Squawk

The term *squawk* that you will often hear is confined to transponder usage, and the instruction following squawk is usually quite clear, for instance: "Squawk ident"; "Squawk code 4000"; "Squawk Mayday" (7700), etc.

Typical Transponder Radio Calls

ATC: "(CALLSIGN), SQUAWK IDENT". Pilot response is to press the transponder IDENT button, allowing the radar controller to identify you positively on his screen.

ATC: "(CALLSIGN), SQUAWK CODE 7340". Pilot response is a read-back of the assigned code: "(callsign), code 7340", and to select the transponder to that code.

ATC: "(CALLSIGN), SQUAWK STANDBY". Pilot response is to move the function switch to STANDBY from ON or ALT position, for a temporary suspension of transponder operation (maintaining present code).

ATC: "(CALLSIGN), SQUAWK NORMAL". Pilot response is to reactivate the transponder from STANDBY to ON or ALT, as appropriate, retaining the existing code.

Further information on SSR operating procedures appears in UK AIP ENR 1-6-3.

*Now complete **Exercises 9 – Radar.***

DME

Slant Distance

Distance-measuring equipment (DME) can provide you with extremely useful information: the distance of your aircraft from a DME ground station. DME uses radar principles to measure this distance, which is the *slant distance* rather than the horizontal distance (or range). For most practical purposes, the DME distance can be considered as range, except when the aeroplane is within a few miles of the DME ground station.

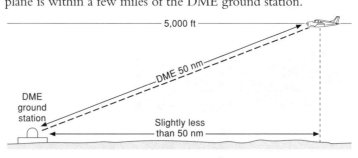

■ *Figure 10-1* **DME measures slant distance**

Passing directly over the DME ground station, the DME indicator in the cockpit will either show the height of the aeroplane in nautical miles (1 nm = 6,000 ft approximately), or the DME indication will drop out.

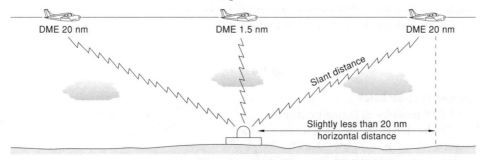

■ *Figure 10-2* **Passing overhead a DME ground station**

DME Cockpit Displays

DME distance is usually displayed in the cockpit as a digital readout. The pilot generally selects the DME using the VHF-NAV radio (since most DMEs are paired with a VOR frequency or a localizer frequency). Once the DME is *locked on,* and a DME reading and *ident* obtained, the DME indications can be used for distance information irrespective of whether the VOR (or localizer) is used for tracking or orientation purposes.

Some airborne DME equipment is capable of computing the rate of change of DME distance (the *rate of closure* of the aeroplane with the DME ground station), and displaying this rate of closure on the DME cockpit instrument. If it is assumed that slant distance equals horizontal distance, and that the aeroplane is tracking either directly towards or directly away from the DME ground station, then the rate of closure read-out will represent **groundspeed (GS),** a very useful piece of information. Some DME indicators can also display **time to the station (TTS)** in minutes at the current rate of closure, by comparing the groundspeed with DME distance.

> *DME measures rate of closure to the ground station and displays your groundspeed and time to the station.*

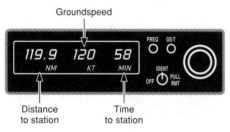

■ *Figure 10-3* **A digital DME panel**

If the DME equipment in the aeroplane does not give a groundspeed read-out, then simply note the DME distance at two particular times, and carry out a simple calculation of GS = distance/time either mentally or on your navigation computer.

EXAMPLE 1 You note DME distance and time as you track towards a DME ground station. Calculate groundspeed.

DME 35	Time 0215 UTC	
DME 25	Time 0220 UTC	
10 nm	5 min	= **GS 120 kt**

Circular Position Lines

The DME provides a circular position line. If the DME reads 35 nm, for instance, then you know that the aeroplane is somewhere on the circumference of a 35 nm circle centred on the DME ground station.

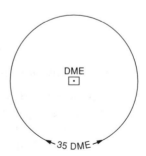

■ *Figure 10-4* **A circular position line from a DME**

Information from another radio aid may assist in positively fixing the position of the aeroplane, provided the two position lines give a good 'cut' (angle of intercept).

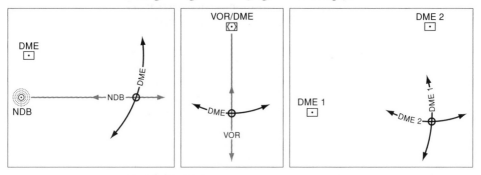

■ Figure 10-5 **Using two radio navaids to fix position**

Some instrument approach procedures (e.g. Carlisle NDB/DME) allow a **DME arc** to be flown, prior to intercepting the final approach track, by maintaining an approximately constant DME reading – achieved by keeping the other aid (e.g. the NDB) approximately on the wingtip.

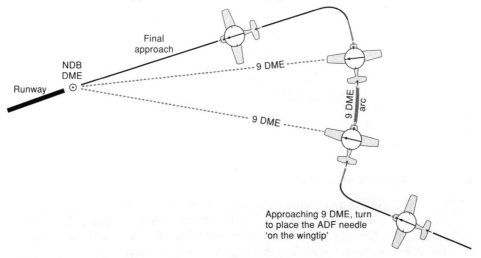

■ Figure 10-6 **Example of a DME arc manoeuvre**

How DME Works

DME uses the principle of secondary radar. Radar is covered thoroughly in Chapter 9, where both primary and secondary radar are discussed. **Primary radar** detects one of its own transmissions that is reflected from some object; **secondary radar** detects a *responding transmission* from a **transponder** activated by an *interrogation* signal.

Distance measuring equipment operates by the airborne transmitter (the *interrogator*) sending out a stream of radio pulses in all directions on the receiving frequency of the DME ground station transponder.

At the target DME ground beacon, these pulses are passed through an electronic *gate*. If the pulses and the gate match up, the DME ground beacon (or transponder) is triggered, and responds by transmitting a strong answering signal. The airborne DME equipment detects this answering signal and measures the time between the transmission of the interrogating pulse from the aircraft and the reception of the ranging reply pulse from the DME ground station. It converts this time to a *distance in nautical miles* and the DME indicator, when it displays this distance with the red OFF flag out of view, is said to have latched on or locked on.

NOTE Do not confuse the DME transponder at the DME ground station (and associated with the airborne DME equipment) with the SSR transponder carried in the aircraft (operated by the pilot and associated with the ground-based secondary surveillance radar).

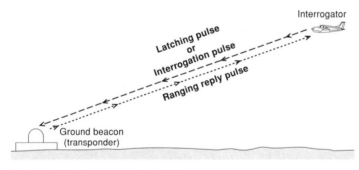

■ *Figure 10-7* **Operation of the DME**

Each DME ground transponder can cope with about 100 different aeroplanes at any one time before becoming saturated, and the system is designed so that there is no possibility of interrogation pulses from one aeroplane causing an incorrect range indication in another aeroplane. Also, because the frequencies are carefully chosen so that stations with like frequencies are situated far apart geographically, there is no likelihood of interference from the wrong DME ground station. DME signals are line-of-sight transmissions (like VHF radio communications, radar and VOR). The approximate usable range in nautical miles is the square root of (1.5 × height in ft).

You must positively identify a DME ground station before using it for navigation.

DME Frequencies

DME operates in the UHF (ultra-high frequency) band from 962 MHz to 1,213 MHz which, with 1 MHz spacing, gives 252 possible frequencies. Each DME channel consists of two frequencies (an interrogation frequency from the aeroplane and a paired response frequency from the ground station).

There are 126 channels currently in use, numbered from 1 to 126, and with X or Y classification after them. You may see references such as DME CH 92Y or DME CH 111X in the AIP, but there is no need for you to know these details, since these numbers are not used by the pilot to select the DME – the DME is automatically selected on many types of VHF-NAV units when you select the VHF-NAV to an appropriate VOR or ILS frequency.

VOR/DME Pairing

Each VOR frequency has a specific DME channel paired with it. For instance, VOR frequency 112.00 MHz has DME channel 57X paired with it, so that the VOR's associated DME will automatically be interrogated when you select the VOR frequency 112.00 on the VHF-NAV. The purpose of this pairing is to reduce your workload in the cockpit, with only one selection instead of two required, and to reduce the risk selecting the right VOR but the wrong DME station. It is normal for only **co-located** VORs and DMEs to be frequency paired. Co-located VORs and DMEs are situated within 800 metres of each other, and each will have the same Morse code ident.

A paired VOR and DME give a very good position fix:
- the radial from the VOR; and
- the distance from the DME.

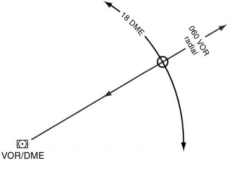

■ Figure 10-8 **Fixing position with VOR and DME**

ILS/DME Pairing

Many instrument landing systems (ILS) have their localizer frequency paired with a DME located very close to the runway threshold. This provides you with very useful information during an ILS or localizer approach to the runway; for example, distance fixes for key positions on the approach (such as the final approach fix), as well as the distance-to-run to the runway threshold.

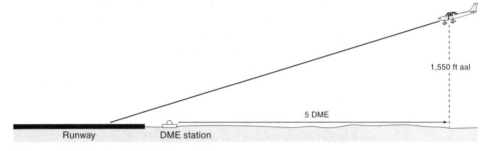

■ Figure 10-9 **Using a paired localizer/DME**

DME Station Information

Further information on individual DME ground stations appears in the ENR 4-1-1 section of the UK AIP.

| STATION | SERVICE | CALL SIGN OR IDENT | EM | TRANSMITS | | RECEIVES | | HOURS OF |
				kHz	MHz	kHz	MHz	WINTER PERIOD
1	2	3	4	5	6	7	8	9
Midhurst	VOR	MID	A9W	–	114.000	–	–	H24
	DME	PON						

RADIO NAVIGATION AIDS EN-ROUTE

| SERVICE SUMMER PERIOD | CO-ORDINATES | LOCATION | | OPERATING AUTHORITY AND REMARKS |
		MAG	NM	
10	11	12	13	14
H24	N5103.20 W00037.40	–	–	NATS. DOC 60 nm/50000 ft (100 nm/50000 ft in Sector 127° to 217° MAG). DME Ch 87X. Aerial Hgt 200 ft amsl.

INFORMATION ONLY
Not for Navigational Purposes

■ Figure 10-10 **Information from AIP ENR 4-1-1 for the Midhurst DME station**

Now complete **Exercises 10 – DME.**

The NDB and the ADF

General Description

The non-directional beacon (NDB) is the simplest form of radio navigation aid used by aircraft. It is a ground-based transmitter that transmits radio energy in all directions, hence its name – the **non-directional beacon.**

The **automatic direction finder** (ADF), fitted in an aeroplane has a needle that indicates the direction from which the signals of the selected NDB ground station are being received. This is extremely useful information for pilots flying in instrument conditions and/or at night. In days past, the combined ADF/NDB system was referred to as the **radio compass.**

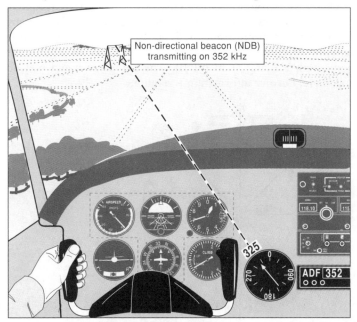

Non-directional beacon (NDB) transmitting on 352 kHz

■ *Figure 11-1* **A correctly tuned ADF indicates the direction of the selected NDB from the aircraft**

Flying to an NDB in an aeroplane is similar to following a compass needle to the North Pole – fly the aeroplane towards where the needle points and eventually you will arrive overhead.

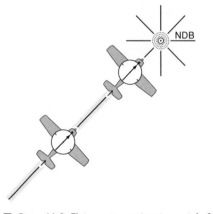

■ *Figure 11-2* **Flying to a station is straightforward**

Flying away from the North Pole, however, with the magnetic compass needle pointing behind, could take the aeroplane in any one of 360 directions. Similarly, flying away from the NDB using only the ADF needle will not lead the aeroplane to a particular point (unlike flying *to* an NDB). The aeroplane could end up anywhere! Further information is required.

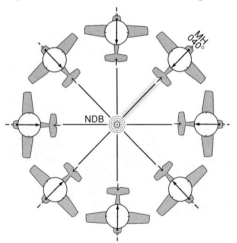

■ *Figure 11-3* **Flying away from a station requires more information than just the needle on the tail**

The ADF and the Heading Indicator

The extra information required by the pilot, in addition to that supplied by the ADF needle, comes from the magnetic compass, or more commonly, from the heading indicator. Accurate navigation can be carried out using the aircraft **ADF needle** which points at an NDB ground station, and a **heading indicator** which indicates the aeroplane's magnetic heading (MH).

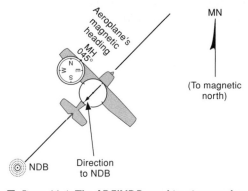

■ Figure 11-4 **The ADF/NDB combination needs support from a magnetic compass (or from a heading indicator)**

NOTE Since a heading indicator will most probably drift slowly out of alignment, it is essential that you periodically realign it with the magnetic compass in straight flight at a steady speed, say every 10 or 15 minutes.

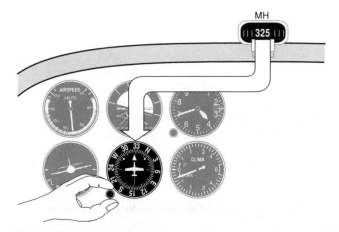

■ Figure 11-5 **Periodically realign the HI with the magnetic compass in steady flight**

The NDB/ADF Combination

Before using an ADF's indications of the bearing to a particular NDB, the aeroplane must be within the promulgated range of the NDB and you must have:
  ☐ **correctly selected** the NDB frequency;
  ☐ **identified** its Morse code ident; and
  ☐ **tested** the ADF needle to ensure that it is indeed 'ADFing'.

If the NDB is 40° to the left of the aeroplane's magnetic heading, say MH 070°M, then the situation can be illustrated as shown in Figure 11-6. The NDB, since it is 40° left of the nose, will have a magnetic bearing (MB) of 030°M from the aeroplane.

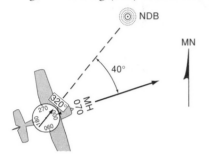

■ *Figure 11-6* **A diagrammatic representation**

The ADF/NDB combination, in conjunction with the heading indicator, can be used:
☐ **to track** to the NDB on any desired track, pass overhead the NDB, and track outbound on whatever track is desired; or
☐ **to fix** the aeroplane's position.

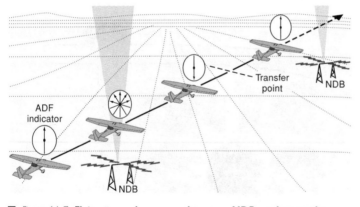

■ *Figure 11-7* **Flying towards, over, and past an NDB, and on to the next one**

The ADF in the aeroplane should, whenever possible, be selected to an NDB relevant to the desired path of the aeroplane. If tracking en route between two NDBs, the point of transfer from one NDB to the next would reasonably be the half-way point, depending of course on their relative ranges.

If the NDB is ahead, the ADF needle will point up the dial; if the NDB is behind, the ADF needle will point down the dial. As the aeroplane passes overhead the NDB, the ADF needle will become very sensitive and will swing from ahead to behind.

If the ADF needle points up, the NDB is ahead.

If the ADF needle points down, the NDB is behind.

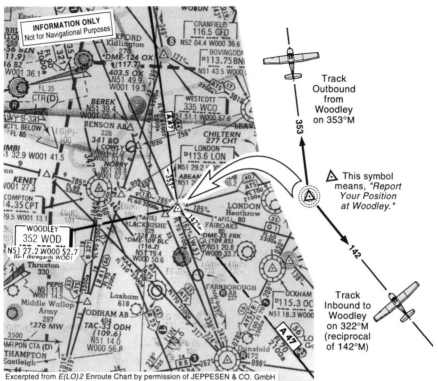

Excerpted from E(LO)2 Enroute Chart by permission of JEPPESEN & CO. GmbH
© 1994 JEPPESEN SANDERSON INC.

■ Figure 11-8 **The Woodley NDB is used as a tracking aid, a turning point and as a reporting point on the A47 air route**

The ADF can also be used for more advanced procedures such as:
□ flying an accurate 'racetrack' holding pattern based on the NDB; or
□ using the NDB for guidance when manoeuvring in the vicinity of an aerodrome, either as a let-down or cloudbreak aid in its own right, or as a lead-in to a precision approach aid such as an ILS (instrument landing system).

NDBs with published approach procedures are referred to as locators (L) (abbreviated 'Lctr' on *Jeppesen* charts). The Luton locator (frequency 345 kHz), shown in Figure 11-9, is available as:
□ **a point over which to hold** in a racetrack pattern:
□ **the sole tracking aid** on an NDB let-down for Runway 26; or
□ **as an additional tracking guide** when using the Runway 26 instrument landing system, and as an outer marker (LOM) or check point on this ILS approach.

NOTE The more you use approach charts or *approach plates,* the simpler they will appear.

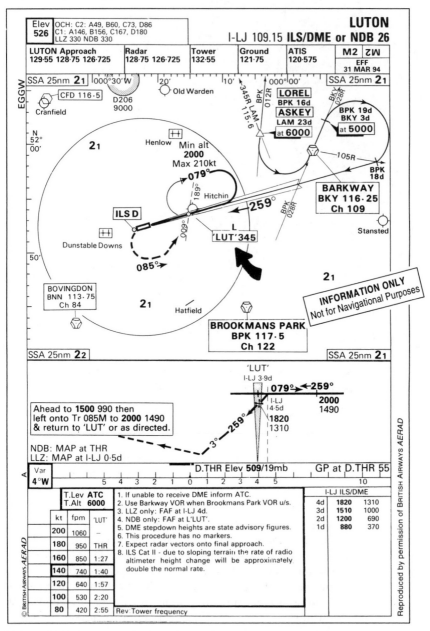

■ *Figure 11-9* **The approach chart for Luton Runway 26, using the**
ILS/DME or NDB

Some NDBs are not available for holding or for instrument approaches, but only for en route navigation. This information is available in the UK AIP ENR 4-1-1 section.

The NDB/ADF combination is the simplest form of radio navigation in theory, yet it takes a good instrument pilot to use it accurately. Other more advanced systems, such as the VOR, are more complicated in principle but easier to use.

The NDB

The NDB is a ground-based transmitter.

The non-directional beacon (NDB) is the ground-based part of the combination. It is called *non-directional* because no particular direction is favoured or differentiated in its transmissions; the NDB radiates identical electromagnetic energy in all directions. Each NDB transmits on a given frequency in the low-frequency or medium-frequency LF/MF bands (somewhere between 200 to 1,750 kHz). The transmission aerial is either a single mast or a large 'T-aerial' slung between two masts.

■ *Figure 11-10* **NDB transmission aerials**

Identify an NDB before using it for navigation.

To avoid confusion between various NDBs, and to ensure that the pilot is using the correct beacon, each NDB transmits its own particular identification signal (or **ident**) in the form of a two- or three-letter Morse code signal, which you should monitor periodically in the cockpit.

EXAMPLE 1 The Plymouth NDB has a frequency of 396.5 kHz and is identified by listening to, and identifying the Morse code symbols for PY, which are: *"dit-dah-dah-dit dah-dit-dah-dah"* or:

· — — ·   — · — —

The normal sources of frequency and ident information for the instrument pilot are the radio navigation charts and/or the approach charts, which are carried in the cockpit.

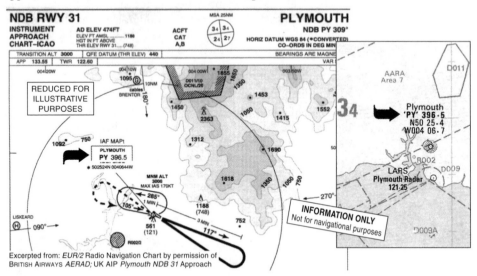

■ *Figure 11-11* **Plymouth NDB information on radio navigation charts**

As mentioned earlier, more detailed information is available in AIP AD 2 or ENR 4-1-1.

RADIO NAVIGATION AND LANDING AIDS				
Type Category (Variation)	IDENT	Frequency	Hours of Operation Winter	Summer
			# and by arrangement	
1	2	3	4	
L	PY	396.5 kHz	0630-2230 #	0530-2130 #

Antenna site co-ordinates	Elevation of DME transmitting antenna	Remarks
5	6	7
*502524N 0040644W		On AD. Range 20 nm.

INFORMATION ONLY
Not for navigational purposes

■ *Figure 11-12* **UK AIP AD 2 extract showing details of Plymouth NDB**

The AIP is used for flight planning, and is not usually carried in the aircraft. Additional information that is available in the AIP, and not available on the radio navigation charts or approach charts, includes:

☐ hours of service;
☐ the operating authority;

☐ **geographical location** in latitude and longitude;
☐ **the precise track and direction** from the NDB to the aerodrome (useful information when flying to an aerodrome after locating the aeroplane over the NDB after an instrument approach);
☐ **range;** and
☐ **other relevant remarks.**

NDB Range

For long-range en route navigation where no other aids are available, a fairly strong NDB with a range of 100 nm or more is usually required. Some NDBs used for long-distance overwater tracking, for instance in the Pacific area, may have a range of 400 nm. In the UK, however, where routes are relatively short and there are many navigation facilities, most NDBs have only a short range.

Lichfield NDB, for instance, near Birmingham, has a range of only 50 nm. The range of each non–directional beacon (NDB) is listed in AIP ENR 4-1-1, and within this promulgated range the NDB should provide bearings accurate to within ±5°. The promulgated range also provides guidance as to when you should shift your attention to the next aid.

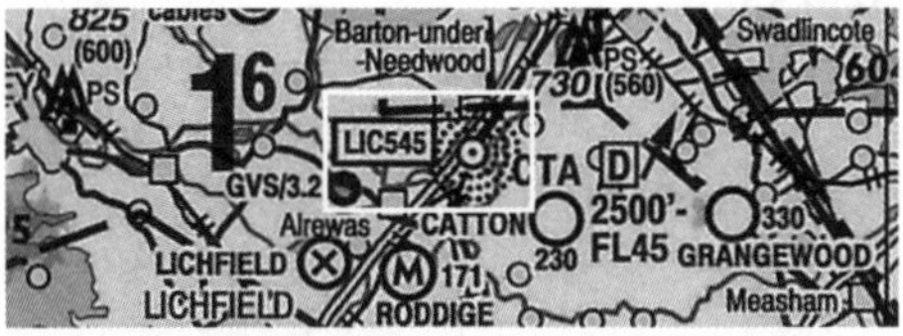

UK AIP   **(18 Jun 98) ENR 4-1-1-3**

ENR 4.1 — RADIO NAVIGATION AIDS — EN-ROUTE						
Name of Station (VOR set Variation)	IDENT	Frequency (Channel)	Hours of Operation (Winter/Summer)	Co-ordinates	DME Aerial Elevation	Remarks
Lichfield NDB	LIC	545.0 kHz	H24	524448N 0014310W	—	Range 50 nm.

■ *Figure 11-13* **Many NDBs have only a short range**

For manoeuvring in the vicinity of aerodromes, only lower-powered NDBs are required. NDBs used for approaches are referred to as locators (*L*, or *Lctr* on *Jeppesen* charts), e.g. the Manchester locator, ident MCR.

If a locator is co-located with an outer marker that serves to fix a position as an aircraft proceeds down an instrument landing system (ILS) approach, then it will be depicted on the ILS approach chart as LOM (locator outer marker).

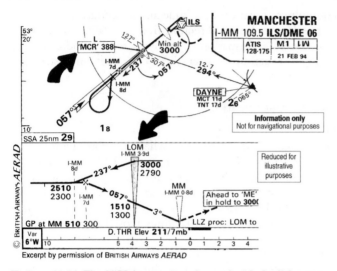

Excerpt by permission of BRITISH AIRWAYS *AERAD*

■ *Figure 11-14* **The MCR locator is co-located with the ILS outer marker, shown as LOM, for the Manchester Rwy 06 ILS**

The range of an NDB depends on:

☐ **transmission power** (10–2,000 watts);

☐ **transmission frequency;** and

☐ **atmospheric conditions** existing at the time – electrical storms, as well as the periods of sunrise and sunset, can distort or reflect the signals from an NDB.

NDB Signal Accuracy

An ideal NDB signal received by an aircraft may be accurate to ±2°; however, various factors may reduce this accuracy considerably. These factors include:

THUNDERSTORM EFFECT causes the ADF needle to be deflected towards a nearby electrical storm (cumulonimbus cloud) and away from the selected NDB.

NIGHT EFFECT when strong skywaves from the NDB returning to earth from the ionosphere cause interference with the surface waves from the NDB, possibly resulting in a fading signal and a wandering ADF needle (most pronounced at dawn and dusk).

INTERFERENCE from other NDBs transmitting on similar frequencies.

MOUNTAIN EFFECT due to reflections of the NDB signals from mountains.

COASTAL EFFECT caused by the NDB signal bending slightly towards the coastline when crossing it at an angle.

NDB Identification

Each NDB or locator is identifiable by a two- or three-letter Morse code identification signal which is transmitted along with its normal signal. This is known as its **ident.**

You must identify an NDB before using it for any navigational purpose within its promulgated range and, if using it for some length of time, periodically re-identify it.

The lack of an ident may indicate that the NDB is out of service, even though it may still be transmitting (say for maintenance or test purposes), and it must not be used for navigation. If an incorrect ident is heard, then those signals must not be used.

If a test or incorrect ident is heard, the NDB must not be used.

	L	L	
	'LUT' 345	'TD' 347.5	'NH' 371.5
Morse code	· — · · · · —	— ·	— — · · — · ·	— · · · · · ·

Monitor the ident frequently if an NDB is the only navaid you are using, as a signal failure will not be indicated on the ADF display.

To identify most NDBs, simply select AUDIO on the ADF, listen to the Morse code signal, and confirm that it is the correct one. (Morse code is shown on the legend of the ICAO 1:500,000 aeronautical chart series.)

Different NDBs have different ident characteristics which are associated with the type of transmission.

All NDBs in the UK can be identified with the ADF mode selector in the ADF position. In Continental Europe, however, there are some NDBs that require the pilot to select BFO (beat frequency oscillator) to enable identification. The BFO imposes a tone onto the NDB carrier wave to make it audible. Such NDBs are shown on charts without inverted commas, e.g. MP at Cherbourg and DEN at Dender, both in France.

Some NDBs carry voice transmissions, such as the automatic terminal information service (ATIS) at some aerodromes. It is also possible, in a situation where the communications radio (VHF-COM) has failed, for ATC to send voice messages to the pilot on the NDB frequency. They can be received on the ADF if AUDIO is selected.

NOTE Broadcasting stations such as the BBC and commercial stations may also be received by an ADF, since they transmit in the LF/MF bands. But it is not good airmanship to use a broadcasting station as a navigational aid, since they are difficult to identify precisely. Even if an announcer says "This is BBC Radio 2", it is possible that the transmission is coming, not from the main transmitter, but from an alternative or emergency transmitter located elsewhere, or even a relay station many miles away from the main transmitter. To use information from a radio broadcasting station, you must be absolutely certain of its geographical position –

something which is difficult to determine. It is not good airmanship to listen to a broadcasting station in flight, as it will distract you from operational tasks and responsibilities.

The ADF

The airborne partner of the NDB is the automatic direction finder, usually referred to as the ADF. It operates on the *radio compass* principle whereby the ADF needle indicates the direction from which the signals are coming.

The ADF is a receiver in the aircraft.

The automatic direction finder has three main components:

THE ADF RECEIVER, which the pilot tunes to the frequency of the desired NDB and verifies with the ident.

THE AERIAL SYSTEM, consisting of a **loop aerial** (or its modern equivalent), plus a **sense aerial,** which together determine the direction from which the signal is coming.

THE ADF COCKPIT DISPLAY, either a fixed-card or a rotatable compass card with a pointer or needle indicating the direction from which the signals are coming. The cockpit instrument is fitted into the instrument panel, usually to the right of the attitude flight instruments, with the top of the dial representing the nose of the aeroplane, and the bottom of the dial representing its tail. Ideally, the ADF needle will point continuously and automatically towards the NDB ground station.

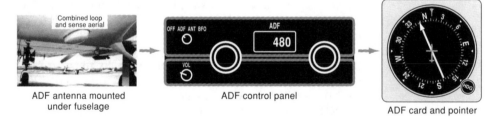

Combined loop and sense aerial

ADF antenna mounted under fuselage

ADF control panel

ADF card and pointer

■ *Figure 11-15* **The airborne ADF equipment**

ADF Aerials

Improved reception on a portable radio is sometimes possible by rotating it to a particular position, because of the directional properties of its receiving antenna. The automatic direction finder works on the same principle.

The Loop Aerial

When the loop aerial is aligned with the plane of a radio wave (in the position shown in Figure 11-16), it will have slightly different voltages induced either side of it because, at any instant, the two sides will be receiving different parts of the radio wave. This will cause a small electric current to flow from one side of the loop to the other, and this current is measurable. The size of the electric current will be greatest when the loop aerial is aligned with the radio wave, which occurs in two positions 180° apart.

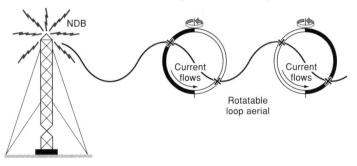

■ Figure 11-16 **The loop antenna having a maximum electric current induced in it by a radio wave**

If the loop aerial is rotated until it is perpendicular to the radio wave, then each side of the loop will be receiving similar parts of the radio wave simultaneously, there will be no difference in potential, no voltage difference across the loop, and hence no current, i.e. a *null* position. The null positions can be thought of as the radio wave slipping through the loop. For one complete 360° rotation of the loop aerial, the null or zero signal will occur in two positions, 180° apart.

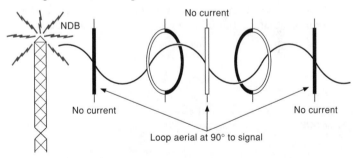

■ Figure 11-17 **The loop antenna in its null position, having zero electric current induced in it by a radio wave**

For one 360° rotation of the loop aerial, the received signal will pass through two maximums and two nulls, with the nulls (zero current) being much more sharply defined than the maximums, as illustrated in Figure 11-18. Small angular deflections of the loop aerial near its null positions produce larger changes in current than similar angular changes near to the loops' maximum positions.

For this reason, a null position of the loop aerial, rather than a maximum position, is used for direction-finding purposes.

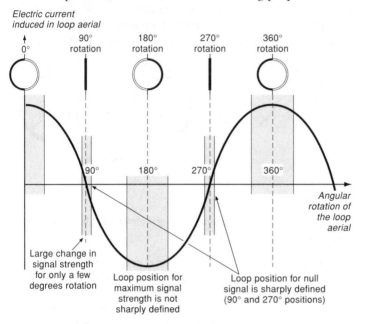

Figure 11-18 **The nulls are sharply defined**

If a loop aerial is rotated into a null position where no current is generated, then the NDB transmitter is either directly ahead of the loop or 180° away and directly behind the loop. This is an ambiguous situation, but it can be resolved using a sense aerial.

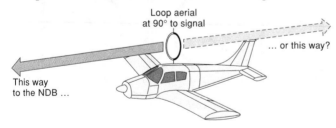

■ *Figure 11-19* **Which way to the NDB (using only a loop aerial)?**

The Sense Aerial

The sense aerial is a single stationary aerial. It has the same sensitivity as the loop in its maximum position and so it generates a continuous maximum current. Unlike the loop aerial, it has no directional properties.

By adding the steady signal from the sense aerial to the alternating signal from the loop signal as it rotates, there is now only one position as the loop rotates 360° at which there is zero current. This acts as a phase reference point, allowing the correct null position to be correctly identified. In other words, the 180° ambiguity has been removed, and the pilot can be certain of the direction to the NDB.

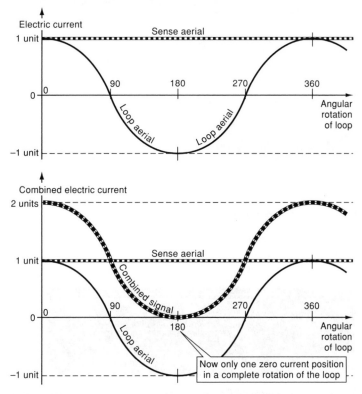

■ *Figure 11-20* **The sense antenna removes the ambiguity from the loop signal**

Modern ADF Aerial Systems

In days gone by, the loop had to be turned manually by the pilot or navigator for the radio compass needle to point towards the ground station. Then came a loop antenna that was rotated electrically, so that the ADF needle pointed continuously and automatically at the NDB.

Modern equipment uses a loop antenna that does not have to be rotated at all, but is rather a fixed loop antenna (or goniometer) that is directionally sensitive to radio signals. This has allowed the ADF aerial system to become very compact.

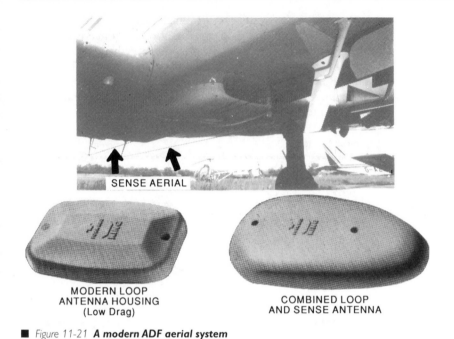

MODERN LOOP
ANTENNA HOUSING
(Low Drag)

COMBINED LOOP
AND SENSE ANTENNA

■ *Figure 11-21* **A modern ADF aerial system**

The ADF Control Panel

ADF units vary from type to type, so you must become familiar
with the set you will be using prior to flight.

■ *Figure 11-22* **Typical ADF control panel**

You must be able to select and positively identify the NDB that
you want to use, and then verify that the ADF needle is indeed
responding to the signals from that NDB. The correct procedure,
any time a new NDB is to be used, is to confirm (verbally if so
desired):

☐ **selected;**
☐ **identified;** and
☐ **ADFing** (and giving a sensible bearing).

The Mode Selector or Function Switch

The mode selector switches between ADF modes of operation:

OFF. Switches the ADF off.

The ADF mode selector is usually selected to ADF.

ADF. The normal position when you want bearing information to be displayed automatically by the needle. Most NDBs can be identified with the mode selector in this position (and the volume knob adjusted suitably).

ANT or REC. Abbreviations for **antenna** or **receiver.** In this position, only the signal from the sense antenna is used, with no satisfactory directional information being available to the ADF needle. The reason for this function position is that it gives the best audio reception to allow easier identification, and better understanding of any voice messages. Never leave the mode selector in this position if you are navigating using the ADF – the ADF needle will remain stationary with no obvious indication that it is not responding! It is possible, however, to identify most NDBs with the mode selector in the ADF position (which is a safer position), and for the ANT position to be avoided.

BFO or CW. Abbreviations for **beat frequency oscillator** or **carrier wave.** This position is selected when identifying the few NDBs that use A0/A1 or A1 transmissions, which are unmodulated carrier waves whose transmission is interrupted in the pattern of the NDB's Morse code identification. Since no audio message is carried on an unmodulated carrier wave, the BFO (as part of the airborne equipment) imposes a tone onto the carrier wave signal to make it audible to the pilot so that the NDB signal can be identified. Again, do not leave the mode selector switch in this position when navigating using the ADF.

TEST. Switching the mode selector to the TEST position will deflect the ADF needle from its current position. Placing the mode selector back to ADF should cause the needle to swing back and indicate the direction of the NDB. This function should be tested everytime as part of the *selected, identified, ADFing* tuning procedure. Some ADF sets have a separate TEST button which only needs to be pressed to deflect the needle, and then released to check the return of the needle.

NOTE On some ADF equipment, the TEST function is achieved using the ANT/REC position, which drives the needle to the 090 position. Returning the mode selector to ADF should see the needle start 'ADFing' again.

VOL. The **volume** knob will probably be separate from the mode selector. With audio selected to the pilot's headset or to the cockpit speakers, the VOL should be adjusted so that the ident or any voice messages on the NDB may be heard. If signal reception is poor in ADF, then try ANT/REC; if there is no signal reception, try BFO/CW. But remember to return the mode selector to ADF!

Frequency Knobs

NDBs transmit on a frequency in the range 200–1,750 kHz, the most common band being 200–400 kHz. To allow easier and accurate selection of any particular frequency, most modern ADFs have knobs that allow digital selection, in 100, 10 and 1 kHz steps. Some ADFs may have a band selector (200–400; 400–1,600 kHz), with either a tuning knob or digital selection for precise tuning.

ADF Cockpit Displays

The basic purpose of an automatic direction finder in an aeroplane is for its needle to point directly towards the selected NDB ground station.

The ADF cockpit display is a card or dial placed vertically in the instrument panel so that:

☐ if the ADF needle points up, the NDB is ahead;

☐ if the ADF needle points down, then the NDB is behind;

☐ if the ADF needle points to one side, then the NDB is located somewhere to that side of the fore–aft axis of the aeroplane.

To convey this information to the pilot, various presentations are used, three of which we will consider:

1. The fixed-card ADF, or relative bearing indicator (RBI);

2. The rotatable-card ADF (the poor man's RMI); and

3. The radio magnetic indicator (RMI).

The Relative Bearing Indicator (RBI)

A fixed-card display has an ADF needle that can rotate against the background of a fixed azimuth card of 360° with 000° (360°) at the top, 180° at the bottom, and so on. The fixed-card ADF is also known as the relative bearing indicator (RBI), and is common in many general aviation aircraft.

> On the fixed-card ADF, the needle indicates the relative bearing of the NDB from the aeroplane.

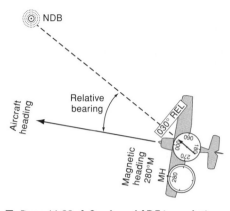

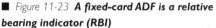

■ Figure 11-23 **A fixed-card ADF is a relative bearing indicator (RBI)**

The **relative bearing** of the NDB from the aircraft is the angle between the aircraft's heading and the direction of the NDB. Usually relative bearings are described clockwise from 000° to 360°, but it is sometimes convenient to describe the bearing of the NDB relative to the nose or tail of the aeroplane.

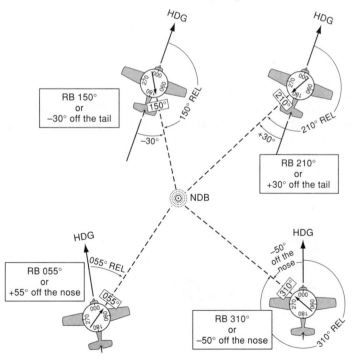

■ Figure 11-24 **The RBI or fixed-card ADF shows relative bearings**

Each time the aeroplane changes its magnetic heading, it will carry the fixed card with it. Therefore:

> With each change of magnetic heading, the ADF needle will indicate a different relative bearing (RB).

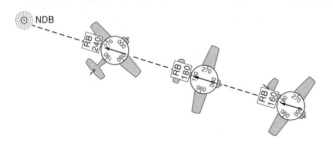

■ *Figure 11-25* **Each time heading is changed, the relative bearing also changes**

Orientation using the RBI

The aeroplane can be orientated with respect to the NDB if you know:

☐ the **magnetic heading** (MH) of the aeroplane (from the compass or heading indicator); plus

☐ the **relative bearing** (RB) of the NDB from the aeroplane.

In practice, magnetic heading is flown using the heading indicator, which should be realigned with the magnetic compass in steady flight every 10 minutes or so. Our illustrations will therefore display the HI instead of the magnetic compass.

In Figure 11-26, the aeroplane is heading 280°M, and the ADF indicates RB 030° to the Bristol locator, i.e. MH 280 and RB 030.

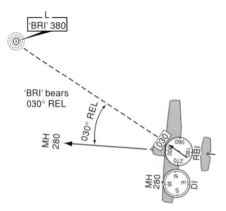

■ *Figure 11-26* **Orientation (Where am I?) using an RBI**

MH 280	+	RB 030	=	310°M to NDB
Aircraft magnetic heading	+	Relative bearing of NDB from aircraft	=	Magnetic bearing of NDB from aircraft

Visualising Magnetic Bearing To the NDB (QDM)

The magnetic bearing of the NDB from the aeroplane is also known as QDM, and in this case is QDM 310.

A quick pictorial means of determining QDM using a relative bearing indicator and a heading indicator is to translate the ADF needle onto the HI, by paralleling a pencil or by using your imagination.

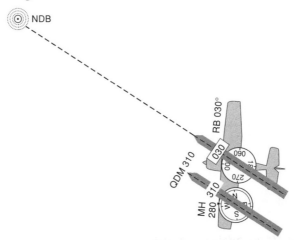

■ Figure 11-27 **A pictorial (but clumsy) method of finding QDM**

Visualising Magnetic Bearing From the NDB (QDR)

The magnetic bearing of the aircraft from the NDB, i.e. the reciprocal to QDM, is known as the QDR, and in Figure 11-27 is QDR 130. QDR can be visualised as the tail of the pencil (or needle) when it is transferred from the RBI onto the HI.

NOTE An easier method of finding reciprocals than adding or subtracting 180°, is to either:
☐ add 200 and subtract 20; or
☐ subtract 200 and add 20.

EXAMPLE 2

QDM 310	QDM 270	QDM 085
−200	−200	+200
+20	+20	−20
QDR 130	QDR 090	QDR 265

The Rotatable-Card ADF

The rotatable-card ADF is an advance on the fixed-card ADF, because it allows you to rotate the card so that the ADF needle indicates, not relative bearing, but magnetic bearing to the NDB (also known as QDM). Do this by aligning the ADF card with the HI compass card each time the aeroplane's magnetic heading is changed.

To align a rotatable-card ADF:
☐ note magnetic heading on the heading indicator; then
☐ rotate the ADF card, setting magnetic heading under the index.

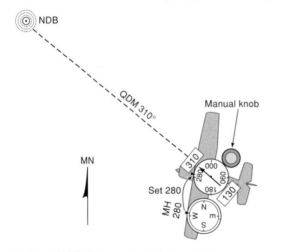

■ Figure 11-28 **Using a rotatable-card ADF**

When the ADF card is aligned with the HI, the ADF needle will indicate QDM, the magnetic bearing to the NDB. This eliminates any need for mental arithmetic. Note also that the tail of the needle, 180° removed from its head, indicates QDR, the magnetic bearing of the aeroplane from the NDB.

> Any time the aircraft changes magnetic heading, you must manually align the ADF card with the HI (ensuring, of course, that the HI is correctly aligned with the magnetic compass).

If desired, the rotatable card can still be used as a fixed card simply by aligning 000 with the nose of the aeroplane and not changing it.

The next step up from a rotatable card is one that remains aligned automatically, a radio magnetic indicator (RMI).

The Radio Magnetic Indicator (RMI)

The RMI display has the ADF needle superimposed on a card that is continuously and automatically aligned with magnetic north. It is, if you like, an automatic version of the rotatable-card ADF – an automatic combination of the heading indicator and RBI.

The RMI is the best ADF presentation, and the easiest to use, but unfortunately the most expensive and usually only encountered in more sophisticated aircraft. In such aircraft, the RMI usually occupies the position in the instrument panel previously occupied by the manually slaved HI.

> The RMI **needle** will always indicate QDM, the magnetic bearing **to** the NDB.
>
> The **tail** of the RMI needle will indicate QDR, the magnetic bearing **from** the NDB.

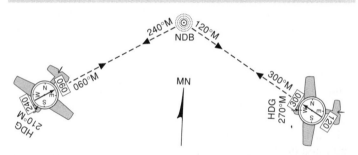

■ *Figure 11-29* **The RMI compass card remains aligned with magnetic north**

As an aeroplane turns and its magnetic heading alters, the RMI card (which automatically remains aligned with magnetic north) will appear to turn along with the ADF needle. In reality, of course, it is the compass card and the RMI needle that remain stationary, while the aeroplane turns about them. Before, during and after the turn, the RMI's needle will constantly indicate the current QDM.

Gyro-Stabilised Compass Equipment

In most aeroplanes fitted with an RMI, the initial magnetic north reference to the RMI card is provided by a **fluxgate** or **fluxvalve**, a detector that is sensitive to magnetic north, and situated in a fairly non-magnetic part of the aeroplane, such as in a wingtip. A **directional gyroscope** is electrically connected to this magnetic reference so that the gyroscope is continually aligned with magnetic north, and it is this directional gyroscope that drives the RMI compass card in a process known as *slaving*.

FLUX VALVE
provides
Magnetic Reference to   DIRECTIONAL   which
                                    GYRO   drives   RMI COMPASS CARD

■ Figure 11-30 **The RMI compass card is driven by a fluxvalve and DG**

Most gyro-stabilised compasses have an **annunciator** near the
compass card. This is a small needle, often triangular in shape, that
oscillates when automatic slaving is in process (which should be
all the time). The annunciator being hard over to one side indicates that the compass card is a long way out of alignment; this can
usually be remedied using a manual knob to quickly re-align the
compass card with the magnetic heading of the aeroplane, after
which the slower, automatic slaving should be sufficient to maintain alignment.

If slaving is not occurring because of some fault in the system
(indicated by the annunciator being stationary and not annunci-
ating) then you can revert to using the RMI as a rotatable-card
ADF or as a fixed-card ADF (relative bearing indicator).

Indicators with Two Pointers
Some aeroplanes are fitted with two ADF receivers, and have two
needles superimposed on the one dial. Sometimes the indicator
has a function switch that causes a needle to point, not at an NDB,
but at a VOR ground station. This gives the pilot more flexibility
in using radio navigation aids.

■ Figure 11-31 **Dual-pointer ADF**

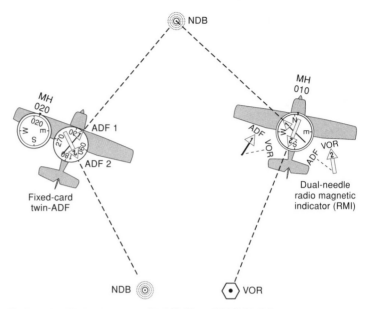

■ *Figure 11-32* ***Dual-pointer ADF (left) and RMI (right)***

What Follows ...

The next two chapters consider in-flight operation of:

☐ **the relative bearing indicator (RBI)** or fixed-card ADF; and
☐ **the radio magnetic indicator (RMI),** including the rotatable card.

Initially you need read only the chapter that applies to the ADF instrument in your training aircraft.

Now complete **Exercises 11 – The NDB and the ADF.**

The Relative Bearing Indicator (RBI)

Operational Use of the RBI

Orientation

Using the RBI to Obtain a Position Line

A position line is a line along which the aeroplane is known to be at a particular moment. A position line (PL) is also referred to as a line of position (LoP). A position line may be obtained by a pilot either visually, or by radio means.

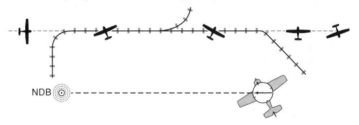

■ *Figure 12-1* **A visual position line, and a radio position line**

Two position lines that cut at a reasonable angle are needed for a fix. For the aeroplane to be on both position lines simultaneously, it must be at the point of intersection. Figure 12-2 shows a radio fix obtained using two NDBs in an aeroplane fitted with two ADFs. It is possible to fix position using a combination of radio aids including ADF/NDB, VOR and DME.

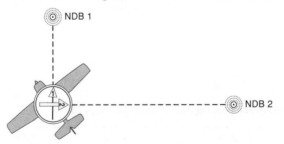

■ *Figure 12-2* **Two position lines with a good cut can provide a fix**

A position line can be considered from two perspectives:
- ☐ **from the aeroplane,** i.e. the position line from the aeroplane to the NDB that a pilot would see, as either a relative bearing (RB) or a magnetic bearing to the station (QDM); or
- ☐ **from the NDB ground station** (which is necessary if the aeroplane's position is to be plotted on a chart) as either a

magnetic bearing from the station (QDR) or a true bearing from the station (known in the Q-code as QTE).

EXAMPLE 1 An aircraft has a magnetic heading of 015°M (MH 015). Its ADF needle points towards a non-directional beacon 75° to starboard (to the right of the nose) on a fixed-card ADF (relative bearing indicator). Magnetic variation is 5°W. Calculate:

(a) the relative bearing (RB) of the NDB from the aeroplane;

(b) the magnetic bearing of the NDB from the aeroplane (MB or QDM);

(c) the magnetic bearing of the aeroplane from the NDB (QDR); and

(d) the true bearing of the aeroplane from the NDB (TB or QTE).

While it is possible to calculate all of this mentally, at this early stage it is a good idea to sketch a clear diagram to help visualise the situation.

Step 1. Sketch the aeroplane on MH 015.

Step 2. Indicate RB 075.

Step 3. Draw in the position line to the NDB.

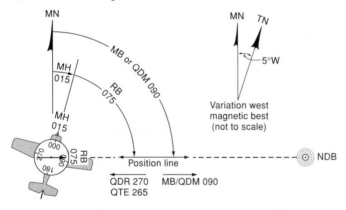

■ *Figure 12-3* **Magnetic heading 015°, relative bearing 075°**

MH 015	MB/QDM 090°M	Variation west,	QDR 270°M
+ RB 075	+ 180	magnetic best	Variation −5
MB/QDM 090°M	QDR 270°M		QTE 265°T

ANSWER RB 075; QDM 090; QDR 270; QTE 265

True Bearings from an NDB (QTE)

Normally when instrument flying, you would not bother to plot positions on a chart. However, if for some reason you decide to, then the easiest method on a visual chart is to use true bearings from a ground station, i.e. bearings from a ground station related to true north (as indicated on the chart by the meridians of longitude). In the 'Q-code', this is known as QTE, a true bearing from a ground station. QTE is easily calculated. In the UK, where variation is west, it is simply:

> *QTE = QDR – west variation*

EXAMPLE 2 MH is 280. RB is 050. What is the true bearing from the NDB (QTE)? Variation in the area is 6°W.

```
MH 280 + RB 050 = QDM 330
                    –200
                    +20
              QDM 150
                     –6   West variation
              QTE   14 ° True
```

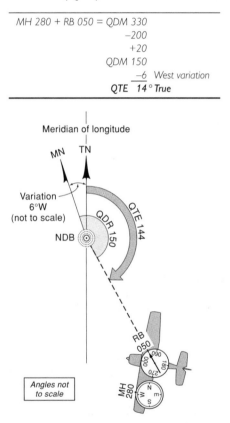

■ *Figure 12-4* **QTE = QDR 150 – 6°W variation = 144°T**

ANSWER QTE 144

NOTE As a matter of interest, QTE can be supplied to you by the radar controller, though prudent pilots would calculate their own by subtracting west variation from QDR.

EXAMPLE 3 Magnetic heading is 120°M. The needle indicates 290° on a fixed card. Variation is 7°W. Calculate:

(a) the relative bearing (RB) of the NDB from the aeroplane;

(b) the magnetic bearing of the NDB from the aeroplane (MB or QDM);

(c) the magnetic bearing of the aeroplane from the NDB (QDR); and

(d) the true bearing of the aeroplane from the NDB (TB or QTE).

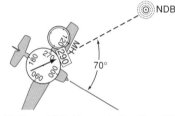

■ Figure 12-5 **Magnetic heading 120°, relative bearing 290°**

MH 120			
+ RB 290			
MB/QDM 410	MB/QDM 050°M	Variation west,	QDR 230°M
– 360	+ 180	magnetic best	Variation –7
MB/QDM 050°M	QDR 230°M		QTE 223°T

ANSWER RB 290; QDM 050; QDR 230; QTE 223

Easy Method of Visualising QDM

A relative bearing, as well as being specified using the 360° method clockwise from the nose of the aeroplane, can be specified as either left or right of the nose (or the tail). For instance, a relative bearing of 290 may be thought of as –70, since the QDM will be 70° less than the magnetic heading. Similarly, RB 030 may be thought of as +30, since it will cause the QDM to exceed the MH by 30°.

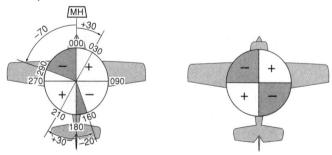

■ Figure 12-6 **Quadrants for converting RBs to QDMs or QDRs**

For angles off the tail of the aeroplane, RB 160 may be thought of as −20 off the tail; and RB 210 as +30 off the tail. This builds up a *quadrantal* approach to relative bearing and QDM/QDR problems that will simplify your visualisation in flight.

EXAMPLE 4 An aeroplane is flying on a magnetic heading of 340. The ADF needle shows RB 010. Determine the QDM.

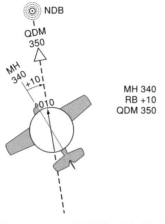

MH 340
RB +10
QDM 350

■ *Figure 12-7* **MH 340 + RB 10 = MB/QDM 350**

EXAMPLE 5 An aeroplane is flying on a magnetic heading of 358. The ADF needle shows RB 352. Determine the QDM.

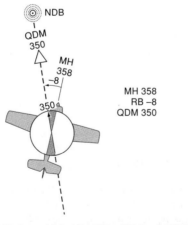

MH 358
RB −8
QDM 350

■ *Figure 12-8* **MH 358 – RB 8 = MB/QDM 350**

Notice that, by coincidence, this aeroplane is on the same QDM as the one in Figure 12-7. In fact, it may even be the same aeroplane, which has simply altered magnetic heading by turning right from 340 to 358.

EXAMPLE 6 An aeroplane is flying on a magnetic heading of 340. The ADF needle shows RB 190. Determine the QDR.

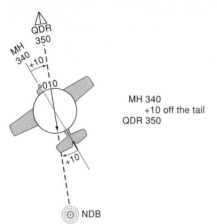

MH 340
  +10 off the tail
QDR 350

■ *Figure 12-9* **MH 340 + 10 off the tail = QDR 350**

EXAMPLE 7 An aeroplane is flying on a magnetic heading of 010. The ADF needle shows RB 160° Determine the QDR.

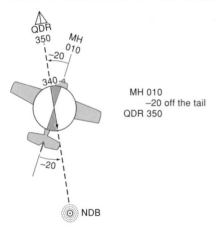

MH 010
  −20 off the tail
QDR 350

■ *Figure 12-10* **MH 010 – 20 off the tail = QDR 350**

Again, notice that, this aeroplane is on the same QDR as the one in Figure 12-9. It also may be the same aeroplane, which has simply altered magnetic heading by turning right from 340 to 010.

Visualising Position on the Heading Indicator

Mentally transferring the RBI needle onto the HI allows quick visualisation of QDM on the head of the needle, and QDR on its tail. If you now imagine a model aeroplane attached to the tail of the needle, with the model aeroplane orientated with the actual heading, you have a very good picture of the whole scene.

EXAMPLE 8 Visualise the situation of MH 070 and RB 260.

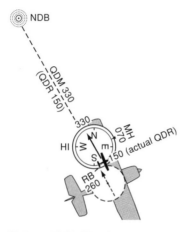

■ *Figure 12-11* **Visualising position on the HI; QDM 330 and MH 070**

Intercepting a Track

Having orientated yourself with respect to an NDB, you know the answer to the question "Where am I?" Now ask "Where do I want to go?" and "How do I get there?"

STEP 1 is always to **orientate the aeroplane** relative to the NDB, and to the desired track.

STEP 2 involves a **turn to take up a suitable intercept heading,** considering where it is that you want to join the track.

STEP 3 involves **maintaining the intercept heading** and waiting:
☐ for the head of the needle to fall if inbound;
☐ for the tail of the needle to rise if outbound:
  – to ±030 for a 30° intercept;
  – to ±045 for a 45° intercept;
  – to ±060 for a 60° intercept;
  – to ±090 for a 90° intercept, etc.

STEP 4 involves a **turn onto the desired track** and allowing for a suitable wind correction angle to maintain it.

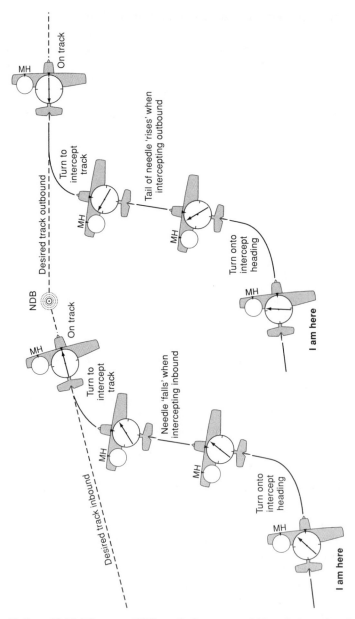

■ Figure 12-12 **Where am I? Where do I want to go? How do I get there?**

Visualising Where You Are, and Where You Want To Go

The heading indicator (HI) can assist greatly in visualising the situation. In Example 8, the situation MH 070 and RB 260 was visualised, the aeroplane being on QDM 330. What if you want to intercept a track of 270 to the NDB?

All you need to do is visualise the desired track on the HI. With a model aeroplane on the tail of the needle tracking as desired, it becomes quite clear what turns are necessary to intercept the desired track.

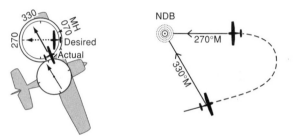

■ *Figure 12-13* **Visualising an intercept on the HI**

The first turn to make is to the left onto a suitable intercept heading, say MH 360 for a 90° intercept of QDM 270 to the NDB.

NOTE If you become disoriented, a simple procedure is to take up the heading of the desired track. Even though not on track, the aeroplane will at least be parallel to it, and the ADF needle will indicate which way to turn to intercept it.

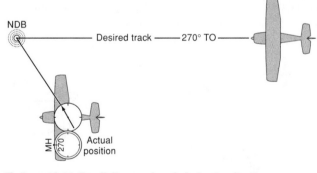

■ *Figure 12-14* **Paralleling track to help in visualisation**

Suppose the situation is MH 340, RB 080, and you want to intercept a track of 090 to the NDB. The current QDM is of course 060°M (MH 340 + RB 080).

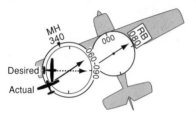

Figure 12-15 **Visualising the intercept**

By continuing to head 340°M, the aeroplane will eventually intercept 090 to the NDB, but it would be a rather untidy intercept, as a turn of 110° would be required.

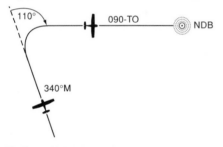

■ Figure 12-16 **An inefficient intercept**

A tidier and more efficient intercept could be achieved by turning onto an initial heading of 360°M for a 90° intercept; or a heading of 030°M for a 60° intercept. (Turning further right onto a heading of 060°M would of course point the aeroplane at the NDB and the 090-*to* track would not be intercepted.)

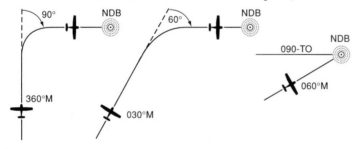

■ Figure 12-17 **More efficient intercepts**

Intercepting an Inbound Track

EXAMPLE 9 You are heading 355°M, and the RBI indicates 005 when turned to a particular NDB. You are requested to track inbound on a track of 340°M to the station, intercepting the track at 60°.

Step 1. Orientate the aeroplane.

MH 355 + RB 005 = QDM 360 or QDR 180.

The aeroplane is south of the NDB and heading 355.

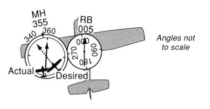

■ *Figure 12-18* **Visualising track**

The desired track is 340°M to the NDB (or 160°M from the NDB), which is to the right of the aeroplane.

Step 2. To intercept the track 340 from the left at 60°, the aeroplane should be turned onto a heading of (340 + 60 = 400) 040°M. As the aeroplane's heading alters, the ADF needle will continue to point at the NDB and so the relative bearing will change (in this case, even though it is not an important calculation, from 005 to –040 or 320 with the 45° right turn).

Step 3. Maintain MH 040 and periodically observe the RBI as the head of the needle falls. Since it is a *plus 60* intercept, wait until the head of the needle falls to *minus 60* (or 300). You are: *heading plus 60, waiting for minus 60.*

Step 4. At QDM 340, or shortly before QDM 340 is reached, and as the needle is falling to –60, turn left to take up the desired track to the NDB, allowing for the estimated crosswind effect on tracking. In this case, a wind correction angle (WCA) of 3° left is used. Maintain the desired track of 340°M to the station by continually checking that MH + RB = QDM 340.

NOTE An aeroplane takes some distance to turn, so you should anticipate the desired track by commencing the turn onto track just before QDM 340 is reached. You could do this by observing the rate at which the ADF needle falls towards –060, and commencing the turn accordingly.

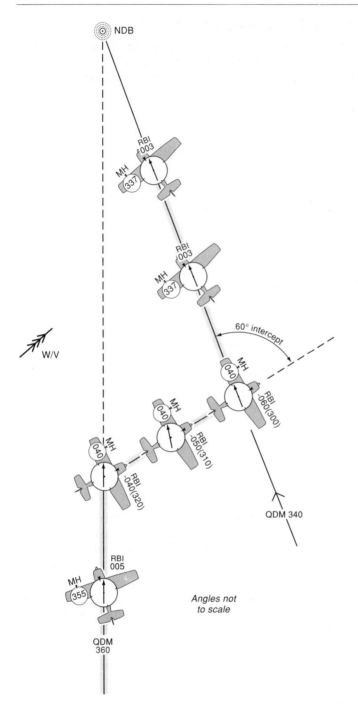

■ Figure 12-19 **Intercepting 340°M inbound, from south of the station**

EXAMPLE 10 You are given a radar heading to steer of 010°M, and instructed to intercept 055°M inbound to an NDB off that heading.

Step 1. Orientate the aeroplane. With radar vector 010 to intercept 055 inbound, the aeroplane must be south of 055 inbound.

Step 2. The intercept has been organised by the radar controller so that the aeroplane will intercept track at 45° (055 – 010 = 45).

Step 3. Maintain MH 010 and periodically observe the RBI as the head of the needle falls. Since it is a minus 45 intercept, wait until the head of the needle falls to +045. *Heading minus 45, waiting for plus 45.*

Step 4. At QDM 055, or shortly before QDM 055 is reached and as the needle falls onto +45, turn right to take up the desired track to the NDB, allowing for the estimated crosswind effect on tracking. In this case, a WCA of 5° right is used, by steering MH 060 with the RBI on –005 (355). Maintain track 055°M to the station by continually checking that MH + RB = QDM 055.

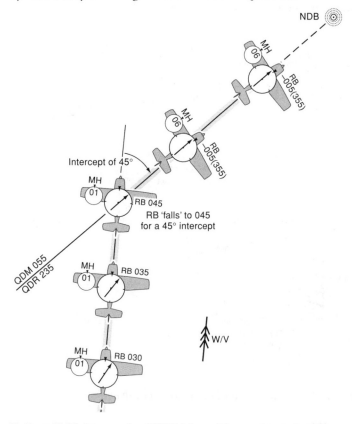

■ Figure 12-20 **Intercepting 055°M inbound from radar vector 010**

Another means of achieving a smooth intercept is to reduce the closing angle as the desired track is approached, say from 45° to 30° to 15° and, finally, to zero as it is intercepted.

Intercepting an Outbound Track

EXAMPLE 11 The radar controller gives a radar vector of 340 to intercept an outbound track of 280.

Step 1. Orientate the aeroplane. It must be south of the outbound track (see inset of Figure 12-21).

Step 2. Consider the intercept. A radar vector of 340 to intercept 280 outbound means a +60° intercept.

Step 3. Monitor the intercept by steering a steady MH 340 and periodically checking the RBI to see the tail of the needle rising to –060 (300). *Heading plus 60, waiting for minus 60.*

Step 4. As QDR (track outbound) of 280 is approached, indicated by the tail of the needle rising to –060, turn left to pick it up, in this case allowing a WCA of 10° for the wind from the right, i.e. MH 290 and RB –010 (350) = QDR 280.

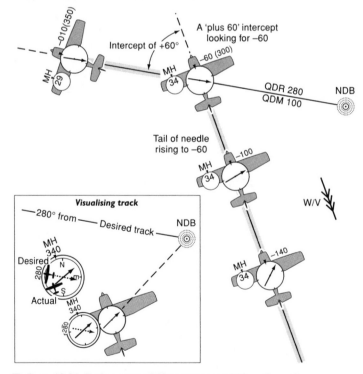

■ Figure 12-21 **Radar vector 340 to intercept 280 outbound**

EXAMPLE 12 You are steering 120°M with RB 080. You want to track outbound from the NDB on 090°M, intercepting as soon as possible.

Step 1. Orientate the aeroplane. MH 120 + RB 080 = QDM 200 or QDR 020. The aeroplane is north-north-east of the NDB and heading 120°M. The desired track is 090°M from the NDB, which is to the right of the aeroplane (see inset of Figure 12-22).

Step 2. Continuing on present MH 120 would give a 30° intercept of 090 outbound. To intercept track 090 outbound as soon as possible, i.e. with a 90° intercept, the aeroplane should be turned onto a heading of (090 + 90) = 180°M.

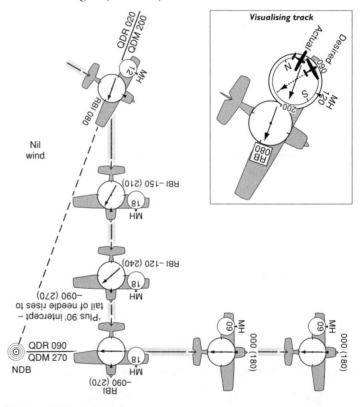

■ *Figure 12-22* **A 90° intercept of 090 outbound**

Step 3. Maintain MH 180 and periodically observe the RBI as the tail of the needle rises. Since it is a *plus 90* intercept, wait until the tail of the needle rises to *minus 90* (270). *Heading plus 90, waiting for minus 90.*

Step 4. At QDR 090, or shortly before QDR 090 is reached and as the tail of the needle approaches −90, turn left to take up the desired track from the NDB, allowing for the estimated crosswind effect on tracking. In this case, with nil wind, steer MH 090. The tail of the ADF needle should be on 000. Periodically check that MH ±ADF tail = QDR 090.

NOTE With such a large intercept angle, you will have to watch the rate at which the tail of the ADF needle rises, and anticipate the turn to intercept the desired track. If you do not anticipate the intercept, the aeroplane will fly through the track, which will then have to be re-intercepted from the other side – not a very tidy manoeuvre.

Tracking

Tracking Inbound to an NDB
The ADF/NDB combination is often used to provide guidance for an aeroplane from a distant position to a position overhead the NDB ground position. This is known as **tracking**. Just how you achieve this depends to a certain extent on the wind direction and speed, since an aeroplane initially pointed directly at the NDB will be blown off course by a crosswind.

Tracking Towards an NDB, with No Crosswind Effect
With no crosswind, a direct track inbound can be achieved by heading the aeroplane directly at the NDB. This is achieved with a heading that maintains the ADF needle on the nose of the aeroplane (RB 000).

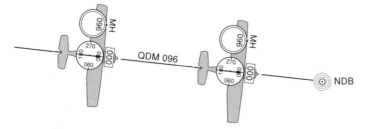

■ Figure 12-23 **Tracking inbound, with no crosswind**

If there is no crosswind to blow the aeroplane off track, then everything will remain constant as in Figure 12-23 – the magnetic heading 096, the relative bearing of 000, and the QDM 096 will all remain constant. This will be the situation in:
☐ nil-wind conditions;
☐ a direct headwind; or
☐ a direct tailwind.

Tracking Inbound with a Crosswind

WITH NO CORRECTION FOR DRIFT made by the pilot, and the aeroplane headed directly at the NDB so that the ADF needle indicates a relative bearing of 000, any crosswind will cause the aeroplane to be blown off track.

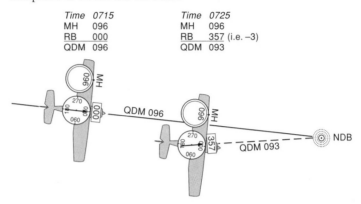

Time 0715
MH   096
RB   000
QDM   096

Time 0725
MH   096
RB   357 (i.e. –3)
QDM   093

■ *Figure 12-24* **Crosswind causes drift**

In Figure 12-24, the wind, with a northerly component, has blown the aeroplane to the right of track. This is indicated by the ADF needle starting to move down the left of the dial. To return to track, the aeroplane must be turned towards the left, i.e. towards the direction in which the head of the needle is moving.

If the pilot turns left to RB 000 to put the NDB on the nose again, then after a short while the aeroplane will again have been blown to the right of track, and the ADF needle will move to the left of the nose. A further turn to the left will be required – and the process will need to be repeated again and again.

In this way, the track made good (TMG) to the NDB will be curved, the aeroplane finally approaching the NDB heading roughly into-wind, and a longer distance will be travelled compared to the direct track from the original position. This rather inefficient means of arriving overhead the NDB is known as **homing** (keeping the NDB on the nose). It is not a very tidy procedure. Professional pilots rarely use it.

WITH CORRECT DRIFT CORRECTION made by the pilot – a far better procedure than homing is to **track direct to the NDB** by heading into wind and laying off a wind correction angle (WCA) to counteract drift. If 5° left is indeed the correct WCA, the aeroplane can achieve a track of 096°M direct to the NDB by the pilot steering MH 091.

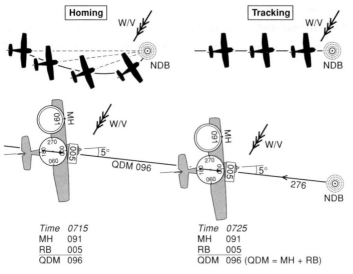

Time   0715   Time   0725
MH   091   MH   091
RB   005   RB   005
QDM   096   QDM   096 (QDM = MH + RB)

■ Figure 12-25 **Tracking direct to the NDB**

Different Winds Require Different Wind Correction Angles

An aeroplane is on track when the relative bearing is equal and opposite to the difference between the actual magnetic heading and the desired track. This is illustrated in Figure 12-26. In each situation, the aeroplane is on the desired track of 010°M, but using a different wind correction angle to counteract the drift under different wind conditions.

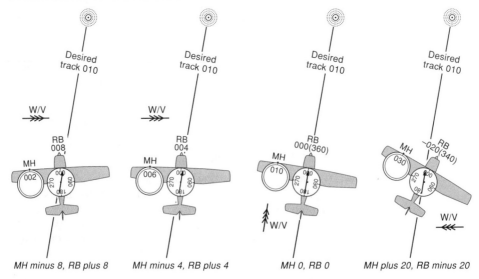

MH minus 8, RB plus 8   MH minus 4, RB plus 4   MH 0, RB 0   MH plus 20, RB minus 20

■ Figure 12-26 **Laying off drift to achieve the desired track**

If the precise wind effect is not known, then use a 'best guess' WCA estimated from the available information as an initial WCA. For the same crosswind, slower aeroplanes will need to allow a greater WCA then faster aeroplanes.

It is possible that the wind effect will change as you track towards an NDB, so regular adjustments to the heading may be required. This is often the case as an aeroplane descends using the NDB as the tracking aid, due to variations in wind velocity and true airspeed.

WITH INCORRECT DRIFT CORRECTION made by the pilot, the aeroplane will move off the desired track, i.e. the QDM (magnetic track to the NDB) will change. If a steady heading is being flown, this will become obvious through a gradually changing relative bearing, with the ADF needle moving left or right down the dial.

Suppose, for instance, the pilot steers a heading with a 5° wind correction angle to the left to counteract the effect of a wind from the left. If the wind effect turns out to be less than expected, then the aeroplane will gradually move to the left of the desired track to the NDB, and the QDM will gradually increase. Typical cockpit indications could be:

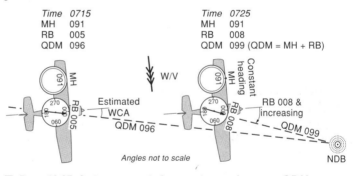

■ *Figure 12-27* **An incorrect wind correction angle causes QDM to change**

The head of the ADF needle falling away to the right indicates that a turn right must be made to track to the NDB. Conversely, the head of the ADF needle falling away to the left indicates that a left turn must be made to track to the NDB. Just how great each correcting turn should be depends on the deviation from track.

NOTE Be careful of terminology. *Drift* is the angle between heading and the actual track made good, which may not be the desired track. The perfect *wind correction angle* will counteract any drift exactly, and the actual TMG will follow the desired track, which is usually the aim of tracking.

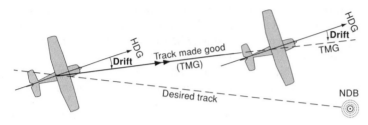

■ *Figure 12-28* **Drift is the angle between heading and TMG**

Maintaining Track

Flying straight and level usually consists of many tiny climbs and descents as the pilot attempts to maintain the desired altitude perfectly. Similarly, it is almost impossible to maintain a perfect track, and so many small turns will usually have to be made by the pilot in an attempt to do so, by correcting any deviations from track.

Re-intercepting a track, having deviated from it, involves the same procedure as the initial intercept of a new track, except that the angles will be smaller provided you are vigilant and do not allow large deviations to occur. Realising that the aeroplane is diverging from the direct track to the NDB, you have several options. You may either:

1. Track direct from the present position (along a new track); or

2. Regain the original track.

1. TO TRACK DIRECT TO THE NDB from the present position (even though it is not the originally desired track) turn slightly right (say 3° in this case), and track direct to the NDB from the present position. In most NDB tracking, this technique is used only when very close to the station (say 1 or 2 nm from the NDB), when there is insufficient distance remaining to regain track.

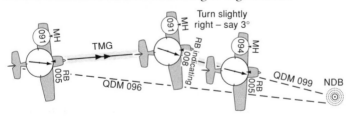

■ *Figure 12-29* **Flying a new track to the NDB**

> *Needle head falling right; turn right.*

2. TO REGAIN THE ORIGINAL TRACK, turn further right initially (say 5° onto MH 096), re-intercept the original track by allowing the wind to blow the aeroplane back onto it and, once the track is regained, turn left and steer a heading with a different wind correction angle (say WCA 3° left instead of 5° left), MH 093 instead of MH 091. This is a very moderate correction, something you would expect to see from an experienced instrument pilot, who would have noticed any deviation from track fairly quickly.

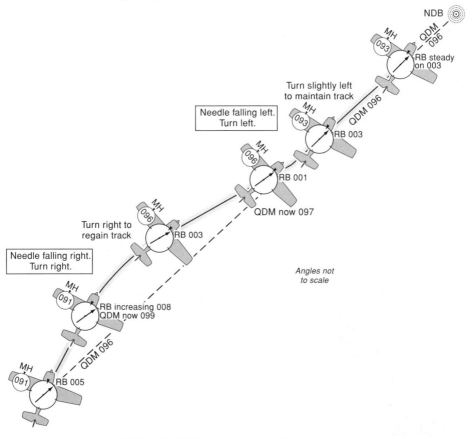

■ *Figure 12-30* **Regain the desired track**

Attempting to maintain the desired track (or remain on the one QDM) is the normal navigational technique when at some distance from the NDB. If, when maintaining a steady magnetic heading, the ADF needle near the top of the dial indicates a constant relative bearing, then the aeroplane is tracking directly to the NDB, and no correction to heading is necessary.

If MH + RB = desired QDM constantly, then ADF tracking is good.

CORRECTING TURNS TO MAINTAIN TRACK. Just how great each correcting turn should be depends on the deviation from track. A simple method is to double the error. If the aeroplane has deviated 10° left indicated by the RBI moving 10° right, then alter heading by 20° to the right. (If you alter heading by only 10° to the right, the result will probably be a further deviation to the left, a further correction to the right, with this being repeated again and again, resulting in a curved *homing* to the NDB).

Having regained track, turn left by only half the correcting turn of 20°, i.e. turn left 10° to intercept and maintain track. This leaves you with a WCA different to the original one (remembering that the original WCA caused you to deviate from track). The new WCA should provide reasonable tracking. If not, make further minor corrections to heading!

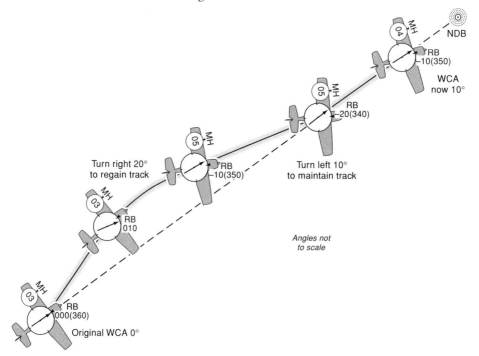

■ *Figure 12-31* **Regaining track by 'doubling the error', and maintaining track thereafter**

Bracketing Track

In practice, an absolutely perfect direct track is difficult to achieve. The actual track made good will probably consist of a number of minor corrections such as those just described, a technique known as **bracketing** the track, i.e. making regular corrections, left or right as required, to maintain or regain the desired track.

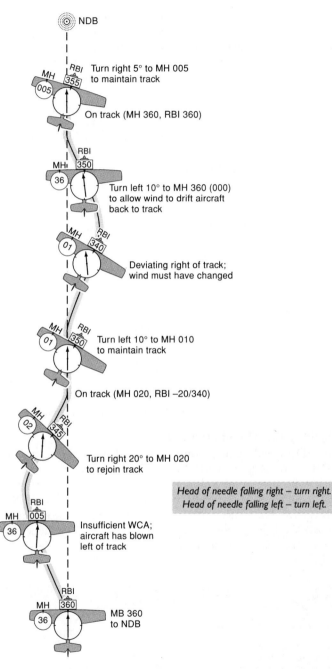

NDB

Turn right 5° to MH 005
to maintain track

On track (MH 360, RBI 360)

Turn left 10° to MH 360 (000)
to allow wind to drift aircraft
back to track

Deviating right of track;
wind must have changed

Turn left 10° to MH 010
to maintain track

On track (MH 020, RBI −20/340)

Turn right 20° to MH 020
to rejoin track

*Head of needle falling right − turn right.
Head of needle falling left − turn left.*

Insufficient WCA;
aircraft has blown
left of track

MB 360
to NDB

■ Figure 12-32 **Bracketing the track**

The aim of bracketing is to find the precise WCA needed to maintain track. If, for instance, a WCA of 10° right is found to be too great and the aeroplane diverges to the right of track, and a WCA of only 5° right is too little and the wind blows the aeroplane to the left of track, then try something in between, say WCA 8° right.

Monitor the tracking of the aeroplane on a regular basis, and make corrections earlier rather than later. The result will be a succession of small corrections rather than just one big correction. However, if a big correction is required as may be the case in strong winds, make it. Be positive in your actions!

Wind Effect

If the wind direction and strength is not obvious, then the best technique is to initially **steer track as heading** (make no allowance for drift). The effect of the wind will become obvious as the ADF needle moves to the left or right. Observe the results, and then make heading adjustments to bracket track.

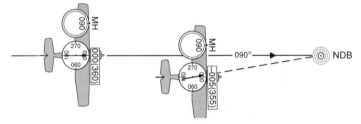

■ *Figure 12-33* **If uncertain of wind, initially steer track as heading**

Tracking Overhead an NDB

The ADF needle will become more and more sensitive as the NDB station is approached. Minor displacements left or right of track will cause larger and larger changes in relative bearing and QDM, and the ADF needle becomes 'agitated' as the NDB is approached. For a very precise track to be achieved, you must be prepared to increase your scan rate as the NDB is approached, and to make corrections more frequently.

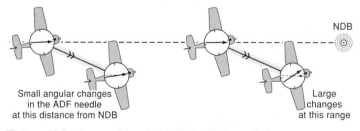

Small angular changes in the ADF needle at this distance from NDB

Large changes at this range

■ *Figure 12-34* **Approaching the NDB, the ADF needle becomes more sensitive**

Close to the station and just prior to passing overhead, however, the ADF needle becomes very sensitive. At this point, you can relax a little and steer a steady heading until the aeroplane passes overhead the NDB, indicated by the ADF needle moving towards the bottom of the dial and settling down.

Having passed overhead the NDB, tracking *from* the NDB should be checked and suitable adjustments made to heading. If the track outbound is different to that inbound, then a suitable heading change estimated to make good the new desired track could be made as soon as the ADF needle falls past the 090 or 270 position on its way to the bottom of the dial.

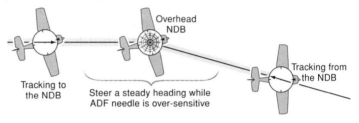

■ *Figure 12-35* **Do not overcorrect when close to the station**

The ADF needle becoming extremely active and then falling rapidly to the bottom of the dial indicates that the aeroplane has passed directly overhead the NDB.

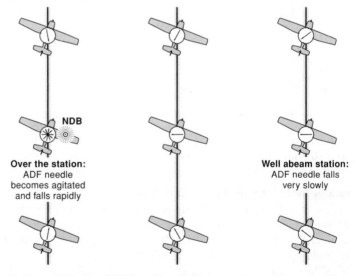

■ *Figure 12-36* **Good ADF tracking (left); reasonable and poor tracking**

The ADF needle moving gradually to one side and slowly falling to the bottom of the dial indicates that the aeroplane is passing to one side of the beacon – the rate at which the needle falls being an indication of the aeroplane's proximity to the NDB. If it falls very slowly, then perhaps your tracking could have been better. Time overhead (or abeam) the NDB can be taken as the needle falls through the approximate 090 or 270 position.

Tracking Away From an NDB

When tracking away from an NDB, the head of the ADF needle will lie towards the bottom of the dial.

Tracking Away From an NDB with No Crosswind Effect

If you track overhead the NDB and then steer track as heading, the aeroplane will track directly away from the NDB with the head of the ADF needle steady on 180, and the tail of the ADF needle steady at the top of the dial on 000.

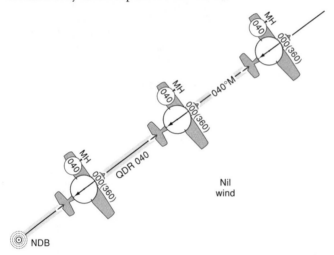

Figure 12-37 **Tracking away from an NDB with no crosswind effect**

The aeroplane shown in Figure 12-37 has a QDR of 040 (magnetic track from the station to the aeroplane), and a QDM of 220 (magnetic track from the aeroplane to the station).

Tracking Away From an NDB with a Crosswind

Suppose that the desired track outbound from an NDB is 040°M, and you estimate that a WCA of 5° to the right is necessary to counteract a wind from the right. To achieve this, you steer MH 045, and hope to see the tail of the ADF needle stay on –005 (i.e. 355). The magnetic track away from the station (QDR) is found from:

QDR = MH ± deflection of the tail of the needle.

In this case, MH 045 – 005 tail = QDR 040, and the chosen WCA and magnetic heading to steer are correct.

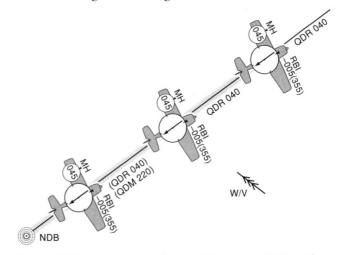

■ *Figure 12-38* **Tracking away from an NDB, with a WCA of 5°**
into wind

If the estimated WCA is incorrect, then the track made good by the aeroplane will differ from that desired. If, in Figure 12-38, the wind is stronger than expected, the aeroplane's actual TMG may be 033°M, and to the left of the desired track of 040°M.

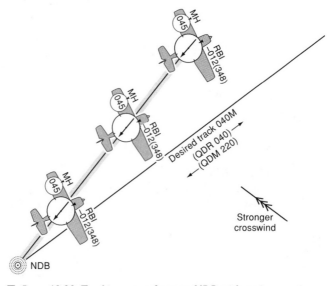

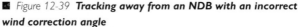

■ *Figure 12-39* **Tracking away from an NDB with an incorrect**
wind correction angle

Whereas inaccurate tracking *to* an NDB is indicated by the ADF needle falling, incorrect tracking away *from* an NDB can occur with the ADF needle indicating a steady reading. Having passed overhead the NDB, an aeroplane can track away from it in any direction. You must always ensure that you are flying away from the NDB along the correct track, and the easiest way to do this is to calculate QDR or QDM using the HI and the RBI.

Regaining Track Away from an NDB in a Crosswind

If an incorrect wind correction angle is flown, the aeroplane will be blown off track. A vigilant pilot will see the incorrect TMG, probably by visualising QDR (from the NDB) or QDM (to the NDB) while a constant magnetic heading is flown.

EXAMPLE 13 In Figure 12-40, the pilot is flying track as heading, i.e. initially making no allowance for drift. If the head of the ADF needle moves right from 180 into the negative quadrant, then the aeroplane must be turned right to regain track.

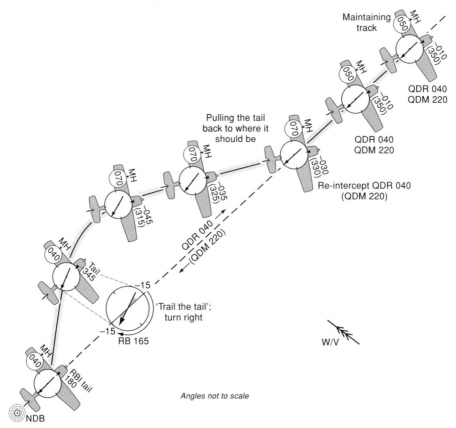

■ Figure 12-40 **Turning right to 'trail the tail' or 'pull the tail around'**

NOTE It is generally easier to work off the top of the dial, since that is where the aeroplane is going, rather than off the bottom of the dial. The right turn necessary to regain track, turning right towards the head of the needle and therefore away from the tail of the needle, can be thought of as *pulling the tail of the ADF needle around* or *trailing the tail*. Some instructors, however, prefer to say that if the head of the needle is moving left, then turn left (and vice versa), even though the head of the needle is at the bottom of the dial. Your instructor will recommend a method.

In Figure 12-40, the aeroplane has been blown to the left of track. The off-track QDR is given by:

MH 040 – 015 tail = QDR 025;
which is left of the desired QDR 040.

To regain track, the pilot has turned right by 30° (double the error) from MH 040 to MH 070, which causes a simultaneous change in the relative bearing of the NDB, the ADF needle tail moving from –015 (345) to –045 (315). (The head of the needle, indicating relative bearing, will move from 165 to 135, but this is not a calculation for the pilot to make, only an observation.)

The relative bearing will naturally change as the aeroplane is turned but, once the aeroplane is flown on its steady intercept heading of MH 070, the tail of the needle will be gradually pulled around.

The pilot will continue with the intercept heading until the aeroplane approaches the desired track, QDR 040. This is indicated to the pilot by MH 070 and the tail of the needle moving up towards –030 (since QDR 040 = MH 070 – 030 tail). For a 30° intercept of 040°M outbound, the pilot is steering + 30 (040 + 30 = MH 070), waiting for the tail of the needle to rise to –030.
Flying track plus 30, waiting for minus 30 on the needle.
As the desired outbound track is approached, the pilot turns left to maintain QDR 040. Estimating a WCA of 10° into wind to be sufficient, the pilot steers MH 050 and checks regularly that the needle tail stays on –010.

EXAMPLE 14 If, on the other hand, the head of the ADF needle moves left from 180 into the positive quadrant, then the aeroplane must be turned left to regain track. Looking at the top of the ADF dial and the tail of the needle, turn left and 'trail the tail'.

In Figure 12-41, the aeroplane has been blown to the right of track. The off-track QDR is given by:

MH 040 + 015 tail = 055;
which is right of the desired QDR 040.

To regain track, the pilot has turned left by 30° from MH 040
to MH 010, which causes a simultaneous change in the relative
bearing of the NDB, the tail of the ADF needle moving from 015
to 045.

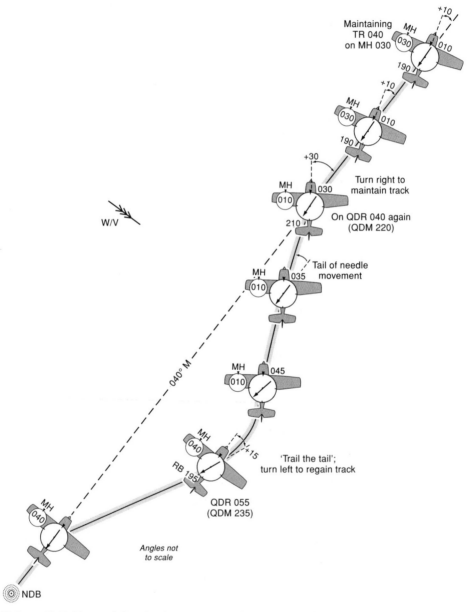

■ Figure 12-41 **Turning left to 'trail the tail' or 'pull the tail around'**

The relative bearing will naturally change as the aeroplane is turned but, once the aeroplane is flown on its steady intercept heading of MH 010, the tail of the needle will be gradually pulled around. For a 30° intercept of 040°M outbound, the pilot is steering −30 (040 − 30 = MH 010), waiting for the tail of the needle to rise to + 030.

Flying track minus 30, waiting for plus 30 on the needle.

The pilot will continue with the intercept heading until the aeroplane approaches the desired track, QDR 040. This is indicated by MH 010 and the tail of the needle moving up towards 030 (since QDR 040 = MH 010 + 030 tail).

As the desired track outbound is approached, the pilot turns right to maintain QDR 040. Estimating a WCA of 10° into wind to be sufficient, the pilot steers MH 030 and checks regularly that the needle tail stays on +010.

NDB Approaches

The NDB/ADF combination is very useful for tracking, and use is made of this in the instrument approach to land known as the **NDB approach** or **NDB let-down**, such as that at Lyneham, shown in Figure 12-42. The top section of the chart shows a plan view for tracking purposes, and the bottom section shows a profile view for vertical navigation (descent).

Prior to being used for tracking, the NDB must have been *selected, identified* and checked that it is *'ADFing'*. Flying towards Lyneham at the end of a cross-country flight, you can track to the NDB (using the ADF) at an altitude no lower than the minimum safe altitude (MSA) for that sector (shown as sector safe altitude, SSA, on *Aerad* charts). From the southwest, the MSA is 3,000 ft amsl.

From overhead the NDB, you may track outbound on 090°M, and descend to 3,000 ft on QNH *(2,533 ft on QFE)*, the height difference in these being due to the threshold elevation of 467 ft. Normal outbound tracking procedures are used, with the ADF needle being very sensitive at first, and becoming less sensitive as the aeroplane flies further away from the NDB. It is good airmanship to monitor the ident of the NDB periodically.

At 8 nm outbound from the NDB, a left turn is commenced to intercept the inbound track of 255°M. During the turn, the aircraft is permitted to descend to 2,500 ft on QNH *(2,033 ft on QFE)*.

When established on the inbound track of 255°M (within ±5°), the aircraft may be descended to the minimum descent altitude (MDA, on QNH), or the minimum descent height (MDH, on QFE). Reference to MDA and MDH combined is often written as MDA(H). (Minima calculation is discussed in

Chapter 22.) The absolute minimum height for an NDB approach by an IMC-rated pilot is 600 ft on QFE (aal), but it could be significantly higher, depending on obstacles in the vicinity.

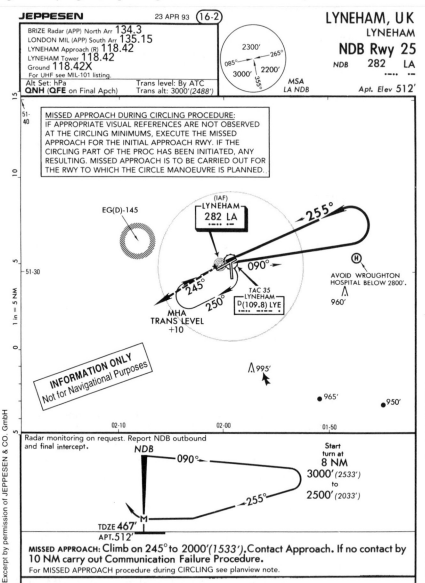

■ Figure 12-42 **Plan and profile of the Lyneham NDB approach for Runway 25 (Jeppesen chart)**

If you become *visual* at or above the MDA(H), you may descend further for a landing. If you do not become visual at the MDA(H), then you may continue tracking to the NDB at the MDA(H) in the hope of becoming visual, but otherwise must make a **missed approach** at the NDB by climbing away on the outbound track of 245°M, to at least the published missed approach altitude of 2,000 ft on QNH. The options then are to return for another approach in the hope that conditions have improved, or to divert to another aerodrome at a safe cruise level.

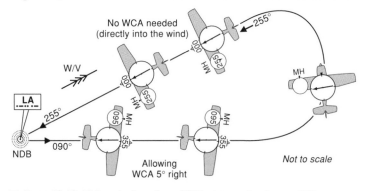

■ *Figure 12-43* **Flying the Lyneham NDB approach using an RBI**

Now complete
Exercises 12 – The Relative Bearing Indicator (RBI).

The Radio Magnetic Indicator (RMI)

The radio magnetic indicator combines the relative bearing indicator and heading indicator into one instrument, where the ADF card is aligned automatically with magnetic north. This considerably reduces pilot workload by reducing the amount of visualisation and mental arithmetic required. Even the rotatable card (which allows you to align the ADF card manually with magnetic north) lightens the workload, since it also reduces the amount of visualisation and mental arithmetic required.

The discussion that follows applies to both the RMI and the rotatable-card ADF, except that whereas:

☐ **the RMI** is continuously and automatically aligned with magnetic north;

☐ **the rotatable card** must be re-aligned with the HI by hand following every heading change (and of course the HI must be re-aligned with the magnetic compass by hand every 10 minutes or so).

■ Figure 13-1 **Radio magnetic indicators with single and double pointers. The RMI card is automatically aligned with magnetic north.**

■ Figure 13-2 **The rotatable-card ADF**

Orientation

An RMI gives a graphic picture of where the aeroplane is:

☐ **the head** of the RMI needle displays QDM (magnetic track *to* the NDB); and

☐ **the tail** of the RMI needle displays QDR (magnetic track *from* the NDB).

EXAMPLE 1 Orientate an aeroplane with MH 320 and RMI 050. Determine the QDM, QDR and QTE (true track from the NDB). The magnetic variation is 7°W.

NOTE RMI 050 means QDM 050°M to the NDB (whereas RBI 030 or ADF 030 means a relative bearing of 030 to the NDB, i.e. relative to the nose of the aeroplane and its heading).

QDM is 050, QDR is 230.

Variation west, magnetic best; so true track to the NDB is given by:

QTE = QDR 230 – 7°W variation = QTE 223.

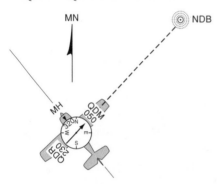

■ *Figure 13-3* **Orientation with an RMI is quite straightforward**

QTE is really only of value for plotting a position line on a visual chart, and so is rarely used in instrument flying.

The Initial Interception of Track

Intercepting an Inbound Track

A common use of the RMI, after you have used it to orientate yourself with respect to the NDB, is to **track to the NDB**. The RMI makes it easy for you to visualise:

☐ where you are;

☐ where you want to go; and

☐ how to get there.

EXAMPLE 2 Your aeroplane has MH 340 and RMI 030. You are requested to intercept a track of 090 to the NDB.

Step 1. Orientating the aeroplane is made easy by the RMI. The QDM (magnetic track to the NDB) in the present position is 030. If you now imagine a model aeroplane attached to the tail of the needle, and on the actual heading (which in this case is MH 340), then you have a very good picture of the situation.

The desired track to the NDB, 090°M-*to*, is ahead of the present position of the aeroplane. If you visualise the desired track on the RMI, with the model aeroplane on the tail of the needle tracking as desired, it becomes quite clear what turns are required to intercept the desired track.

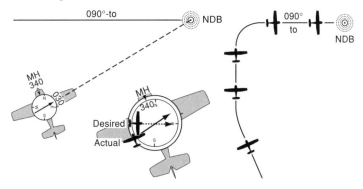

■ *Figure 13-4* **Visualising track on an RMI**

Step 2. To intercept the track 090 to the NDB, the aeroplane should be turned onto a suitable intercept heading, such as one of those illustrated in Figure 13–5.

Step 3. Maintain the chosen intercept heading and periodically observe the RMI needle as it falls towards the desired inbound track of 090°M.

Step 4. As the 090 track is approached, indicated by the RMI needle approaching 090, turn right to take up the desired track to the NDB, allowing for any estimated crosswind effect on tracking. In this case, a WCA of 10° right has been used. With MH 100, and the RMI steady on 090, the aeroplane now tracks 090 to the NDB.

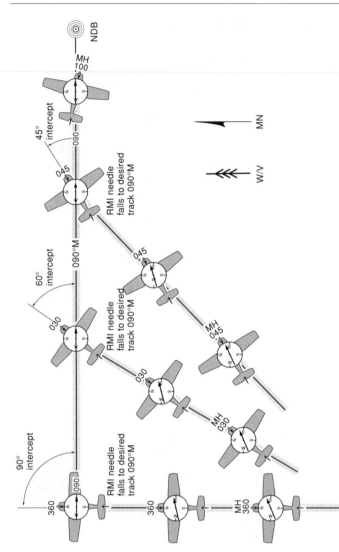

EXAMPLE 3 An aeroplane is given a radar vector by ATC to steer a heading of 010°M, and then to make an intercept 055°M inbound to an NDB.

Visualising the situation confirms that radar vector 010 will intercept the 055-*to* track, and it will in fact be a 45° intercept (055 – 010 = 45). The RMI needle falls towards 055 approaching the desired track inbound, and you should commence a turn shortly before reaching it to avoid overshooting it. This is known as **leading in** (which is really anticipating), and the amount of lead-in can be judged by the *rate* at which the needle is falling, and the distance required for the aeroplane to turn onto a suitable heading to track inbound. Another way to achieve a smooth intercept is to reduce the closing angle as the desired track is approached, say from 45° to 30° to 15° and, finally, to zero as it is intercepted.

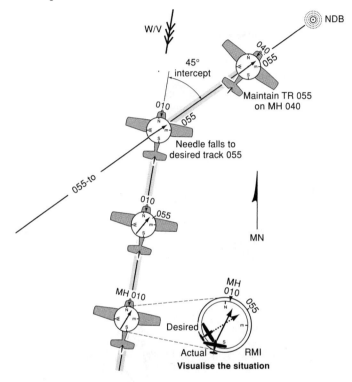

■ *Figure 13-6* **Intercepting 055°M inbound from radar vector 010**

In this case, the pilot has chosen to track inbound with a WCA of 15° left to counteract drift caused by a strong northerly wind. Correct tracking to the NDB will be confirmed by the RMI needle staying on 055.

Intercepting an Outbound Track

EXAMPLE 4 The pilot is given a radar vector of 340 to intercept 280 outbound from an NDB.

Step 1. Orientate the aeroplane.

Step 2. Consider the intercept, 60° in this case (340 − 280 = 60). Visualise the situation. Again, the model aeroplane imagined on the tail of the needle helps.

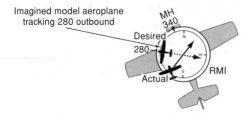

■ Figure 13-7 **Visualise the situation**

Step 3. Monitor the intercept by steering a steady MH 340 and periodically checking the tail of the RMI needle rising to 280.

Step 4. As the desired track 280 outbound (or QDR 280) is approached and as the tail of the needle approaches 280, the pilot turns left to pick it up, in this case allowing no wind correction angle, since no crosswind effect is expected.

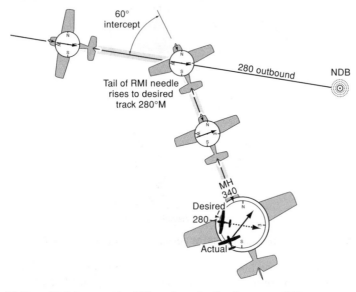

■ Figure 13-8 **Intercepting 280 outbound off radar vector 340**

Maintaining Track

Tracking Towards an NDB, with No Crosswind Effect

With no crosswind, a direct track inbound can be achieved by heading the aeroplane directly at the NDB. The magnetic heading will, in this case, be the same as the desired track, and the RMI needle will be on the nose indicating the track.

If there is no crosswind to blow the aeroplane off track, then everything will remain constant as in the case shown in Figure 13-9 – the magnetic heading 250 and the RMI 250 will remain constant. This will be the situation in:

☐ nil-wind conditions;
☐ a direct headwind; or
☐ a direct tailwind.

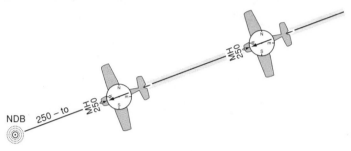

■ *Figure 13-9* **Tracking inbound on 250°M using an RMI, with no crosswind**

Tracking Inbound with a Crosswind

WITH NO CORRECTION FOR DRIFT made by the pilot, and the aeroplane headed straight at the NDB with the RMI needle initially on the nose, any crosswind will cause the aeroplane to be blown off track.

Time 0715	Time 0725
MH 250	MH 250
RMI 250 (QDM)	RMI 255 (QDM)

In the case shown in Figure 13-10, the wind, with a northerly component, has blown the aeroplane to the left of track. This is indicated by the head of the RMI needle starting to move down the right of the dial. To return to track, the aeroplane must be turned towards the right, i.e. towards the direction in which the head of the needle is moving.

If the pilot turns left to put the NDB on the nose again (MH = RMI 255), then after a short period the aeroplane will again be blown to the left of track, and the RMI needle will move to the right of the nose. Another turn to the right will be required.

In this way the path to the NDB will be curved, with the aeroplane finally approaching the NDB heading roughly into wind, and a longer distance will be travelled compared to the direct track from the original position. This is known as **homing** (keeping the NDB on the nose). It is not a very tidy procedure. Professional pilots rarely use it!

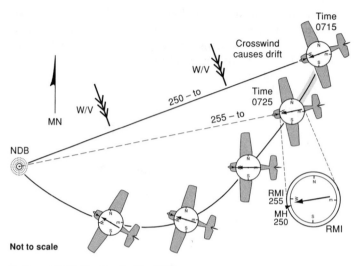

■ *Figure 13-10* **Homing to the NDB**

WITH CORRECT DRIFT CORRECTION made by the pilot – a much better procedure than homing – the aeroplane tracks direct to an NDB by heading into wind and laying off a wind correction angle (WCA) to counteract drift. If 15° right is indeed the correct WCA, then the aeroplane will track 250°M direct to the NDB by steering MH 265.

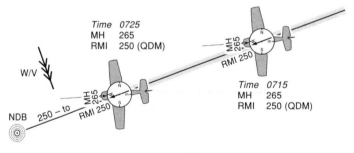

■ *Figure 13-11* **Tracking direct to the NDB**

Different Winds Require Different Wind Correction Angles

An aeroplane is on track when the RMI indicates track. This is illustrated in Figure 13-12. In each situation, the aeroplane is on the desired track of 355°M, but using a different wind correction angle to counteract the drift under different wind conditions.

If the precise wind effect is not known, then use a 'best guess' WCA estimated from the available information as an initial WCA. For the same crosswind, slower aeroplanes will need to allow a greater WCA than faster aeroplanes.

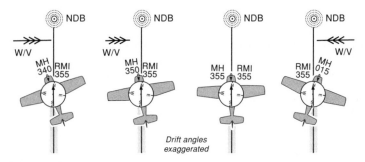

■ Figure 13-12 **Laying off drift to achieve the desired track**

It is possible that the wind effect will change as you track towards an NDB, and so regular alterations of heading may be required. This is often the case as an aeroplane descends using the NDB as the tracking aid.

WITH INCORRECT DRIFT CORRECTION made by the pilot the aeroplane will move off the desired track, i.e. the QDM (magnetic track to the NDB) will change. This will become obvious through a gradually changing RMI reading (as the RMI indicates QDM).

Modify the wind correction angle to maintain course by altering heading.

Suppose, for instance, you steer a heading with a 5° wind correction angle to the right to counteract the effect of a wind from the right. If the wind effect turns out to be greater than expected, the aeroplane will gradually deviate to the left of the desired track to the NDB, and the RMI reading (QDM) will gradually increase. Typical cockpit indications could be:

Time 0715	Time 0725
MH 020	MH 020
RMI 015 (QDM)	RMI 018 (QDM)

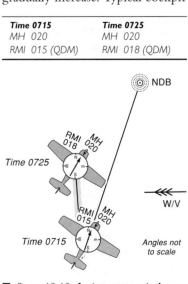

■ Figure 13-13 **An incorrect wind correction angle causes RMI reading (QDM) to change**

The head of the RMI needle falling away to the right indicates that a right turn must be made to track to the NDB. Conversely, the head of the RMI needle falling away to the left indicates that a left turn must be made to track to the NDB. Just how great each correcting turn should be depends on the deviation from track.

Maintaining Track

Re-intercepting a track, once having deviated from it, uses the same procedure as the initial intercept of a new track, except that the angles will be smaller, provided you are vigilant and do not allow large deviations to occur. Realising that the aeroplane is diverging from the direct track to the NDB, you have several options. You may either:

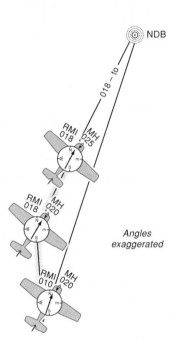

1. Track direct to the NDB from the present position even though it is slightly off the original track; or

2. Regain the original track.

METHOD 1. Turn slightly right (say 5° in this case), and track direct to the NDB from the present position, even though it is not on the originally desired track. In most NDB tracking this technique is used only when very close to the station (say 1 or 2 nm).

■ *Figure 13-14* **Method 1: flying a new track to the NDB**

Needle falling right; turn right.

METHOD 2. Turn further right initially (say 10° onto MH 030), and re-intercept the original track, indicated by the RMI needle moving down to read 015 again. Once track is regained, turn left (say by half the correcting turn of 10°) onto MH 025. This is a very moderate correction, something you would expect to see from an experienced instrument pilot. (See Figure 13-15.)

If MB + RB = desired MB constantly, then ADF tracking is good.

Attempting to maintain the desired track (or remain on the one QDM) is the normal navigational technique when at some distance from the NDB. If the RMI remains on a steady reading, then the aeroplane is tracking directly to the NDB.

CORRECTING TURNS. Just how great each correcting turn should be depends on the displacement from track and the distance from the station. A simple method is to initially alter heading by double the error. If the aeroplane has deviated 10° left (indicated by the RMI moving 10° right), then alter heading by 20° to the right. (If you alter heading by only 10° to the right, the result will probably be a further deviation to the left, a further correction to the right, resulting in a curved homing to the NDB.)

HAVING REGAINED TRACK, turn left by only half the correcting turn of 20°, i.e. turn left 10° to intercept and maintain track. This leaves you with a WCA different to the original one (that caused you to deviate from track), and one that should provide reasonable tracking. If not, make further corrections to heading!

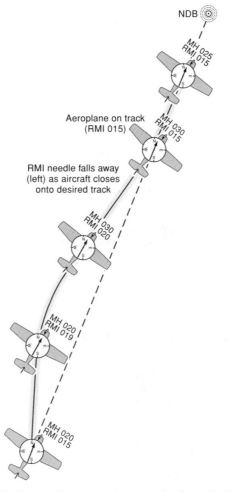

■ Figure 13-15 **Method 2: regain the desired track**

Bracketing Track

In practice, an absolutely perfect direct track is difficult to achieve. The actual track made good will probably consist of a number of minor corrections such as those just described, a technique known as **bracketing** the track, i.e. making regular corrections, left or right as required, to maintain or regain the desired track.

The aim of bracketing is to find the precise WCA needed to maintain track. If, for instance, a WCA of 10° right is found to be too great and the aeroplane diverges to the right of track, and a WCA of only 5° right is too little and the wind blows the aeroplane to the left of track, then try something in between, say WCA 8° right.

A precise instrument pilot will monitor the tracking of the aeroplane on a regular basis and make corrections earlier rather than later, the result being a number of small corrections rather than just one big correction.

■ Figure 13-16

Bracketing the track

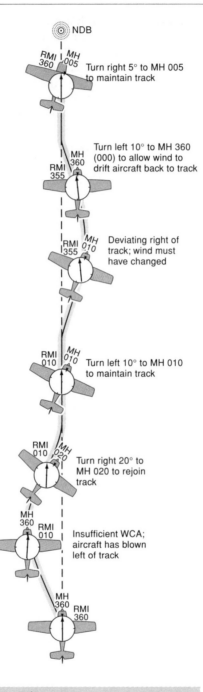

◎ NDB

RMI 360 | MH 005 — Turn right 5° to MH 005 to maintain track

MH 360 / RMI 355 — Turn left 10° to MH 360 (000) to allow wind to drift aircraft back to track

RMI 355 / MH 010 — Deviating right of track; wind must have changed

RMI 010 / MH 010 — Turn left 10° to MH 010 to maintain track

RMI 010 / MH 020 — Turn right 20° to MH 020 to rejoin track

MH 360 / RMI 010 — Insufficient WCA; aircraft has blown left of track

MH 360 / RMI 360

Head of needle falling right – turn right.
Head of needle falling left – turn left.

Wind Effect

If the wind direction and strength is not obvious, then a useful technique is to initially steer the track to the station as heading (i.e. make no allowance for drift), observe the results, and then make heading adjustments to bracket track. This is illustrated in Figure 13-16.

Tracking Overhead an NDB

The RMI needle will become more and more sensitive as the NDB station is approached, minor movements left or right of track causing larger and larger changes in the RMI reading; i.e. the RMI needle becomes 'agitated' as the NDB is approached. For a very precise track to be achieved, you must be prepared to increase your scan rate and respond more frequently.

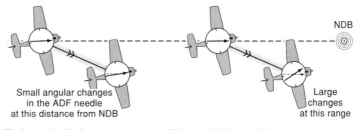

Small angular changes
in the ADF needle
at this distance from NDB

NDB

Large
changes
at this range

■ *Figure 13-17* **Approaching the NDB, the RMI needle becomes more sensitive**

Close to the station and just prior to passing overhead, however, you can relax a little and steer a steady heading until the RMI needle moves towards the bottom of the dial and settles down, at which time tracking from the NDB should be checked and suitable adjustments made to heading. If the track outbound is different to that inbound, then a suitable heading change estimated to make good the new desired track could be made as soon as the RMI needle falls past the mid-position on its way to the bottom of the dial.

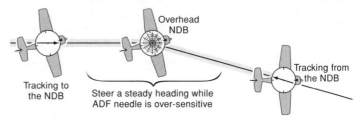

Overhead
NDB

Tracking to
the NDB

Steer a steady heading while
ADF needle is over-sensitive

Tracking from
the NDB

■ *Figure 13-18* **Do not overshoot when close to the station**

The RMI needle becoming extremely active and then falling rapidly to the bottom of the dial indicates that the aeroplane has passed directly overhead the NDB. The RMI needle moving gradually to one side and slowly falling to the bottom of the dial indicates that the aeroplane is passing to one side of the beacon, the rate at which the needle falls being an indication of the aeroplane's proximity to the NDB. If it falls very slowly, then perhaps your tracking could have been better. Time overhead (or abeam) the NDB can be taken as the needle falls through the approximate mid-position.

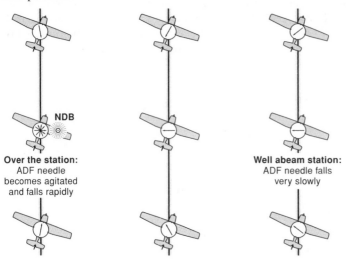

Over the station:
ADF needle
becomes agitated
and falls rapidly

Well abeam station:
ADF needle falls
very slowly

■ *Figure 13-19* **Good ADF tracking (left); reasonable and poor tracking**

Tracking Away From an NDB
When tracking away from an NDB, the head of the RMI needle will lie towards the bottom of the dial, and the tail of the RMI needle will be towards the top of the dial.

Tracking Away From an NDB with No Crosswind Effect
If you track overhead the NDB and then steer track as heading, the aeroplane will track directly away from the NDB with the head of the RMI needle steady at the bottom of the dial, and the tail of the RMI needle steady at the top of the dial under the MH lubber line.

■ *Figure 13-20* **Tracking away from an NDB with no crosswind effect**

The aeroplane in Figure 13-20 has a QDR of 090 (magnetic track from the station to the aeroplane) indicated by the tail of the RMI needle, and a QDM of 270 (magnetic track from the aeroplane to the station) indicated by the head of the RMI needle. Since it is track *outbound* that is being considered here, the position of the *tail* of the needle is of more use.

Tracking Away From an NDB with a Crosswind

Suppose that the desired track outbound from an NDB is 340°M, and you estimate that a WCA of 12° to the right is necessary to counteract a wind from the right. To achieve this, you steer MH 352, and hope to see the tail of the RMI needle stay on 340, the desired outbound track.

In Figure 13-21, the chosen WCA and MH are correct, and the desired track of 340°M outbound is maintained.

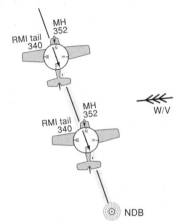

■ *Figure 13-21* **Tracking away from an NDB with a WCA of 12° into wind**

If the estimated WCA is incorrect, then the actual track made good by the aeroplane will differ from that desired. If the wind is stronger than expected, the aeroplane's actual TMG may be 335°M, and to the left of the desired track of 340°M (Figure 13-22).

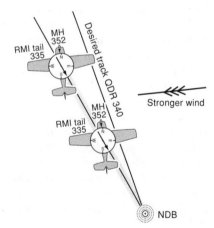

■ *Figure 13-22* **Tracking away from an NDB with an incorrect wind correction angle**

Whereas inaccurate tracking *to* an NDB is indicated by the ADF needle falling, incorrect tracking away *from* an NDB can occur with the RMI needle indicating a steady reading – but the aeroplane may be on the *wrong* QDR. Having passed overhead the NDB, an aeroplane can track away from it in any direction. You must always ensure that you are flying away from the NDB along the correct track, and the easiest way to do this is to *observe the QDR on the tail of the RMI needle*.

Regaining Track Away from an NDB in a Crosswind

If an incorrect wind correction angle is flown, then the aeroplane will of course be blown off track. The vigilant pilot/navigator will observe the incorrect TMG (track made good), probably by noting that the tail of the RMI needle is indicating something other than the desired outbound track.

NOTE It is generally easier to work off the top of the dial, since that is where the aeroplane is going, rather than off the bottom of the dial. The left turn necessary to regain track (turning left towards the head of the needle and therefore away from the tail of the needle) can be thought of as *pulling the tail of the RMI needle around* or *trailing the tail*. Some instructors, however, prefer to use the head of the needle – in this case, the head of the needle (now at the bottom of the dial) moves left, indicating that a correcting turn to the left is required. Your instructor will recommend a method.

EXAMPLE 5 In the situation illustrated in Figure 13-23, the pilot is flying track as heading, i.e. initially making no allowance for drift. If the tail of the RMI needle moves right, then the aeroplane must be turned left to regain track.

In Figure 13-23, the aeroplane has been blown to the right of the desired track QDR 035, onto QDR 043 indicated by the tail of the RMI needle.

To regain track, the pilot has turned left by 16° (double the error) from MH 035 to MH 019. As the aeroplane is flown on its steady intercept heading of MH 019, the tail of the needle will be gradually pulled around.

The pilot will continue with the intercept heading until the aeroplane approaches the desired track, QDR 035. This is indicated by the tail of the RMI needle moving up the dial towards 035.

As the desired track outbound is approached, the pilot turns right to maintain the RMI tail on 025, i.e. QDR 035. Estimating a WCA of 8° into wind to be sufficient, the pilot steers MH 027 and checks regularly that the tail of the RMI needle stays on 035.

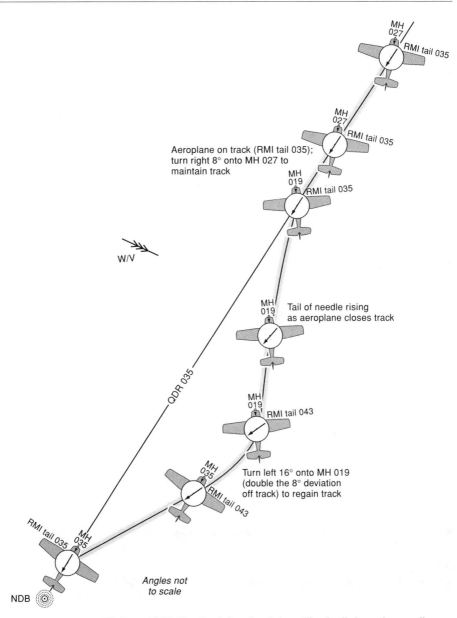

MH 027 / RMI tail 035

MH 027 / RMI tail 035

Aeroplane on track (RMI tail 035); turn right 8° onto MH 027 to maintain track

MH 019 / RMI tail 035

W/V

Tail of needle rising as aeroplane closes track

MH 019

QDR 035

MH 019 / RMI tail 043

MH 035 / RMI tail 043

Turn left 16° onto MH 019 (double the 8° deviation off track) to regain track

RMI tail 035 / MH 035

NDB

Angles not to scale

■ Figure 13-23 **Turning left to 'trail the tail' or 'pull the tail around'**

Similarly, if the tail of the RMI needle is left of where it should be, then the desired track is out to the right, and a right turn should be made to trail the tail (Figure 13-24).

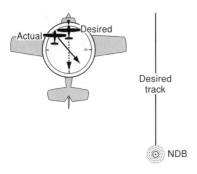

■ Figure 13-24 **Turn right to 'trail the tail'**

NOTE If using the head of the needle is the preferred technique, then the need for a left turn is indicated by the head of the needle moving to the left of the datum QDM 215.

NDB Approaches
The NDB approach discussed at the end of Chapter 12 is made simpler with an RMI to use for NDB tracking, rather than an RBI. The actual NDB let-down procedure for the pilot to follow is identical for all ADF presentations.

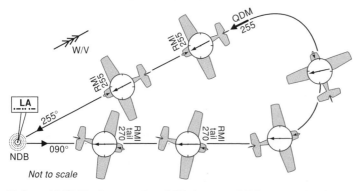

Not to scale

■ Figure 13-25 **Tracking using an RMI during an NDB approach**

Now complete
Exercises 13 – The Radio Magnetic Indicator (RMI).

The VOR

The VOR (pronounced *"vee-oh-are"*) is a very high frequency radio navigation aid that is extensively used in instrument flying. Its full name is the **very high frequency omni-directional radio range,** commonly abbreviated to the VHF omni range, VOR, or omni.

A VOR ground station can be selected on the VHF-NAV radio set.

Each VOR ground station transmits on a specific VHF frequency between 108.00 and 117.95 megahertz (MHz), which is a lower-frequency band than that used for VHF communications. A separate VHF-NAV radio is required for navigation purposes, but is usually combined with the VHF-COM in a NAV-COM set.

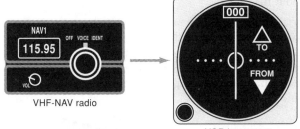

VHF-NAV radio

VOR instrument

■ *Figure 14-1* **Cockpit VOR equipment**

The VOR was developed in the United States during the late 1940s, and was adopted by the International Civil Aviation Organisation (ICAO) as the standard short-range radio navigation aid in 1960. When introduced, it offered an immediate improvement over existing aids such as the ADF/NDB combination, most of which operated in lower frequency bands than the VOR and suffered significant limitations, such as night effect, mountain reflections, interference from electrical storms, etc.

Principal advantages of the VOR include:
- ☐ **reduced susceptibility** to electrical and atmospheric interference (including thunderstorms);
- ☐ **the elimination of night effect,** since VHF signals are line-of-sight and not reflected by the ionosphere (as are NDB signals in the LF/MF band).

The reliability and accuracy of VOR signals allows the VOR to be used with confidence in any weather conditions, by day or by night, for purposes such as:
- ☐ **orientation** and position fixing (Where am I?);

☐ **tracking** to or from a VOR ground station;

☐ **holding** (for delaying or manoeuvring action); and

☐ **instrument approaches** to land.

Many VORs are coupled with a DME (distance-measuring equipment providing a measure of distance from the station in nautical miles), so that selection of the VOR on the VHF-NAV set in the cockpit also selects the DME, thereby providing both tracking and distance information.

> *VORs are often paired with a DME.*

How the VOR Works

The VOR ground station transmits two VHF radio signals:

1. **the reference phase,** which is omni-directional (the same in all directions); and

2. **the variable phase,** which rotates uniformly at a rate of 1,800 revolutions per minute, with its phase varying at a constant rate throughout the 360°.

The aerial of the VOR aircraft receiver picks up the signals, whose **phase difference** (the difference between the wave peaks) is measured, this difference depending on the bearing of the aeroplane from the ground station. In this manner, the VOR can determine the **magnetic bearing** of the aeroplane from the VOR ground station.

■ *Figure 14-2* **Typical VOR aerials**

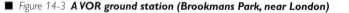

■ *Figure 14-3* **A VOR ground station (Brookmans Park, near London)**

The two signals transmitted by the VOR ground station are:
- in phase on magnetic north, which is the reference for VOR signals;
- 90° out of phase at magnetic east 090°M;
- 180° out of phase at magnetic south 180°M;
- 270° out of phase at magnetic west 270°M; and
- 360° out of phase (back *in* phase) at magnetic north 360°M, or 000°M.

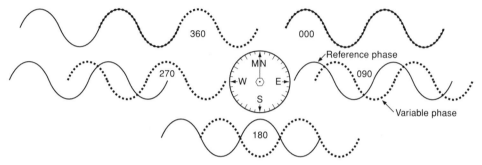

■ *Figure 14-4* **The VOR transmits two VHF signals with a phase difference between them**

Check the Morse code ident before using a VOR.

Every 10 seconds or so a Morse code **ident** signal is transmitted, allowing you to positively identify the VOR. Some VORs may also carry voice transmissions with a relevant automatic terminal information service (ATIS).

The VOR is a very high frequency aid operating in the frequency band 108.0 MHz to 117.95 MHz. It allows high-quality *line-of-sight* reception as there is relatively little interference from atmospheric noise in this band. Reception may be affected by the terrain surrounding the ground station, the height of the VOR beacon, the altitude of the aeroplane and its distance from the station.

VOR Range

The VOR signal is line-of-sight.

The approximate maximum range of a VHF signal is given by the formula (which you do not need to remember):

$$VHF\ range\ in\ nm\ =\ \sqrt{1.5 \times altitude\ in\ feet}$$

EXAMPLE 1 At 7,000 ft amsl, approximate VHF range:

$$= \sqrt{1.5 \times 7,000}$$
$$= \sqrt{10,000}$$
$$= 100\ nm$$

Different VOR stations may operate on the same frequency, but they should be well separated geographically so that there is no interference between their VHF line-of-sight signals. The higher the aeroplane's altitude, however, the greater the possibility of interference. The AIP specifies a designated operational coverage (DOC) for each VOR above which interference is possible. Within the DOC coverage, VOR reception should be reliable. *Detling VOR,* for instance, has a DOC of 60 nm/50,000 ft (see AIP ENR 4-1-1).

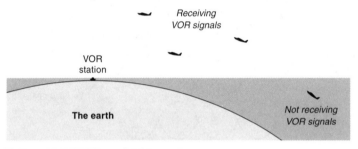

■ *Figure 14-5* **VHF line-of-sight signals**

Tracking with a VOR

The VOR can be used to indicate the **desired track** and the aeroplane's **angular deviation** from that track. For a desired track of 015°M, expect to steer a heading of approximately 015°M, plus or minus a wind correction angle (WCA). By selecting an omni bearing of 015 under the course index of the VOR cockpit display, you can obtain tracking information, as illustrated in Figures 14-6 and 14-7.

The VOR cockpit display is not heading sensitive, which means that the display will not change as a result of the aeroplane changing heading. Figure 14-7 shows the same aeroplane as Figure 14-6, except that a wind correction angle of 10° right is being used by the pilot to counteract a wind from the right, and so the aeroplane's magnetic heading is now MH 025 (rather than MH 015 previously).

Note that:
- ☐ the VOR indication depends on the **angular deviation** of the aeroplane relative to the selected track;
- ☐ the VOR indication will *not* change with any heading change of the aeroplane.

It is usual, when tracking en route from one VOR to another, to select the next VOR when the aeroplane is approximately halfway between them, as in Figure 14-8. This allows the use of the stronger signal, although intervening mountains which might shield the signal of a VOR may affect your decision in this regard.

Change VORs at the approximate mid-point between them.

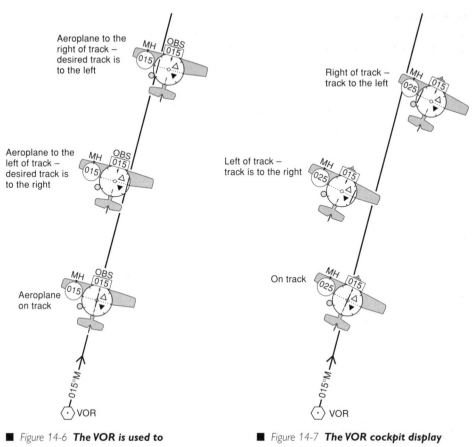

Aeroplane to the right of track – desired track is to the left

Right of track – track to the left

Aeroplane to the left of track – desired track is to the right

Left of track – track is to the right

Aeroplane on track

On track

VOR

VOR

■ Figure 14-6 **The VOR is used to indicate track**

■ Figure 14-7 **The VOR cockpit display is not heading sensitive**

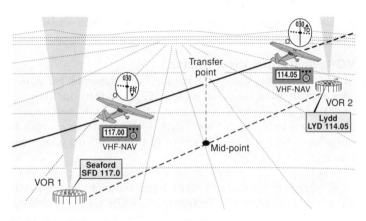

Transfer point

VOR 2

Lydd
LYD 114.05

Mid-point

Seaford
SFD 117.0

VOR 1

■ Figure 14-8 **Tracking between two VORs**

VOR Radials

As its name *omni* suggests, a VOR ground transmitter radiates signals in all directions. Its most important feature, however, is that the signal in any particular direction differs slightly from all the adjacent signals. These individual directional signals can be thought of as *tracks* or *position lines* radiating out from the VOR ground station, in much the same way as spokes from the hub of a wheel.

By convention, 360 different tracks away from the VOR are used, each separated from the next by 1°, and each with its direction related to magnetic north. Each of these 360 VOR tracks or position lines is called a radial.

> A **radial** is the magnetic bearing outbound FROM a VOR.

NOTE A specific VOR radial is the same as QDR. For instance, the 293 radial is QDR 293, which is a track of 293° magnetic away *from* the VOR ground station.

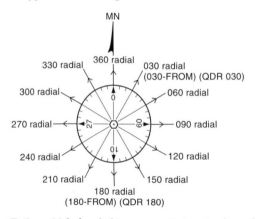

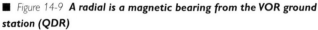

■ *Figure 14-9* **A radial is a magnetic bearing from the VOR ground station (QDR)**

VORs on Aeronautical Charts

Most aeronautical charts show the position, frequency and Morse code identification (ident) of each VOR ground station. Information on a particular VOR may be found in the UK Aeronautical Information Publication (AIP ENR 4-1-1), and any changes to this information will be referred to in NOTAMs (to which you may refer prior to flight).

A VOR ground station may be represented in various ways on a chart – the common representations are shown in Figure 14-10. Since magnetic north is the reference direction for VOR radials, a magnetic north arrowhead usually emanates from the VOR symbol, with a compass rose heavily marked each 30°, and the

> VOR radials are based on magnetic north.

radials shown in 10° intervals on the rose. This is generally adequate for in-flight estimation of track to an accuracy of ±2°; however, when flight planning, it is advisable to be more accurate.

At the flight planning stage, use a protractor or plotter for precise measurement of track, although in some cases this may not be necessary because some much-used tracks are published on Radio Navigation Charts (RNCs) in degrees magnetic. If you measure the track in degrees true (°T), then magnetic variation needs to be applied to convert to degrees magnetic (*variation west, magnetic best*).

CAA 1:500,000 Aeronautical Chart (no radials are marked on this chart)

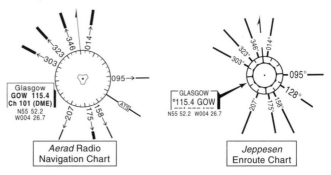

■ Figure 14-10 **A VOR and its radials represented on different charts**

It is usual for instrument-rated pilots to use the Radio Navigation Charts (published by *Aerad* and *Jeppesen*), and IMC-rated pilots to use the CAA 1:500,000 (half-million) ICAO Topographical Charts, already well known from visual navigation.

Further Information on VORs

The UK AIP carries information regarding radio navigation aids in its ENR 4-1-1 section. For example, the AIP extract for *Goodwood*, shown in Figure 14-11, includes:

☐ Frequency, 114.75 MHz (also found on the charts).

☐ Callsign, or identification, 'GWC' (also found on the charts) which, in Morse code, is *"dah-dah-dit dit-dah-dah dah-dit-dah-dit"*.

☐ Hours of service (24 hours a day, summer and winter).

☐ Location in latitude and longitude (if you cannot find it on the chart).

☐ Remarks that:

　　– the VOR is an approach aid to Chichester/Goodwood aerodrome (and there will therefore be an instrument approach chart available for it from *Jeppesen*, *Aerad* and the CAA); and

　　– it has a designated operational coverage (DOC) of 80 nm up to 50,000 ft amsl, above which there may be interference from distant VORs using the same frequency.

RADIO NAVIGATION AIDS — EN-ROUTE

Name of Station (VOR set Variation)	IDENT	Frequency (Channel)	Hours of Operation (Winter/Summer)
1	2	3	4
Goodwood VOR/DME (4.0°W - 1996)	GWC	114.75 MHz (Ch 94Y)	H24

INFORMATION ONLY
Not for navigational purposes

Co-ordinates	DME Aerial Elevation	Remarks
5	6	7
AD Purpose: 505118.78N 0004524.25W ENR Purpose: 505119N 0004524W	113 ft amsl	APCH Aid to Chichester/ Goodwood. DOC 80 nm/50000 ft.

■ *Figure 14-11* **UK AIP ENR extract for Goodwood VOR**

RADIO NAVIGATION AIDS — EN-ROUTE

Name of Station (VOR set Variation)	IDENT	Frequency (Channel)	Hours of Operation (Winter/Summer)
1	2	3	4
Guernsey VOR/DME (4.4°W - 1996)	GUR	109.40 MHz (Ch 31X)	H24

Co-ordinates	DME Aerial Elevation	Remarks
5	6	7
AD Purpose: 492613.45N 0023613.67W ENR Purpose: 492613N 0023614W	347 ft amsl	APCH Aid to Guernsey. DOC 60 nm/50000 ft (80 nm/ 50000 ft in Sector 022°-067°M).

INFORMATION ONLY
Not for navigational purposes

Excerpted from *EUR/2* Radio Navigation Chart by permission of BRITISH AIRWAYS *AERAD*

■ *Figure 14-12* **Guernsey VOR/DME, in AIP ENR and Aerad chart**

Also, the beginning pages of AIP ENR advise not to use any VOR if it cannot be identified by its Morse code ident. It may be that the VOR is radiating signals on test, in which case the ident is suppressed or the Morse letters 'TST' (for test) are transmitted, to indicate that the facility is not to be used for navigation.

VORs that have a DME (distance-measuring equipment) station associated with them may be described as VOR/DMEs. The DME is automatically tuned when you select the VOR frequency on the VHF-NAV radio. Guernsey has such a facility, see the AIP ENR and chart extract in Figure 14-12.

As the VOR is a VHF radio navigation aid, its line-of-sight signals can be stopped or distorted by high mountains in some locations. AIP ENR should contain a warning, as is the case in Figure 14-13, where Inverness VOR has reduced coverage in the sector between 154°M and 194°M from the VOR ground station.

STATION	SERVICE	CALL SIGN OR IDENT	EM	TRANSMITS		RECEIVES		HOURS OF
				kHz	MHz	kHz	MHz	WINTER PERIOD
1	2	3	4	5	6	7	8	9
Inverness	VOR	INS (Reduced coverage in Sector R154°-R194°. Flag alarms may occur in this sector when aircraft are 30 nm or more from the VOR and flying at or below 7000 ft).	A9W	–	109.200	–		H24 INFORMATION ONLY Not for navigational purposes

■ Figure 14-13 **AIP ENR extract for Inverness**

VOR Cockpit Instruments

There are various types of VOR cockpit display, but they are all reasonably similar in terms of operation. The VOR cockpit display is often referred to as the **omni bearing indicator,** or **OBI.** It displays the omni bearing selected by the pilot on the course card using the **omni bearing selector** (OBS), a small knob which is geared to the card.

If the aeroplane is on the selected radial, then the VOR needle, known as the **course deviation indicator** or **CDI,** will be centred. If the aeroplane is not on the selected track, then the CDI will not be centred.

Whether the selected track would take the aeroplane to or from the VOR ground station is indicated by the TO/FROM flags.

The OBI is only to be used for navigation if:
☐ the red OFF warning flag is hidden from view;
☐ the correct Morse code ident is heard.

When a VOR is operating normally, the radials are transmitted to an accuracy of at least ±2°.

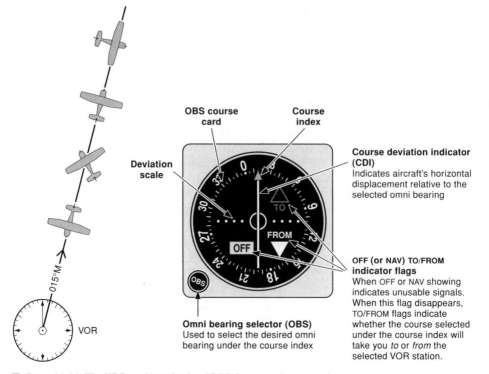

■ *Figure 14-14* **The VOR cockpit display (OBI) for aeroplanes on the**
015 radial

NOTE *Course* is an American term with the same meaning as *track*.
Since most aviation radio equipment is manufactured by US
companies, American terminology is used. In the UK, *course*
sometimes refers to heading; however, it will not be used in this
sense in *The Air Pilot's Manual*.

Course Deviation Indicator (CDI)

The course deviation indicator (CDI) in the VOR cockpit instrument indicates off-track deviation in terms of *angular deviation from
the selected track*. At all times, the reference when using the VOR
is the selected track under the course index. (This is a totally
different principle to that of the ADF needle which simply points
at an NDB ground station and indicates its relative bearing.)

The amount of *angular* deviation from the selected track is
referred to in terms of *dots*; there are 5 dots either side of the
central position. The inner dot on both sides is often represented
by a circle passing through them. Each dot is equivalent to 2°
track deviation.

- If the aeroplane is on the selected track, the CDI is centred.
- If the aeroplane is 2° off the selected track, the CDI is displaced 1 dot from the centre (i.e. on the circumference of the inner circle).
- If the aeroplane is 4° off the selected track, the CDI is displaced 2 dots.
- If the aeroplane is 10° or more off the selected track, the CDI is fully deflected at 5 dots.

A 1-dot deviation of the CDI on the VOR cockpit display represents 2°. Full-scale deflection at 5 dots represents 10° or more.

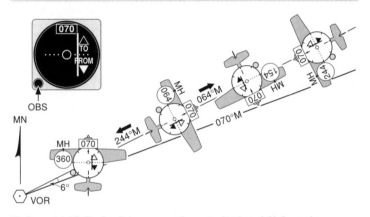

■ *Figure 14-15* **Each of these aeroplanes is displaced 6° from the 070 radial**

Since the CDI indicates *angular* deviation, the actual *distance* off track for a given CDI indication will be smaller the closer the aeroplane is to the ground station. In a manner of speaking, the aeroplane is 'funnelled' in towards the VOR ground station.

To or From

The 090 radial, which is QDR 090 (a magnetic bearing away *from* the station) of 090°M, is the same position line as QDM 270 *to* the station. If an aeroplane is on this position line, then the CDI will be centred when *either* 090 *or* 270 is selected with the OBS. Any ambiguity in your mind regarding the position of the aeroplane relative to the VOR ground station is resolved with the TO/FROM indicators.

The TO or FROM flags or arrows indicate whether the selected omni bearing will take you *to* the VOR ground station, or away *from* it.

In Figure 14-16, the pilot could centre the CDI by selecting either 090 or 270 (reciprocals) with the OBS. A track of 090°M would take the aeroplane *from* the VOR, whereas a track of 270°M would lead it *to* the VOR.

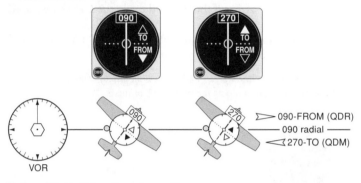

■ *Figure 14-16* **Using the TO/FROM flag**

EXAMPLE 2 Illustrate two indications on the omni bearing indicator that would inform you that the aeroplane is on the 235 radial. The 235 radial is either:

☐ 235°M *from* the VOR; or
☐ 055°M *to* the VOR.

So, with the CDI centred, the VOR cockpit display could indicate either 235-FROM or 055-TO.

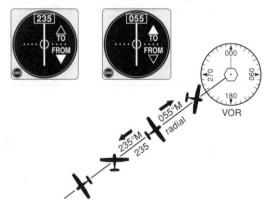

■ *Figure 14-17* **Indications that the aeroplane is on the 235 radial**

> At all times, the reference when using the OBI is the track
> selected under the course index. It determines:
> • CDI deflection; and
> • whether the TO or the FROM flag shows.

Different Presentations of the Omni Bearing

There are various presentations of VOR information. In all cases, full-scale deflection is 10° either side of the selected omni bearing (a total arc of 20°), with five dots either side of centre. In many VOR cockpit displays the two inner dots are joined by the circumference of a circle.

The course deviation indicator (CDI) may also differ between instruments. It may move laterally as a whole, or it may hinge at the top and swing laterally.

Similarly, the means of displaying the selected omni bearing may differ between instruments. It may be shown under a course index, or it may be shown in a window. In some equipment, the TO and the FROM flags may be displayed in the one window, in others they may have separate windows.

The VOR cockpit display usually doubles as the ILS (instrument landing system) display, with vertical dots marked to indicate glideslope (GS) deviation (using a second needle which lies or is hinged horizontally so that it can move up or down). When being used for the VOR (and not the ILS), the glideslope cross bar (or needle) may be biased out of view, and there may be a **red GS warning flag** showing.

Operational Use of the VOR

Preparing the VOR for Use

Always select, tune and identify a VOR before use.

A radio navigation aid is of little value if you do not use it correctly. Prior to using the VOR, you must:

- ensure electrical power is available, and switch the VHF-NAV ON;
- select the desired frequency (e.g. 114.3 MHz for Aberdeen VOR as found on navigation charts or in AIP ENR);
- identify the VOR (*dit-dah dah-dit-dit dah-dit,* which is ADN in Morse code as shown on the navigation charts for AberDeeN);
- check that the OFF flag is not showing (i.e. the signal is usable, otherwise the OFF flag would be visible).

Orientation

Using a Single VOR Position Line

Orientation means 'to determine one's approximate position'. The first step in orientation is to establish a position line (PL) along which the aircraft is known to be at a particular moment.

To obtain a position line using the VOR display:

- rotate the OBS (omni bearing selector) until the CDI (course deviation indicator) is centred; and
- note whether the TO or the FROM flag is showing.

EXAMPLE 3 You rotate the OBS until the CDI is centred – this occurs with 334 under the course index and the TO flag showing. Illustrate the situation.

Could another OBI (omni bearing indicator) reading be obtained with the course deviation indicator centred?

In the aircraft's location, the CDI will be centred with either:
☐ 334-TO; or
☐ 154-FROM.

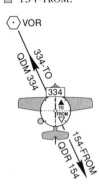

■ Figure 14-18 **On the 154 radial**

Using Two Position Lines to Fix Position

One position line alone does not allow you to positively fix the position of the aircraft overhead a particular point, it only provides a line somewhere along which the aircraft lies.

It requires two or more position lines to positively fix the position of an aircraft. Also, to be of any real value for position fixing, the two PLs need to intersect at an angle of at least 45°. Any 'cut' less than this decreases the accuracy of the fix.

Radio position lines can be provided by any convenient radio navigation aid, including VORs, NDBs and DMEs.

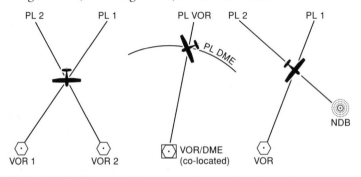

■ Figure 14-19 **Fixing position requires two position lines with a good 'cut' (angle of at least 45°)**

Two VORs

Some aeroplanes are fitted with two independent VHF-NAV systems, enabling two different VORs to be tuned at the same time, and thus two PLs from two different VOR ground stations can be obtained simultaneously. In an aeroplane fitted with only one VHF-NAV set, you can obtain two PLs using the one VHF-NAV by retuning it from one VOR to another.

EXAMPLE 4 An aeroplane fitted with two VHF-NAVs is tracking 134°M from Prestwick to Manchester via Dean Cross, and obtains the following indications:

☐ VOR 1. Dean Cross 115.2 is selected, and the CDI centres with 134-TO.

☐ VOR 2. Talla 113.8 is selected, and the CDI centres with 220-FROM.

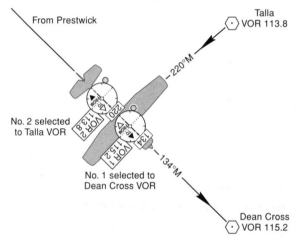

■ *Figure 14-20* **Fixing position using two VORs**

Figure 14-20 shows that the aeroplane is on track (134°M between Prestwick and Dean Cross) and passing the Talla 220 radial. The two position lines cut at a good angle, and the pilot has a fairly positive indication of where the aeroplane is.

VOR and a DME

Probably the most common form of en route position fixing between aids is the VOR/DME fix, based on a ground station where the DME (distance-measuring equipment) is co-located with the VOR ground station. The VOR can provide a straight position line showing the radial that the aeroplane is on, and the DME can provide a circular position line showing the distance that the aeroplane is from the ground station. The intersection of the lines is the position of the aeroplane.

EXAMPLE 5 An aircraft tracking north from Brecon (ident BCN, frequency 117.45 MHz) has the cockpit indications of:
☐ BCN VOR 008-FROM; and
☐ BCN DME 31 nm.

Where is the aircraft?

As can be seen from Figure 14-21, the aircraft is at the RADNO position, an in-flight position determined purely by radio navaids.

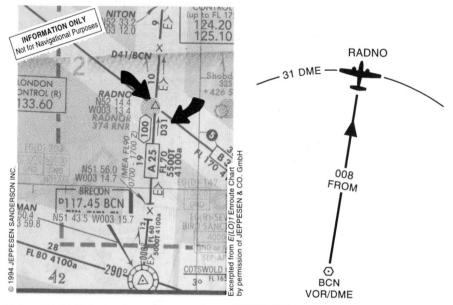

■ *Figure 14-21* **Fixing position using a co-located VOR/DME**

Overhead a VOR

As an aircraft approaches overhead a VOR, the CDI will become more and more agitated as the ±10° funnel either side of track becomes narrower.

As the aircraft passes through the **'zone of confusion'** over the VOR ground station, the CDI may flick from side to side, before settling down again as the aircraft moves away from the station. The TO/FROM flag will also change from TO to FROM (or vice versa), and the red OFF flag may flicker in and out of view because of the temporarily unusable signal.

The zone of confusion can extend in an arc of 70° overhead the station, so it may take a minute or so for the aircraft to pass through it before the CDI and the FROM flag settle down, and the OFF flag totally disappears.

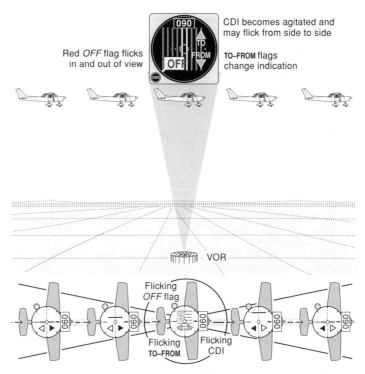

■ *Figure 14-22* **Fixing position overhead a VOR**

Passing Abeam a VOR

A common means of checking flight progress is to note the time passing abeam (to one side of) a nearby VOR ground station. The most straightforward procedure is to:
- [ ] select and identify the VOR; and
- [ ] under the course index, set the radial perpendicular (at 90°) to your track.

EXAMPLE 6 An aircraft is tracking 350°M, and will pass approximately 20 nm abeam a VOR ground station out to its right. The VOR radial perpendicular to track is the 260 radial, and so 260 should be set with the OBS. The CDI will be fully deflected to one side if the aircraft is well away from the abeam position, and will gradually move from full deflection one side to full deflection on the other side as the aircraft passes through the ±10° arc either side of the selected radial. The aircraft is at the abeam position when the CDI is centralised.

The abeam position can also be identified by setting the QDM *to* the VOR under the course index (rather than the QDR or radial *from* the VOR), in which case the movement of the CDI will be from the opposite side.

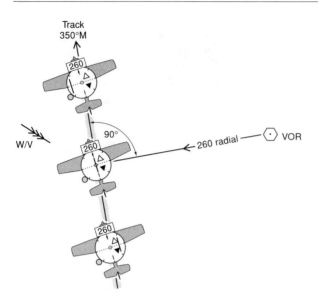

■ Figure 14-23 **Passing abeam a VOR**

The 1-in-60 rule, frequently used in navigation, states that 1 nm off-track in 60 nm subtends an angle of 1°. In rough terms, this means that, as the aircraft flies at right angles through the 10° from when the CDI first starts to move to when it is centred, it will travel approximately 10 nm abeam the VOR when it is located 60 nm from the VOR ground station (or 5 nm at 30 nm, etc.). At say GS 120 kt (2 nm/min), passing through a 10° arc abeam the VOR will take 5 minutes at 60 nm, or 2.5 minutes at 30 nm.

Crossing a Known Radial from an Off-Track VOR

It is a simple procedure to identify passing a known radial from an off-track VOR and, indeed, some en route reporting points are based on this.

EXAMPLE 7 UPTON reporting point en route on the track between Ottringham and Wallasey VORs is specified by the 330 radial from Gamston VOR.

▢ With two VOR displays in the cockpit, it would be normal procedure to track using VOR 1 on Ottringham (and later Wallasey), and check UPTON using VOR 2 tuned to Gamston.

▢ With only one VOR set fitted in the aircraft, it would be normal procedure to leave it on the main tracking aid (Ottringham) until almost at UPTON (say two minutes before ETA), and then select Gamston and the 330 radial. Having crossed this radial, the VOR could be selected to a tracking aid (Ottringham or Wallasey).

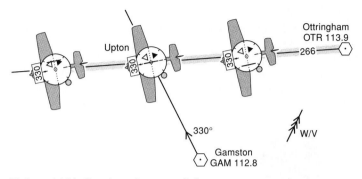

■ Figure 14-24 **Crossing a known radial**

If a 1:500,000 aeronautical chart is being used (rather than a Radio Navigation Chart), you can construct your own checkpoints along track using nearby off-track VORs. In Figure 14-25, the pilot has chosen to check position crossing the 105, 075 and 045 radials from an off-track VOR. By measuring the distance between these planned fixes en route and noting the time of reaching them, the pilot can calculate the groundspeed and revise estimates for positions further along track.

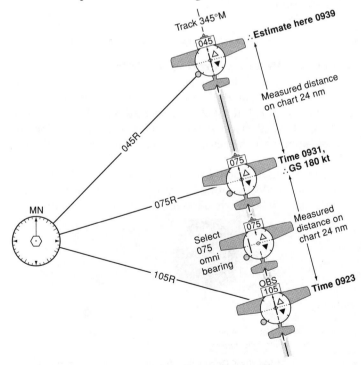

■ Figure 14-25 **Using an off-track VOR to monitor progress**

The VOR Display

The VOR indicates the position of the aeroplane with respect to the selected VOR track, and the VOR display in the cockpit will be the same irrespective of the aeroplane's heading. Each of the aeroplanes in Figure 14-26 will have the same VOR display, provided the same track is set under the course index with the OBS.

> The CDI position will **not** change as the aeroplane changes heading.

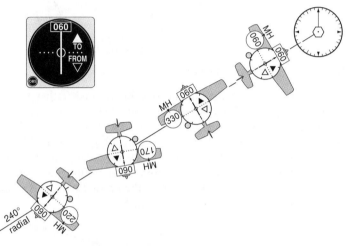

■ Figure 14-26 **The VOR cockpit display is not heading sensitive**

Orientation Without Altering the OBS

It is possible, without altering the omni bearing selector, to determine which quadrant the aeroplane is in with respect to the selected track. In Figure 14-27, the selected omni bearing is 340.

- The CDI is deflected left, which indicates that, when looking in direction 340, the aeroplane is out to the right (of the line 340–160); and
- The FROM flag indicates that tracking 340 would take the aeroplane *from* the VOR ground station, i.e. the aeroplane is ahead of the line 250–070 when looking in the direction 340.

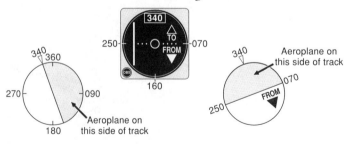

■ Figure 14-27 **Using the CDI and the** TO/FROM **flag for orientation without moving the omni bearing selector**

This puts the aeroplane in the quadrant away from the CDI, and away from the TO/FROM flag – between 340 and 070 radials (omni bearings from the VOR ground station).

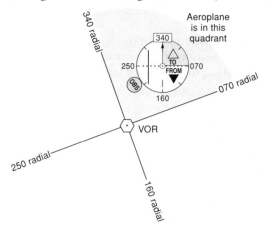

■ *Figure 14-28* **The aeroplane is in the quadrant away from the CDI and TO/FROM flag**

NOTE No information is available from the VOR cockpit display regarding aeroplane heading. Heading information in °M must be obtained from the heading indicator.

EXAMPLE 8 With 085 under the course index, the OBI reads CDI deflected right with the TO flag showing. Position the aeroplane with respect to the VOR.

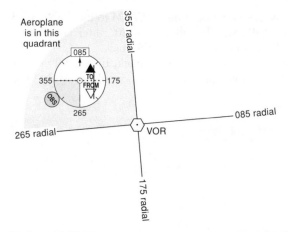

■ *Figure 14-29* **The aeroplane is between the 355 and 265 radials**

This method is a quick way to determine the approximate position of the aeroplane in relation to the VOR ground station.

VOR Tracking

Tracking To a VOR

To track *to* a VOR:

- [ ] **select** the VOR frequency;
- [ ] **identify** the station (Morse code ident);
- [ ] **check** that the red OFF warning flag is not displayed; and
- [ ] **select the omni bearing** of the desired track with the OBS.

Orientate the aeroplane with respect to the desired track, and then take up a suitable intercept heading using the heading indicator (aligned with the magnetic compass). If the aeroplane is heading approximately in the direction of the desired track, the centre circle will represent the aeroplane, and the CDI the desired track. To intercept track in this case, turn towards the CDI.

This is using the OBI as a **command instrument.** This commands you to turn towards the CDI to regain track. Be aware, however, that this only applies when the aeroplane's heading is roughly in the same direction as the selected omni bearing.

On intercepting track, steer a suitable heading to maintain it, considering wind direction and strength. If the desired track is maintained, the CDI will remain centred.

EXAMPLE 9 In Figure 14-30, with the desired track 030 set in the OBI, the CDI is out to the right. Since the aeroplane's initial heading agrees approximately with the track of 030, the pilot concludes that the track is out to the right of the aeroplane. The CDI out to the right *commands* a right turn to regain track and centre the CDI.

The pilot has taken up a heading of 050°M to intercept a track of 030 *to* the VOR, which will give a 20° intercept. This is satisfactory if the aeroplane is close to the track.

If the aeroplane is well away from track, then a 60° or 90° intercept might be more appropriate. This would be MH 090 or MH 120.

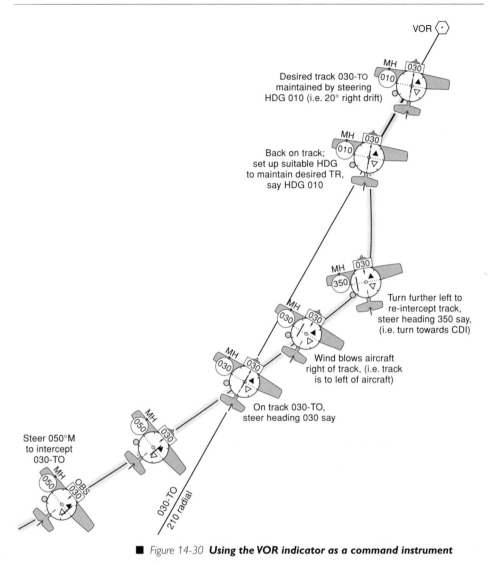

VOR

MH 030
Desired track 030-TO maintained by steering HDG 010 (i.e. 20° right drift)
MH 010

MH 030
Back on track; set up suitable HDG to maintain desired TR, say HDG 010
MH 010

MH 030
Turn further left to re-intercept track, steer heading 350 say, (i.e. turn towards CDI)
350

MH 030
Wind blows aircraft right of track, (i.e. track is to left of aircraft)
MH 030

On track 030-TO, steer heading 030 say
MH 050 030

Steer 050°M to intercept 030-TO
MH 050 OBS 030

030-TO
210 radial

■ Figure 14-30 **Using the VOR indicator as a command instrument**

Determining Drift Angle

When tracking inbound on 360 *to* a VOR with 360 set under the course index, MH 360 will allow the aeroplane to maintain track provided there is no crosswind component.

If, however, there is a westerly wind blowing, then the aeroplane will be blown to the right of track unless a wind correction (WCA) is applied and the aeroplane steered on a heading slightly into wind. This is MH 352 in the centre diagram of Figure 14-31.

If, on the other hand, there is an easterly wind blowing, the aeroplane will be blown to the left of track, unless a wind correction angle (WCA) is applied and the aeroplane steered on a heading slightly into wind, such as MH 005 in the right-hand diagram of Figure 14-31.

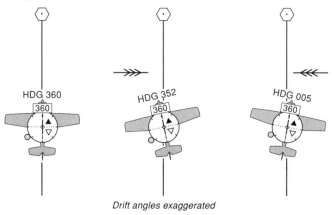

Drift angles exaggerated

■ *Figure 14-31* **Tracking inbound and allowing for drift**

Just how great the WCA need be is determined in flight by trial and error (although any pre-flight calculations using the navigation computer when flight planning may suggest a starting figure for WCA). If the chosen WCA is not correct, and the aeroplane gradually departs from track, causing the CDI to move from its central position, then heading should be altered, the track regained (CDI centred), and then a new magnetic heading flown with an improved estimate of WCA. This process of achieving a suitable WCA is known as **bracketing.**

Of course, in the real world the wind frequently changes in both strength and direction, and so the magnetic heading required to maintain track will also change from time to time. This becomes obvious by gradual movements of the CDI away from its central position, which you will notice in your regular scan of the radio navigation instruments, and correct by changes in magnetic heading. See Figure 14-32.

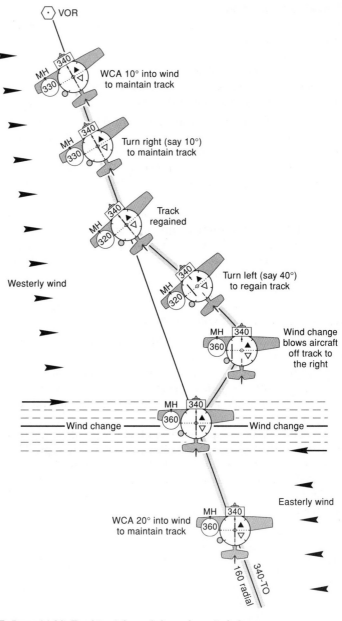

■ Figure 14-32 **Tracking inbound through a wind change**

Tracking From a VOR

To track *from* a VOR (assuming the VOR has not already been selected and identified):

☐ **select** the VOR frequency;

☐ **identify** the station (Morse code ident);

☐ **check** that the red OFF warning flag is not displayed; and

☐ **select the omni bearing** of the desired track with the OBS.

Orientate the aeroplane with respect to the desired track, and then take up a suitable intercept heading using the heading indicator (aligned with the magnetic compass). If the aeroplane is heading approximately in the direction of the desired track, the centre circle will represent the aeroplane, and the CDI the desired track.

To intercept track in this case, turn toward the CDI. This is using the OBI as a **command instrument.** This commands you to turn towards the CDI to regain track. Be aware, however, that this only applies when the heading is roughly in the same direction as the selected omni bearing.

On intercepting track, steer a suitable heading to maintain it, considering the wind direction and strength. If the desired track is maintained, the CDI will remain centred.

EXAMPLE 10 In Figure 14-33, with the desired track 140 set in the OBI, the CDI is out to the right.

Since the aeroplane's initial heading agrees approximately with the track of 140, the pilot concludes that the track is out to the right of the aeroplane (or, in this case, straight ahead and to the right).

The pilot has taken up a heading of 220°M to intercept a track of 140 *from* the VOR, which will give an 80° intercept. This is satisfactory if the aeroplane is well away from the track.

If the aeroplane is close to track, then a 60° or 30° intercept might be more applicable, which, in this case, would be MH 200 or MH 170.

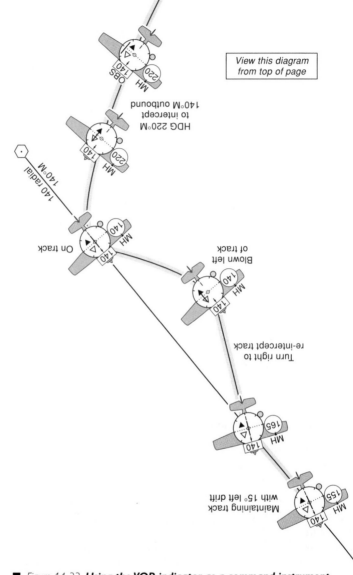

■ Figure 14-33 **Using the VOR indicator as a command instrument**

Use the OBI as a Command Instrument

Use the OBI as a **command instrument** whenever possible. With the desired track set in the OBI, and the aeroplane headed at least roughly in the same direction as the selected track, the omni bearing indicator will act as a command instrument. By flying *towards* the deflected CDI, you can centre it, and thereby regain track. For example:

☐ tracking 060 *to* the VOR, set 060 under the course index;
☐ tracking 030 *from* the VOR, set 030 under the course index.

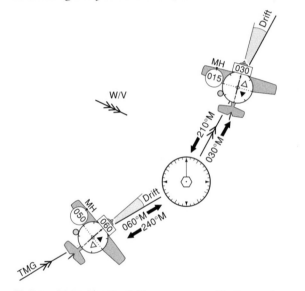

■ *Figure 14-34* **Use the OBI as a command instrument**

A minor complication can arise when the aeroplane is steered on a heading approximating the *reciprocal* of the omni bearing selected on the OBI. It causes the VOR cockpit display to be no longer a command instrument.

EXAMPLE 11 You have been tracking 140 *from* a VOR, with 140 selected in the OBI and by steering MH 140. The aeroplane has drifted left of track, and so the CDI will be deflected to the right of centre. To regain the 140-FROM track, you must turn towards the needle, in this case towards the right, i.e. heading and OBI selection are similar, so it is used as a command instrument.

Now you want to return to the VOR ground station on the reciprocal track, which is 320 *to* the VOR, so turn through approximately 180° onto MH 320 without altering the 140 set under the course index. The omni bearing indicator, because it is not heading sensitive, indicates exactly as it did before the turn, with the CDI as seen by the pilot out to the right of centre.

The VOR indicator is not heading sensitive.

To regain track on this reciprocal heading, turn, not towards the CDI, but away from it. Turning towards the CDI on this reciprocal heading to the selected track would take you further away from the selected track, i.e. it is no longer a command instrument, which is a pity!

This inconvenience can be easily removed, and the OBI returned to being a command instrument, by selecting the new desired track under the course index, 320, which approximates the heading being flown. The immediate effect will be for:

☐ the TO flag to appear, replacing the FROM flag, and

☐ the CDI to swing across to the other side.

The CDI will now be out to the left, and a turn towards it will bring the aeroplane back towards the selected track. The OBI is once again a command instrument, easier to understand, and easier to fly.

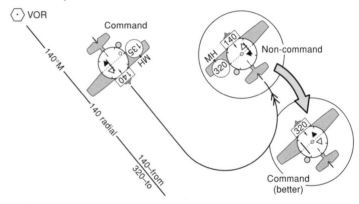

■ Figure 14-35 **For ease of operation, use the OBI as a command instrument**

To keep the OBI as a command instrument when flying on a VOR (so that you can regain track by flying towards the CDI), set the desired track in the direction nearest to the heading to be flown.

A good example of this is the (Goodwood) Chichester VOR 32 instrument approach, which uses a base turn let-down:

☐ outbound on 160-FROM, where the pilot should set 160 with the OBS; and

☐ inbound on 325-TO, where the pilot should set 325 with the OBS.

The 15° between the 2-minute outbound leg and the inbound leg of the descent in still air allows sufficient arc for a rate-1 turn or less to align the aeroplane very nicely for the final descent inbound to the VOR.

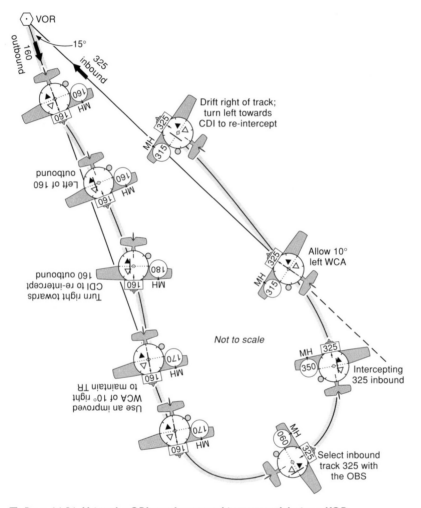

■ *Figure 14-36* **Using the OBI as a 'command instrument' during a VOR base turn**

Slow aircraft carrying out a rate-1 turn will have a smaller turning radius than fast aircraft (for which the approach plates are designed), and so may tend to undershoot the inbound track (unless there is a strong tailwind in the turn). To avoid under-shooting the inbound leg, the aeroplane should be rolled out of the rate-1 base turn onto a suitable heading to allow for a reasonable intercept of the inbound leg (say a 60°, 45° or 30° intercept).

A lot depends on the wind strength and direction on the day. For instance, a strong tailwind during the base turn will cause the aeroplane to intercept the inbound leg more quickly than in nil-wind or headwind conditions.

NOTE The instrument landing system (ILS) uses the same cockpit instrument as the VOR. Whereas you can select any VOR track, there is only one ILS track. This is discussed in detail in Chapter 15, *The Instrument Landing System (ILS)*, but the main points are:

☐ **when flying inbound** on the ILS track (known as the localizer), the cockpit display is a command instrument (fly towards the CDI to centre it and regain track); but

☐ **when flying from overhead** the aerodrome back towards where the ILS procedure commences, i.e. flying outbound on the localizer, course-sensing is reversed and the cockpit indicator is no longer a command instrument.

Intercepting a Track using the VOR

Orientation

You need to know:

☐ Where am I?;

☐ Where do I want to go?; and

☐ How do I get there?

The easiest method of orientating the aircraft using the VOR is to rotate the OBS until the CDI centres. This can occur on one of two headings (reciprocals of each other); choose the one with the omni bearing that most resembles the aircraft's magnetic heading. If the aircraft is heading towards the VOR ground station, then the TO flag will show; if it is heading away from the VOR, then the FROM flag will show.

Select the desired track in °M using the omni bearing selector (OBS). Determine which way to turn to intercept the desired track, and then take up a suitable intercept heading.

Intercepting an Outbound Track

The VOR is just as useful tracking away from a VOR ground station as tracking towards it, and it is much easier to use than the NDB/ADF combination. The next example illustrates the normal method of doing this.

EXAMPLE 12 You are tracking inbound on the 170 radial to a VOR (350-TO). ATC instructs you to take up a heading to intercept the 090 radial outbound (090-FROM).

Orientation is not a problem since you already know where you are (the usual situation). The best way to track inbound on the 170 radial (which is the same as QDR 170, making the inbound QDM 350), is to have 350 set in the OBI course index, since the aeroplane is tracking 350 *to* the VOR. This ensures that the indicator is a command instrument (fly towards the CDI needle to regain the selected track).

Visualise the situation:
- [ ] tracking northwards towards the VOR;
- [ ] the desired track, 090-FROM, lies ahead to the right.

To intercept the 090-FROM track:
- [ ] set 090 under the course index;
- [ ] take up a suitable intercept heading (MH 030 for a 60° intercept); and
- [ ] maintain MH 030 until the CDI moves from full-scale deflection towards the centre. To avoid overshooting the track, anticipate the interception, and 'lead-in' by commencing a turn just prior to intercepting track.

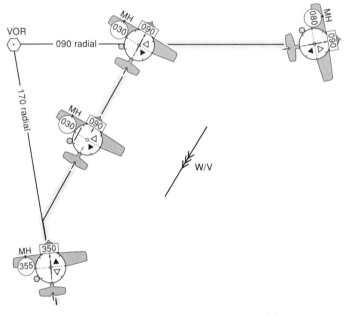

■ *Figure 14-37* **Intercepting a track outbound from a VOR**

Intercepting an Inbound Track

EXAMPLE 13 ATC instructs you to track inbound on the 010 radial to a particular VOR.
Select and identify the VOR; then
- [ ] Orientate yourself with respect to it (perhaps by centring the CDI suitably).
- [ ] Set the desired track under the course index – *inbound* on the 010 radial (QDR) is 190-TO (QDM) – and determine the position of this track.
- [ ] Take up a suitable intercepting heading, and wait for the CDI to centre.

In Figure 14-38:

☐ the CDI centres on 050-FROM (it would also centre on 230-TO);

☐ you have chosen a 90° intercept, steering MH 280 to intercept 190-TO; and

☐ as the CDI starts to move (within 10° of the selected track), lead in to smoothly join track, and allow a wind correction angle of 5°.

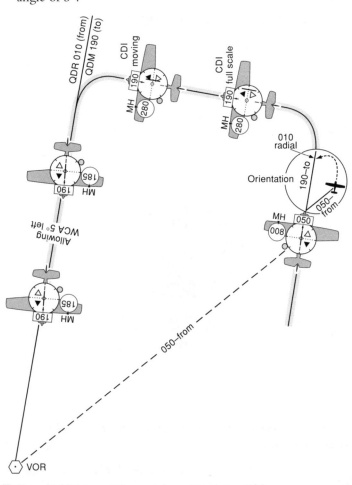

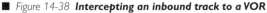

■ Figure 14-38 **Intercepting an inbound track to a VOR**

Other VOR Cockpit Displays

There are various presentations of the VOR cockpit display (as discussed earlier) with which you should be familiar. In some aircraft, it is also possible to use an RMI needle to point to the VOR ground station as if it were an NDB. This can, on occasions, be very useful.

The Radio Magnetic Indicator (RMI)

The radio magnetic indicator (RMI) combines a heading indicator and a relative bearing indicator into one instrument. The RMI compass card is continually aligned with magnetic north, and the RMI needles point at the ground stations to which they are tuned. These ground stations, on many RMIs, may be either an NDB or a VOR, the selection of either ADF or VOR being made with small switches at the base of the RMI.

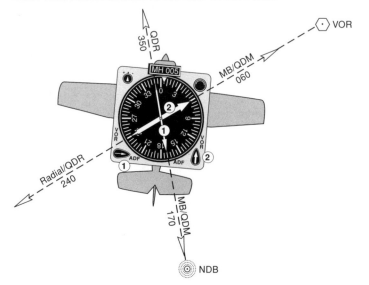

■ *Figure 14-39* **RMI needle 1 indicating the NDB; RMI needle 2**
indicating the VOR

In Figure 14-39, the pilot has selected RMI needle 1 to the ADF, hence:

☐ the head of needle 1 indicates magnetic bearing *to* the NDB (QDM); and

☐ the tail of needle 1 indicates magnetic bearing *from* the NDB (QDR).

RMI needle 2 has been selected to the VOR, hence:

☐ the head of needle 2 indicates magnetic bearing *to* the VOR (QDM);

☐ the tail of needle 2 indicates magnetic bearing *from* the VOR (radial or QDR).

Using the RMI with one needle selected to a VOR allows the VOR to be used as if it were an NDB for orientation and tracking purposes. Refer to Chapter 13.

Orientation

Orientation with one needle on the RMI selected to VOR is easy, and does not involve altering the OBS (omni bearing selector). In Figure 14-40, RMI needle 2 indicates that the QDM (magnetic bearing to the VOR) is 043 (hence the aeroplane is on the 223 radial).

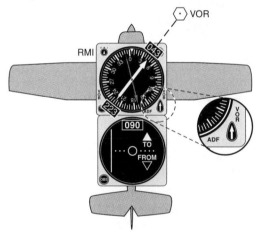

■ *Figure 14-40* **The RMI indicates 043 to the VOR**

Note that there is no need to alter the OBS to determine this, as would be necessary if an RMI were not fitted. Without an RMI, the pilot would have had to alter the OBS until the CDI centred at either 043-ᴛᴏ or 223-ꜰʀᴏᴍ.

Intercepting a Track

If you want to intercept the 090 inbound track to the VOR, then you would (since you have already orientated the aeroplane using the RMI):

☐ set 090 under the course index with the OBS (already done); and

☐ take up a suitable intercept heading.

If uncertain of your orientation, you can use the ADF technique of imagining:

☐ the aeroplane on the tail of the needle in its current situation: and

☐ the aeroplane on the tail of the needle where you want to go (090-TO).

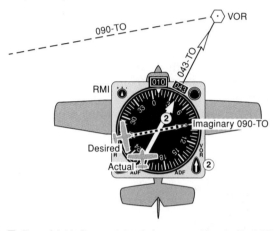

■ *Figure 14-41* **Determining 'where to go' using the RMI**

On MH 010, it would be an 80° intercept. If you wanted a 60° intercept, you would turn onto MH 030. Tracking on MH 030, the RMI needle will gradually fall towards 090. Once the aeroplane is within 10° of the selected track on the OBI, the CDI will start to move.

The Horizontal Situation Indicator (HSI)

The HSI is a remote indicating compass with a VOR indicator superimposed on it. It provides you with an easily understood pictorial display of the aircraft's 'situation' relative to the selected VOR radial. The HSI is one of the most popular navigation instruments ever devised. It shows the magnetic heading and the position of the aeroplane relative to the selected track (course).

A wonderful feature of the HSI over the traditional VOR indicator is that the HSI is always a command instrument. If the aeroplane turns, the remote indicating compass card turns, carrying the VOR display with it, so the HSI will always show the CDI deflection towards the selected track.

In Figures 14-42 and 14-43, the selected track is out to the left. If the aeroplane turns 180°, to MH 190, the HSI will show the selected track 040 out to the right of the aeroplane, as indeed it is. An HSI exhibits no reverse sensing.

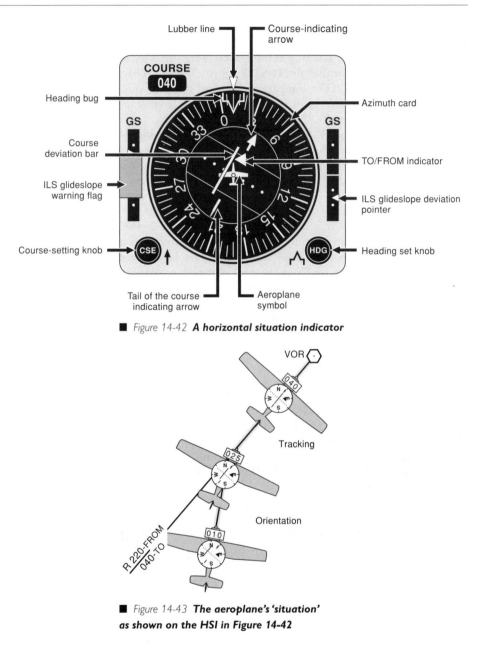

■ Figure 14-42 **A horizontal situation indicator**

■ Figure 14-43 **The aeroplane's 'situation'**
as shown on the HSI in Figure 14-42

VOR Instrument Approaches

The VOR is used as the tracking aid when carrying out a VOR approach such as the **Sumburgh Rwy 27** approach (*Aerad* chart shown in Figure 14-44). The top part of the chart is a plan view for tracking, and the bottom part of the chart is a profile view for vertical navigation (descent).

The pilot tracks to the VOR at or above the sector safe altitude (SSA) (referred to as minimum safe altitude, MSA, on *Jeppesen* charts) and then takes up the outbound track of 096°M (the 096 radial or QDR 096), maintaining it using the VOR. This is most easily achieved by having 096 selected with the OBS. Descent may be carried out to 1,520 ft on QNH *(1,500 ft on QFE)*.

At 6 DME, a left turn may be commenced to intercept 264°M inbound to the VOR, most easily intercepted and maintained if 264 is selected with the OBS. (264°M inbound may be referred to as the 084 radial.) From 5 DME, descent may be commenced to the calculated **minimum descent altitude** on QNH, or **minimum descent height** on QFE – often abbreviated as MDA(H).

Calculation of your particular MDA(H) is covered in detail in Chapter 22 but, for any VOR let-down carried out by an IMC-rated pilot, it will not be less than an absolute minimum of 600 ft aal, and could be considerably higher if there are obstacles in the approach area.

If you become visual at or above MDA(H), then further descent for a landing is permissible. If you do not become visual, then you may continue tracking to the missed approach point (MAPt) not below the MDA(H) in the hope of becoming visual. At the MAPt a missed approach should be commenced (at the VOR, without DME; or at 1.5 DME, with DME) – climb straight ahead on track 264°M to 2,000 ft on QNH, then turn left to return to the VOR.

Now complete **Exercises 14 – The VOR.**

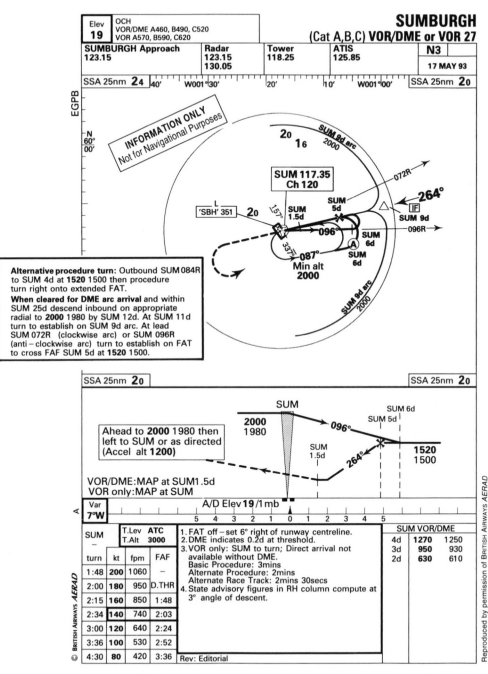

■ Figure 14-44 **The VOR/DME approach for Sumburgh Runway 27**
(Aerad chart)

The Instrument Landing System (ILS)

The instrument landing system is known as the ILS (pronounced *"eye-ell-ess"*). It enables a suitably equipped aeroplane to make a **precision approach** to a particular runway. A precision approach is one in which slope guidance, as well as tracking guidance, is given. Each ILS is known by the runway it serves – for example, the *Liverpool ILS Rwy 27*.

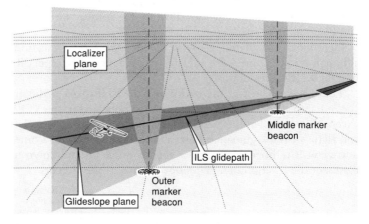

■ *Figure 15-1* ***The instrument landing system***

The instrument landing system has three main elements:

1. **The localizer** (LLZ), which provides tracking guidance along the extended centreline of the runway (guidance in *azimuth* left or right of the extended centreline).

2. **The glideslope,** which provides vertical guidance towards the runway touchdown point, usually at a slope of approximately 3° to the horizontal, or 1:20 (vertical guidance above or below the glideslope).

3. **Marker beacons,** which provide accurate range fixes along the approach (usually an outer marker and a middle marker).

On some ILS approaches, locator beacons may be substituted for the marker beacon(s) and, on others, a DME distance may be substituted for the outer marker. These can be used in place of marker beacons to provide the pilot with an accurate fix along the approach.

The ideal flightpath on an ILS approach, where the localizer plane and the glideslope plane intersect, is referred to as the **glidepath.** The word *glide* is really a misnomer carried over from earlier days, since modern aircraft make powered approaches down the glidepath, rather than glide approaches. However, the term is still used.

Since ILS approaches will often be made in conditions of poor visibility or at night, there is always associated visual information that can be used once the pilot becomes 'visual'. This may include approach lights leading towards the runway, runway lights, touch-down lights, and centreline lights.

There may also be a **VASIS** (visual approach slope indicator system) to provide slope guidance during the visual stage of the approach. This, and other visual information, will assist the pilot to maintain a stable descent path down to the runway surface and complete the flare and landing.

Lighting is considered in detail in the *Night Flying* section, although it is, of course, also valuable in daylight hours, especially in poor weather conditions.

The ILS is selected in the cockpit on the VHF-NAV radio. Its cockpit display is usually the same instrument as for the VOR except that, as well as the 'vertical' localizer needle that moves left and right for track guidance, there is a second needle that comes into view. It is 'horizontal', and is able to move up and down to represent the position of a glideslope relative to the aircraft.

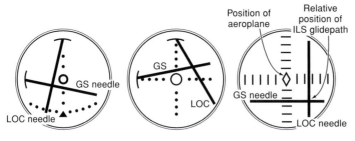

■ *Figure 15-2* **The ILS cockpit display**

The Localizer

The localizer provides directional guidance along the extended centreline of the landing runway. Its transmitting aerial, which may be 20 metres wide and 3 metres high, is positioned at the far end of the runway (the stopping end), and typically 300 metres beyond the end so as not to be an obstacle to aeroplanes taking off.

The localizer transmits on a frequency in the VHF band between 108.10 and 111.95 MHz. The specific frequency is published on charts.

■ Figure 15-3 **Localizer transmitting aerials**

Localizer Ground Equipment

The localizer aerial at the far end of the runway transmits two overlapping lobes of radio energy on the localizer's carrier frequency (e.g. 110.10 MHz at Birmingham). The lobe on the left hand side of the approach path is modulated at 90 Hz (traditionally known as the *yellow* sector), and the lobe on the right hand side of the approach path is modulated at 150 Hz (the *blue* sector). The two lobes overlap to provide a path 5° wide in line with the extended centreline of the runway, 2.5° either side of the extended centreline.

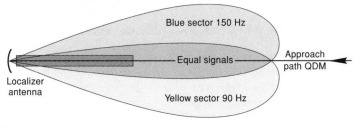

■ Figure 15-4 **The localizer's radiation pattern**

The main function of the localizer is to provide guidance in azimuth to an aeroplane on final approach to a particular runway. The signal transmitted out along the approach path is sometimes called the localizer **front beam.** It is calibrated (and flight-checked) out to 10 nm from the runway threshold (as is the glideslope), and protected from interference from other stations out to 25 nm. Usable localizer signals may be received out to 25 nm within +10° of the localizer front-course line, and out to 17 nm when in the area 10° to 35° either side of the front-course line.

A few localizers also transmit a **back beam.** This can be used for tracking – for instance when continuing overhead the runway and straight ahead following a missed approach. In the UK, the back beam is usually suppressed.

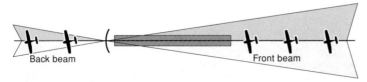

■ *Figure 15-5* **A localizer with both a front beam and a back beam**

The back beam of a localizer does not have an associated glide-slope for an approach in the opposite direction (although false glideslope signals might exist), nor is it maintained to the same accuracy as the front beam. Do not confuse the back beam of a localizer with an ILS for the reciprocal runway, which will be a totally different installation with its own transmitting aerials.

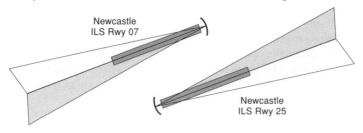

■ *Figure 15-6* **Two different ILSs serving opposite runways**

Localizer Aircraft Equipment

The localizer transmits on a frequency in the VHF band between 108.10 and 111.95 MHz. The specific frequency is published on the relevant instrument approach chart. You can select this frequency on the VHF-NAV radio, and must identify the localizer by its Morse code **ident** before using it. It will begin with the letter 'l' (*dit-dit*) and will usually, but not always, consist of a three-letter group.

Always positively identify a localizer before using it for navigation.

Identifying the localizer serves to identify the ILS (including the glideslope). The Birmingham Runway 33 ILS, for instance, has an ident of 'IBM' (*dit-dit dah-dit-dit-dit dah-dah*). The ILS in the opposite direction, on Runway 15, has an ident 'IBIR' (*dit-dit dah-dit-dit-dit dit-dit dit-dah-dit*). Correct identification is essential before an ILS (or any radio aid for that matter) is used.

For the localizer to be usable, it must be identified, and there should be no red OFF flag covering the vertical needle. If the OFF flag is visible, then the signal being received at the aeroplane is not sufficiently strong, and so the CDI (course deviation indicator) indications will be unreliable.

The aeroplane's VHF–NAV receiver, when tuned to a localizer frequency, compares the strengths of the two signals (150 Hz and 90 Hz) it receives, and produces a voltage that energises the localizer needle in the cockpit. If the 150 Hz signal is stronger (which will occur if the aeroplane on approach is out to the right), then a voltage is fed to the localizer needle that moves it to the left. This indicates that the localizer centreline is to the left of the aeroplane on approach. On some instruments, the needle will point to a blue marking, as a further indication that the aeroplane is to the right of centreline and in the blue sector.

If the signals are of equal strength, the localizer needle will be centred, providing an *on track* indication. If the 90 Hz signal predominates, then the voltage fed to the localizer needle moves it to the right, indicating that the aeroplane is in the yellow sector and, on approach, will need to move to the right to get back on centreline.

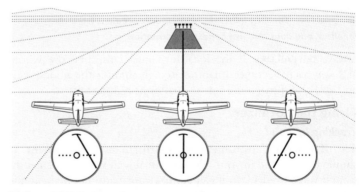

■ *Figure 15-7* **An aeroplane on approach**

Full-scale deflection will occur when the aeroplane is displaced 2.5° or more from the centreline. This means that the VHF–NAV display (with its five dots either side of centre) is four times more sensitive when it is tuned to a localizer (0.5° per dot), compared to when it is tuned to a VOR (2° per dot, to provide an indication

10° either side of the selectedVOR radial). Usable localizer signals may be obtained up to ±35° from course centreline (giving full-scale deflection beyond ±2.5°). Outside this signal area, the OFF flag will come into view.

The localizer course is a *single* fixed beam, unlike the VOR which gives the pilot a choice of 360 radials using the omni bearing selector (OBS). With an ILS or localizer selected on the VHF-NAV, however, the OBS has absolutely no significance, and changing it will have no effect on the indications of the CDI needle. It is good operating procedure, however, to dial in the inbound track of the localizer (using the OBS) simply as a reminder.

The localizer cockpit indicator does not give any heading information, but only *position* information. It displays how many degrees the aeroplane is displaced from the localizer track, and in which sector (blue or yellow).

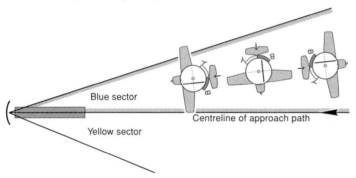

■ *Figure 15-8* **The CDI indicates angular displacement from the localizer, and does not give heading information**

LOCALIZER FAILURE. If the localizer signal fails, then the whole ILS approach becomes unauthorised (including the glideslope), and an ILS approach in such a situation is not permitted.

Flying the Localizer

Tracking Inbound

The ILS cockpit instrument is a **performance instrument.** It should be included in your selective radial scan when information from it is required. Having gained that information (which, in this case, is the position and/or movement of the localizer needle), your eyes should return to the attitude indicator. Any corrections to heading to regain or maintain the localizer track can then be made with a small coordinated turn on the AI. The heading indicator can be checked for heading, and the ILS cockpit indica-tor can be checked again for position and/or movement of the localizer needle.

Apply a wind correction angle that will keep the airplane on centreline.

The aim is to fly a heading that will maintain the aeroplane on centreline. If a crosswind exists, a wind correction angle will be required, and the aeroplane heading will differ slightly from the published inbound track of the localizer. The wind will probably back and weaken in strength as the aeroplane descends, and there will be gusts and lulls, so continual adjustments to heading can be expected. The localizer beam narrows as the runway is approached, a bit like a 'funnel', so the corrections should become smaller and smaller (hopefully). This is the same bracketing technique used for tracking on the NDB or VOR, except that the localizer is far more sensitive (four times as sensitive as the VOR).

Inbound to a localizer, the CDI is a command instrument – fly towards the needle.

For an aeroplane on approach, the localizer needle indicates which way the aeroplane should move to regain the centreline. If the localizer needle is to the right, then the aeroplane should be moved right. On approach, the CDI acts as a **command instrument;** to regain centreline, fly towards the needle.

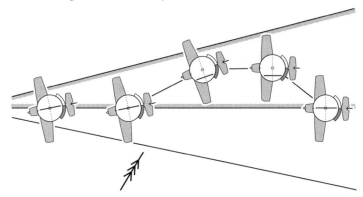

■ Figure 15-9 **Typical heading corrections for a deviation right of centreline**

It is usual to make many heading corrections on the one approach to regain and maintain the localizer centreline. This is to be expected, since the wind effect almost certainly will vary along the approach. Because the CDI needle displays *angular* displacement from the centreline, it will become more and more sensitive as the runway is approached, and so the heading corrections should become finer and finer. Aim to capture the localizer early on the approach, so that small deviations are corrected before they have a chance to become large deviations.

NOTE A typical heading bug on a heading indicator has an angular width of about 12°, 6° either side of centre. If such a heading bug is used as a heading datum on the HI, then most heading changes to maintain the localizer can be contained within its angular width.

The localizer is usable out to about 25 nm from the runway; however, it is not usually intercepted until within approximately 10 nm of the aerodrome at 3,000 ft aal or less.

Tracking Outbound

When tracking outbound on a localizer, which may occur when positioning the aeroplane for an ILS, the CDI needle will still indicate which sector the aeroplane is in (blue or yellow), and will display the angular displacement from centreline as if the aeroplane were on approach. This means that, when flying outbound, to regain centreline the aeroplane must be turned away from the CDI needle. In other words, it acts as a non-command instrument when the aeroplane is flying outbound.

> When tracking outbound from a localizer, the CDI is a non-command instrument.

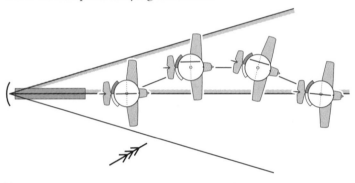

■ Figure 15-10 **Tracking outbound on a localizer**

Additional tracking guidance is always useful (especially when tracking outbound on a localizer using a non-command instrument), and in many ILSs this additional guidance can be obtained from a locator NDB.

NOTE Some advanced instruments combine a compass card with the CDI to form a horizontal situation indicator (HSI), which simplifies tracking outbound on the localizer. The HSI is described briefly on page 280.

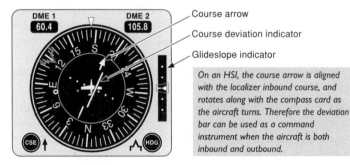

> On an HSI, the course arrow is aligned with the localizer inbound course, and rotates along with the compass card as the aircraft turns. Therefore the deviation bar can be used as a command instrument when the aircraft is both inbound and outbound.

■ Figure 15-11 **Horizontal situation indicator (HSI)**

The Glideslope

The most suitable approach to a runway for large modern aircraft is a glideslope of approximately 3° to the horizontal (a gradient of 1 in 20, or 5%) which intersects the runway approximately 300 metres in from the threshold. The 3° slope provides a loss of approximately 300 ft in height for every 1 nm travelled, which gives a reasonable rate of descent for most aeroplanes at typical approach speeds – 600 ft/min at 120 kt groundspeed, for instance, and 450 ft/min at 90 kt groundspeed. With a slope of 300 ft per nautical mile, you can expect the glideslope to be:

- 3,000 ft aal at approximately 10 nm to touchdown;
- 2,100 ft aal at approximately 7 nm; and
- 1,500 ft aal at approximately 5 nm.

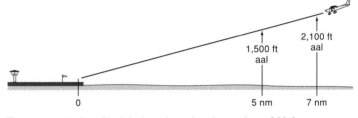

■ *Figure 15-12* **The 3° glideslope loses height at about 300 ft per nautical mile**

The approximate height on slope can be checked by multiplying the distance from the runway in nautical miles by 300. For example, at 3 DME the aeroplane should be at 900 ft QFE.

Glideslope Ground Equipment

The glideslope transmitting aerial is usually situated about 300 metres in from the runway threshold to ensure that any aeroplane flying the glideslope will have adequate wheel clearance over the threshold and any objects and/or terrain on approach. The threshold crossing height (TCH) of the glideslope is published on the ILS chart. The main wheels on some larger aircraft follow a much lower flightpath than the glideslope receiving antenna, which could be located near the nose of the aeroplane or somewhere else significantly higher than the wheels.

The aim when flying a glideslope is not to touch down on the 'piano keys', but to touch down in the **touchdown zone** near where the glideslope intersects the runway. On some runways, the glideslope transmitting aerial may be further in than 300 metres if there are high and restricting obstacles on the approach path.

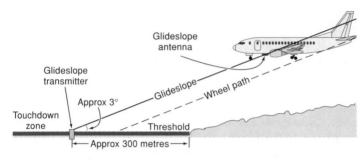

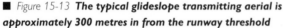

■ *Figure 15-13* **The typical glideslope transmitting aerial is approximately 300 metres in from the runway threshold**

As well as being some 300 metres in from the threshold, the **glideslope transmitting aerial** is usually situated some 100 to 200 metres to the side of the runway to avoid being an obstacle to aircraft operating on the runway, and to reduce interference with the glideslope signal to these aircraft. The glideslope is transmitted on an ultra-high frequency (UHF) carrier wave using a similar principle to the localizer transmission (that of two overlapping lobes), but the transmission pattern is slightly more complex.

A large 90 Hz lobe overlaps a 150 Hz lobe in the vertical plane. The actual glideslope, formed where the two signals are equal, is typically at 3° to the horizontal, but some glideslopes may be shallower, at 2.5°, and others may be steeper at 3.5°. It may not seem much of an approach angle, but a 4° approach angle is extremely steep, very noticeable in the cockpit and possibly difficult to maintain in some jet transports.

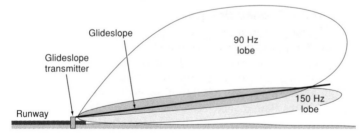

■ *Figure 15-14* **The glideslope**

The area of overlap of the two signals is about 1.4°, i.e. the useful signals extend 0.7° above and below the precise glideslope. The glidepath is calibrated out to 10 nm, although signals can be received at greater distances. The approximate 3° glideslope is protected in the range 1.35° to 5.25° above the horizontal, and is accurate within ±8° of the localizer centreline.

Unfortunately, due to ground reflection of some of the transmissions, there may be more than one overlapping of the lobes, giving rise to one or more **false glideslopes** at different angles to the horizontal, and well above the true glideslope. The false glideslopes may occur at multiples of the true glideslope angle (typically 3°), i.e. at 6°, 9°, 12° and 15°. You should be aware that one or more false glideslopes may exist, and not be surprised when a false on-slope indication is given in the cockpit, for instance above 12,000 ft aal when only 10 nm from the aerodrome, or when manoeuvring around the aerodrome to intercept the ILS.

The glideslope needle in the cockpit may oscillate as the aeroplane meets one of the false glideslopes, or it may exhibit other abnormal indications such as reverse sensing, but it will be fairly obvious that the signal is a false one. If the localizer transmits a back beam, then there will probably be false glideslope signals in that area, which can cause the glideslope OFF flag to flicker in and out of view. Be prepared to recognise a false glideslope signal for what it is, and then disregard it.

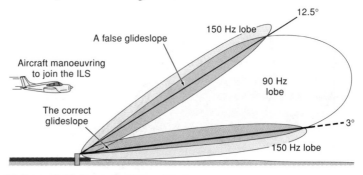

■ *Figure 15-15* **Beware of false glideslopes**

*False glideslopes will not occur **below** the true glideslope, so intercept the glideslope from below.*

The problem of false glideslopes is easily solved if the pilot has in mind the height/distance relationship of the real glideslope (300 ft/min). Also, and most importantly, there will be no false glideslope below the true glideslope – any false glideslopes will be above it, and will be at approximately 6° (or more) to the horizontal. For this reason it is recommended to intercept the glideslope from below. For instance, it may be preferable to fly in from 10 nm at 2,500 ft aal to intercept the glideslope at about 7 nm to run, than to carry out a very steep descent from above the glideslope in an attempt to intercept it.

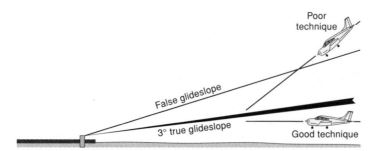

■ *Figure 15-16* **Ideally, intercept the glideslope from below**

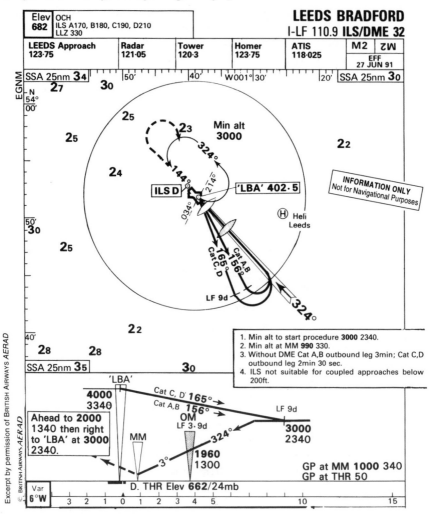

■ *Figure 15-17* **Plan and profile of the Leeds Bradford ILS/DME Rwy 32**

The electronic glideslope of the ILS is accurate from approximately 10 nm, but descent on the glideslope should not be commenced until the aeroplane has first intercepted the localizer. In the **Leeds Bradford ILS/DME Rwy 32**, the published procedure starts overhead the runway at 4,000 ft amsl on QNH *(3,340 ft aal on QFE)* and proceeds outbound on 156°M (or 165°M for the faster aeroplanes with the larger turning radii) on descent to 3,000 ft amsl *(2,340 ft aal)* at 9.0 DME LF (the identifier for the Runway 32 DME, selected automatically with the Runway 32 ILS, and which is the zero point for the approach – the runway threshold).

During the turn inbound, the published path is beneath the glideslope, and so the localizer inbound track of 324° can be intercepted before descent on the glideslope is commenced, when it is intercepted from below after 9.0 DME inbound.

Aircraft Glideslope Equipment

The position of the glideslope relative to the aircraft is indicated by the 'horizontal' needle of the VHF-NAV cockpit display. To be certain that the glideslope signal is usable, the red OFF flag should be biased out of view. The vertical glideslope scale on the usual cockpit indicator consists of 5 dots above and below the central position, although the first dots *up* and *down* may be part of a centre circle.

■ Figure 15-18 **Different glideslope cockpit displays**

A particular glideslope transmission frequency is always *paired* with the same localizer frequency, so that the associated glideslope is automatically selected when the pilot selects the localizer on the VHF-NAV. For instance, a frequency of 329.300 MHz in the ultra-high frequency band for the glideslope is always paired with a localizer frequency of 108.900 MHz. So by selecting the Edinburgh Rwy 25 localizer frequency, which is published on charts as 108.900 MHz, you are automatically selecting its paired glideslope frequency without even knowing what it is.

The glideslope receiver in the aircraft compares the relative strength of the two signals, producing a voltage that positions the glideslope needle. If the 90 Hz signal is stronger because the aeroplane is above the glideslope, then the glideslope needle moves down. This indicates that the aeroplane must *fly down* to recapture the glideslope. It is the aircraft which moves to the glideslope (and not vice versa).

Conversely, if the aircraft is below the glideslope, the needle will move up – known as a *fly up* indication. This does not mean that the aircraft must actually climb to recapture the glideslope. Flying level, or even just reducing the rate of descent, as the aircraft flies towards the runway may be sufficient.

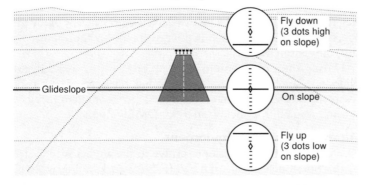

■ *Figure 15-19* **The glideslope needle indicates where the glideslope is with respect to the aircraft**

A full-scale *fly up* indication means that the aircraft is at 0.7° or more below the glideslope. Deviation from the glideslope is referred to in terms of 'dots' rather than degrees, there being 5 dots up and 5 dots down on the instrument.

Keep the aircraft right on glideslope (to the best of your ability), and do not exceed more than one-half full-scale *fly up* deviation below slope, to retain adequate obstacle clearance towards the end of the approach. This would put the aeroplane 0.3° or 0.4° below slope, which is significant since the slope is only 3° thick. As a general rule, make a strong effort to stay right on glideslope throughout the approach.

Do not go below the glideslope by more than half the full-scale fly up deflection.

Conversely, a full-scale *fly down* indication means that the aircraft is 0.7° or more above the slope. Full-scale deflections once the ILS approach has been commenced are not acceptable, since the deviation from slope is at least 0.7°, but it could be anything! There is no indication on the cockpit display of just how far the aircraft is above or below slope when the glideslope needle is fully deflected.

The 1.4° overlap (0.7° above and below the perfect slope) is equivalent to about 140 ft in 1 nm (using the familiar 1:60 rule and the approximation that 1 nm = 6,000 ft), which means that the vertical thickness of the overlapping glideslope beam is:

☐ 1,400 ft at 10 nm (from full-scale *up* to full-scale *down*);
☐ 700 ft at 5 nm;

☐ 420 ft at 3 nm;

☐ 280 ft at 2 nm;

☐ 140 ft at 1 nm; and

☐ a few feet thick at the runway threshold.

The glideslope signal is only approved for navigational use down to the lowest authorised decision height (DH) for that particular ILS, and any reference to glideslope indications below that height must be supplemented by visual reference to the runway environment.

A Category 1 ILS is approved down to DH 200 ft, a Category 2 ILS is approved down to DH 100 ft, a Category 3 ILS is approved down to DH 0 ft – all of which are well below the decision heights allowed for an IMC-rated pilot carrying out an ILS approach (an absolute minimum of 500 ft aal, or higher).

GLIDESLOPE FAILURE. If the glideslope fails, but not the localizer, then the pilot is still permitted to carry out a (non-precision) localizer approach, using the localizer for guidance in azimuth, and using range markers (such as the marker beacons, DME distances or a locator) for descent to suitable heights which will be marked on the profile part of the approach chart.

Referring back to the **Leeds Bradford ILS/DME Rwy 32** profile (page 296) a localizer checkpoint can be seen when crossing the outer marker (OM), 3.9 DME, at 1,960 ft amsl *(1,300 ft aal)*. Because of the lack of glideslope guidance, the decision height (DH) for an IMC-rated pilot on a localizer approach will be 600 ft aal or higher (compared to the DH for the full ILS approach of 500 ft aal or higher).

Flying the Glideslope

Flying the glideslope is very similar to flying straight and level, except, of course, that the aim is to keep the aeroplane on a *constant descent plane,* rather than on a level plane at constant altitude. In level flight, the altimeter is checked regularly to ensure height is being maintained; during an ILS, the glideslope needle is checked regularly to ensure that the desired slope is being maintained.

The ILS cockpit instrument is a performance instrument. It should be included in the selective radial scan when information from it is desired. Having gained that information (which, in this case, is the position and/or movement of the glideslope needle), the eyes should return to the attitude indicator. Any corrections to regain or maintain the glideslope can then be made with a small pitch attitude change on the AI. The ILS cockpit indicator can be checked again for position and/or movement of the glideslope needle.

A process similar to bracketing track is used to regain and then maintain the glideslope, except that in this case it is pitch attitude that is altered slightly, rather than heading.

If, for instance, the aeroplane goes below slope while a particular pitch attitude is held, then it should be raised slightly and held until the glideslope is regained. Once back on slope, the pitch attitude can be lowered slightly (but not quite as low as before) so that the glideslope is maintained.

There is also a target airspeed to be achieved on an ILS approach and, as in level flight, it can be controlled with power. With pitch attitude changes to regain and maintain glideslope, small airspeed changes will occur. Fluctuations of ±5 kt are normally acceptable, but any trend beyond this should be corrected by a power alteration (typically 1 inch of manifold pressure or 100 rpm is sufficient, although greater power changes may be required in strong and gusty wind conditions or in windshear).

Maintaining glideslope and airspeed is one sign of a good instrument pilot. Flightpath and airspeed (in other words the *performance* of the aeroplane) are controlled by attitude and power on an ILS approach. If you have a good scan and quick response, then small deviations from the glideslope will be corrected immediately, and not develop into large deviations which might require a power adjustment as well.

Flying the glideslope involves energy transfer. If the aeroplane is slightly below slope and slightly fast, then the excess speed can be converted to height (or to a reduced rate of descent) by raising the pitch attitude on the AI, and flying up to regain slope. Conversely, if the aeroplane is above slope, the pitch attitude on the AI can be lowered slightly, and the aeroplane flown down to regain slope, possibly with a small speed increase.

Hold the glideslope with pitch attitude on the AI.

Hold the desired airspeed with power.

Since it displays angular displacement, the glideslope needle will become more accurate and more sensitive as the aeroplane flies closer to the runway. Therefore, corrections on the attitude indicator to hold glideslope should become finer and finer as the runway is approached.

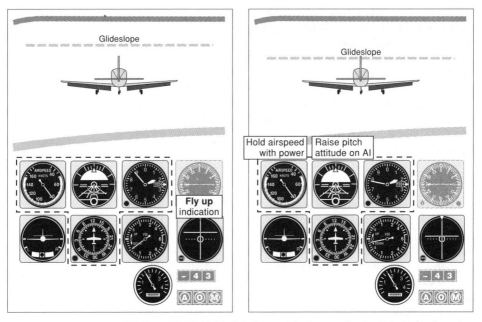

■ *Figure 15-20* **Hold glideslope with elevator (attitude indicator), and airspeed with throttle**

Marker Beacons

ILS marker beacons transmit a vertical elliptical pattern, often described as 'fan-shaped', which can be received by an aircraft as it passes overhead. Because the radio energy is transmitted upwards, it is not possible to track to a marker beacon (unlike an NDB or locator, whose energy is transmitted in all directions).

A typical ILS has two markers along the localizer to provide *range* check points. They are:

☐ **the outer marker** (OM) at approximately 5 nm; and
☐ **the middle marker** (MM) at 3,500 ft (0.6 nm).

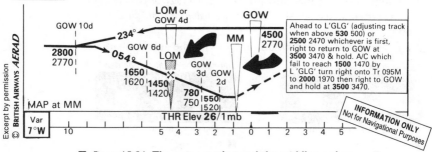

■ *Figure 15-21* **The outer marker and the middle marker**

Both markers operate on the same VHF frequency of 75 MHz, but each is amplitude-modulated differently to provide aural Morse code identification.

The aircraft glideslope equipment consists of a marker receiver which indicates passage over a marker by a light flashing in the cockpit and an aural Morse code ident. The ident can be heard through the headset or cockpit speaker, and the light (one of three colour-coded lights on the instrument panel) can be seen flashing. The pilot does not have to make any specific selection to receive the marker beacons.

Outer Marker

The outer marker (OM) is located between 3 and 7 nm from the runway threshold, usually at about 4 or 5 nm. The aeroplane, if it is on glideslope, should therefore be at approximately 1,200–1,500 ft aal as it passes overhead the OM. The precise height crossing the OM (both amsl and aal) is specified on the profile diagram of the particular ILS, and the pilot should check this on the altimeter as the aircraft passes over the OM. The cockpit indications of passage over the outer marker are:

☐ an aural series of low-pitched (400 Hz) dashes transmitted at two per second (*-dah-dah-dah-dah-dah-dah-*); and

☐ a flashing blue light synchronised with the aural 'dah-dahs'.

Middle Marker

The middle marker (MM) is located approximately 3,500 ft (0.6 nm) from the runway threshold, where the glideslope is approximately 200 ft aal. This is near the decision height and missed approach point for fully instrument-rated pilots, but much lower than the more conservative decision height required for IMC-rated pilots (which is 500 ft aal or higher). The middle marker crossing height may or may not be specified on the charts, since at this stage in the approach the pilot should be visual.

The cockpit indications of passage over the middle marker are:

☐ an aural series of medium-pitched (1.3 kHz) dots and dashes transmitted at six per second (*-dah-dit-dah-dit-dah-dit-dah-dit-*); and

☐ a flashing amber light synchronised with the aural 'dah-dits'.

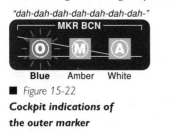

"dah-dah-dah-dah-dah-dah-dah-"

Blue Amber White

■ *Figure 15-22*

Cockpit indications of
the outer marker

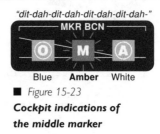

"dit-dah-dit-dah-dit-dah-dit-dah-"

Blue **Amber** White

■ *Figure 15-23*

Cockpit indications of
the middle marker

The signals will increase in strength fairly quickly as the aeroplane nears the marker beacon, be very strong for a number of seconds, and then fade away as the aircraft moves further along the approach. Some aircraft receivers have a HIGH/LOW sensitivity switch – LOW sensitivity giving a much narrower vertical pattern. For instrument approaches, the sensitivity switch is set to HIGH. Because the aircraft will be at a low level during the instrument approach, the marker beacon signal will only be heard and seen for a few seconds.

A typical ILS with two marker beacons on the localizer track is **Belfast Aldergrove Rwy 17 ILS.**

The published glideslope (GS) crossing height at the OM is 1,870 ft amsl on QNH *(1,660 ft aal on QFE).* This is what the altimeter will read in ISA conditions if exactly on slope. In air significantly colder than ISA, however, the altimeter will read slightly higher due to density error. Conversely, in air significantly warmer than ISA, the altimeter will read slightly lower than the published figure.

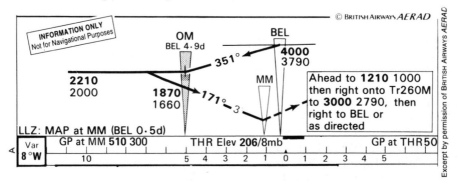

■ *Figure 15-24* ***Belfast Aldergrove ILS Runway 17 profile***

On this ILS profile chart at Belfast Aldergrove:

☐ **The inbound track** of the localizer is 171°M.

☐ **GS crossing height** at the OM is 1,870 ft *(1,660 ft)* with 5 nm to run.

☐ **MM** is (4.9 – 0.5) = 4.4 nm beyond the OM, at 0.8 nm from the zero point (the runway threshold).

☐ **GS crossing height** at MM is 510 ft *(300 ft).*

☐ **ILS glideslope threshold crossing height** (TCH) is 50 ft.

☐ **Runway 17 threshold elevation** is 206 ft amsl (the 8 mb referring to the pressure difference between QNH and QFE).

☐ **The BEL VOR,** which is located on the airport, can be selected to provide useful DME information.

☐ **Airport elevation** for Belfast Aldergrove, 267 ft amsl (the highest point on any of the runways), appears at the top of the *Aerad* chart for the approach (not shown in excerpt above).

Inner Markers

A few ILSs have inner markers situated very close to the threshold, indicated by high-pitched (3 kHz) dots at six per second (*-dit-dit-dit-dit-dit-dit-*), and a synchronised flashing white light. These have little significance to IMC-rated pilots.

Airways Fan Markers and Z markers

Airways fan markers along airways and Z markers over LF radio range sites are no longer used in the UK, although they may be encountered elsewhere. They have a high-pitched (3 kHz) ident and cause a white marker light (labelled A or FM/Z) to flash.

NOTE A locator beacon (NDB) is often co-located with the ILS outer marker and labelled 'LOM' – **locator outer marker.** The advantage of the locator is that it can be used for tracking purposes when positioning the aircraft to commence an ILS, or it can be used for holding.

Other Means of Checking Glideslope

Not all ILS installations have an outer marker and/or middle marker. **Blackpool ILS DME Rwy 28,** for instance, does not have an outer marker. The glideslope, however, can be checked at different DME distances:

☐ 2,000 ft on QNH *(or 1,970 ft on QFE)* at 6.0 DME;

☐ 1,680 ft *(1,650 ft)* at 5.0 DME;

☐ 1,360 ft *(1,330 ft)* at 4.0 DME; as well as

☐ 370 ft *(340 ft)* at the middle marker – although, by this stage in the approach, the IMC-rated pilot will have already reached his decision height and either continued the approach visually or made a missed approach.

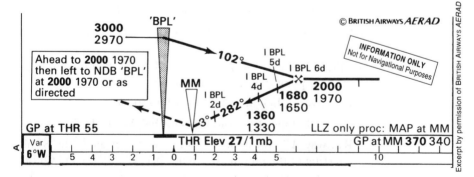

■ *Figure 15-25* **Blackpool ILS DME Rwy 28**

A DME that is *frequency-paired* with an ILS will be automatically selected on many VHF-NAV receivers when the ILS frequency is selected. The DME is arranged to give a zero-range indication at the threshold of the ILS runway. Precise range will only be indicated by the DME when the aeroplane is in line with the runway on the approach path.

Flying a Typical ILS

Check the relevant instrument approach chart for currency, and study it in detail well before commencing the approach. Even though the chart can be referred to during the actual approach, it is helpful to build up an overall view of where the aeroplane is and what path it will follow. As an example, the published **Manchester ILS Rwy 06** chart (in plan and profile) follows (Figure 15-28), accompanied by an illustration of how the approach will be flown (Figure 15-29).

DECISION HEIGHT. Calculate the appropriate **decision height** to be used. In this case the decision height is the greater of:

☐ published DH 200, + 50 altimeter correction, + 200 IMC-rating allowance = 450 ft QFE; or

☐ the IMC-rating absolute minimum for any ILS, which is 500 ft QFE.

So, our decision height is 500 ft QFE (or, since the threshold elevation is 211 ft, 711 ft QNH).

MISSED APPROACH PROCEDURE. Review the missed approach procedure, and plan alternative action if there is any doubt that a successful landing can be made. Low cloud fluctuating about the decision height, poor visibility, heavy rain, or anything else that might prejudice your arrival, should lead you to consider suitable alternate aerodromes.

There is always a remote possibility that an essential ground aid required for the landing will become unserviceable. Possible causes are lightning strikes or flooding during a storm.

FUEL. Consider the fuel situation, and calculate the minimum fuel on board required for diversion. Allow for reserves. Is there fuel enough for more than one approach before diverting? How much fuel is available for holding? Is the weather at the alternate still suitable for a visual approach, etc?

PREPARATION FOR THE APPROACH. Prepare for the approach well before reaching the aerodrome, so that, once there, you can devote your complete attention to flying the approach.

Track to the aerodrome following the normal route, using the normal en route tracking aids, not descending below the relevant sector safe altitude (SSA) or minimum sector altitude (MSA)

published on the charts. All radio aids must be Morse code identified before use. ATC may assist with radar vectors, which can
save distance and time, and will provide adequate obstacle clearance. Read back all clearances, headings, altitudes and pressure
settings passed by ATC.

HOLDING PATTERNS. If you have to enter a holding pattern, plan
to use the correct entry procedure based on the aircraft's heading
when it reaches the holding fix. Vertical separation between
different aircraft in the same holding pattern should be 1,000 ft or
greater.

Stacking aircraft in holding patterns until a 'slot' in the ILS
becomes available is common during busy periods at major
airports. As each aircraft leaves the bottom of the stack and
proceeds into the ILS, the others in the stack can be cleared down
one at a time.

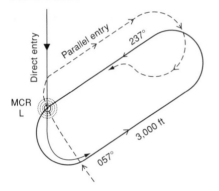

■ Figure 15-26 **Holding pattern entry**

DME ARCS. Some instrument
approach procedures show a
DME arc, which may be flown
to position the aircraft for the
approach. One advantage of
this procedure is that there will
usually be less manoeuvring
involved to reach the final
approach fix, which often saves
time and is more comfortable
for passengers.

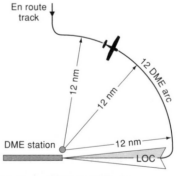

■ Figure 15-27 **A DME arc**

Manchester Runway 06 ILS
In Figure 15-29, the aeroplane has flown en route to the VOR at
the aerodrome, and then turned to track out to the locator outer
marker, where it will commence the ILS procedure.

<table>
<tr><td style="width:30%">*Thorough preparation will reduce your workload during the approach.*</td><td>Integrate the normal operational requirements into the approach so that the whole thing flows smoothly, without undue haste or panic. In addition to flying the ILS, you still need to attend to radio calls, pre-landing checks, configuration and airspeed changes – the sorts of things that occur on all approaches. Thorough early preparation for the approach will reduce the workload later on, and you should be able to sit back (more or less) and calmly follow the procedure, attending briefly to other duties as required.</td></tr>
</table>

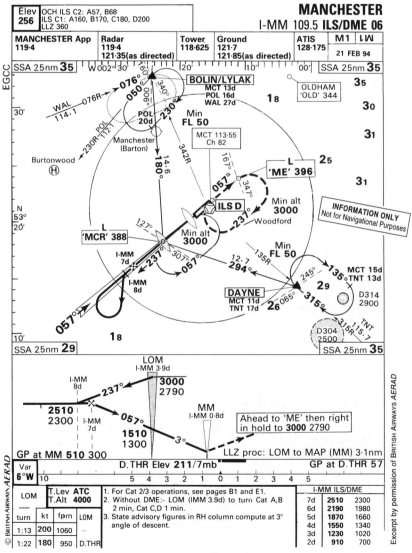

■ Figure 15-28 **Plan and profile of the Manchester Runway 06 ILS**

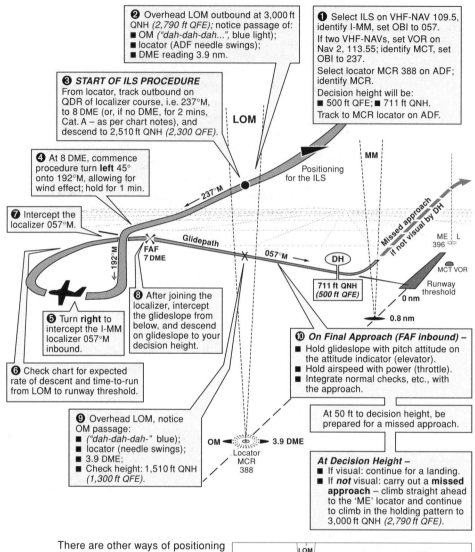

② Overhead LOM outbound at 3,000 ft QNH *(2,790 ft QFE)*; notice passage of:
■ OM *("dah-dah-dah...",* blue light);
■ locator (ADF needle swings);
■ DME reading 3.9 nm.

❶ Select ILS on VHF-NAV 109.5, identify I-MM, set OBI to 057.
If two VHF-NAVs, set VOR on Nav 2, 113.55; identify MCT, set OBI to 237.
Select locator MCR 388 on ADF; identify MCR.
Decision height will be:
■ 500 ft QFE; ■ 711 ft QNH.
Track to MCR locator on ADF.

❸ *START OF ILS PROCEDURE*
From locator, track outbound on QDR of localizer course, i.e. 237°M, to 8 DME (or, if no DME, for 2 mins, Cat. A – as per chart notes), and descend to 2,510 ft QNH *(2,300 QFE)*.

LOM

❹ At 8 DME, commence procedure turn **left** 45° onto 192°M, allowing for wind effect; hold for 1 min.

Positioning for the ILS

MM

237°M

❼ Intercept the localizer 057°M.

Missed approach if not visual by DH

ME L 396

Glidepath

192°M

FAF 7 DME

057°M →

DH

MCT VOR

Runway threshold

❺ Turn **right** to intercept the I-MM localizer 057°M inbound.

❽ After joining the localizer, intercept the glideslope from below, and descend on glideslope to your decision height.

711 ft QNH *(500 ft QFE)*

0 nm

0.8 nm

❻ Check chart for expected rate of descent and time-to-run from LOM to runway threshold.

❿ *On Final Approach (FAF inbound)* –
■ Hold glideslope with pitch attitude on the attitude indicator (elevator).
■ Hold airspeed with power (throttle).
■ Integrate normal checks, etc., with the approach.

❾ Overhead LOM, notice OM passage:
■ *("dah-dah-dah-"* blue);
■ locator (needle swings);
■ 3.9 DME;
■ Check height: 1,510 ft QNH *(1,300 ft QFE)*.

OM ◄ ► 3.9 DME
Locator MCR 388

At 50 ft to decision height, be prepared for a missed approach.

At Decision Height –
■ If visual: continue for a landing.
■ If *not* visual: carry out a **missed approach** – climb straight ahead to the 'ME' locator and continue to climb in the holding pattern to 3,000 ft QNH *(2,790 ft QFE)*.

There are other ways of positioning for the ILS approach. For instance, you could hold over over the MCR locator, at say 5,000 ft (or FL 50, as appropriate) while another aircraft makes an approach, and then descend in the holding pattern to 3,000 ft QNH when ready to commence the ILS approach.

Note: There will only be one aircraft holding at any one level.

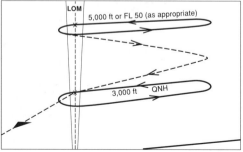

LOM
5,000 ft or FL 50 (as appropriate)
3,000 ft   QNH

■ *Figure 15-29* **Manoeuvring for the Manchester ILS Runway 06**

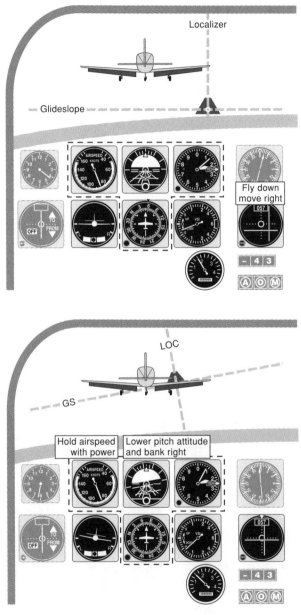

■ Figure 15-30 **Flying the ILS on final approach**

Now complete
Exercises 15 – The Instrument Landing System (ILS).

VHF Direction Finding (VDF)

General Principle

Some aerodromes are equipped with radio aerials that can sense the direction of VHF-COM signals (normal voice signals) received from an aeroplane.

This information is presented to the air traffic controller (usually the approach controller) as a radial line on a cathode ray tube similar to a radar screen or, with the most modern VDF equipment, as a very accurate digital readout of bearing.

VDF enables a controller to determine the direction a VHF-COM signal is coming from.

The controller can then give the pilot the bearing of the aircraft relative to the aerodrome. This is known as **very high frequency direction finding,** and is often abbreviated to VDF or VHF D/F.

An advantage of VDF is that no specific aircraft equipment is required other than a VHF-COM – normal VHF communications radio.

A typical VDF air–ground exchange would be a pilot requesting ATC to provide QDM (magnetic bearing to the ground station), followed by the controller advising it. For example:

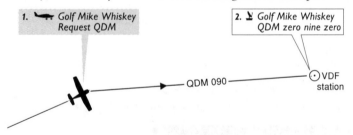

■ *Figure 16-1* **QDM is magnetic bearing to the VDF ground station**

By steering the QDM, the pilot is able to *home to,* or head towards, the ground station.

Ground stations that are equipped to provide VDF are designated by the term **homer,** e.g. *Shoreham Homer,* which operates on the VHF communications frequency of 123.15 MHz.

Whereas no special equipment is required in the aeroplane for VDF other than a VHF-COM radio, it does require a special installation at the ground station. Two typical designs for VDF aerials at aerodromes are the H-type aerial (a double-H dipole aerial in technical terms), or the Doppler-type VDF aerial.

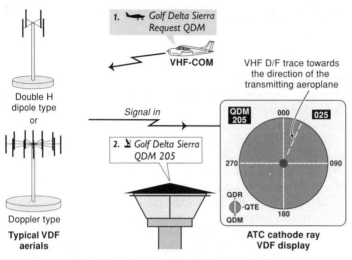

■ Figure 16-2 **Ground equipment for VHF direction finding**

VDF ground equipment from years ago was known as a **manual homer,** and used an ADF–type null–seeking aerial which the operator had to rotate manually to determine the direction of the aeroplane. It also required long transmissions from the aeroplane while the operator sought the null position.

Modern equipment is fully automatic. The direction of the aeroplane is displayed automatically following only a short VHF-COM transmission from the pilot.

Information Available from VDF

Bearings that a pilot may request from a VDF operator are:

VDF BEARINGS	
QDM	magnetic bearing **to** the station
QDR	magnetic bearing **from** the station (the reciprocal of the QDM)
QTE	true bearing **from** the station

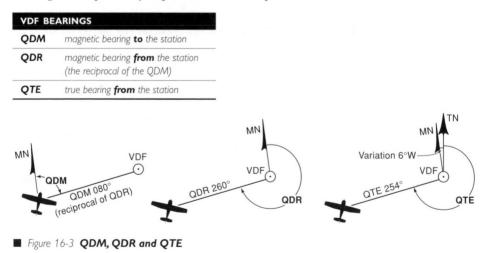

■ Figure 16-3 **QDM, QDR and QTE**

QDR

QDR, the magnetic bearing from the station, is useful for orientation (Where am I?). QDR is similar information to a VOR radial. QTE, the true bearing from the station, is useful if you want to plot a position line from the VDF ground station to the aeroplane on a map (against true north). However, it is QDM, the magnetic bearing to the station, that is the most commonly used and requested VDF bearing.

QDM

QDM is the most commonly requested bearing. It is the heading to steer direct to the VDF station provided no crosswind exists. In a crosswind, however, a wind correction angle (WCA) into wind must be used to counteract the drift if a reasonably straight track is to be achieved, rather than a curved (and inefficient) homing.

At typical light aircraft speeds, it is reasonable for the pilot to request a QDM each half-minute or so to check tracking, and to modify heading if necessary.

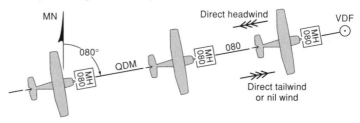

■ *Figure 16-4* **Steering QDM to a VDF ground station in nil-crosswind conditions is satisfactory**

If QDM is steered as heading in crosswind conditions, then the aeroplane will drift downwind, and its QDM will gradually change. The next QDM passed by the ground operator will be different from the first.

In Figure 16-5, an original QDM 080 has become QDM 075, and so the pilot would turn slightly left from a heading of 080°M to a heading of 075°M (the new QDM) to continue homing to the station.

There would be further changes to QDM advised by the operator as the aeroplane continued on, the end result being a curved path with the aeroplane arriving overhead the ground station heading roughly into wind – not a particularly professional arrival!

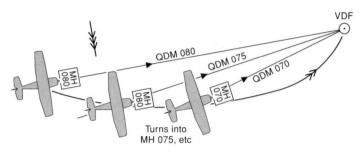

■ *Figure 16-5* **An inefficient homing to a VDF ground station**

A more efficient arrival can be achieved by allowing for wind effect, i.e. tracking using a wind correction angle into wind to counteract drift, rather than homing to the station by flying a continually changing QDM as heading.

VDF Bearing Accuracy
The quality of the bearings obtained by VDF is classified by the VDF ground operator to the pilot as:

Class A	Accurate to within ± 2°
Class B	Accurate to within ± 5°
Class C	Accurate to within ± 10°
Class D	Less accurate than Class C (CAP 46 lists some Class D VDF stations with accuracy less than ± 10°)

Most modern equipment is generally accurate to ± 1°, although accuracy may be decreased by:
☐ **VDF site errors** such as reflection from nearby uneven ground, buildings, aircraft or vehicles; and
☐ **VHF propagation errors** caused by irregular propagation over differing terrain, especially if the aeroplane is at long range from the VDF ground station.

VDF Tracking

Tracking Inbound using QDM
To achieve a desired track to a VDF ground station, the pilot should try to maintain a **datum QDM** which is the same as the **desired track**. For instance, to maintain a track of 080°M to the VDF ground station, the pilot should fly a heading so that QDM 080 is consistently maintained.

While VDF ground operators can advise QDM, they will not advise heading to steer to counter any crosswind effect. The pilot must determine this if a direct track to the VDF station is to be achieved. If the selected WCA is perfectly correct, then the ground operator will advise, on request for QDM, the same QDM as previously.

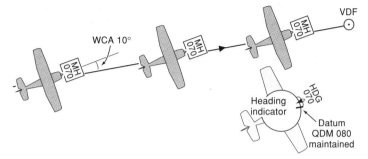

■ Figure 16-6 **Perfect allowance for drift**

The supply of QDMs by ATC may be thought of as a 'talking RMI'. You can, by mentally placing the QDM onto the direction indicator, form the same picture as that given to you by an RMI.

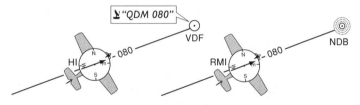

■ Figure 16-7 **The stated QDM is like a talking RMI**

If the stated QDM moves to the right of the datum QDM, then the aeroplane has drifted to the left of the desired track, and should be turned right to re-intercept the desired track (to re-establish the datum QDM). This is exactly the same response as for the head of an RMI needle moving to the right of the datum QDM.

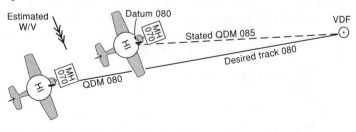

■ Figure 16-8 **Tracking towards a VDF ground station; if QDM moves right of the datum, turn right**

In this case, while flying on a magnetic heading of 070, the actual QDM has moved to the right of the datum QDM 080, indicated by ATC stating QDM 085. To regain the desired track, the pilot should turn right and increase heading (to say MH 090), and then request QDMs until the desired QDM 080 is reached. At this time, a more suitable heading to maintain QDM 080 would be flown, say MH 075.

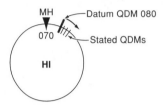

■ *Figure 16-9* **If QDM moves right of datum, turn right**

If the stated QDM moves to the left of the datum QDM, then the aeroplane has drifted to the right of the desired track, and should be turned left to re-intercept the desired track (to re-establish the datum QDM). This is exactly the same response as for the head of an RMI needle moving to the left of the datum QDM.

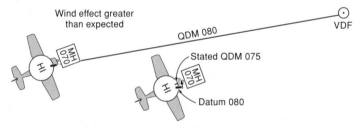

■ *Figure 16-10* **Tracking towards a VDF ground station; if QDM moves left of the datum, turn left**

In this case, the stated QDM has moved left of the datum QDM 080 to 075. The pilot should turn left and decrease heading (to say MH 060), and request QDMs until the desired QDM 080 is reached. At this time, a more suitable heading to maintain QDM 080 would be flown, say MH 065.

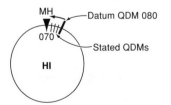

■ *Figure 16-11* **QDM moving left of datum, turn left**

IN KNOWN WIND CONDITIONS, use a 'best-guess WCA' as a starting point in estimating a magnetic heading to maintain the datum QDM, making modifications to heading if the actual or stated QDM gradually moves away from the datum QDM.

IN UNKNOWN WIND CONDITIONS, when unable to estimate a suitable wind correction angle to counter drift, a simple procedure is to steer the QDM as heading, and see what develops. Suitable corrections can then be made as changes in the QDM become apparent.

WHEN TRACKING TOWARDS THE VDF STATION:

> • turn right if actual QDM moves to the right of datum;
> • turn left if actual QDM moves to the left of datum.

The aim is to establish a wind correction angle that allows for drift and results in the desired track being maintained – indicated by the QDM remaining constant. The process of finding a suitable WCA by trial and error is known as **bracketing.** Typically, it will take a number of heading changes to establish the WCA required to maintain track.

Changes to heading will also be required if the wind effect changes, which is often the case. Like most instrument flying, VDF tracking will consist of a continuing series of small (and sometimes not so small) corrections.

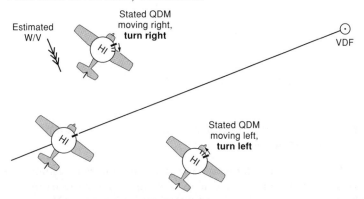

■ Figure 16-12 **Tracking towards a VDF ground station**

Tracking Outbound

When tracking away from a VDF ground station, the datum QDM is the reciprocal of the outbound track. For instance, to maintain a track of 060°M away from the VDF ground station, the aeroplane should be flown so that datum QDM 240 is maintained.

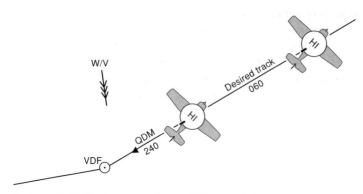

■ *Figure 16-13* **Tracking away from a VDF ground station**

If the stated QDM moves to the right of the datum QDM, the aeroplane has drifted to the left of the desired track, and should be turned right to re-intercept the desired track (to re-establish the datum QDM). This is exactly the same response as for the head of an RMI needle moving to the right of the datum QDM.

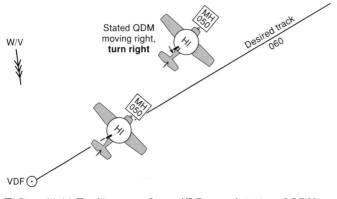

■ *Figure 16-14* **Tracking away from a VDF ground station; if QDM moves right of the datum, turn right**

In this case, the pilot would turn right and increase heading (to say MH 060), which would allow the wind to blow the aeroplane back onto track, and request QDMs until the desired QDM 240 is reached. At this time, a more suitable heading to maintain datum QDM 240 would be flown, say MH 055.

If the stated QDM moves to the left of the datum QDM, the aeroplane has drifted to the right of the desired track, and should be turned left to re-intercept the desired track (to re-establish the datum QDM). This is exactly the same response as for the head of an RMI needle moving to the left of the datum QDM.

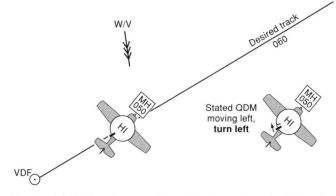

■ *Figure 16-15* **Tracking away from a VDF ground station; if QDM moves left of the datum, turn left**

In this case, since MH 050, allowing for an estimated 10° of drift, has taken the aeroplane to the right of track, the pilot should turn left and decrease heading (to say MH 040), and then request QDMs until the desired QDM 240 is reached. At this time, a more suitable heading to maintain QDM 240 should be flown, say MH 045, allowing a WCA of 15° into wind.

IN KNOWN WIND CONDITIONS, use a 'best-guess' WCA as a starting point in an attempt to maintain the datum QDM, making modifications to heading if the actual QDM changes from the datum.

IN UNKNOWN WIND CONDITIONS, when unable to estimate a suitable wind correction angle to counter drift, a simple procedure is to steer the reciprocal of the QDM as heading, and see what develops. Suitable corrections can then be made as changes in the QDM become apparent.

WHEN TRACKING AWAY FROM THE VDF STATION:

• turn right if actual QDM moves to the right of datum;
• turn left if actual QDM moves to the left of datum.

Note that these are exactly the same rules as for tracking towards the VDF ground station.

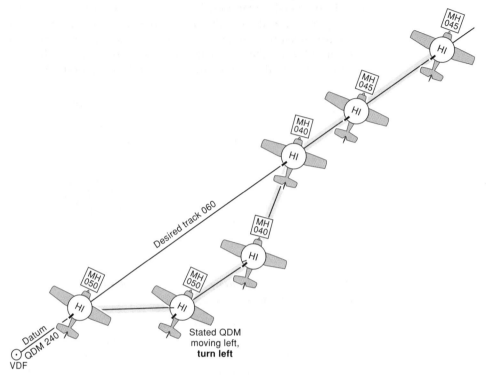

■ *Figure 16-16* **Tracking away from a VDF ground station**

VDF Tracking Rules

1. Determine datum QDM for the desired track;
  - inbound: datum QDM = desired track;
  - outbound: datum QDM = reciprocal of desired track.

2. Use best-guess WCA to establish an initial heading in an attempt to maintain datum QDM.

3. Both inbound and outbound from the VDF ground station:
  - if stated QDM moves left of datum, turn left;
  - if stated QDM moves right of datum, turn right; (treat the stated QDM on the DI as a command instrument).

Flying Overhead the VDF Ground Station

As the aeroplane passes overhead (or near to overhead) the VDF ground station, the ground operator will be unable to determine the direction from which VHF-COM signals are received, even though the actual voice communications will be received normally. He will report this to the pilot as "No bearing".

If the outbound track differs significantly from the inbound track, then the pilot will need to take up a suitable intercept heading until the datum QDM for the outbound track is established, at which time normal tracking to maintain it should occur.

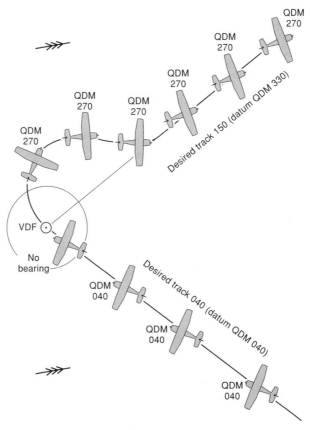

■ *Figure 16-17* **Flying overhead the VDF ground station, and intercepting an outbound track**

Requests for QDM by the pilot should be more frequent the closer the aeroplane is to the ground station so that suitable adjustments to heading can be made.

Approaches

The VDF Instrument Approach

VHF direction finding and the tracking procedures discussed previously can be used by a pilot (in conjunction with the ground controller who will periodically pass the current QDM) to track to overhead the station.

It can also be used to carry out published let-down procedures at certain aerodromes, by tracking outbound from overhead the station, then turning and tracking inbound on the published QDM, and descending to not below a specified height until visual. VDF let-downs approved by the CAA are published by *Aerad* and *Jeppesen,* and are described in UK AIP AD 2.

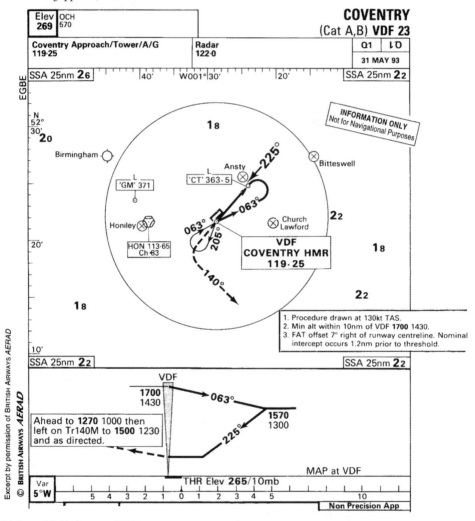

■ *Figure 16-18* **A typical VDF instrument approach**

Pilots flying cross-country may arrive overhead the VDF ground station by requesting QDMs from ATC, and altering heading appropriately. At least the minimum safe altitude (MSA) for the sector should be maintained until overhead, at which time the ground operator will advise "No bearing".

10 NM OUT. At least 10 nm prior to reaching the aerodrome, you should have requested the weather conditions to enable a suitable approach to be planned, and the en route (FREHA) and icing checks should have been completed. Slow the aeroplane to flap extension speed prior to reaching the station to allow for better manoeuvrability and immediate flap selection when descent is permissible.

OVERHEAD. When overhead the station, take up a suitable heading to intercept the outbound track. Frequent QDMs will be required to allow an efficient interception of the track close to the station. Start the stopwatch to enable accurate timing of the outbound leg, with allowance made for any strong wind effect.

For instance, with a 20-knot tailwind outbound, a reduction of 20 seconds per minute will result in a more appropriate track over the ground that does not extend too far from the station (e.g. a published 3-minute outbound leg could be reduced to 2 minutes), and does not require an exceptionally 'long-haul' upwind leg back to the station.

TRACKING OUTBOUND. Once you have intercepted the outbound track, maintain it by flying a heading that allows for drift, e.g. 063°M plus or minus the estimated WCA (wind correction angle). Make periodic requests for QDM to check tracking accuracy. The desired QDM for the final approach on the Coventry VDF procedure (at left) is 225 (a magnetic bearing of 225° to the station), which will be used as the datum. The aim is to establish a heading that allows this datum QDM to be maintained.

If the ground operator advises a QDM that is moving to the left of the datum, then turn left. If the advised QDM is moving to the right of the datum, then turn right.

WITHIN 5° OF TRACK. When within ±5° of track, you may descend to 1,570 ft on QNH, or 1,300 ft on QFE (the difference equals the runway threshold elevation of 265 ft, rounded off to the nearest 10 ft). Carry out pre-landing checks during the intermediate approach.

3 MINUTES OUTBOUND. After 3 minutes' flight time outbound (adjusted for wind effect), you may make a left turn to intercept QDM 225°M inbound to the station. Ideally, a request for QDM halfway through the turn will result in the 'mid-QDM' being advised. If not, adjust the turn for an efficient intercept of the inbound QDM, which now becomes the datum QDM. You may need to remove bank angle temporarily part-way through the turn and fly wings-level for a short while to get closer to the inbound track before completing the intercept turn.

Exactly the same tracking rules apply inbound as outbound. If the ground operator advises a QDM that is moving to the left of

the datum, turn left. If the ground operator advises a QDM that
is moving to the right of the datum, turn right.

TRACKING INBOUND. When established inbound, you are permitted to descend to the MDA (minimum descent altitude) with
QNH set on the altimeter, or MDH (minimum descent height)
with QFE set. For IMC-rated pilots this will be no lower than an
absolute minimum of 600 ft aal, but it could be significantly
higher at certain aerodromes with obstacles in the approach area.
The calculation of MDA(H) for any particular approach is
covered in Chapter 22, *Instrument Minima*.

Once at the MDA(H), you must not descend further unless you
become visual. If not visual at the MDA(H), you may proceed to
the station at the MDA(H), and if still not visual, make a missed
approach by climbing straight ahead to 1,270 ft (1,000 ft QFE),
then a climbing left turn on track 140°M, and follow the remain-
der of the published missed approach procedure.

The QGH Approach

The QGH approach is a VDF-type approach where the air traffic
controller will provide, not QDM information as for a VDF let-
down, but tracking guidance in the form of headings-to-steer
accompanied by descent instructions. Consequently, the QGH
approach is easier for a pilot than a VDF approach, even though
the same let-down path might be followed.

It is up to you to request a QGH approach if so desired,
provided ATC has the capability to provide one at the aerodrome.

Other Uses for VDF

Bearings obtained by VDF can be used for a number of common
navigational purposes. For instance, you may request a QDM
from an abeam VDF station to verify that you are indeed flying
abeam it.

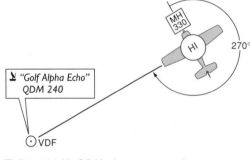

■ Figure 16-19 **QDM abeam a ground station**

A position line given by a VDF bearing can be used together with another position line from say a VOR, NDB or even another VDF station to fix the position of the aeroplane.

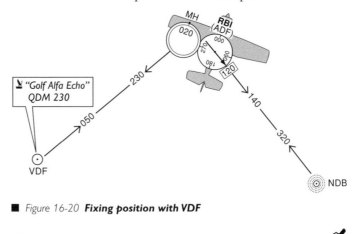

■ Figure 16-20 **Fixing position with VDF**

Now complete **Exercises 16 – VHF Direction Finding (VDF).**

Introduction to RNAV

General Description

> A waypoint is a geographical position used to define a route.

Area navigation (RNAV) allows you to fly point-to-point on a direct course without having to overfly ground-based radio aids. Instead of flying from VOR/DME-to-VOR/DME along or beneath airways on what might be a circuitous route, you can fly direct from your departure airport to the destination airport, or from waypoint-to-waypoint, using RNAV. A **waypoint** is a geographical position usually specified by latitude and longitude, or by radial and distance from a VOR/DME, and used to define a route.

Some RNAV systems can define a waypoint internally when the pilot inserts the desired waypoint latitude and longitude into the computer. The RNAV system then derives data from navigation systems such as LORAN, inertial navigation systems (INS), VLF/Omega systems, and Doppler radar which enables the airplane to be flown to the desired waypoint. Other RNAV systems define waypoints relative to a VOR/DME, using radial and distance (or latitude and longitude) to create 'phantom' VOR/DMEs, known as pseudo-VOR/DMEs.

Pseudo-VOR/DMEs

Many general aviation aircraft have a course line computer system which, when used in conjunction with the VHF-NAV radio selected to a VOR/DME, can electronically relocate that VOR/DME, so that a pseudo-VOR/DME is created at any desired waypoint. It does this by electronically adding a vector (radial and distance) to the position of the actual VOR/DME.

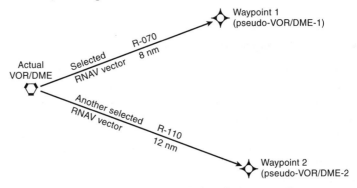

■ Figure 17-1 **Creating a phantom VOR/DME electronically**

Operational Use

You can locate pseudo-VOR/DMEs wherever you like, provided they are within signal reception range of the parent VOR/DME, and thereby create a series of waypoints along your desired route.

The normal VHF-NAV receiver is selected to the parent VOR/DME, and the computer is programmed to electronically add the vector (radial and distance) to received VOR/DME signals. How this is done depends on the actual equipment in the cockpit – refer to equipment information in your Pilot's Operating Handbook.

The course deviation indicator (CDI) in the cockpit receives its input via the computer, and indicates deviation from course between the waypoints – not an angular deviation as for normal VOR flying, but a lateral deviation in nautical miles, or fractions thereof.

The course between waypoints is maintained by keeping the CDI centered. Because it indicates lateral deviation in nautical miles, known as crosstrack error, rather than angular deviation, there is no 'funneling' effect using the RNAV CDI.

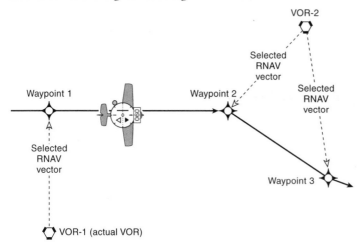

■ Figure 17-2 **Tracking between waypoints**

Distance to the waypoint is shown on the normal DME indicator.

The waypoints can normally be preset on the RNAV equipment, and then instantaneously recalled as you need them. As the flight progresses, you will proceed through the waypoints in order, keeping within signal range of each parent VOR/DME by flying at a suitable altitude and distance from it. If the usable signal range is exceeded, the CDI OFF flag will show.

Typical RNAV systems can provide you with:
- crosstrack deviation from the selected course in nm with TO/FROM information;
- distance to the waypoint in nm;
- groundspeed in knots;
- time-to-waypoint in minutes.

■ Figure 17-3 **A typical RNAV display**

LORAN-C

General Description

LORAN-C is a long-range navigation system originally designed for maritime use. In earlier days, it required rather complicated charts, a large table to spread them out on, and a trained navigator to interpret signals and plot the position on the chart – obviously not a perfect system for small aircraft. However, the development of the microprocessor has changed all that. What were complicated calculations are now performed automatically at high speed and with great accuracy, with position and other information presented to the pilot in the cockpit in digital form.

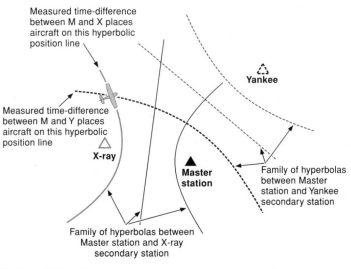

■ Figure 17-4 **LORAN-C computes position using hyperbolas**

The cost of the equipment is within the range of the small
aircraft owner, and has become a popular means of light aircraft
navigation.

The LORAN-C system is a hyperbolic system. It measures the
difference in time of arrival of radio pulses from a chain of trans-
mitters which are separated by hundreds of miles. One station is
the master station, and the others are secondary stations whose
signals are synchronized with those from the master station.

The time-difference between the arrival of the various pulses
from different directions allows the microprocessor to compute
the position of the aircraft. All points having the same time-
difference between pulses from two stations lie on a curve known
as a hyperbola. With signals from a number of stations, more than
one hyperbolic position line is known, and the intersection of two
or more of these hyperbolas defines the position of the aircraft.

■ *Figure 17-5* **A typical LORAN set**

The capability of the microprocessor is taken advantage of to
provide you with many pieces of information – in fact, so much
that you must discriminate and only access what you need. There
are differences between sets from various manufacturers, but a
typical set can provide you with:
- position (as latitude/longitude or radial/distance);
- track and groundspeed;
- wind speed and direction (using MH and TAS data);
- crosstrack error (lateral deviation from course in nautical
  miles);
- estimated time en route;
- memory storage of all airports and radio navigation aids in the
  United Kingdom and elsewhere, plus anything else that you
  care to add;
- airways specifications; and
- track and distance to any selected point (no matter how far) –
  very useful when considering diverting to an alternate airport.

LORAN-C is currently giving way to GPS navigation.

Global Positioning System (GPS)

General Description

The global positioning system (GPS) is an extremely accurate area navigation aid for all classes of aviation as well as other modes of transport. GPS was developed for the United States Department of Defense, but has now been made available for civil use.

In early 1994 the Federal Aviation Administration approved the use of GPS as an operational in-flight navigational aid. With an FAA-approved GPS system and supporting software, GPS may now be used to fly en route under Instrument Flight Rules, and, in some cases in the USA, for nonprecision instrument approaches. The GPS instrument approach procedures are presently overlayed on other established instrument approach procedures, such as VOR approaches. Dedicated GPS approaches will soon be introduced. No doubt the UK and Europe will follow.

GPS should not be used as the primary navigation method.

IFR and VFR pilots may also use GPS as an aid to navigation, including information relating to aircraft, speed and track over the ground, wind velocity and distance/time to waypoints or destination. GPS is very accurate, but as satellites can become unserviceable etc., it should not be considered as such for more than 95% of the time. Therefore GPS should not be used as the primary navigation method, only as an aid to other methods.

Basically, GPS is comprised of three elements:
- a space element, consisting of a constellation of 21 active satellites orbiting the earth every 12 hours, in six orbital planes with four in each plane, at an altitude of 11,000 nm (21,300 km);
- a satellite control ground network (control station plus monitor stations), responsible for orbital accuracy and control; and
- navigation receiver/computers in aircraft capable of receiving and identifying signals from satellites in view at a particular time and place.

Basic Operating Principle

Each satellite transmits its own computer code packet on frequency 1575.42 MHz (for civilian use), 1,000 times per second. The satellite continually broadcasts its position and the exact time UTC. By knowing the exact position of the satellite at the time of transmission, and then by measuring the time taken for the data packet to reach the receiver from the satellite, the distance between the satellite and the receiver can be determined. The satellite constellation configuration usually guarantees that at least four satellites are in view at any given time.

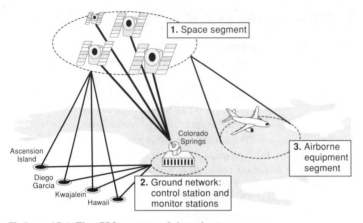

■ Figure 17-6 **The GPS consists of three basic segments**

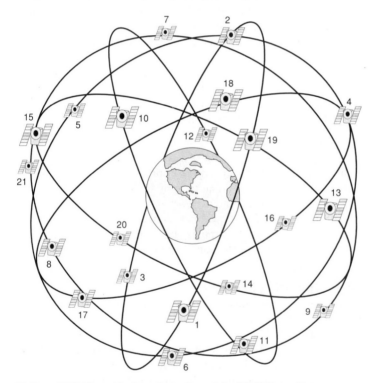

■ Figure 17-7 **The orbital configuration of the 21 GPS satellites**

Each transmitted data packet contains a precise timing reference. GPS receivers use accurate clocks and appropriate software to ascertain position by receiving and computing data from at least three satellites for a two-dimensional fix, and four satellites for a three-dimensional fix, such as ground position and altitude.

■ *Figure 17-8* **Signals from satellites are received to establish position**

Now complete **Exercises 17 – Introduction to RNAV.**

Section **Three**

Instrument Procedures

Preparation for Flight

Flight Planning

Planning for a flight on instruments is most important, especially since the safety advantages of visual flight may not be present during the flight. As an instrument pilot flying in cloud or at night, you must be very conscious of **high terrain** or **obstacles** that cannot be seen, and ensure that a safe height above them is maintained.

You must be aware of the danger of **icing** (both airframe and carburettor icing) and take appropriate precautions. You must have an **alternate airfield** in mind in case a diversion becomes necessary, and you must have **sufficient fuel** to get there and still have a safety margin remaining in the tanks. The best time to organise these things is prior to flight.

> *Good flight planning is essential.*

Flight planning procedures discussed in earlier volumes of *The Air Pilot's Manual* (Volume 3) will have prepared you thoroughly. As a reminder of some of the vital points, a number of the exercises that follow will test your knowledge in these areas. Do not be afraid to review the relevant chapters. Always remember that the pilot-in-command is responsible for the safety of the flight.

Whether the submission of a flight plan is optional or compulsory for a particular flight is discussed in UK AIP ENR 1-10.

Some Icing Considerations

Flying IFR often means flying in cloud or rain, i.e. in 'visible moisture'. If the temperature of the aeroplane is zero or below, ice can form on the exposed parts of the airframe and on the propeller. Icing conditions are commonly defined as:

1. Visible moisture; and

2. Temperature at or below zero.

Many IFR aircraft are fitted with anti-icing and/or de-icing equipment – anti-icing equipment to prevent the formation of ice, de-icing equipment to remove ice that has already formed. Of course, there are some icing conditions that are so severe that even the best equipment cannot cope with them, and so you will find that most smaller IFR aircraft are certified only for light to moderate icing conditions, and not for severe icing conditions. Often 'severe icing conditions' also means CBs, with associated severe turbulence and windshear – the sort of area in which no sensible pilot would fly. Light icing conditions might lead to a centimetre of ice forming in 40 nm flight distance, whereas in moderate conditions the centimetre would form in about 20 nm.

If your IFR aeroplane is not fully equipped to handle icing conditions, then you should not enter an area where icing is possible. This does not mean that you should avoid cloud or other visible moisture altogether, but it does mean that you should avoid it if the temperature is zero or below. You can do this by ensuring that your IFR cruising level in cloud or visible moisture is lower than the freezing level (and do not forget to ensure that it is also above your safety altitude!)

Almost all IFR aircraft are fitted with pitot heaters to ensure that ice does not form over or in the pitot tube, and so cause faulty airspeed indications. Since the compass is usually 'swung' (calibrated) with the pitot heaters on, you should always have them on in flight to ensure reasonably correct compass indications. This may or may not apply to windshield heaters, if fitted. The conditions under which your particular compass was swung will be specified on the deviation card in the cockpit.

Anti-icing and De-icing Equipment

There are two main types of anti-icing/de-icing equipment.

DE-ICING FLUID can be spread onto the leading edge of the wings, the tailplane and the propellers, preventing the formation of ice and removing any ice that has formed. It is usual to check this system during the pre-flight walk-around by switching it on and checking that the de-icing fluid bubbles out of the de-icing orifices on the leading edge. This ensures that the system is purged of air. (If not, ice could form over the outlets and the de-icing fluid would not be able to get at the ice because of an airlock.) You must ensure that only the correct type of de-icing fluid is used. Normally this system is engaged in anti-icing mode before you enter icing conditions. If ice does form, then you can switch to de-ice mode, which doubles the flow rate of the fluid.

DE-ICING BOOTS operate pneumatically – inflating and breaking up any ice that has formed, and then deflating. The ice meanwhile is blown away in the airstream. It is usual to check for punctures, possibly caused by stones thrown up by the propellers, during the pre-flight walk-around. A puncture wound, as well as degrading the inflation/deflation cycle, can also cause moisture to be drawn in and form ice within the boots. Normally this system is used for de-icing, and is switched on after ice has formed. Five millimetres of ice thickness is typical before the de-icing boots are activated. If the de-icing boots are cycled too soon, the thin layer of ice crystals may be pushed out by the expanding boots but not broken up and dislodged. Further icing may form on this displaced layer, but the boots will be operating inside the layer, not touching it, and therefore unable to dislodge it. It is good airmanship to test the de-icing boots by cycling them before you enter icing conditions.

Pre-Flight Considerations for an IMC Flight

Pre-flight considerations include:

☐ Am I properly qualified (IMC rating or instrument rating)?

☐ Is the aeroplane suitably equipped (serviceable radios, anti-icing equipment, lighting, etc.)?

☐ What is the weather? Are changes expected? Check aerodrome forecasts (TAFs) and en route forecasts (e.g. area forecasts, such as provided by the AIRMET service and updated four times daily).

☐ Is the departure aerodrome suitable for my operation?

☐ Is the destination aerodrome suitable for my operation?

☐ Is an alternate aerodrome required (or more than one)?

☐ What routes are suitable in terms of terrain, weather and available en route radio navigation facilities?

☐ Are there any important messages contained in NOTAMs, AICs or obtainable from a briefing office, such as serviceability of Radio Navigation Facilities, serviceability of aerodromes, changes to procedures if, for instance, a purple airway for a royal flight has been declared, etc.?

☐ Is a flight plan required to be submitted (for instance, to enter Class D controlled airspace at a busy aerodrome)?

☐ Preparation of charts (en route charts, approach charts, etc.).

☐ Compilation of a flight log (with tracks, distances, times, minimum safe altitudes and cruising levels calculated).

☐ Compilation of a fuel log, with adequate fuel reserves.

☐ Preparation of the aircraft, and check of the weight and balance.

☐ Organising the cockpit for flight – keeping charts, torch, etc., handy.

☐ Briefing of passengers.

SAFETY ALTITUDE. Calculation of a minimum safety altitude is important, since terrain and other obstacles may not be seen in IMC conditions. An IMC-rated pilot planning with a visual chart, such as the CAA half-million series, may calculate a safety altitude based on 1,000-foot vertical clearance from any obstacle within 5 nm of track. Published **maximum elevation figures** (MEFs) for the latitude–longitude quadrangles en route are useful in determining a safety altitude. Adding a suitable buffer, e.g. 1,000 ft, to the highest MEF en route can give a suitable safety altitude (or safety height). Radio Navigation Charts will specify lowest safe altitudes for published routes.

CRUISING LEVELS. Cruising levels should be chosen according to the IFR cruising level table – the quadrantal rule based on magnetic track (Rule 30). When flying over congested areas, attention should be paid to the Low Flying Rule (Rule 5).

FUEL. Fuel requirements should be calculated carefully, with consideration to arriving at a diversion airfield with adequate fuel reserves on board. Being tight on fuel significantly increases the stress level of a pilot if an unexpected diversion becomes necessary.

REVIEW RADIO PROCEDURES. A review of AIP ENR 1-6 and AD 2 radio failure procedures should be made from time to time by every IMC-rated pilot, to ensure competence.

Following Start-Up

After start-up and prior to take-off, all radio navigation equipment should be checked for correct operation. This includes the VHF-COM, VHF-NAV, DME, ADF/RMI, marker lights and transponder. The altimeter should be checked for the correct subscale setting – check that QFE and QNH give a sensible value of airfield elevation between both readings.

During taxi, the instruments should be checked:

TURNING LEFT:
- HI/RMI/compass decreasing;
- ADF/RMI tracking;
- Turn coordinator shows left turn;
- Balance ball shows skidding right;
- AI steady.

TURNING RIGHT:
- HI/RMI/compass increasing;
- ADF/RMI tracking;
- Turn coordinator shows right turn;
- Balance ball shows skidding left;
- AI steady.

Radio Procedures

Communication between air traffic service units (ATSU) on the ground and an aeroplane is important, and is best achieved if correct radio procedures are used. Some typical radiotelephony

(R/T) calls follow, but you should refer to CAP 413 for a full discussion of these. Being prepared to handle the radio professionally, using correct procedures, will simplify any flight, but especially a flight in IMC conditions.

On initial R/T contact, the full callsign of the aircraft should be used, e.g. "Golf Bravo Foxtrot Romeo Mike" for the registration G-BFRM. The 'G' indicates that it is a UK registration. Once communication has been established, the callsign may be shortened by the ATSU to "Golf Romeo Mike" in which case it is appropriate for the pilot to use the abbreviated callsign also.

READBACK. As a general principle, all messages from an ATSU should be acknowledged by use of the aircraft callsign. Executive instructions should be acknowledged with an abbreviated readback of the instructions and the callsign.

> ☗ *Golf Alpha Charlie*
> *Aircraft landing Runway 35*
> *Hold position*
>
> ➤ *Holding – Golf Alpha Charlie*

A full readback should be made to instructions containing any of the following:
- ☐ Level instructions.
- ☐ Heading instructions.
- ☐ Speed instructions.
- ☐ Airways or route clearances.
- ☐ Runway in use.
- ☐ Clearance to enter, land on, take off, backtrack or cross an active runway.
- ☐ SSR operating instructions.
- ☐ Altimeter settings.
- ☐ VDF information.
- ☐ Changes of radio frequency.

> ➘ *Golf Mike Echo*
> *Descend to two thousand*
> *QNH one zero one five*
>
> ➤ *Descend to two thousand*
> *QNH one zero one five*
> *Golf Mike Echo*
>
> ➘ *Golf Zulu November*
> *Contact London Control one two five decimal eight*
>
> ➤ *London one two five decimal eight*
> *Golf Zulu November*

POSITION REPORTS. Pass en route position reports in the form:
- Aircraft callsign.
- Position and time over that position.
- Altitude or flight level.
- Estimate next position and time over it.

> ✈ *Golf Charlie Delta*
> *Inverness at three five*
> *Flight level seven five*
> *Estimate Aberdeen at five six*

NOTE Position reports are required in the circumstances listed in AIP ENR 1-1-1-4.

If an ATSU requests '**details**', pass them in the form:
- Aircraft callsign and type.
- Position and heading.
- Altitude or flight level.
- Flight conditions.

> ↘ *Golf Mike Whiskey*
> *Pass your details*
>
> ✈ *Golf Mike Whiskey*
> *Cessna one seven two*
> *One six miles north of Bodmin*
> *Heading zero eight zero*
> *Three thousand*
> *VMC*

Any request for '**route**' (in addition to details) from an ATSU should be passed in the form:
- Departure aerodrome.
- Route, including an estimate for a position en route, and destination.
- True airspeed in knots.
- Any other relevant information.

> ↘ *Golf Mike Whiskey*
> *Pass your details and route*
>
> ✈ *Golf Mike Whiskey*
> *Cessna 172, one six miles north of Bodmin*
> *Heading 280*
> *Three thousand*
> *VMC*
> *From Land's End*
> *Estimating Okehampton zero four*
> *To Exeter*
> *One three five knots*

RADAR SERVICES. A non-radar service is known as a **procedural service,** whereby separation between aircraft, for instance, is established by laid down time and/or distance separation standards. Details, route, position reporting and estimate over the next position are important, since the procedural separation will be based on these reports.

To make use of the **Lower Airspace Radar Service (LARS),** you should, when within approximately 40 nm of a participating aerodrome, establish two-way R/T communication on the appropriate frequency. The response you receive will probably contain a request for 'details', which should be passed in the form detailed on page 342.

> ➤ *Pilot: St. Mawgan*
> *Golf Alpha Charlie X-ray Delta*
> *Request Lower Airspace Radar Service*

When operating in a radar environment, you may request a:

Be aware that under a radar service, the pilot is still responsible for terrain clearance.

☐ **Radar Information Service (RIS)** in which information regarding conflicting or nearby traffic is given (but no avoiding action in terms of heading changes is offered: this is left to the pilot to initiate); or

☐ **Radar Advisory Service (RAS)** in which both traffic information and avoidance action is given by ATC to the pilot.

To carry out a particular instrument approach, you should request it.

> ➤ *Exeter Approach*
> *Golf Foxtrot Hotel India Lima*
> *Request QGH approach*

During a QDM approach, you may have to request QDMs.

> ➤ *Exeter Tower*
> *Golf Juliett Yankee*
> *Request QDM*
>
> ▼ *Golf Juliett Yankee*
> *Exeter Tower*
> *QDM 050*
> *Class Bravo*

NOTE *Class Bravo* indicates the bearing is accurate to within ±5°.

For radio failure procedures, see AIP ENR 1-6, AD 2, Appendix 3 of this manual, and Vol. 7 of *The Air Pilot's Manual.*

Now complete **Exercises 18 – Preparation for Flight.**

Instrument Departures

You should not take off unless you are certain that conditions at the departure aerodrome are suitable, and that conditions at the destination or alternate aerodrome(s) will allow a landing to be made. This is not to say that it is unsafe to operate in bad weather, but it is strongly recommended that a careful decision whether to operate or not is made, taking into account all the available relevant information, especially the weather information. UK PPL holders must determine their own minima (and this is fully discussed in Chapter 22).

Bad weather can be said to exist if conditions are:
☐ cloud ceiling worse than 1,000 ft aal;
☐ in-flight visibility worse than 1,800 metres; and
☐ runway visual range (RVR)/aerodrome visibility worse than 1,500 m.

The UK AIP recommends that, for non-public transport flights, the minimum weather conditions for take-off in a single-engined aeroplane should never be less than:
☐ **600 ft cloud ceiling;** and
☐ **1,800 metres visibility.**

Following an unexpected engine failure in these minimum conditions, an experienced and current pilot of a relatively slow and manoeuvrable aircraft will have a reasonable chance of viewing a suitable forced landing field, and avoiding obstacles in an attempt to reach it. However, realistically speaking, the average IMC-rated pilot should only fly in conditions well in excess of these (such as 1,500-foot cloud ceiling and 3 km flight visibility).

Prior to an instrument departure, ensure that your radio navaids and instruments are set correctly, with the aids identified (by Morse code). At a controlled airport you will need an ATC departure clearance specifying your route and altitude or flight level, and possibly a transponder code, and then you will need another ATC clearance to enter the runway and take off. If you experience radio failure, taxi clear of the runway.

If you are airborne in uncontrolled airspace (Classes F and G) and wish to enter controlled airspace, ensure that ATC has your flight plan details (position, level, and proposed track), and then obtain an ATC clearance to enter. Compliance with Rule 5 (Low Flying Rule), and two-way radio communication are necessary. If you experience radio failure before entering controlled airspace, then stay clear of it and land at the nearest suitable airport.

Setting Course

Most departures on an instrument flight involve manoeuvring after take-off to intercept the departure track to or from a particular radio navigation aid. It is good airmanship to have in mind, prior to take-off, the direction of turns required and the approximate time it will take to intercept the track.

Figure 19-1 shows an aeroplane taking off and intercepting the 270°M track outbound from an NDB near the aerodrome.

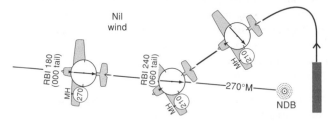

■ *Figure 19-1* **Intercepting the departure track using an NDB**

In Figure 19-2, an aeroplane is taking off and intercepting the 030°M track to a VOR (the 210 radial), and then tracking outbound on the 090 radial.

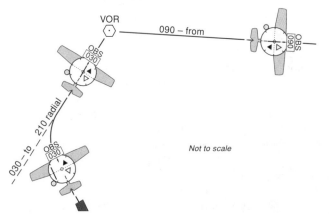

■ *Figure 19-2* **Intercepting the departure track using a VOR**

QNH is normally set in the altimeter subscale for departure on cross-country flights so that the altimeter indicates height amsl.

When cruising, the appropriate setting is:

☐ **Regional QNH** for cruising at or below the transition altitude (usually 3,000 ft in the UK) when outside controlled airspace and not in the vicinity of an aerodrome; and

☐ **1013.2 mb** when cruising IFR at or above the transition level, preferably at a quadrantal level appropriate to the magnetic track.

NOTE If departing an aerodrome located beneath a TMA, the QNH of an aerodrome beneath the TMA should be used for the period of flight beneath the TMA. The same applies to flight beneath any other controlled airspace. (Vertical navigation is discussed in detail in Volume 3 of *The Air Pilot's Manual*.)

Standard Instrument Departures

At some busy controlled aerodromes, standard instrument departures (SIDs) are published. SIDs considerably simplify the issue of departure clearances by ATC. ATC simply names the SID without having to describe any further tracking details, because the pilot can obtain these in diagrammatic and textual form from SID charts. *"Perth Three Alpha"* at Glasgow is a typical SID.

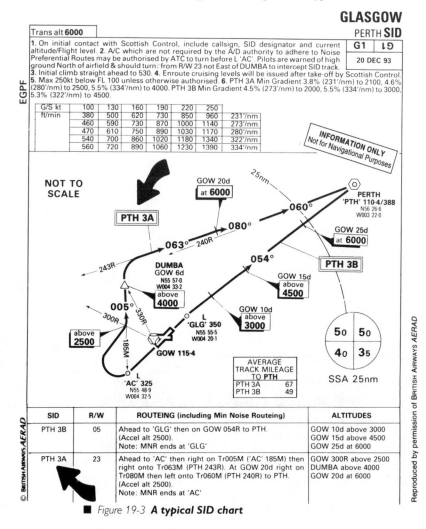

■ Figure 19-3 **A typical SID chart**

SIDs are generally designed to separate departing traffic from arriving traffic, to provide an efficient interception of the outbound track (considering that some airspace around these aerodromes may be busy), and avoid noise-sensitive areas. Radio transmissions are also considerably reduced, which reduces workload and frees communications frequencies. SIDs are generally available only to instrument-rated pilots (and not to IMC-rated pilots).

Not all instrument departures are complicated, as the White-gate SIDs from Birmingham Airport in Figure 19-4 show.

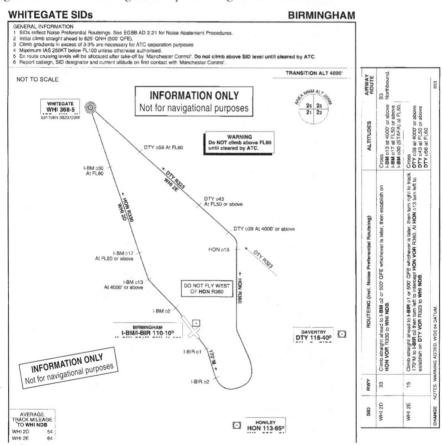

■ Figure 19-4 **AIP AD excerpt for the Whitegate SIDs from Birmingham**

En Route Charts

En route Radio Navigation Charts for IFR pilots are published by both *Aerad* and *Jeppesen*, on which certain IFR tracks are specified, along with a lot of other details. Study of these charts and their legends is necessary for instrument-rated pilots, and is recommended for IMC-rated pilots. Sample excerpts follow.

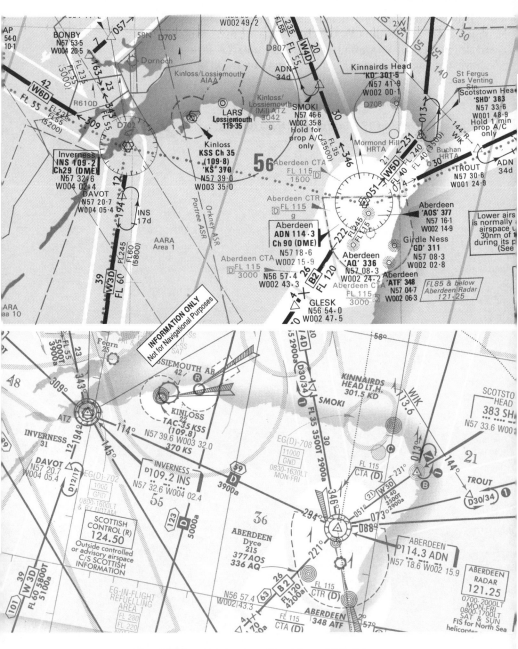

Reproduced with permission from *Aerad* EUR/3 and *Jeppesen* E (LO) 1A charts

■ Figure 19-5 **Excerpts from Aerad (top) and Jeppesen en route charts**

IMC-rated pilots are generally able to plan IMC flights using a visual chart such as the CAA 1:500,000 series, measuring desired tracks and calculating minimum safe altitudes (at least 1,000 ft above the highest obstacle within 5 nm of track) in a similar manner to preparing for visual cross-country flights (see Vol. 3 of *The Air Pilot's Manual*).

Now complete **Exercises 19 – Instrument Departures.**

Holding and Manoeuvring

Holding Patterns

Joining a holding pattern is an efficient and convenient means of delaying an aircraft in a prescribed pattern at a given location. Further progress of the flight ceases until the aeroplane is cleared to proceed.

The delaying action could be required for a number of reasons, such as waiting for an onward en route clearance, or waiting until other aircraft have commenced an ILS approach and an approach slot has become available, or waiting until a storm has moved away from the intended aerodrome of landing.

A holding pattern is generally a *racetrack* shape, and has five basic elements:

☐ the holding fix;
☐ the holding radial or bearing;
☐ the location of the holding radial or bearing relative to the eight main points of the compass;
☐ the direction of turns; and
☐ the timing.

A typical holding pattern, as shown in Figure 20-1, is a one-minute, right-hand pattern, south of the 250 VOR radial, inbound 070. The holding fix is the VOR.

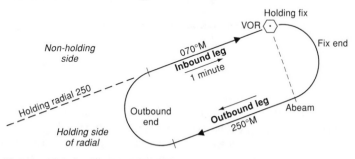

■ Figure 20-1 **A typical holding pattern**

Holding patterns are shown on charts in sufficient detail for a pilot to join and maintain one correctly. There may be other details superimposed on the chart, but, with experience, the details of the holding pattern are easily read. Most patterns are based on a radio navigation aid (e.g. at *Southend* on the NDB, at *Glasgow* on the VOR), or on a combination of aids (e.g. *Biggin Hill* 243° inbound on the 063 VOR radial with the fix at 7 DME).

As well as the details listed above, they may also show the minimum holding altitude (MHA), which is 1,800 ft on QNH (and normally 2,000 ft by ATC instruction) at Biggin Hill (BIG), and 3,500 ft on QNH at Glasgow (GOW).

Do not be concerned with the technical-sounding descriptions given above – instrument flying has its own jargon which you will quickly learn.

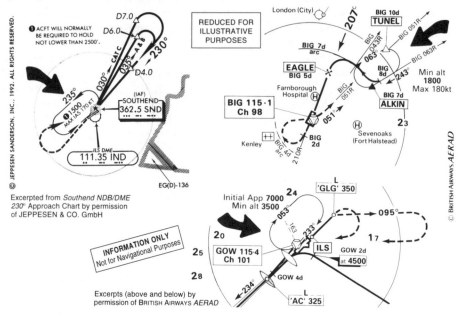

Excerpted from *Southend NDB/DME* 230° Approach Chart by permission of JEPPESEN & CO. GmbH

Excerpts (above and below) by permission of BRITISH AIRWAYS *AERAD*

■ *Figure 20-2* **Examples of holding patterns on instrument approach charts**

A complete one-minute holding pattern will, if flown perfectly, take four minutes. In nil-wind conditions, the straight inbound and outbound legs will each take one minute, as will the rate-1 180° turns at each end, making a total of four minutes. Normal timing commences from either abeam the beacon outbound, or from wings-level after rolling out of the turn if the abeam position cannot be determined (whichever is the latter).

In a two-minute holding pattern, the straight legs are increased to two minutes, the complete pattern then taking six minutes, and occupying more airspace.

Occasionally, the delay required during holding is less than four minutes, in which case the timing of the outbound leg can be adjusted for the aeroplane to arrive overhead the fix at the desired time – for instance, at an expected approach time (EAT) for an ILS approach that has been nominated by ATC.

Tracking in Holding Patterns

The main tracking leg of a holding pattern is the inbound leg towards the specified aid – usually an NDB or a VOR. Follow normal tracking procedures, allowing for drift to maintain the desired track.

Monitor the tracking periodically on the ADF or VOR cockpit display, which act as navigation performance instruments. Most of your attention will be on the attitude flying instruments (monitoring height, airspeed and direction), with an occasional scan of the navigation instruments (ADF, VOR, DME). Make any adjustments to heading with reference to the attitude indicator and the heading indicator.

During the turns and the outbound leg there is no direct tracking aid. Both the turns and the outbound leg of the holding pattern are modified according to the estimated wind effect, so that the rate-1 turn to rejoin the inbound track will bring the aeroplane out right on track. Checking the instruments in the cockpit during this turn inbound will enable you to determine if you will overshoot or undershoot the inbound track, and enable you to take early corrective action.

Wind Corrections in Holding Patterns

The aim of a standard holding pattern is to achieve an approximate total time of four minutes around the pattern, with a fairly tidy turn from the outbound leg onto the inbound leg to the fix.

In nil-wind conditions, the ground track of the holding pattern will be a straightforward *racetrack* pattern. Outbound timing will begin as the aeroplane passes abeam the fix, and the outbound leg (where there is no tracking aid) will simply be the reciprocal of the inbound leg, flown for 1 minute.

In a tailwind, reduce the outbound leg by 1 second per knot of tailwind.

TAILWIND. If there is a strong tailwind outbound, however, then 1 minute outbound will carry the aeroplane much further than in still wind conditions, and it will be carried even further downwind during the turn inbound. With an airspeed of 90 kt, for instance, the groundspeed will be 110 kt outbound with a 20 kt tailwind and only 70 kt inbound. It will be a long haul (well in excess of 1 minute) back to the fix – unless a correction to the outbound timing is made.

A reasonable correction is to reduce the 1 minute outbound by 1 second per knot of tailwind. For instance, with a 20 knot tailwind outbound, reduce the timing to 40 seconds outbound before commencing the rate-1 turn inbound.

In a headwind, increase the outbound leg by 1 second per knot.

HEADWIND. Conversely, in strong headwind outbound, add 1 second per knot. The timing is commenced when abeam the fix and on heading – another use for the stopwatch.

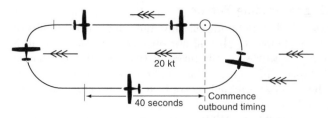

■ *Figure 20-3* **Adjust outbound timing to allow for head/tail wind**

CROSSWIND. In strong crosswind conditions, the aeroplane will tend to be carried downwind both on the straight legs and during the turns. The inbound track to the fix is the easiest part of the pattern, since it has a direct tracking aid, and a suitable drift allowance for the inbound leg can be found by normal tracking corrections.

For the turns and the outbound leg, however, measures to counter the wind effect can only be estimated, since there is no direct tracking aid. One turn will be downwind, the outbound leg will have a crosswind, and the other turn will be into a head-wind. With common sense and a little experience, however, you will handle this effectively.

EXAMPLE 1 In the pattern in Figure 20-4, a strong tailwind on the rate-1 turn outbound will increase its *ground radius*, the path it follows over the ground. If the aeroplane then flies the published outbound heading without any adjustment for wind, it will be carried even further downwind. The rate-1 turn inbound, with its much smaller ground radius into wind, will then place the aeroplane well short of the required inbound track, and the attempt to regain it will require a long haul back into wind. The result is an unsatisfactory holding pattern but, with some thought, this may be remedied.

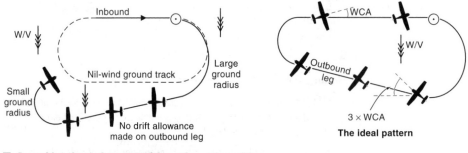

■ *Figure 20-4* **Apply 3 times WCA on the outbound leg**

On the outbound leg, simply applying a comparable drift allowance to that inbound will cause the aeroplane to parallel the inbound leg. However, it will not overcome the problem of the different ground radii of the turns. To allow for this, it is recommended that, when a particular wind correction angle is used on the inbound leg, you apply a triple wind correction angle into wind on the outbound leg to a maximum of 30°.

For instance, if a 8° WCA to the left is used inbound, then a 24° right WCA should be applied outbound. This means that the rate-1 turn outbound will be modified to 294° in this case. The rate-1 turn onto the inbound leg at the far end of the holding pattern will then be much neater.

The triple drift allowance can be thought of as one drift allowance to allow for the wind effect during the outbound turn, plus a second to allow for the drift on the outbound leg, plus a third to allow for the wind effect during the turn onto the inbound leg. If the triple drift allowance (to a maximum of 30°) results in an outbound heading within 30° of the wind direction, then there will be little drift on the outbound leg itself, in which case the correction can be reduced to a double drift allowance (2 × WCA), just to allow for the wind effect in the turns.

The success of the outbound leg drift allowance will be discovered when turning to rejoin the inbound leg. It is unlikely that it will have been perfect. If too great a correction was made, then the aeroplane will fly through the inbound track. If the correction was too small, then the turn inbound will have to be stopped early until the inbound track is regained. Aim to regain the inbound track without delay, and then make suitable adjustments to tracking and timing for the next run around the pattern.

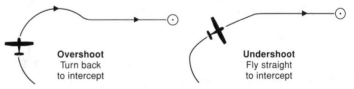

Overshoot
Turn back
to intercept

Undershoot
Fly straight
to intercept

■ *Figure 20-5* **Rejoining the inbound leg**

Holding Pattern Wind Corrections Summary

1. *Apply a triple wind correction angle outbound, to a maximum of 30°. If the resulting outbound heading is within 30° of the wind direction, reduce it to a double WCA.*

2. *Reduce the outbound timing by 1 second per knot of tailwind (and increase it by 1 second per knot for a headwind component).*

Joining a Holding Pattern

There will usually be some manoeuvring required to join a holding pattern, since an aeroplane may approach the holding fix from
any direction and, surprisingly, this is often the most difficult
manoeuvre to perform. Three types of **sector entry** have been
devised, based on the direction of the inbound holding track and
an imaginary line angled at 70° to the inbound holding track.
How the aeroplane joins the pattern depends on the aircraft's
heading, since this determines the sector from which it is
approaching.

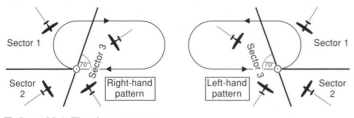

■ *Figure 20-6* **The three sectors**

A Sector 1 Entry is a parallel entry

☐ Fly to the fix and turn onto an outbound heading to fly parallel
to the inbound track. Do not backtrack on it – just fly parallel
to it on the non-holding side for a period of 1 minute (plus or
minus 1 sec/kt wind correction).

☐ Turn in the direction of the holding side through more than
180° to either intercept the inbound track or return to the fix.

☐ On reaching the fix, turn to follow the holding pattern.

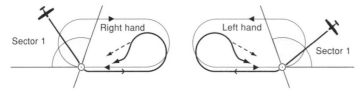

■ *Figure 20-7* **The sector 1 parallel entry**

A Section 2 Entry is an Offset entry

☐ Fly to the fix and turn onto a heading to fly a 30° teardrop, i.e.
to make good a track within the pattern (on the holding side)
at 30° to the reciprocal of the inbound leg for a period of
1 minute (plus or minus wind correction).

☐ Turn in the direction of the holding pattern to intercept the
inbound track.

☐ Track to the fix, and proceed with normal holding patterns.

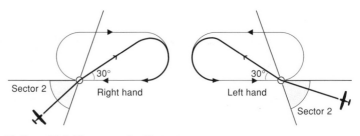

■ *Figure 20-8* **The sector 2 offset entry**

A Sector 3 Entry is a Direct Entry
☐ Fly to the fix and turn to follow the holding pattern.
☐ If a full 180° turn (or greater) is required to take up the outbound heading, then commence turning immediately you reach overhead the fix. If, however, the turn onto the outbound leg is less than 180°, then hold heading for an appropriate time past the fix before commencing the rate-1 turn. For instance, if the turn is less than 180° by 45° (which at rate 1 of 3°/sec would take 15 sec), maintain the original heading for 15 seconds before turning.

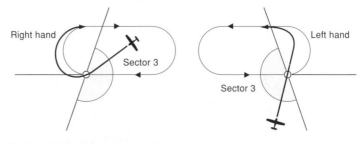

■ *Figure 20-9* **The sector 3 direct entry**

Entering a holding pattern correctly and efficiently (if one has to be entered) is a sign of a good instrument pilot. Holding patterns often precede an instrument approach, so a good holding pattern is a good start to the let-down.

Using the ADF to Enter and Maintain a Holding Pattern
Many holding patterns use an NDB or locator as the fix. In Figure 20-10, typical ADF indications are shown as the pilot initially tracks to the NDB, and then joins the holding pattern.

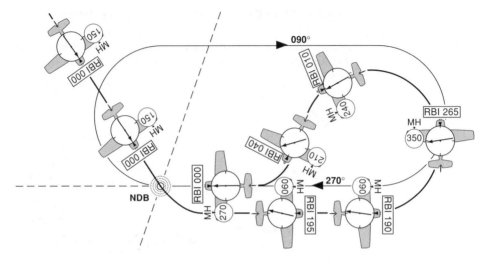

■ Figure 20-10 **Making a sector 1 entry using the ADF**

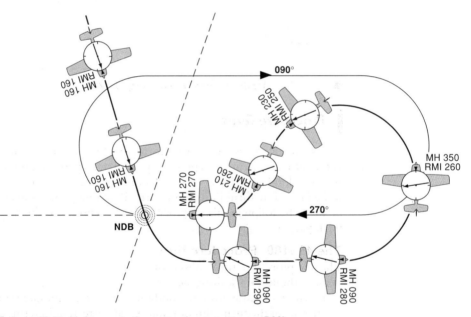

■ Figure 20-11 **Making a similar sector 1 entry using an RMI**

Using the VOR to Enter and Maintain a Holding Pattern

Some holding patterns use a VOR ground station as the fix. In Figure 20-12, typical VOR cockpit indications are shown as the pilot initially tracks to the VOR, and then joins the racetrack pattern.

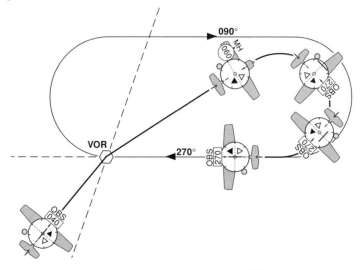

■ *Figure 20-12* **Making a sector 2 entry using the VOR**

Procedure Turns

Unless suitable fixes, or radar vectoring by ATC, permits a direct entry into an instrument approach procedure, a positioning turn of some kind may be necessary. Course reversals can be made using procedure turns or teardrop turns. Positioning turns can also be made by following the appropriate sector entry into the race-track pattern.

The 45°/180° Procedure Turn

The 45° procedure turn consists of:
- ☐ an outbound track from the fix;
- ☐ a turn of 45° away from the outbound track for 1 minute from the start of the turn (plus or minus wind correction in terms of both drift and time); and then
- ☐ a 180° turn in the opposite direction to intercept the inbound track.

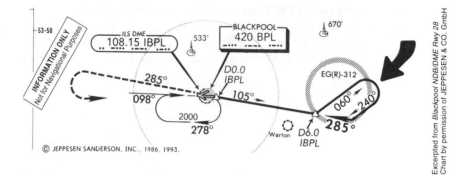

■ *Figure 20-13* **The 45° procedure turn**

Left or *right* in a description of the procedure turn refers to the direction of the initial turn.

The 80°/260° Procedure Turn

The 80° procedure turn is less common in the UK. It consists of:
☐ an outbound track away from the fix;
☐ a turn of 80° away from the outbound track;
☐ followed almost immediately by a 260° turn in the opposite direction to intercept the inbound track.

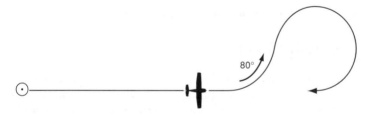

■ *Figure 20-14* **The 80° procedure turn**

If the initial turn is into a strong headwind, then the 80° heading can be held for a brief time (e.g. an extra one second per knot of headwind), before the 260° turn is commenced.

If the initial turn puts a strong tailwind behind the aeroplane, then stop turning before 80° is reached, and gently roll immediately into the reversal turn.

The Base Turn

The base turn, used to reverse direction by more than 180°, is a teardrop pattern which consists of:
☐ a specified outbound track and timing or distance limit;
☐ followed by a turn to intercept the inbound track.

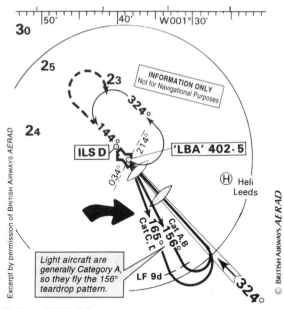

■ Figure 20-15 **A base turn**

Positioning in a Racetrack Pattern for an Approach

Many instrument approaches commence at the holding fix, and simply by carrying out a sector entry to the holding pattern (even if a full pattern is not required) the aeroplane is in position to commence the approach. For example, an aeroplane approaching the LBA NDB at *Leeds Bradford* from the east, could enter the holding pattern with a sector 1 parallel entry, and be ready immediately on reaching the fix on the inbound leg of the pattern to begin the approach. If there is any delay in approval to begin the approach, the aeroplane can simply remain in the holding pattern.

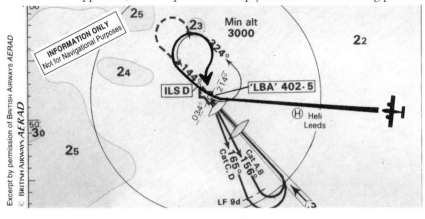

■ Figure 20-16 **Positioning in a holding pattern**

Sometimes alternative procedures are marked on the instrument approach chart. On the *Norwich* chart, for instance, there is a 45° procedure turn specified, but there is also an alternative, and simpler, procedure: "Extend the outbound leg of the holding pattern to 2 minutes, and then turn left to intercept the localizer." Only one turn will be required, instead of three.

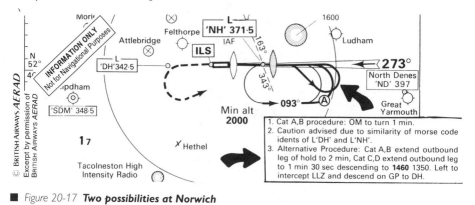

■ *Figure 20-17* **Two possibilities at Norwich**

Now complete **Exercises 20 – Holding and Manoeuvring.**

Instrument Approaches

Vertical Navigation

Correct vertical navigation is vital during instrument flight, when terrain, obstacles and other traffic may not be seen. Vertical navigation is based mainly on the indications of the altimeter, therefore winding in the correct altimeter subscale setting is essential. It is also important that each new altimeter setting advised by ATC is read back by the pilot as confirmation.

Read back all altimeter settings for confirmation.

The datum for vertical navigation is mean sea level. QNH is the subscale setting that allows the altimeter to indicate altitude, the vertical distance of the aircraft above mean sea level (amsl).

Aerodrome Procedures

Aerodrome elevation is the vertical distance in feet above mean sea level of the highest point on the landing area of the aerodrome. It is published on all instrument approach charts (usually near the top of the page) as *Elev* or *Apt. Elev* (airport elevation).

Set QFE for visual manoeuvring at aerodromes.

For visual manoeuvring at an aerodrome, it is usual in the UK to have Aerodrome QFE set in the subscale, so that the altimeter indicates height above the aerodrome elevation.

On straight-in instrument approaches to a particular runway that has a threshold elevation published (which may be the case if it is 7 ft or more below aerodrome elevation), the altimeter may be set to **Threshold QFE** to indicate vertical dis-

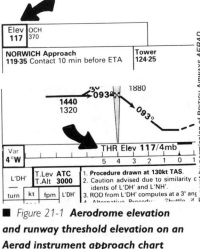

■ *Figure 21-1* **Aerodrome elevation and runway threshold elevation on an Aerad instrument approach chart**

tance above the runway threshold. For a 30 ft difference between aerodrome and threshold elevations, Threshold QFE will be 1 mb greater than Aerodrome QFE.

Set Regional QNH or 1013 mb en route.

When taking off for a cross-country flight you will be given Aerodrome QNH before take-off so that the altimeter will indicate altitude (amsl). For en route cruising, fly at a level based on:

☐ **1013.2 mb** when cruising IFR at or above the transition level, and preferably at a quadrantal level; and

☐ **Regional QNH** when cruising at or below the transition altitude (usually 3,000 ft in the UK) when outside controlled airspace and not in the vicinity of an aerodrome.

Arriving aircraft will initially be given Aerodrome QNH, and ATC reference to vertical position will be in terms of altitude until the aircraft commences final approach. **Minimum sector altitudes (MSAs)** are published on instrument approach charts and will provide at least 300 metres (1,000 ft) vertical clearance within 25 nm of the homing facility for the instrument approach.

If the aircraft remains at or above the relevant MSA, then it should be clear of terrain and obstacles as it tracks to the aerodrome prior to making the approach. Some aerodromes have instrument approaches with an MSA that applies to all sectors (e.g. *East Midlands*), but most aerodromes have different MSAs for different sectors, depending on the direction from which the aircraft is arriving and the terrain over which it has to pass (e.g. *Leeds Bradford ILS/DME Rwy 32,* and *Chichester VOR 32*).

☐ *Jeppesen* publishes MSAs in a circle at the top of its charts, with the sectors delineated by magnetic bearings from the homing facility. See Figure 21-2.

☐ *Aerad* publishes the information differently, as four sector safe altitude (SSA) boxes, one in each corner of the plan section of the instrument approach chart. An SSA of 2,300 ft amsl within 25 nm of the aerodrome will be published as SSA 25 nm 23.

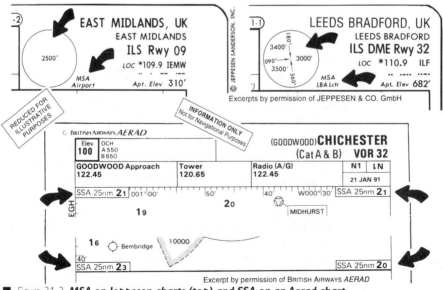

■ *Figure 21-2* **MSA on Jeppesen charts (top) and SSA on an Aerad chart**

If visual manoeuvring (circling) around the aerodrome is required, then Aerodrome QFE will be given; if a straight-in landing is possible, then Runway Threshold QFE may be given.

Set QNH on a missed approach.

After a missed approach, vertical position will be referred to in terms of altitude, so QNH will be the more appropriate subscale setting at this stage (except at military aerodromes, which normally use a QFE procedure). See Figure 21-3.

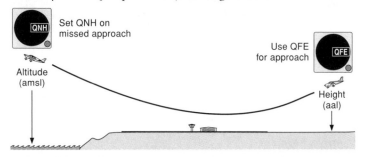

■ *Figure 21-3* **Altimeter subscale settings in the vicinity of an aerodrome**

The Instrument Approach

Having arrived in instrument conditions at the homing facility (which may be a locator, VOR, etc.), the aircraft is then in a position to commence the instrument approach. Delaying action, if necessary, can be taken by entering a holding pattern.

When an instrument approach is designed by an aircraft performance specialist, the initial consideration is the final approach track to a minimum altitude (or minimum height). The procedure is then designed backwards from this desirable final approach track through a number of segments, with the aim of providing a suitable flightpath between the en route phase of the flight and final approach.

Generally, the fewer the turns, the less complicated the approach, and the better it is for the pilot and for ATC.

The Segments of an Instrument Approach
The complete instrument approach procedure may be divided into up to five separate segments that blend into each other:

1. Arrival segment.

2. Initial approach segment.

3. Intermediate approach segment.

4. Final approach segment.

5. Missed approach segment.

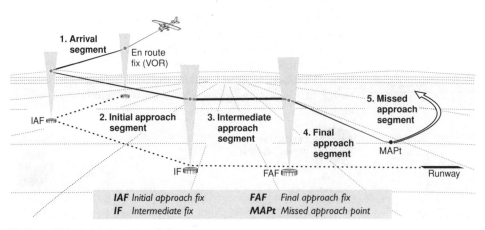

■ *Figure 21-4* **A simple and well-designed instrument approach**

1. Arrival Segment

The arrival segment is the route followed from the en route phase of the flight to the **initial approach fix (IAF).** It usually starts at an en route fix and ends at the initial approach fix (IAF), usually the first navigational facility associated with the procedure. The arrival segment may also be referred to as a *feeder route* or *terminal route*. An example of an arrival segment is shown in Figure 21-5: the feeder route from the LANAK fix (at 20 DME on the 127° Glasgow VOR radial) toward the Glasgow (GOW) VOR, on a track of 307°M, probably at or above 4,500 ft amsl (since the procedure starts at 4,500 ft amsl); turning left at 2 DME from GOW VOR to track outbound on the Rwy 05 localizer course.

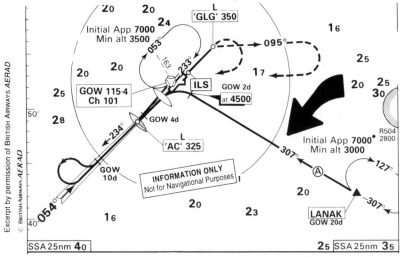

■ *Figure 21-5* **Arrival segment for Glasgow ILS Rwy 05 approach (Aerad)**

There may be a number of feeder routes into the one instrument approach procedure to cater for aircraft arriving from different directions, or there may be none. Many procedures do not require an arrival segment – for instance, if the en route tracking ends at the initial approach fix.

2. Initial Approach Segment

In the initial approach segment, the aircraft is manoeuvred to enter the intermediate segment. The initial approach segment commences at the initial approach fix (IAF), and may consist of a particular track, VOR radial, arc, procedure turn, holding pattern, radar vector – or any combination of these.

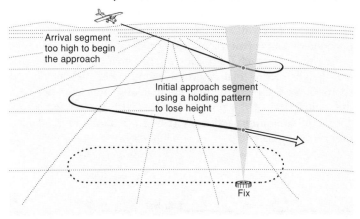

Arrival segment too high to begin the approach

Initial approach segment using a holding pattern to lose height

Fix

■ *Figure 21-6* **The initial approach segment**

3. Intermediate Approach Segment

The intermediate approach segment blends the initial approach segment and the final approach segment. It is the segment in which aircraft configuration, speed and positioning adjustments should be completed prior to entering the final approach segment, by which time all cockpit pre-landing checks should normally be completed, with the aircraft established in a suitable condition for landing. Your flying instructor will explain the procedures to use for your particular aircraft.

The intermediate approach segment ends at the **final approach fix (FAF),** and may begin either:

☐ at a designated intermediate approach fix (such as an NDB or locator outer marker); or

☐ on completion of a dead-reckoning track, or a reversal or race-track procedure.

4. Final Approach Segment

The final approach segment of a non-precision approach (such as an NDB let-down) begins at the final approach fix (FAF), and is the segment in which the alignment and descent for landing are accomplished. It ends at the **missed approach point (MAPt)**. In some instrument approaches, the final approach fix is the same as the initial approach fix (e.g. the IAF may be the locator outer marker, LOM, when flying outbound, and the FAF is the same LOM when flying inbound). Figure 21-7 shows one such approach.

Final approach may be made to a runway for a **straight-in landing,** or it may be made for a **circling approach** (visual manoeuvring for at least a partial circuit) to a runway with which the final approach of the instrument procedure is not aligned, provided of course that the pilot becomes visual at a suitable time.

The final approach fix should be crossed at or above the specified height before final descent is commenced. Where no final approach fix is shown, the final approach segment commences at the completion of the procedure turn, with the aircraft within ±5° of the **final approach track (FAT),** whereupon final descent may be commenced.

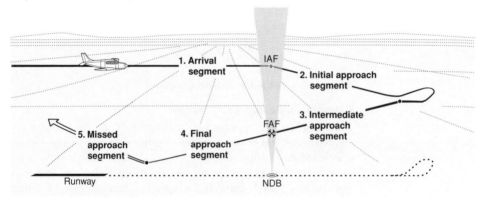

■ *Figure 21-7* **The five segments of a typical NDB approach**

Step-down fixes, if published on the chart profile diagram, are limiting heights, and should be crossed at or above their minimum crossing heights.

Where a suitable DME exists, especially a DME located at the runway threshold, some descent slope guidance may be provided for non-precision approaches in the form of a table of *altitude* or *height versus DME distance.* It is not mandatory to follow this information precisely – it is intended to assist pilots in carrying out straight-in and non-precision approaches.

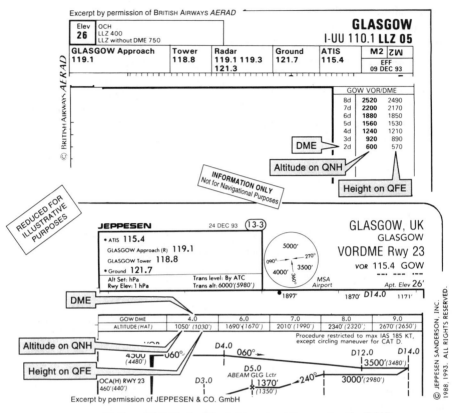

■ Figure 21-8 **Typical final descent guidance using the DME**

The final approach segment for a precision approach is considered to commence at the **final approach point (FAP),** where the intermediate segment of the procedure intersects the glidepath for the precision part of the ILS. It is marked on *Aerad* and *Jeppesen* charts with a Maltese cross. If this point coincides with a suitable fix (e.g. a LOM), it is called a **final approach fix (FAF).**

The ILS approach is designed so that the aeroplane will intercept the glideslope from below, generally by flying level until the slope is intercepted, to avoid the possibility of following one of the false glideslopes that may exist at steep angles such as 6°, 9°, 12°, etc.

> *Avoid false glideslopes! Intercept the glideslope on an ILS from below.*

Final descent slope guidance on an ILS is provided by the electronic glideslope. Descent on the glidepath should not be initiated unless the aircraft is on track (within half-scale deflection of the localizer). A fix or facility, usually the outer marker (OM) (but it could be a locator [L] or a DME distance), is provided to allow the pilot to verify the *glidepath/altitude* relationship at one point on the precision approach. Descent below the published crossing altitude at the fix or facility should not occur before passing the fix or facility.

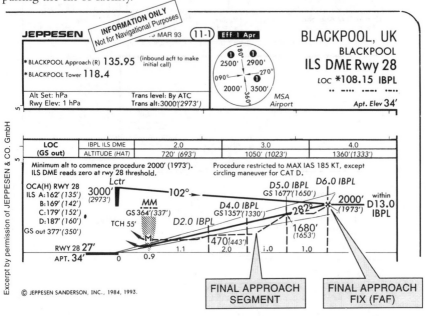

■ *Figure 21-9* **The final approach segment of an ILS**

It is most important that you do *not* descend below your minimum permitted altitude/height for a particular approach unless you have become 'visual' and can continue the approach to land visually, with the runway environment and nearby ground features in view.

The calculation of the minimum altitude/height should be done well before the instrument approach is even commenced, in a period when the workload is not as high – possibly as far back as on the cruise, or even pre-flight on the ground at the flight planning stage.

The starting point in calculating minima is the OCA(H) published on the instrument approach chart, to which significant additions must be made. OCH is the obstacle clearance height above the aerodrome level (and so is applicable when using QFE). OCA is the obstacle clearance altitude above mean sea level (and is applicable when using QNH).

On *Aerad* charts for the UK, where QFE is the altimeter setting most commonly used on final approach, the information is shown as OCH (in the box beside the field elevation, in the top left corner of the chart).

On *Jeppesen* charts, the minimum is shown as OCA(H). For example, on the *Leeds Bradford ILS DME Rwy 32,* the minimum is written as 832′(170′). The difference (662) equals the runway threshold elevation. Different OCA(H)s are published for different categories of aeroplane, based on speed (and manoeuvrability) – most training planes are in Category A.

Take the greater of **OCA(H) plus required additions** and the **absolute minimum** to obtain your personal minimum for the approach. The absolute minima are:

☐ **500 ft decision height** on QFE for a precision approach, such as an ILS; or

☐ **600 ft minimum descent height** on QFE for a non-precision approach, such as an NDB let-down or a VOR let-down.

Be very careful calculating minima! More about this in Chapter 22, *Instrument Minima.*

5. Missed Approach Segment

If you have not become visual by a particular point or minimum height on final descent, you must make a missed approach.

PRECISION APPROACHES. For a precision approach, such as the instrument landing system, the **missed approach point (MAPt)** is defined by the intersection of the glidepath with the pilot's decision height, and therefore is not shown on approach charts. Unless visual, the pilot should commence a missed approach *immediately* the DH is reached on an ILS.

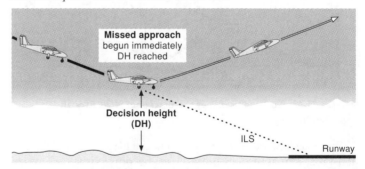

Missed approach begun immediately DH reached

Decision height (DH)

ILS

Runway

■ *Figure 21-10* **If not visual, commence the missed approach on reaching the decision height on a precision approach**

NON-PRECISION APPROACHES. For a non-precision approach, the **missed approach point (MAPt)** is defined by either a fix, facility or timing, and is shown on both the plan and profile diagrams as a dotted line. It is also described in text. If a turn is specified in the missed approach procedure, then it should not be commenced until the aeroplane has passed the MAPt and is established in the climb.

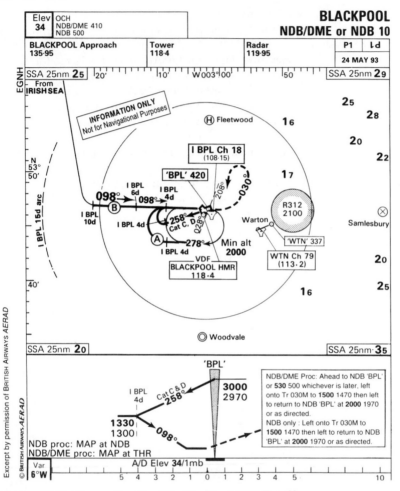

Elev	OCH				P1	Ld
34	NDB/DME 410			**BLACKPOOL**		
	NDB 500			**NDB/DME or NDB 10**		
BLACKPOOL Approach 135·95		Tower 118·4		Radar 119·95	24 MAY 93	

■ *Figure 21-11* **Plan and profile of the Blackpool NDB Rwy 10 approach (Aerad)**

You may not descend below your calculated MDA(H) on a non-precision approach unless you become visual. However (unlike on a precision approach), you may track in as far as the MAPt at or above this level in the hope of becoming visual, before beginning a missed approach. It is possible that you may become visual in a position from which it is not possible to complete a straight-in landing safely, in which case some manoeuvring to position the aeroplane will be necessary.

The missed approach segment is considered to be completed at an altitude/height sufficient to allow either:

☐ initiation of another instrument approach;

☐ return to a designated holding pattern; or
☐ resumption of en route flight to a diversion aerodrome.

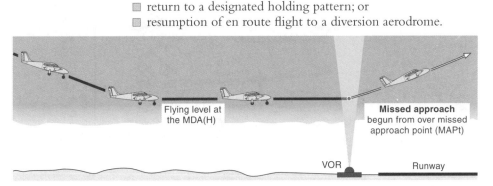

Flying level at
the MDA(H)

Missed approach
begun from over missed
approach point (MAPt)

VOR   Runway

■ *Figure 21-12 **If not visual on a non-precision approach, you may track
in to the MAPt at the MDA(H) before executing a missed approach***

*Set QNH on a
missed approach.*

Instructions from ATC during the missed approach will be in terms of *altitude,* and so it may be necessary to alter the subscale setting from QFE to QNH. During the missed approach, pilots may continue to use the altimeter setting selected for the final approach, but reference to the vertical position of the aircraft exchanged in communication with ATC should be expressed in terms of altitude on aerodrome QNH, unless otherwise instructed by ATC. See AIP ENR 1-7-2).

Becoming Visual on an Instrument Approach

Of course, the aim of an instrument approach is to become visual and then to go ahead and make a safe landing. Some instrument approaches position you ideally for a straight-in landing, whereas others may put you in a position where some visual manoeuvring (circling) is necessary to position the aeroplane for a landing.

Visual manoeuvring after an instrument approach is discussed in Chapter 22.

Instrument Approach Charts

Instrument approach charts provide a graphic presentation of:
☐ holding procedures (if required prior to commencing the instrument approach);
☐ the instrument approach procedure; and
☐ the missed approach procedure (in case the approach has to be discontinued at any time).

Instrument approach charts are designed to be readable in the cockpit, although some difficulty may be experienced in turbulence and/or poor light. The actual instrument approach will be shown in both plan and profile on the chart, along with other significant features such as aerodromes and obstructions.

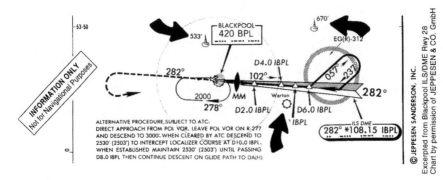

■ *Figure 21-13* **Excerpt from a Blackpool chart, showing Warton aerodrome and obstructions (Jeppesen)**

Instrument approach charts are available for all aerodromes where instrument approach procedures have been established and approved by the CAA. The various types of chart in use that are acceptable to the UK CAA are those published by:

☐ *British Airways/Aerad;*
☐ *Jeppesen;* and
☐ the CAA.

Aerad and *Jeppesen* are the most commonly used charts in commercial operations. A chart list for CAA charts can be found in UK AIP.

You must study carefully the instrument approach charts that you will be using, since presentation of the same instrument approach by the different publishers is not identical. The symbols and abbreviations used will also differ. We have used a variety of charts in this manual to expose you to both publishers: *Aerad* and *Jeppesen*. A description of each approach is given in UK AIP, and during your learning phase, it is worthwhile comparing this with the actual charts.

Use only current instrument approach charts! They are regu-larly revised and amendments made available. Changes to the actual procedure, the appearance of significant new obstacles – such as buildings or masts in the approach or missed approach areas, changes to radio frequencies, or the addition of new radio navigation facilities relevant to that approach, etc., will require issue of either a new chart or an amendment to the old chart.

Keep your approach charts up to date.

Urgent amendments of a timely nature may be advised to pilots by NOTAM. Always check the date at the top of the chart, and check the NOTAMs for any amendments.

Elements of an Instrument Approach Chart

The information provided on an instrument approach chart includes:

☐ identification of the particular approach;

☐ a plan view of the approach and the missed approach;

☐ a profile view of the approach and the missed approach;

☐ holding procedures associated with the approach;

☐ full details of radio facilities associated with the approach, missed approach and holdings;

☐ necessary aerodrome, topographical and cultural information (coastlines, significant lakes and rivers, relief, built-up areas, etc.) pertinent to the safe execution of the approach; and

☐ a landing chart, showing the runway layout.

Identification of an Instrument Approach Chart

An instrument approach chart is normally identified in the top right-hand side by:

☐ the name of the aerodrome;

☐ an abbreviation of the type of facility (further identified by the runway served in the case of a *runway approach* as against an *aerodrome approach*); and

☐ additional information to distinguish between separate charts for the same aerodrome.

There will be further information, such as the frequency of the radio navigational facility on which the approach is based, and its Morse code identification signal. The aerodrome elevation (highest point on the landing area) is usually shown in this section of the chart. The date of the chart will also appear at the top.

Radio Communications Frequencies

Relevant VHF communications frequencies, usually in the order in which they will be used, are also listed near the top of the chart.

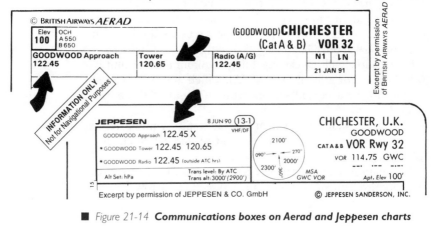

■ *Figure 21-14* **Communications boxes on Aerad and Jeppesen charts**

Plan View of the Instrument Approach

The plan view is a conformal projection that displays correct angular relationships. The scale is such that the approach charts are of a conveniently small size for use in the cockpit, yet large enough to show the intermediate approach area as well as the final approach and missed approach areas. A scale of 5 nm to the inch is typical. A graduated scale line will often be found down the left-hand side of the plan view (remember that 1 minute of latitude is 1 nm).

A reference circle of 5-nm radius or 10-nm radius is centred on the aerodrome to emphasise any obstructions or features close to the aerodrome. Horizontal distances along the approach are given in *nautical miles* to facilitate use of the DME (which reads in nm); however, remember that runway distances and runway visual range (RVR) are in *metres*.

The aerodrome is clearly shown on the plan view, including the runway pattern and any other distinctive patterns perhaps formed by taxiways or aprons. (Aerodrome elevation is shown in the top left box on *Aerad* charts, and in the top right area of *Jeppesen* charts, immediately above the plan view.) Restricted and Danger Areas are shown, as are nearby aerodromes (to avoid mis-identification once visual). Even large aeroplanes have been landed at incorrect aerodromes, often in good weather when the instrument-rated pilot has become visual well away from the destination aerodrome and not paid sufficient attention to tracking details to the aerodrome as shown on the instrument approach chart. An aerodrome symbol on the chart will alert you to this danger.

Even though obstacle clearance is provided for in the design of the instrument approach, significant topographical and other data, although not part of the actual instrument approach, may be shown on the chart to assist pilots when and if they become visual. It is very handy, for instance, to know the runway layout and the position of any nearby obstacles to expect when and if becoming visual on final approach.

Information will appear regarding minimum sector altitudes (MSA), or sector safe altitudes (SSA), which are the lowest safe altitudes in the specified sectors within 25 nm of the homing facility.

The plan position of each of the radio aids required for the procedure is shown, with frequencies, ident, and defined tracks in *degrees magnetic*.

The **main procedure track** is generally shown as a heavy, solid line with its magnetic direction and a directional arrow.

The **missed approach** is generally shown as a heavy, dashed line, with a directional arrow. The latest point at which to commence a missed approach according to the procedures is referred to as the missed approach point (MAPt).

The **holding pattern,** which, strictly speaking, is not part of most approaches, is generally shown as a light, solid or dotted line, with magnetic direction and a directional arrow. Some approaches, however, use the racetrack pattern as part of an alternative intermediate segment, replacing a procedure turn. The minimum holding altitude may also be shown near the holding pattern, as may any special distance or time requirements.

Profile View of an Instrument Approach Chart

The profile view of the instrument approach is published directly beneath the plan view. The aerodrome or a specific runway will be shown in the profile diagram, probably with its elevation stated nearby. Relevant radio facilities are also shown in profile.

The **main procedure track** is a solid line with a directional arrow and magnetic track. In the profile view, the angles shown are generally not to scale, but exaggerated for graphic effect. Approach slopes are really quite gentle (a typical ILS glideslope, for instance, is only 3° to the horizontal — a gradient of 1 in 20). The profile view of any reversal or procedure turn is shown as a horizontal line, which may have associated altitude, distance or time requirements stated nearby.

Vertical distances required along the instrument procedure are shown in feet on UK charts, both as *altitudes* (feet above mean sea level, amsl) based on the QNH altimeter setting, and as *heights* above aerodrome level (aal) based on the QFE altimeter setting.

The heights of obstructions will be shown as feet amsl. European charts may show vertical distances in *metres*.

The missed approach procedure will generally be shown as a dotted line with a directional arrow, with a written description nearby.

Obstacle Clearance Section

Somewhere on the chart will be stated the obstacle clearance information for final approach, from which you may calculate your decision altitude (height) for a precision approach, or minimum descent altitude (height) for a non-precision approach.

☐ *Jeppesen* **charts** present the basic information as OCA(H), the obstacle clearance altitude (height).

☐ *Aerad* **charts** specify the minimum as OCH, obstacle clearance height (aal, based on QFE). (*Aerad* also has a green page with aerodrome operating minima at the front of each aerodrome group.)

Groundspeeds vs. Descent Rates on Final, and Timing to MAPt

Some charts have a table towards the bottom that provides guidance regarding the *rate of descent* required at a particular *groundspeed* to maintain the aeroplane on the published approach slope.

To maintain a given slope, the faster the aeroplane is moving over the ground, the greater its rate of descent must be. To use this table, you need to apply the wind component to your airspeed to obtain groundspeed, and then read (or interpolate) the approximate rate of descent required to maintain the slope.

For a non-precision approach where the approach aid is well away from the aerodrome and acts as the final approach fix (FAF), *Jeppesen* charts also show the *time* from the FAF to the MAPt. *Aerad* gives a time from the FAF to the runway threshold (see Figure 21-15).

Gnd speed-Kts		70	90	100	120	140	160
Descent Grad.	6.0%	426	547	608	730	851	973
Lctr to MAP	4.3	3:41	2:52	2:35	2:09	1:51	1:37

Excerpted from *Glasgow NDB Rwy 05* Approach Chart by permission of JEPPESEN & CO. GmbH

kt	fpm	FAF
200	1060	–
180	950	THR
160	850	2:15
140	740	2:34
120	640	3:00
100	530	3:36
80	430	4:30

© BRITISH AIRWAYS *AERAD*

Excerpted from *London/Stansted ILS/DME 23* Approach Chart by permission of BRITISH AIRWAYS *AERAD*

■ *Figure 21-15* **Groundspeed/rate of descent/time tables: (above) Jeppesen non-precision approach chart; (right) Aerad precision approach chart**

On ILS charts, the *GS/RoD/time* information is useful in situations where the electronic glideslope is not available, and a localizer approach has to be made.

Holding Procedures Associated with the Approach

Any holding patterns associated with the approach are shown on the plan diagram. Initially, they may appear to clutter the chart, but, with familiarity, it is easy to distinguish the various components. In some procedures the holding pattern may actually form part of the approach – a *reversal of the outbound track* using a procedure turn may sometimes be avoided by using a published alternative (and simpler) procedure of tracking outbound in the holding pattern and then turning inbound to intercept the final approach track (FAT).

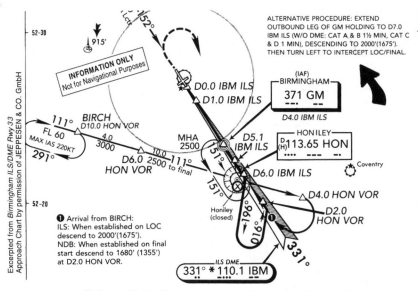

■ *Figure 21-16* **Alternative reversal procedure for the Birmingham Rwy 33 ILS/DME**

Typical Instrument Approach Charts

Examples of *Jeppesen* and *Aerad* instrument approach charts for some UK approaches follow.

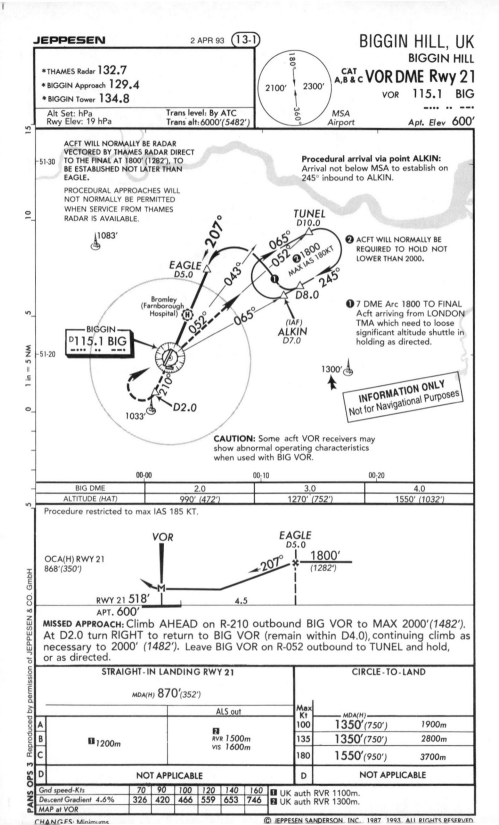

JEPPESEN 2 APR 93 (13-1)

BIGGIN HILL, UK
BIGGIN HILL
CAT A,B & C **VOR DME Rwy 21**
VOR **115.1 BIG**
---- .. ---

* THAMES Radar **132.7**
* BIGGIN Approach **129.4**
* BIGGIN Tower **134.8**

Alt Set: hPa	Trans level: By ATC
Rwy Elev: 19 hPa	Trans alt: 6000'(5482')

MSA Airport — 180° 2100' / 2300' 360°

Apt. Elev **600'**

ACFT WILL NORMALLY BE RADAR VECTORED BY THAMES RADAR DIRECT TO THE FINAL AT 1800' (1282'), TO BE ESTABLISHED NOT LATER THAN EAGLE.

PROCEDURAL APPROACHES WILL NOT NORMALLY BE PERMITTED WHEN SERVICE FROM THAMES RADAR IS AVAILABLE.

Procedural arrival via point ALKIN: Arrival not below MSA to establish on 245° inbound to ALKIN.

❷ ACFT WILL NORMALLY BE REQUIRED TO HOLD NOT LOWER THAN 2000.

❶ 7 DME Arc 1800 TO FINAL Acft arriving from LONDON TMA which need to loose significant altitude shuttle in holding as directed.

TUNEL D10.0
EAGLE D5.0 — 207° — 043° — 065° — 052° — ❷1800 MAX IAS 180KT — ❶ — 245° D8.0
Bromley (Farnborough Hospital) (H) — 052° — 065°
BIGGIN D115.1 BIG ---- .. ---
(IAF) ALKIN D7.0
R-210 — D2.0
1083'
1033'
1300'
1300'

INFORMATION ONLY Not for Navigational Purposes

CAUTION: Some acft VOR receivers may show abnormal operating characteristics when used with BIG VOR.

	00-00	00-10	00-20
BIG DME	2.0	3.0	4.0
ALTITUDE (HAT)	990' (472')	1270' (752')	1550' (1032')

Procedure restricted to max IAS 185 KT.

VOR — EAGLE D5.0 — ←207° — 1800' (1282')

OCA(H) RWY 21 868'(350')

M — RWY 21 **518'** — 4.5 — APT. **600'**

MISSED APPROACH: Climb AHEAD on R-210 outbound BIG VOR to MAX 2000'(1482'). At D2.0 turn RIGHT to return to BIG VOR (remain within D4.0), continuing climb as necessary to 2000' (1482'). Leave BIG VOR on R-052 outbound to TUNEL and hold, or as directed.

STRAIGHT-IN LANDING RWY 21		CIRCLE-TO-LAND	
MDA(H) **870'**(352')			

		ALS out	Max Kt	MDA(H)	
A			100	**1350'**(750')	1900m
B	❶1200m	❷ RVR 1500m VIS 1600m	135	**1350'**(750')	2800m
C			180	**1550'**(950')	3700m
D	NOT APPLICABLE		D	NOT APPLICABLE	

Gnd speed-Kts	70	90	100	120	140	160	❶ UK auth RVR 1100m.
Descent Gradient 4.6%	326	420	466	559	653	746	❷ UK auth RVR 1300m.
MAP at VOR							

CHANGES: Minimums

PANS OPS 3   Reproduced by permission of JEPPESEN & CO. GmbH

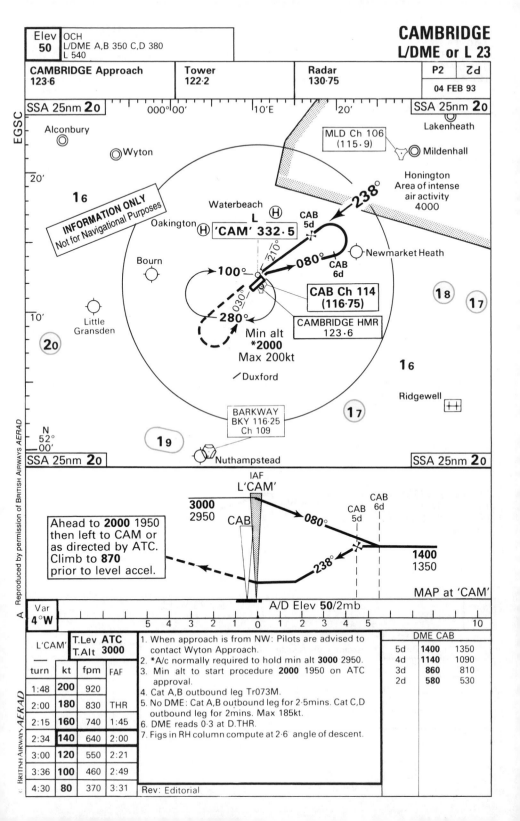

CAMBRIDGE
L/DME or L 23

Elev 50	OCH L/DME A,B 350 C,D 380 L 540		

CAMBRIDGE Approach 123·6	Tower 122·2	Radar 130·75	P2 / Zd
			04 FEB 93

EGSC

SSA 25nm **2**o

Alconbury

Wyton

MLD Ch 106 (115·9)

Lakenheath

Mildenhall

1 6

INFORMATION ONLY
Not for Navigational Purposes

Waterbeach

Oakington

L 'CAM' 332·5

238°

CAB 5d

Honington
Area of intense
air activity
4000

Bourn

080°

CAB 6d

Newmarket Heath

100°

210°

CAB Ch 114 (116·75)

18   **1**7

030°

280°

CAMBRIDGE HMR 123·6

Min alt *2000 Max 200kt

Little Gransden

2o

Duxford

16

Ridgewell

BARKWAY BKY 116·25 Ch 109

17

19

Nuthampstead

N 52° 00'

SSA 25nm **2**o

IAF
L'CAM'

3000 2950

CAB

080°

CAB 5d

CAB 6d

Ahead to **2000** 1950 then left to CAM or as directed by ATC. Climb to **870** prior to level accel.

238°

1400 1350

MAP at 'CAM'

A/D Elev **50**/2mb

Var 4°W

| | 5 | 4 | 3 | 2 | 1 | 0 | 1 | 2 | 3 | 4 | 5 | | 10 |

L'CAM'	T.Lev **ATC** T.Alt **3000**		
turn	kt	fpm	FAF
1:48	**200**	920	
2:00	**180**	830	THR
2:15	**160**	740	1:45
2:34	**140**	640	2:00
3:00	**120**	550	2:21
3:36	**100**	460	2:49
4:30	**80**	370	3:31

1. When approach is from NW: Pilots are advised to contact Wyton Approach.
2. *A/c normally required to hold min alt **3000** 2950.
3. Min alt to start procedure **2000** 1950 on ATC approval.
4. Cat A,B outbound leg Tr073M.
5. No DME: Cat A,B outbound leg for 2·5mins. Cat C,D outbound leg for 2mins. Max 185kt.
6. DME reads 0·3 at D.THR.
7. Figs in RH column compute at 2·6 angle of descent.

Rev: Editorial

DME CAB		
5d	**1400**	1350
4d	**1140**	1090
3d	**860**	810
2d	**580**	530

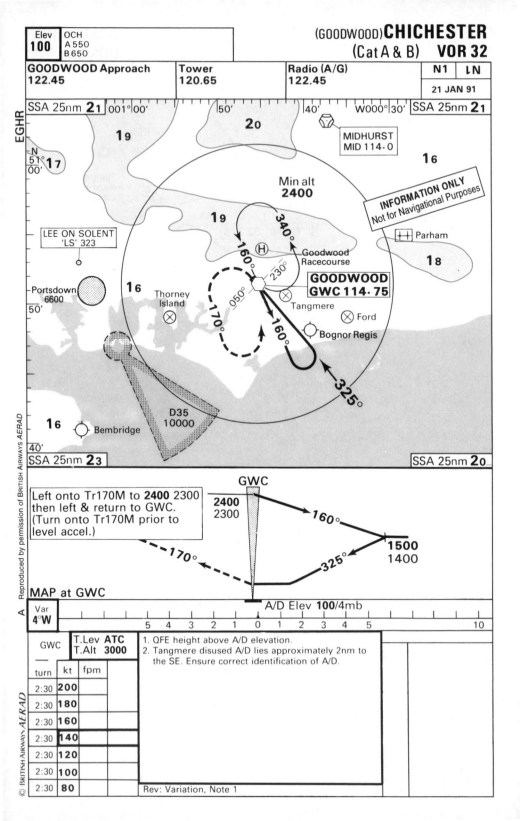

| Elev **100** | OCH A 550 B 650 | | | | N1 | LN |

| GOODWOOD Approach **122.45** | Tower **120.65** | Radio (A/G) **122.45** | 21 JAN 91 |

EGHR

SSA 25nm **21**   001°00'   50'   40'   W000°30'   SSA 25nm **21**

1 9

2 0

MIDHURST
MID 114·0

N 51° 00' **1 7**

1 9

Min alt **2400**

INFORMATION ONLY
Not for Navigational Purposes

1 6

Parham

1 8

LEE ON SOLENT 'LS' 323

160°

340°

230°

(H)

Goodwood
Racecourse

**GOODWOOD
GWC 114·75**

Portsdown 6600

1 6

Thorney Island

050°

170°

160°

Tangmere

Ford

Bognor Regis

325°

1 6

Bembridge

D35 10000

40'

SSA 25nm **23**

SSA 25nm **2 0**

Reproduced by permission of BRITISH AIRWAYS AERAD

GWC

Left onto Tr170M to **2400** 2300 then left & return to GWC. (Turn onto Tr170M prior to level accel.)

2400 2300

160°

170°

325°

1500 1400

MAP at GWC

A

| Var **4°W** |

A/D Elev **100**/4mb

5 4 3 2 1 0 1 2 3 4 5 ... 10

1. QFE height above A/D elevation.
2. Tangmere disused A/D lies approximately 2nm to the SE. Ensure correct identification of A/D.

GWC —	T.Lev **ATC** T.Alt **3000**	
turn	kt	fpm
2:30	**200**	
2:30	**180**	
2:30	**160**	
2:30	**140**	
2:30	**120**	
2:30	**100**	
2:30	**80**	

Rev: Variation, Note 1

© BRITISH AIRWAYS *AERAD*

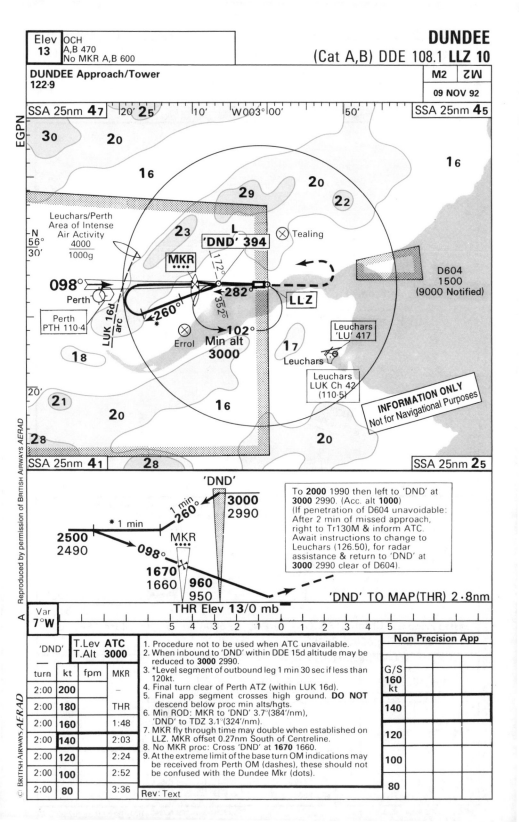

DUNDEE
(Cat A,B) DDE 108.1 LLZ 10

Elev 13	OCH A,B 470 No MKR A,B 600

DUNDEE Approach/Tower
122·9

M2 | ZW
09 NOV 92

EGPN

SSA 25nm **4**7   20' **2**5   10'   W003°00'   50'   SSA 25nm **4**5

3 0   2 0   1 6   1 6

2 9   2 0   2 2

Leuchars/Perth
Area of Intense
Air Activity
4000 / 1000g

2 3   L
'DND' 394   ⊗ Tealing

MKR ••••   172°

098°   282°   D604
Perth   352°   LLZ   1500
(9000 Notified)

260°

Perth
PTH 110·4   102°
⊗ Errol   Min alt
3000

LUK 16d arc

Leuchars
'LU' 417

1 7
Leuchars

Leuchars
LUK Ch 42
(110·5)

1 8

2 1

INFORMATION ONLY
Not for Navigational Purposes

2 8   2 0   1 6   2 0

SSA 25nm **4**1   **2**8   SSA 25nm **2**5

'DND'

To **2000** 1990 then left to 'DND' at
3000 2990. (Acc. alt **1000**)
(If penetration of D604 unavoidable:
After 2 min of missed approach,
right to Tr130M & inform ATC.
Await instructions to change to
Leuchars (126.50), for radar
assistance & return to 'DND' at
3000 2990 clear of D604).

3000 2990

1 min **260°**

* 1 min

2500 2490   **098°**

MKR ••••

1670 1660   **960** 950

'DND' TO MAP(THR) 2·8nm

THR Elev **13**/0 mb

5   4   3   2   1   0   1   2   3   4   5

Var
7°W

'DND'	T.Lev ATC T.Alt 3000			Non Precision App		
turn	kt	fpm	MKR	G/S 160 kt		
2:00	200		–			
2:00	180		THR	140		
2:00	160		1:48			
2:00	140		2:03	120		
2:00	120		2:24	100		
2:00	100		2:52			
2:00	80		3:36	80		

1. Procedure not to be used when ATC unavailable.
2. When inbound to 'DND' within DDE 15d altitude may be reduced to **3000** 2990.
3. *Level segment of outbound leg 1 min 30 sec if less than 120kt.
4. Final turn clear of Perth ATZ (within LUK 16d).
5. Final app segment crosses high ground. **DO NOT** descend below proc min alts/hgts.
6. Min ROD: MKR to 'DND' 3.7°(384'/nm), 'DND' to TDZ 3.1°(324'/nm).
7. MKR fly through time may double when established on LLZ. MKR offset 0.27nm South of Centreline.
8. No MKR proc: Cross 'DND' at **1670** 1660.
9. At the extreme limit of the base turn OM indications may be received from Perth OM (dashes), these should not be confused with the Dundee Mkr (dots).

Rev: Text

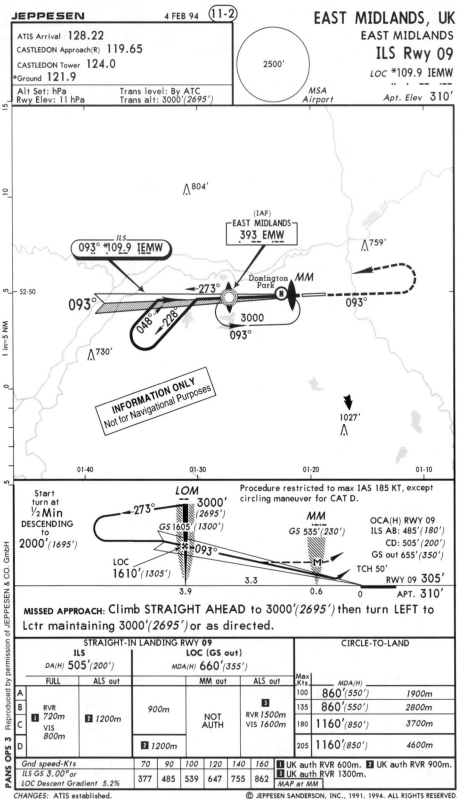

EAST MIDLANDS, UK
EAST MIDLANDS
ILS Rwy 09
LOC *109.9 IEMW
.. -- .. -- ... ---

ATIS Arrival **128.22**	
CASTLEDON Approach(R) **119.65**	
CASTLEDON Tower **124.0**	
*Ground **121.9**	

Alt Set: hPa	Trans level: By ATC
Rwy Elev: 11 hPa	Trans alt: 3000'(2695')

2500'
MSA
Airport

Apt. Elev **310'**

Plan view

804'

(IAF)
EAST MIDLANDS
393 EMW

759'

ILS
093° *109.9 IEMW

273°
Donington
Park
MM
H
093°

52-50
093°
048° 228°
3000
093°

730'

INFORMATION ONLY
Not for Navigational Purposes

1027'

01-40   01-30   01-20   01-10

1 in=5 NM

Profile

Start
turn at
½ Min
DESCENDING
to
2000'(1695')

LOM
273° 3000'
(2695')
GS 1605'(1300')
LOC
1610'(1305')
*
093°

Procedure restricted to max IAS 185 KT, except
circling maneuver for CAT D.

MM
GS 535'(230')
M

3.3

3.9   0.6   0

TCH 50'
RWY 09 **305'**
APT. **310'**

OCA(H) RWY 09
ILS AB: 485'(180')
CD: 505'(200')
GS out 655'(350')

MISSED APPROACH: Climb STRAIGHT AHEAD to 3000'(2695') then turn LEFT to
Lctr maintaining 3000'(2695') or as directed.

STRAIGHT-IN LANDING RWY 09						CIRCLE-TO-LAND		
ILS		LOC (GS out)						
DA(H) **505'(200')**		MDA(H) **660'(355')**			Max Kts	MDA(H)		
	FULL	ALS out		MM out	ALS out			
A			900m			100	860'(550')	1900m
B	RVR **1** 720m	**2** 1200m		NOT AUTH	**3** RVR 1500m VIS 1600m	135	860'(550')	2800m
C	VIS 800m					180	1160'(850')	3700m
D		**2** 1200m				205	1160'(850')	4600m

Gnd speed-Kts	70	90	100	120	140	160	
ILS GS 3.00° or LOC Descent Gradient 5.2%	377	485	539	647	755	862	MAP at MM

1 UK auth RVR 600m. **2** UK auth RVR 900m.
3 UK auth RVR 1300m.

PANS OPS 3

CHANGES: ATIS established.

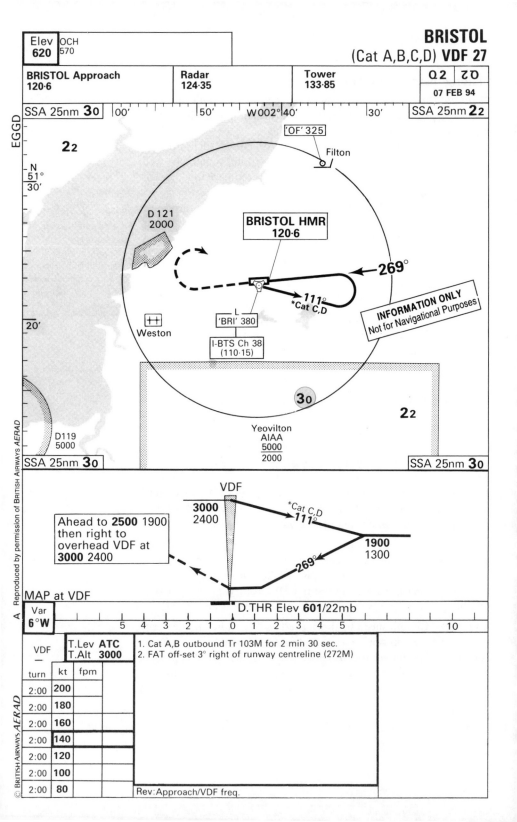

Making Instrument Approaches

PREPARATION. It is most important that the cockpit be well organised prior to commencing an instrument approach, as your workload during the approach will be high.

The instrument approach procedures to be used, including the missed approach, should be reviewed en route, preferably well before the aerodrome, and even prior to commencing descent from cruise level.

Given a choice of instrument approaches to an aerodrome or to a particular runway, a precision approach, such as an ILS, is generally preferable to a non-precision approach. As well as making it easier to fly an accurate final descent, the glideslope guidance of a precision approach will permit a lower minimum height, possibly making the difference between becoming visual and having to make a missed approach.

Precision approaches are generally preferable to non-precision approaches. The best approach, however, may be the one that allows a straight-in approach into the wind.

CHARTS. The charts required should be arranged in order, calculations of minima completed, and the intended action determined in the case of a missed approach (e.g. diversion, return for second approach, etc.). Fuel on board is an important consideration, especially if a diversion is necessary.

NAVIGATION AIDS. The radio navigation aids required for the approach should be set up as early as convenient, although there may be some delays necessary – for instance, if the VHF-NAV needs to remain selected to a VOR for en route tracking prior to the commencement of an ILS approach. Make use of every available means of navigation to assist you in forming a picture of exactly where the aeroplane is. Do not leave the VHF-NAV, ADF or DME idle if they can be tuned to useful aids, even if those aids are not part of the published procedure.

ALTIMETER SETTING. Ensure that the altimeter is set correctly for precise vertical navigation (Aerodrome QNH during the en route descent and, normally in the UK, to Aerodrome QFE for an aerodrome approach, or to Threshold QFE for a runway approach – although some pilots may choose to use Aerodrome QNH).

AIRSPEED. If a high speed has been used on the cruise and descent, then it may be appropriate to slow the aeroplane down to a more suitable manoeuvring speed before reaching the initial approach fix, and to complete any necessary cockpit checks at this time.

FINAL APPROACH TRACK. If the instrument approach uses the same facility for the initial approach fix (IAF) and the final approach fix (FAF), the pilot will track outbound from the IAF, reverse the track by making a procedure turn inbound, and then track to the final approach fix.

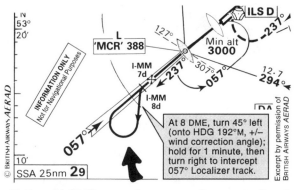

■ *Figure 21-17* **The procedure turn used to reverse direction**

Some instrument approaches are designed so that a base turn (rather than a procedure turn) is used to align the aeroplane on the final approach track.

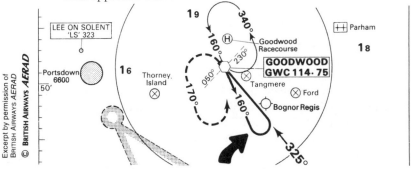

■ *Figure 21-18* **The base turn as part of an intermediate segment**

Under radar control, you may be radar vectored directly to the final approach track of any instrument approach, and cleared to descend to suitable altitudes by ATC, so that a smooth intercept of final approach may be made. If feeder routes are published for the particular approach, then you may be routed by ATC via one of these. Sometimes it is possible to track via a DME arc from the en route track to intercept the final approach track (FAT). In all of these cases, reversal turns may be avoided.

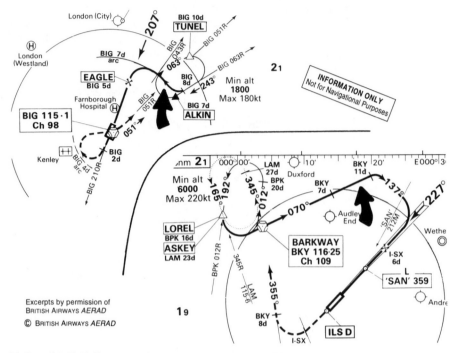

■ Figure 21-19 **Different methods used to avoid reversal turns**

MINIMUM ALTITUDE. The minimum altitude (height) at which you may fly in any particular segment will be shown on the chart, although ATC may assign a higher level.

During the intermediate approach segment, the aeroplane is manoeuvred to be positioned on final approach at a suitable height and airspeed. The actual configuration of the aeroplane (position of the flaps and undercarriage), and the speed at which it should be flown at various stages in the approach, will vary between aeroplane types, and clear instructions in this regard will be given by your flying instructor, and the Pilot's Operating Handbook.

> Review your airspeed, altitude, and mental attitude for the approach during the intermediate segment.

FLYING THE APPROACH. During final approach, normal attitude-flying techniques should be used, with constant reference to the flight instruments, and regular reference to the navigation instruments. During an ILS, the glideslope should be maintained with small adjustments of pitch attitude on the attitude indicator using the elevator, and the airspeed should be maintained on the ASI with power adjustments made with the throttle. For a non-precision approach, a suitable steady rate of descent should be established, preferably that suggested on the approach chart for a particular groundspeed, otherwise approximately 500 ft/min.

During final approach, have your minimum clearly fixed in your mind, along with the missed approach procedure. If not visual with the runway environment in sight at the calculated minumum height:

☐ **for a precision approach,** a missed approach should be commenced immediately at decision altitude (height); and

☐ **for a non-precision approach,** the aeroplane may continue tracking at the minimum descent altitude (height) to the missed approach point (MAPt) if visual flight does not become possible.

What is Visual Reference at the DH or MDH?

Be prepared to miss the approach at all times, even after you have transitioned to VFR.

Visual reference is the minimum visual reference that you should have in view before continuing the approach below the DH or MDH. The visual segment should contain sufficient physical features (approach lights, runway lights, runway markings, and features in the general runway environs) to ensure that the position of the aircraft relative to the desired flightpath can be positively ascertained. This enables you to make an informed judgement at DH/MDH, and thereafter maintain a stable descent path towards the runway.

A precision approach such as an ILS will be aligned with the extended runway centreline and the electronic glideslope will provide an ideal slope to the touchdown zone. Therefore, if you have flown a stable ILS approach in clouds with localizer and glideslope needles centred, you should be in a good position, when and if you become visual, to continue the stable approach without any dramatic alterations of heading or rate of descent (unless necessitated by windshear or turbulence).

The localizer allows you to track accurately along the extended runway centreline – so remember that, if a significant crosswind exists, you can expect to see the runway, not directly straight ahead through the windshield, but slightly left or right depending on the wind direction. Do not make any large changes of heading immediately you become visual – wait briefly to see if you already have the correct wind correction angle – likely to be the case if you have tracked accurately down the localizer. Of course, you may have to make some minor adjustments to heading to keep your flightpath aligned with the extended runway centreline.

Non-precision approaches using a VOR or an NDB may or may not be aligned with the runway centreline – you can determine this from the approach charts – so you should prepare yourself and know where to look for the runway when and if you become visual. If not aligned with the centreline and/or if not on a suitable approach slope, when you become visual you should manoeuvre into a position so that you can fly a straight and stable last few hundred feet to the touchdown zone on the runway.

Even when you are out of the clouds and visual, you should always be prepared to make a **missed approach:**

☐ if you think your approach is too unstable or too far out of alignment with the runway centreline; or

☐ if you are unable to maintain a safe rate of descent to the touchdown zone or to control the airspeed sufficiently well; or

☐ if the runway is obstructed.

Make use of any VASI to assist you in achieving the correct approach slope. If at the MDA on a non-precision approach and the VASI lights are all red (you are well below slope), then fly level at the MDA until you are on slope.

Keep in mind the runway, its length and surface conditions (wet, slushy, etc.) and the possibility of wake turbulence or low-level windshear. There is a lot to think about on approach but, with practice and experience, it becomes a lot easier. Remember: a good landing requires a good approach.

Visual

Not visual

■ *Figure 21-20* **Visual or not visual**

Now complete **Exercises 21 – Instrument Approaches.**
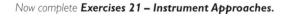

Instrument Minima

Calculation of Minima

Pilots are required to satisfy themselves before take-off that a flight can be made safely. When poor weather exists, they must be certain (before taking off) that conditions at the destination or alternate aerodrome will allow a landing to be made. Take-off conditions at the departure aerodrome must also be suitable. Do not take off unless you are sure that you can land.

UK PPL holders must determine their own minima, based on the sound recommendations given in the UK AIP AD 1-1-2. If the planned flight will be conducted in instrument conditions, the aeroplane must be properly equipped and the pilot properly rated, with either an instrument rating or an IMC rating. As well, the pilot needs to be in current practice.

Careful consideration should therefore be given to studying the available weather reports and forecasts, a detailed explanation of which appears in Vol. 2 of *The Air Pilot's Manual*. **Bad weather** can be said to exist if conditions are:

☐ **cloud ceiling** worse that 1,000 ft aal;
☐ **in-flight visibility** worse than 1,800 metres; and
☐ **runway visual range** (RVR)/aerodrome visibility worse than 1,500 metres.

Prior to operating, a pilot must consider:

☐ **for take-off** – the minimum visibility and cloud ceiling;
☐ **for approach and landing**;
  – **the minimum height** to which an approach on instruments should be continued for a straight-in landing (a decision height or a minimum descent height) or a circling approach to land on another runway (visual manoeuvring height); and
  – **the minimum visibility** and visual reference required to continue the approach to a safe landing.

The pilot must also consider:

☐ **runway surface** conditions (dry, wet, standing water, slush, ice);
☐ **crosswind**;
☐ **aeroplane performance** (take-off or landing distance required).

Minimum Weather Conditions for Take-Off

A prime consideration for take-off in a single-engined aeroplane is the ability for a safe forced landing to be made following engine failure.

The UK AIP states that, for non-public transport flights, the minimum weather conditions for take-off should never be less than:
☐ **600 ft cloud ceiling** (recommended); and
☐ **1,800 metres in-flight visibility** (mandatory).

Visibility is the distance at which prominent unlit objects by day, and a moderate-intensity light by night, can be seen and identified.

Following an unexpected engine failure on take-off in these minimum conditions, an experienced and in-practice pilot of a relatively slow and manoeuvrable aeroplane will have a reasonable chance of viewing a suitable forced landing area, and being able to avoid obstacles in attempting to reach it. Realistically, however, an IMC-rated pilot should be very wary about flying in conditions worse than 1,500 ft cloud ceiling and 3 km visibility.

Minimum En Route Weather Conditions

Following the take-off, the aeroplane should be climbed to a safe cruising level for the journey. While the above minimum conditions might be suitable for take-off, they are not suitable for a visual transit flight cross-country or to another aerodrome. Flying visually cross-country under such poor conditions is generally not possible.

VMC MINIMA. If a visual flight is to be undertaken, then the usual visual requirements (shown below) must be met.

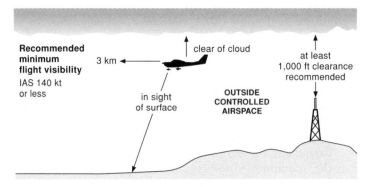

■ *Figure 22-1* **Requirements for a visual flight**

IMC MINIMA. If the flight is to proceed in Instrument Meteorological Conditions (IMC), then a suitable **safety altitude** must be used. It is suggested that you fly at least 1,000 ft above the highest obstacle within 5 nm either side of track, or above the maximum elevation figure (MEF). MEFs are shown in latitude-longitude quadrangles on the half million aeronautical chart series. The *quadrantal rule* should also be considered when selecting the cruise level. These aspects of vertical navigation are fully covered in Vol. 3 of *The Air Pilot's Manual*.

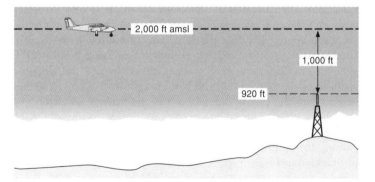

2,000 ft amsl

1,000 ft

920 ft

■ Figure 22-2 **In IMC, maintain at least 1,000 ft above any obstacles within 5 nm**

Minimum Conditions for Landing

Determining the minimum conditions for landing is more complicated. The main considerations are as follows:

☐ Is there an instrument approach procedure published for the destination?

☐ Is it a precision approach (ILS), or a non-precision approach (NDB/VOR)?

☐ Is obstacle clearance a problem?

☐ What is the particular system minimum (e.g. ILS 200 ft, NDB/VOR/VDF 300 ft, 350 ft)?

☐ Is a correction for altimeter position error correction (PEC 50 ft) required?

☐ What pilot qualification do I hold – IMC rating or instrument rating? (IMC-rated pilots must add an extra 200 ft.)

☐ Am I current, i.e. with recent experience? (Either do not fly in instrument conditions if out of practice, or else add extra height to any decision height.)

☐ Is the visibility at least 1,800 metres (for IMC-rated pilots)?

☐ Is the runway suitable (runway length, surface friction, cross-wind component)?

An instrument approach consists of a non-visual phase, followed (hopefully) by a visual phase that will allow a safe touch-down and landing to be made. During the non-visual phase, the instruments will provide tracking guidance, and on some approaches, slope guidance is provided as well. This divides instrument approaches into two families, precision and non-precision approaches.

PRECISION APPROACHES. A precision approach is one in which both *tracking* and *slope* guidance is given – the most common precision approach being the ILS. The minimum height calculated for a precision approach is known as a **decision height (DH)** – based on QFE and height above the runway – or **decision altitude (DA)** – based on QNH and height amsl. The DA will be greater than the DH by the amount of the runway elevation.

Tracking and slope guidance is given in a precision approach.

Jeppesen charts show the two figures as, for example, DA(H) 227'(200'), with the decision altitude 227' based on QNH coming first, followed by the decision height 200' based on QFE in brackets and italic type. On *Aerad* charts, the two minima are shown one above the other, with the QNH figure at the top and in **bold** type.

The visibility required for an IMC-rated pilot to proceed below the DA(H) is 1,800 metres. If satisfactory visual reference is not acquired at or before reaching the DA(H) on a precision approach, then a missed approach should be initiated *immediately.*

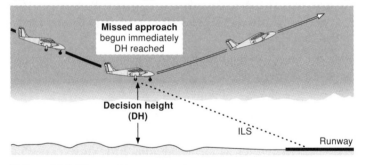

■ *Figure 22-3* **The precision approach**

NON-PRECISION APPROACHES. A non-precision approach is one in which *tracking* guidance only is given, without accurate slope guidance. The NDB and VOR let-downs are non-precision approaches, as is an ILS approach without the glideslope (known as a localizer approach). The minimum height calculated for a non-precision approach is known as a **minimum descent height (MDH)** – based on QFE – or **minimum descent altitude (MDA)** – based on QNH.

Tracking guidance only is given in a non-precsision approach.

The aircraft should not be descended below the MDA(H) unless satisfactory visual reference is acquired. The visibility required for an IMC-rated pilot to proceed below the MDA(H) is 1,800 metres.

If satisfactory visual reference is *not* acquired by the MDA(H), which may be reached some distance from the aerodrome, the aircraft may be flown level at (but not below) this height until either adequate visual reference for landing is acquired, or the missed approach point (MAPt) is reached and a missed approach begun.

This is different to the precision approach procedure where, if visual reference is not acquired on reaching the DA(H), the missed approach is begun immediately.

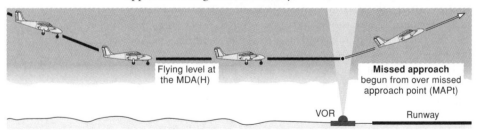

■ Figure 22-4 **Going around from a non-precision approach**

The minimum height to which it is safe to descend on instruments alone depends on a number of items, the most important ones being:

☐ **obstacles** in the vicinity of the approach path (obstacle clearance height – OCH);

☐ **the minimum height** to which a particular non-visual aid (e.g. ILS, VOR, NDB) may be flown (known as the system minimum); and

☐ **the qualifications** and recent experience of the pilot.

Obstacle Clearance Height (OCH)

The designer of the approach calculates, according to strict criteria, a safe **obstacle clearance height (OCH).** The OCH at a particular aerodrome will be lower for the precision aids because of the smaller area in which obstacles need to be considered for a precision approach compared to a non-precision approach. On a precision approach such as an ILS, the descent should be on slope, and the aeroplane should not arrive at the minimum height earlier than required.

For example, the *Blackpool Runway 28 ILS* OCH for Category A aircraft is 135 ft, while the NDB OCH is 500 ft. The ILS provides approach slope guidance, whereas the NDB alone does not. If a Runway 28 NDB/DME approach is carried out (with a DME to provide range, as well as the NDB to provide track guidance), more guidance on slope is given when compared to the NDB alone, the area to be considered for obstacles is less, and consequently the OCH has been lowered from 500 ft for the NDB alone to 450 ft aal for the combined NDB/DME.

Another factor that can reduce OCH is **aeroplane speed.** A slower aeroplane is assumed to lose less height due to inertia when commencing a missed approach, whereas a faster aeroplane may lose more height during the transition from final descent to the missed approach climb-out.

As well as the lower obstacle clearance height, there is a further advantage for slower aircraft in the visual manoeuvring phase following the instrument approach and when circling to land on another runway. Because they are more manoeuvrable and have a smaller turning radius, slower aircraft such as *Cessnas* and *Pipers* can circle in a smaller area compared to *Boeings* and *Airbuses,* and therefore are likely to be exposed to fewer obstacles. Consequently (and logically), slower aeroplanes are permitted to operate at a visual manoeuvring height (VMH) based on obstacles in a reduced circling area, which means their VMH may be lower than that for the faster aircraft.

The aeroplane categories are based on the **nominal threshold speed (V_{AT})**, which is $1.3 \times$ *indicated stalling speed* in the approach configuration at the maximum landing weight. V_{AT} is the speed at which you would normally plan to cross the threshold when at maximum landing weight, so it is a fixed value at all times for the one aeroplane, which therefore is always in the one category. Most light aircraft fall into Category A or B. You should know the category of your aeroplane. The categories (which are listed in UK AIP AD 1-1-2) are as follows:

AIRCRAFT CATEGORIES	
Category A	V_{AT} less than 91 kt
Category B	V_{AT} between 91 and 120 kt
Category C	V_{AT} between 121 and 140 kt
Category D	V_{AT} between 141 and 165 kt
Category E	V_{AT} between 166 and 210 kt

A typical set of published OCHs for the different aeroplane categories is that for the *Blackpool ILS/DME Rwy 28:*

A 135   B 142   C 152   D 160

If you are flying a Category A aeroplane (such as a typical training aeroplane), then OCH 135 is the figure you use when commencing to calculate your decision height.

NOTE If you require visual manoeuvring to land (a circling manoeuvre) following the instrument approach, then the *visual manoeuvring OCH* should be substituted for the procedure OCH in determining your *circle-to-land MDH.*

System Minima

A precision approach is capable of guiding a pilot to a lower height than a non-precision approach. The minimum height to which a particular type of non-visual aid can be flown (the system minimum as listed in UK AIP AD 1-1-2) is considered to be as stated below. These are *not* the heights to which you may descend in instrument conditions – they (like OCH) are an early consideration to which additions must be made in the calculation of your **personal minimum height.**

SYSTEM MINIMA	
Precision Approach System Minima	
ILS	200 ft
Non-Precision Approaches System Minima	
ILS (no glidepath)	250 ft
SRA (terminating at 0.5 nm)	250 ft
VOR, NDB, VDF (QDM or QGH)	300 ft
SRA (terminating at 2 nm)	350 ft

Calculation of DH for a Precision Approach, or MDH for a Non-Precision Approach

1. Take the higher value of OCH or system minimum.

2. For a precision approach (ILS), **add 50 ft** altimeter position error correction (PEC) (50 ft is considered adequate for light aircraft). The correction has already been included for non-precision approaches.

This gives the DH/MDH for a pilot with an instrument rating (and is listed in UK AIP AD 2).

3. An IMC-rated pilot must **add a further 200 ft** and then take the greater of this figure and the **absolute minima** of 500 ft for a precision approach and 600 ft for a non-precision approach.

EXAMPLE 1 *Bristol Rwy 27 ILS/DME* OCH for Category A is 176. What is the DH for an IMC-rated pilot?

1. Greater of OCH 176 and ILS system minimum 200 ft (the system minimum is more limiting than any obstacles).

2. For ILS, add altimeter PEC 50 ft to give 250 ft (as in AIP AD 1-1-2 for an instrument rating).

3. For IMC rating only, add 200 ft, to give 450 ft; compare with the IMC rating absolute minimum for an ILS of 500 ft. The greater is 500 ft DH.

ANSWER 500 ft DH.

It is suggested that pilots who have not flown instrument approaches within the previous few weeks should deliberately avoid making an approach in bad weather. If, however, such an approach is unavoidable, then a further addition of at least 100 ft to the calculated DH is advisable.

EXAMPLE 2 *Blackpool NDB Rwy 10* OCH is 500 ft. What is the MDH for an IMC-rated pilot?

1. Greater of OCH 500 and NDB system minimum 300 ft is 500 ft (there are significant obstacles).

2. This is a non-precision approach, so there is no requirement to add the altimeter PEC. (The 500 ft calculated so far is listed in AIP AD 1-1-2 for a pilot with an instrument rating.)

3. For an IMC rating only, add 200 ft, to give 700 ft: compare with the IMC absolute minimum for a non-precision approach of 600 ft. The greater is 700 ft MDH.

ANSWER 700 ft MDH.

It is perhaps easier to calculate DH or MDH using a table, such as that in Figure 22-5, since there is quite a bit to remember.

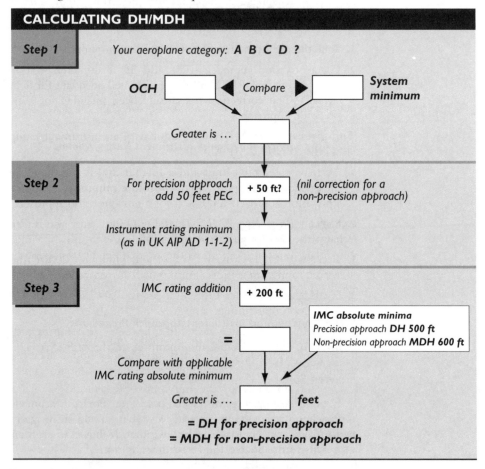

■ *Figure 22-5* **Tabular method of calculating DH/MDH**

Published Minima

The obstacle clearance heights (OCH) can be found:

- on *Jeppesen* and *Aerad* approach plates;
- in UK AIP for Category A aeroplanes, and for all other categories;
- on CAA instrument approach charts; and
- in *Pooley's Flight Guide* for Category A aeroplanes only.

Missed approach points are shown on the approach charts.

Jeppesen, Pooley's Flight Guide and AIP also give DH/MDH and the required RVR/visibility for each procedure. *Aerad* and AIP AD 1-1-2 minima are calculated in the manner described in Figure 22-5, except that *Aerad* does not include the altimeter corrections in the DH. The *Jeppesen* method for calculating minima is acceptable if the altimeter correction to the DH is added. *Pooley's Flight Guide* minima are for IMC-rated pilots.

Refer to Figure 22-6. Pilots planning to use this procedure for a *straight-in* landing may descend to their calculated decision height, which is the latest point at which they must become visual for the approach to be continued. Pilots planning to use this procedure for a circle-to-land approach onto Runway 27 must not descend in instrument conditions below their calculated *circle-to-land* minimum.

Air Traffic Services may Advise Instrument Rating Minima

In conditions where the visibility is 1,500 metres or less, or the cloud ceiling is at or below the visual manoeuvring height, the aerodrome traffic services in the UK will advise the pilots of non-public transport flights of the recommended minima for approach and landing. These minima apply only to pilots with instrument ratings flying in Category A aeroplanes. Pilots with an IMC rating must make further additions to the advised height, as previously discussed. This is an advisory service only by ATS, and does not absolve pilots from determining their own minima, but merely serves as a reminder.

Aerodromes without Instrument Approach Procedures

Instrument approaches are to be made only using published instrument approach procedures. If intending to land at an aerodrome for which there is no published IAP, two possibilities are:

- Descend en route to the minimum safe altitude (allowing 1,000 ft clearance above the highest obstacle within 5 nm of track) and not contravening any low flying rules. If the aeroplane encounters visual conditions, then the flight can proceed visually to the destination aerodrome; or

☐ Use a published instrument approach procedure at a nearby aerodrome to become visual, and then proceed visually to the destination aerodrome. Refer to Figure 22-7.

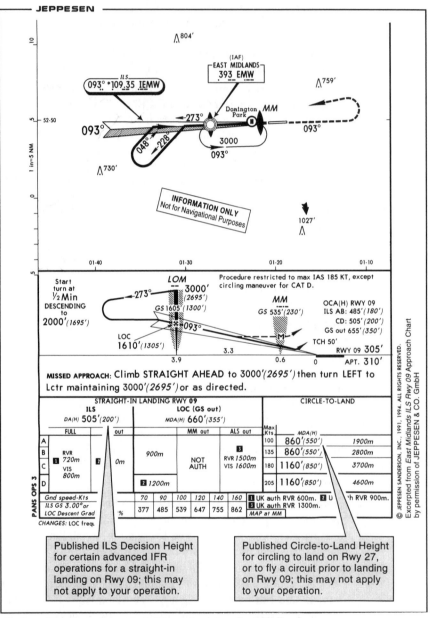

■ *Figure 22-6* **Part of a typical approach plate – East Midlands**
Rwy 09 ILS (Jeppesen)

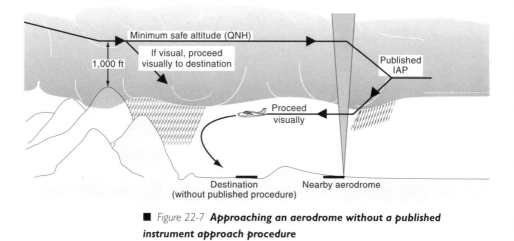

Minimum safe altitude (QNH)

1,000 ft

If visual, proceed
visually to destination

Published
IAP

Proceed
visually

Destination
(without published procedure)

Nearby aerodrome

■ Figure 22-7 **Approaching an aerodrome without a published instrument approach procedure**

Now complete **Exercises 22 – Instrument Minima.**

Visual Manoeuvring

If the final approach direction of an instrument procedure does not align the aeroplane within ±30° of the landing runway, or position it suitably so that a reasonable flightpath to the touchdown point can be achieved comfortably, then it is technically no longer a straight-in procedure, and significant visual manoeuvring (probably involving at least a partial circuit) will be required to align the aeroplane with the landing runway.

Visual manoeuvring is also known as *circling,* or as a *circle-to-land* manoeuvre, and these terms are used to describe the visual phase of flight after completing an instrument approach, with the aim of manoeuvring an aircraft into position for a landing on a runway which is not suitably located for a straight-in approach.

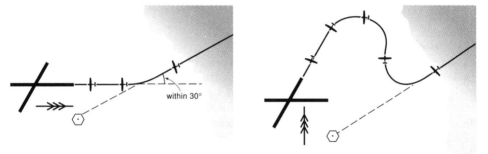

■ *Figure 23-1* **A straight-in approach**   ■ *Figure 23-2* **A circling approach**

The most common use of visual manoeuvring in the UK is after becoming visual at or above the circle-to-land minimum following an instrument approach based on an out-of-wind runway, and then manoeuvring visually for a landing on the into-wind runway, e.g. using a Runway 27 ILS to become visual, followed by a circling approach and landing on Runway 09.

The flightpath that you choose to fly will vary depending on the situation – for instance, you might choose to circle in a direction that avoids high terrain, low cloud, a heavy shower, etc.

> Circling approaches require accurate attitude flying and a good lookout.

A circling approach is a more difficult manoeuvre than a straight-in approach, because it often involves close-in manoeuvring under a low cloud base and in rain or poor visibility. It will require precise attitude flying, with close attention to maintaining height, while flying a suitable flightpath to position the aeroplane for a landing and keeping a very good lookout.

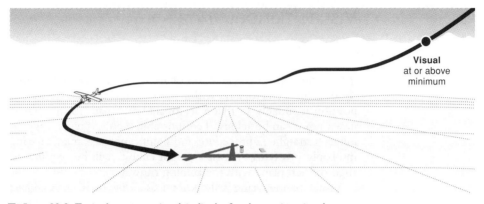

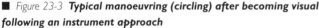

■ *Figure 23-3* **Typical manoeuvring (circling) after becoming visual following an instrument approach**

The *circle-to-land MDH* for a particular approach procedure that is aligned with a runway will generally be higher than the *straight-in DH.*

The Visual Circling Manoeuvre

If you become visual at or above the minimum descent height for the instrument approach, then you should maintain this height until within the circling area. When within the circling area, and remaining visual, you may fly at the **visual manoeuvring obstacle clearance height** (which at some aerodromes is lower than the MDH for the instrument approach). The visual manoeuvring obstacle clearance height may be referred to as the *visual manoeuvring OCH,* the *circling height,* or the *visual manoeuvring height (VMH).*

A circling approach is a visual flight manoeuvre, and you must remain visual throughout, otherwise a missed approach is to be carried out.

Each circling situation is different because of variables such as:
- [ ] **the final approach direction** of the instrument approach;
- [ ] **the runway layout;**
- [ ] **wind direction and speed,** and the selected runway for landing;
- [ ] **local terrain;**
- [ ] **meteorological conditions** (especially cloud base and visibility).

For instance, wind direction and strength usually determine which runway should be used for landing. Cloud base usually determines what circuit height (at or above visual manoeuvring OCH) is flown. If there is a fog bank on one side of the aerodrome, then a circling approach on the other side of the aerodrome in good visibility is preferable, irrespective of whether a left or right circuit is involved.

Generally, though, it is advisable to follow the normal circuit pattern, which at most aerodromes is left-handed to provide the captain in the left seat with a good view of the runway, and at the usual 1,000 ft aal. Should the cloud be lower, a circling approach is legal at heights down to the visual manoeuvring OCH.

> **Keep your circle-to-land approach as close to a normal circuit as the conditions permit.**

The term *circling* does not imply that the visual manoeuvring should follow a circular pattern, but rather that the circuit pattern should be adjusted to suit the conditions. As a general rule, circling should be as close to a normal circuit as conditions allow. This helps other traffic in the circuit, as well as ATC, and keeps things as standard as possible for the pilot.

If, for instance, you become visual at 2,000 ft aal on the instrument approach, well above the permitted minimum, then you should continue descent to normal circuit height and fly a normal circuit, rather than descend to the visual manoeuvring obstacle clearance height, which may be as low as 400 ft aal. While training, however, your instructor may ask you to fly a circuit assuming a particular cloud base, even though actual conditions do not require it.

> **Control your attitude, airspeed and altitude carefully during a circle-to-land approach.**

Good attitude control is essential in the circling manoeuvre, with bank angle limited to 20° or rate 1 (maximum 30°), altitude maintained at or above visual manoeuvring obstacle clearance height, and airspeed as desired. The aeroplane must also be configured for landing (with the landing gear and flaps extended as required), and all checks completed, before the landing is made.

A well-flown circling approach is the sign of a competent pilot.

Descent Below the Visual Manoeuvring Height

Descent below the visual manoeuvring obstacle clearance height should not be made until:

- [ ] visual reference with the aerodrome environment is established and maintained;
- [ ] the landing threshold is in sight; and
- [ ] the required obstacle clearance can be maintained on approach and the aeroplane is in a position to carry out a landing.

> *The most appropriate time to commence the descent from the visual manoeuvring OCH for a landing is when the normal landing descent profile is intercepted.*

The lower the circling height, the closer this will be to the aerodrome. If, for instance, the aeroplane is circling at the lowest permissible visual manoeuvring OCH at an aerodrome with no obstacles (which is 400 ft aal), the landing descent will not be commenced until on final. For higher visual manoeuvring OCHs, the descent for a landing may be commenced earlier to avoid unnecessarily high descent rates on final.

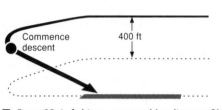

■ *Figure 23-4* **Achieve a normal landing profile**

Pilot Initiative and Judgement is Required

It is impossible to design a single procedure that will cater for all situations – this is an area for pilot judgement and decision. Because the circling manoeuvre may have to be carried out in poor conditions, you must be able to make firm decisions quickly. This ability will come with experience and good planning. The basic assumption in circling approaches is that, after initial visual contact, the runway environment (the runway, the runway threshold or approach lighting aids, or other markings identifiable with the runway) should be kept in sight while manoeuvring in the circuit at or above the visual manoeuvring height.

CLOUD BASE. The actual height to be flown while manoeuvring in the circling area will be governed by the visual manoeuvring obstacle clearance height and the cloud ceiling. It is unusual for a cloud base to be perfectly flat; normally it is rather 'furry' or 'lumpy', and fluctuates in height. For this reason, it is recommended that a gap of at least 200 ft exist between the aeroplane (flying at visual manoeuvring height or higher) and the estimated cloud base. This gap is impossible to measure accurately, of course, so it requires realistic estimation by the pilot, who must:

Allow 200 ft between the cloud base and the visual manoeuvring OCH.

☐ **remain visual;** and
☐ **not descend below** the visual manoeuvring obstacle clearance height until in a position for a safe descent for landing.

If, for example, the visual manoeuvring OCH published for a particular aerodrome is 550 ft aal, then you know, seeing a forecast cloud base of 800 ft aal, that you will probably be operating in marginal conditions where 200 ft above the circling OCH may or may not exist. You must not circle at a lower height than the visual manoeuvring OCH, no matter what the cloud does. Your way out, of course, is a missed approach.

VISIBILITY. While not specified in the AIP, it is recommended that to continue a circling approach there should be a visibility of at least 2,000 metres, assuming a circuit speed of 100 kt or less. (Faster aeroplanes with a greater turning radius and requiring

At least 2,000 metres visibility is required for a circling approach.

more manoeuvring area may need greater visibility – about 200 metres for each additional 10 kt.)

The precise visibility is impossible to measure in flight, but you can estimate it, and must feel confident and comfortable that sufficient visibility exists for safe visual manoeuvring. Ideally, keep the runway in sight at all times.

Do not hesitate to make a missed approach if circumstances require it.

If at any time during the visual manoeuvring for a circling approach you feel uncomfortable for any reason (such as a lowering cloud base, decreasing visibility, heavy rain or hail, turbulence, windshear, or if you lose visual contact, etc.), execute a missed approach.

The Visual Manoeuvring (Circling) Area

The visual manoeuvring area (or circling area) is the area around an aerodrome in which **obstacle clearance** has been considered by the state authority (which in the UK is the CAA) for aircraft having to manoeuvre visually before landing. To avoid penalising slower and more manoeuvrable aircraft (which require less manoeuvring area than faster aeroplanes), different aircraft categories based on maximum speed for circling have been devised.

Most training aeroplanes have a maximum speed for circling of less than 100 kt (known as Category A for visual manoeuvring purposes), and the circling area considered for obstacle clearance under the current ICAO PANS-OPS requirements for such aeroplanes is 1.68 nm radii from the runway thresholds.

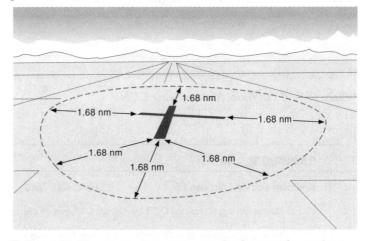

■ *Figure 23-5* **The visual manoeuvring area for Category A aeroplanes (less than 100 kt)**

NOTE For aeroplanes with a maximum speed for circling between 100 and 135 kt, the radii are increased to 2.66 nm.

Obstacle Clearance in the Visual Manoeuvring (Circling) Area

Once the state authority has established its circling area, obstacles within this area are surveyed and a **safety margin** added to ensure clearance from these obstacles. A visual manoeuvring (circling) obstacle clearance height, VM(C) OCH, is then determined for each category of aircraft.

For Category A aeroplanes, the circling area has a radius of 1.68 nm and maximum circling speed 100 kt (AIP ENR 1-5). The safety margin for visual manoeuvring in the circling area is a minimum of 300 ft above obstacles.

If, for example, the highest obstacle in the circling area is a tower 290 ft aal, then the visual manoeuvring obstacle clearance height, VM(C) OCH, is (290 + 300) = 590 ft aal.

If there are no specific obstacles, then 100 feet is allowed for the growth of trees, etc., and the 300 ft safety margin added to this to give a lowest permissible VM(C) OCH at any aerodrome of (100 + 300) = 400 ft aal.

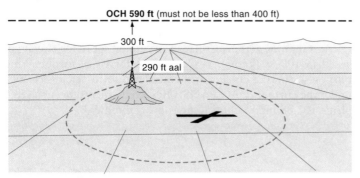

■ Figure 23-6 **Calculation of visual manoeuvring OCH**

Where to Find the Visual Manoeuvring OCH

The visual manoeuvring OCH (or circling OCH) for each aerodrome is published in AIP AD 2 (Instrument Approach Charts).

CAMBRIDGE - General		
1 **Minimum Sector Altitudes** (ft):	Northeast: **1800**	Southeast: **1800**
2 **Visual Manoeuvring (Circling) OCH** by Aircraft Category (ft aal):	A/B: 600	

■ Figure 23-7 **The visual manoeuvring OCH for circling at Cambridge**

Cambridge obviously has a significant obstacle in its circling area, raising its circling OCH to 600 ft aal for Category A aircraft, whereas Alderney (Figure 23-8) does not, since its circling height is the lowest permitted, 400 ft aal.

ALDERNEY - General			
1	**Minimum Sector Altitudes** (ft):	Northeast: **2000**	Southeast: **2000**
2	**Visual Manoeuvring (Circling) OCH** by Aircraft Category (ft aal):		A: 400

■ *Figure 23-8* **The visual manoeuvring OCH for circling at Alderney**

Visual Manoeuvring OCH and MDH

> *The visual manoeuvring OCH may be lower than the circling minimum descent height for the instrument approach procedure.*

The visual manoeuvring OCH (the lowest height permitted for manoeuvring in the circling area to achieve adequate obstacle clearance) should not be confused with the minimum descent height MDH for the instrument approach itself when used prior to a circle-to-land manoeuvre. The two are arrived at using different criteria:

1. **The instrument approach MDH** provides safe obstacle clearance along the instrument approach path and also throughout the missed approach;

2. **The visual manoeuvring OCH** provides safe obstacle clearance in the circling area around the aerodrome.

It is possible that the visual manoeuvring obstacle clearance height is less than the appropriate *circle-to-land* minimum descent height for the instrument approach procedure. In such cases, once you are visual and within the circling area around the aerodrome, it is permissible to descend to the visual manoeuvring obstacle clearance height if necessary. The situation could arise if there is a significant obstacle beneath the instrument approach obstacle clearance plane, but lying outside the visual manoeuvring (circling) area.

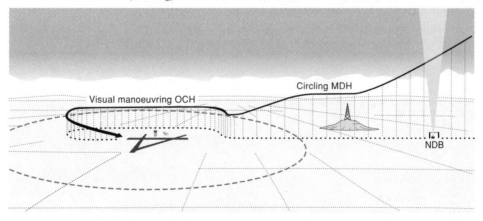

■ *Figure 23-9* **Visual manoeuvring OCH at some aerodromes is less than MDH for the instrument approach**

NOTE It is also possible that visual manoeuvring OCH is the same as the circling MDH, but it will never be greater, since this would lead to the illogical procedure of becoming visual on the instrument approach, and then having to climb to a greater circling height.

As the visual manoeuvring obstacle clearance height and the instrument approach circling MDH may differ, you must be certain (even before commencing the instrument approach) which minimum height applies to which phase of the approach:

☐ **minimum descent height (MDH)** applies to the instrument approach; and

☐ **visual manoeuvring OCH** applies once within the circling area.

Sectorised Visual Manoeuvring (Circling) Areas

The lower the visual manoeuvring obstacle clearance height, the more accessible the aerodrome is in poor weather, since it will allow pilots to operate beneath a lower cloud base. In an attempt to achieve lower circling heights, the state authority can exclude from the circling area a sector that contains a particularly high and restrictive obstacle, provided that it lies outside the final approach and missed approach areas.

If the state authority does exercise this option, and thereby lowers the visual manoeuvring OCH, then you are *prohibited* from circling at this lowered height within the excluded sector that contains the obstacle(s).

For example, an obstacle 800 ft aal in the normal circling area requires a visual manoeuvring height of (800 + 300) = 1,100 ft aal, which operationally is very restrictive. By removing a sector that contains this obstacle from the permissible circling area, the state authority may lower the visual manoeuvring obstacle clearance height appropriately. In Figure 23-10 the visual manoeuvring OCH has been lowered to (150 + 300) = 450 ft aal in this way.

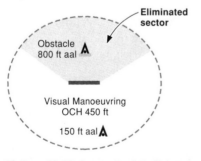

■ *Figure 23-10* **A sectorised circling area**

A typical example of the advantages to be obtained using a sectorised circling area is Blackpool.

BLACKPOOL - General	INFORMATION ONLY Not for navigational purposes	

1	**Minimum Sector Altitudes** (ft):	Northeast: **2900**	Southeast: **3500**
	Note: Subject to ATC approval, aircraft may descend to not below **2000** ft after passing 15 DME		
2	**Visual Manoeuvring (Circling) OCH** by Aircraft Category (ft aal):		A: 550
	Sectorized VM(C) OCH for aircraft south of Runway 10/28 :		A: 400
3	**Holding Procedure:**		
	1-minute race-track pattern approaching NDB(L) BPL on track 097° MAG turning right at the faci		
4	**Notes:**		
4.1	Reversal Procedures to Runway 28: During reversal procedures to Runway 28 using DME aircr∉		
4.2	Lowest altitude to start procedure **2000** ft after holding or missed approach.		

■ *Figure 23-11* **Extract for Blackpool in AIP**

Obviously, if the cloud base at Blackpool is as low as 600 ft, you are better off confining your manoeuvring to that part of the circling area south of Runway 10/28, where the visual manoeuvring obstacle clearance height is only 400 ft aal. If you operate in the area to the north of this runway, the visual manoeuvring OCH becomes 550 ft aal.

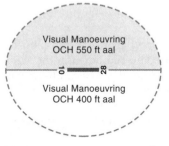

■ *Figure 23-12* **Sectorised circling area at Blackpool**

The Missed Approach Procedure when Circling

If you lose visual reference when circling to land after an instrument approach, then the missed approach procedure for that particular instrument approach should be followed.

The aeroplane may be in a slightly awkward position for a missed approach depending on its position in the circuit, but you are expected to make an initial climbing turn towards the landing runway and overhead the aerodrome, where you will continue climbing on the published missed approach track to the required altitude. This should keep the aeroplane clear of obstacles, first of all in the circling area, and then in the missed approach area.

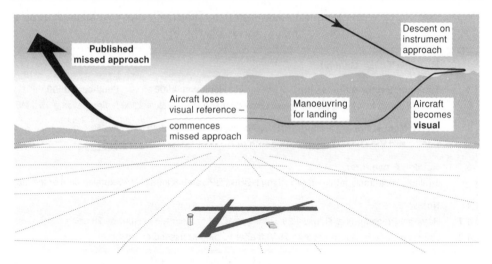

■ *Figure 23-13* **Making a missed approach when circling**

Since the circling manoeuvre may be accomplished in more than one direction, and since the aeroplane could be anywhere in the circuit when visual reference is lost, you will have to devise and follow a suitable flightpath to establish the aeroplane on the prescribed missed approach track. This would depend on the aeroplane's position in the circling manoeuvre at the time visual reference is lost and the climb-away commenced, and also on the nature of the missed approach track.

When you decide to execute a missed approach, you must fly the aeroplane according to the procedure laid down in the aeroplane's Flight Manual – transitioning smoothly to a climb-away in a positive manner with prompt and precise attitude and power changes. A typical missed approach procedure may be:

☐ adopt the missed approach **attitude** and simultaneously apply go-around **power;**

☐ assume the missed approach **configuration** (gear up when a positive climb is achieved, flaps as required).

As soon as comfortably established in the climb (there need be no rush!), turn towards the runway and the missed approach track. Attitude flying will require most of your attention, so at least from the time you commence the circling manoeuvre you should have in mind:

☐ an initial heading to turn to if you lose visual contact;

☐ the missed approach track; and

☐ the missed approach altitude.

When convenient, and once comfortably established in the climb-away, advise ATC that you have commenced a missed approach. Remember that any altitude given by ATC at this time (e.g. "climb to three thousand") will be based on QNH (height amsl). If QFE has been set in the altimeter subscale, it should be reset to QNH.

Remember the order of importance:
- **aviate** (fly the aeroplane!);
- **navigate** (head it towards where you have to go); and, finally,
- **communicate** (advise ATC).

■ Figure 23-14 **Aviate, navigate, then communicate**

Circling at Aerodromes Without a Published Approach

If arriving at an aerodrome which does not have a published instrument approach procedure, you should, where possible, become visual well away from the aerodrome to allow time for orientation and planning the visual circuit. The options available to achieve this are:

1a. Descend in Visual Meteorological Conditions (VMC), with visual contact with the ground, and then fly to the destination in compliance with the Visual Flight Rules and the Minimum Height Rule; or

1b. Descend through cloud using a published instrument approach procedure at a nearby aerodrome, and transit visually to the destination aerodrome (in accordance with the Visual Flight Rules and the Minimum Height Rule).

If either of these options is not available:

2. Obtain an accurate en route fix and descend to not lower than 1,000 ft above the highest obstacle within 5 nm of the aircraft and, once visual, proceed visually to the destination aerodrome (in accordance with the Visual Flight Rules and the Minimum Height Rule).

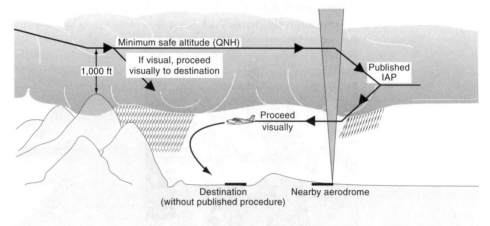

■ *Figure 23-15* **Arriving at a destination aerodrome which does not have a published instrument approach**

Having become visual, you need to remain visual for the transit to the destination aerodrome, and for the circuit and landing.

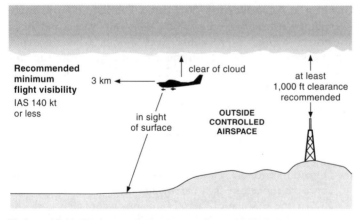

■ *Figure 23-16* **Requirements for a typical visual PPL flight**

In the circling area around an aerodrome, the minimum cloud ceiling recommended is the higher of:
- 600 ft above the highest obstacle within 4 nm of the aerodrome; and
- 800 ft above aerodrome level (aal).

NOTE Information on obstacles within 4 nm of an aerodrome appears in UK AIP AD 2-10.

For more experienced pilots (at least 100 hours as pilot-in-command) flying circuits at aerodromes with which they are familiar, the minimum cloud ceiling may be reduced to allow only 400 ft above the highest obstacle within a 4 nm radius of the aerodrome. Flying a circuit at a low level requires a lot of concentration and makes it more difficult to cope with problems such as an unexpected forced landing, or a circuit and landing with one or more engines inoperative.

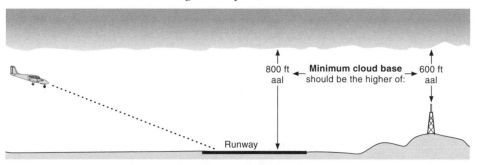

■ *Figure 23-17* **Visual criteria in the circuit of an aerodrome**

Read the AIP
Read those sections of UK AIP AD 1-1-2 & ENR 1-5 related to visual manoeuvring (circling), and periodically revise them.

A Warning from the AIP
Pilots should never commence or continue an instrument approach when:
- **cloud ceiling** is reported to be at or below their calculated DH; or the
- **reported RVR/visibility** is below minimum required (1,800 m, IMC rating).

Therefore a flight should not be planned to terminate in conditions below the relevant minima. Should the destination weather deteriorate below minima after departure, a diversion to a suitably planned alternate should be made forthwith.

Special VFR

The IMC Rating (Aeroplanes) entitles holders to be pilot-in-command of an aeroplane, provided:

☐ they do not fly on a Special VFR (SVFR) flight in a Control Zone in a flight visibility less than 3 km; and

☐ they do not act as such when the aeroplane is taking off or landing at any place if the flight visibility below cloud is less than 1,800 m.

Now complete ***Exercises 23 – Visual Manoeuvring.***

Section **Four**

Night Flying

Aerodrome Lighting

The main aeronautical lighting provided at aerodromes to assist pilots to manoeuvre aircraft at night consists of:

☐ taxiway lighting;
☐ runway lighting;
☐ approach lighting; and
☐ visual approach slope indicators (VASI).

Particulars of aerodrome lighting are shown in the AD 2-14 section of the UK AIP, and on landing and approach charts.

Taxiway Lights

Taxiways are lit for the guidance of pilots with either:

☐ one line of **green centreline** taxiway lights; or
☐ two lines of **blue sideline** taxiway lights.

At some aerodromes, there is a mixture of the two types, centreline green on some taxiways, and sideline blue on others.

At certain points on the taxiway, there may be **red stop bars,** to indicate the position where an aeroplane should hold; for instance, before entering an active runway.

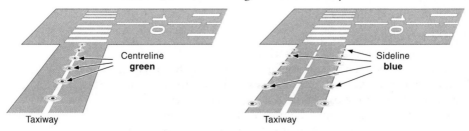

■ *Figure 24-1* **Taxiway lighting**

Runway Lights

Runway edge lighting is **white.** The runway edge lights may be directional and visible only to aeroplanes aligned with the runway, or they may be visible equally in all directions. Some runway lights are flush with the surface, and others are elevated (indicated in AIP AD 2-14 by the word *elev*). If paraffin flares only are available (rather than electrical lighting), this will be indicated in AD 2-14 by the word *goosenecks*.

The approach threshold of the runway will have **green threshold lights** across its width if the lights are of the flush type – if they are of the elevated type, the central area of the approach threshold may be left clear. Sometimes there are wingbars outboard of the runway edge lights for use in poor visibility or to mark a displaced threshold. At the far end of the runway there will be **red runway end lighting.**

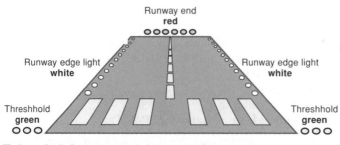

■ Figure 24-2 **Basic runway lighting at night**

On runways for which there is a published instrument approach, the colour of the runway edge lighting over the **caution zone,** which is the last 600 metres, may be yellow. This is an indication to a pilot landing in very poor visibility conditions (far less than that allowed for IMC-rated pilots), that the aeroplane on its landing run is approaching the stopping end of the runway.

Precision approach runways at major aerodromes may have flush **runway centreline lights** that are white, but become red at the stopping end of the runway. There may also be **touchdown zone lighting,** which consists of rows of white lights on either side of the runway during its first 900 metres.

Approach Lighting

At many major aerodromes, approach lighting extends out from the approach end of the runway, to well beyond the physical boundaries of the runway. It consists of extended centreline lighting, with up to three crossbars sited at 300-metre intervals back along the approach path from the threshold. If more crossbars are used, they may be sited at 150-metre instead of 300-metre intervals.

The approach lighting, because of its extent, may have components outside the boundaries of the aerodrome, possibly in forested or even built-up areas. Approach lights do *not* mark the boundaries of a suitable landing area – they simply act as a lead-in to a runway.

To pilots making an approach, the approach lighting provides a visual indication of how well the aeroplane is aligned with the extended runway centreline, as well as helping in estimating the distance the aeroplane has to fly to touchdown. It is very useful to pilots who have become visual during the latter stages of an instrument approach, especially in conditions of low visibility. In situations where no visible horizon exists, it can assist pilots to judge bank angle visually.

Advanced precision approach runways may have additional red approach lights, but these need not concern IMC-rated pilots.

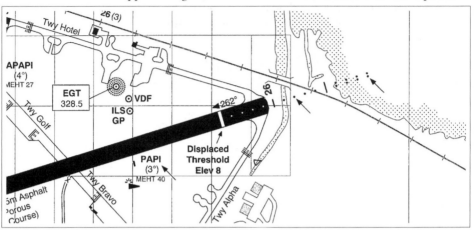

■ *Figure 24-3* **Approaching an instrument runway**

Visual Approach Slope Indicators (VASI or VASIS)

In conditions of poor visibility and at night, when the runway environment and the natural horizon may not be clearly visible, it is often difficult to judge the correct approach path of the aeroplane towards the touchdown zone of the runway. A number of very effective devices have been invented to assist pilots in this situation.

Two-Bar VASI

Red over white: *you are all right.* **White over white:** *you are high as a kite.* **Red over red:** *you are dead.*

The typical two-bar VASI has two pairs of wingbars extending outbound of the runway, usually at 150 metres and 300 metres from the approach threshold. It is sometimes known as the *red/white system,* since the colours seen by the pilot tell him if he is right on slope, or too high or too low. He will see:

☐ **all bars white** if high on approach;

☐ the **near bars white** and the **far bars red** if right on slope; and

☐ **all bars red** if low on slope.

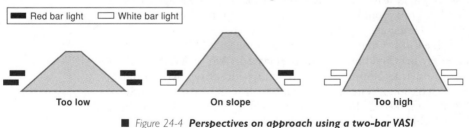

■ *Figure 24-4* **Perspectives on approach using a two-bar VASI**

During the approach, the aeroplane should be maintained on a slope within the white sector of the near bars and the red sector of the far bars. If the aeroplane flies above or below the correct slope, the lights will change colour, with a pink transition stage between red and white.

The plane of the VASI approach slope provides obstacle clearance in an arc 10° left or right of the extended centreline out to a distance of 4 nm from the runway threshold. Before using VASI information, therefore, the aeroplane should be within this arc, and preferably aligned with the extended runway centreline.

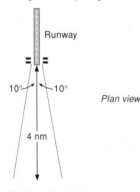

■ Figure 24-5 **The extent of useful VASI information**

In general, therefore, an approach descent using VASI should not be initiated until the aeroplane is visually aligned with the extended runway centreline. On instrument approaches, once the VASI comes into view you may use it to adjust your approach path.

There are some other operational considerations to be borne in mind when using the red/white VASI. At maximum range, the white bars may become visible before the red bars, because of the nature of red and white light. In haze or smog, or in certain other conditions, the white lights may have a yellowish tinge about them. When extremely low on slope, the two wingbars (all lights red) may appear to merge into one red bar – at close range to the threshold this would indicate a critical situation with respect to obstacle clearance, requiring immediate corrective action.

Some VASI systems use a reduced number of lights, in which case they may be known as an **abbreviated VASI** or **AVASI**.

At some aerodromes there is a **low-intensity two-colour approach slope system (LITAS),** which is similar to the VASI, but is composed of lower-intensity indicators installed singly in the upwind and downwind VASI wingbar positions, usually on the left-hand side of the runway only. It is interpreted in the same way as the two-bar VASI.

Three-Bar VASI

The three-bar VASI has an extra far wingbar added to assist the pilots of long-bodied aeroplanes such as the *Boeing 747* and *Airbus A300*. The approach slope guidance given by any VASI depends on the position of the pilot's eyes. Since the wheels of a long-bodied aeroplane will be much further below the pilot's eyes, it is essential that his eyes follow a parallel but higher slope to ensure adequate clearance over the runway threshold. An additional wingbar further into the runway makes this possible.

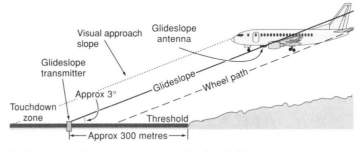

■ *Figure 24-6* **Wheel clearance over the threshold**

Pilots of such aeroplanes should use the second and third wing-bars, and ignore the first. When the pilot's eyes are positioned on the correct slope for a long-bodied aeroplane, he will see the top bar red, the middle bar white (and ignore the lower bar which is also white).

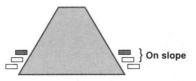

■ *Figure 24-7* **Correct view for the pilot of a long-bodied aeroplane using the three-bar VASI**

Pilots of smaller aeroplanes should refer to only the two nearer wingbars, and ignore the further 'long-bodied' wingbar. On slope, the indications should be (top bar red and ignored), middle bar red and lower bar white.

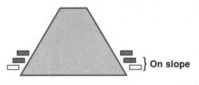

■ *Figure 24-8* **Correct view for the pilot of a smaller aeroplane using the three-bar VASI**

PAPI

The **precision approach path indicator (PAPI)** is a development of the VASI, and also uses red/white signals for guidance in maintaining the correct approach angle, but the lights are arranged differently and their indications must be interpreted differently. PAPI has a single wingbar, which consist of four light units on one or both sides of the runway adjacent to the touchdown point. There is no pink transition stage as the lights change from red to white.

If the aeroplane is on slope, the two outer lights of each unit are white and the two inner lights are red. Above slope, the number of white lights increase, and below slope the number of red lights increase.

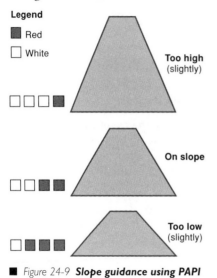

Legend

■ Red

□ White

□□□■ Too high (slightly)

□□■■ On slope

□■■■ Too low (slightly)

■ *Figure 24-9* **Slope guidance using PAPI**

Night Flying at an Aerodrome

Night flying involves a mixture of visual and instrument flying skills. The take-off run at night, for instance, is made with *visual reference* to the runway. But shortly after take-off, there may be no visible features at all to be seen, and transferring your attention from outside the cockpit to *the instruments* in the cockpit at or before that time is essential. In contrast, by day and in good weather conditions your attention can remain outside the cockpit.

Adaptation of the Eyes to Darkness

Protect your night vision. It takes a considerable time for your eyes to re-adjust to darkness after seeing bright light.

Your eyes are very important when flying, and they should always be looked after. However, at night there are some special considerations regarding your vision. Since your attention during night flying will be both inside and outside the cockpit, care should be taken to ensure that eyes can function at near maximum efficiency. It takes the eyes some minutes to adapt to a dark environment, as most of us have experienced when walking into a darkened cinema, stumbling across other patrons in an attempt to find an empty seat.

The rate at which the eyes adapt to darkness depends to a large extent on the contrast between the brightness of light previously experienced, and the degree of darkness of the new environment.

While bright lighting within the previous few minutes has the strongest effect, that experienced for some period within the previous few hours will also have an effect. Bright lighting, therefore, is best avoided prior to night flying. Generally, this is difficult to achieve, since flight planning in a well-lit room and pre-flight inspection with a strong torch or on a well-lit tarmac will almost always be necessary. The best that can be achieved in many cases is to dim the cockpit lighting prior to taxiing, and to avoid looking at bright lights during those few minutes prior to take-off.

Night vision can also be affected by lack of oxygen, so ensure that you use oxygen when flying above 10,000 ft amsl. On a more mundane level, avoid cigarette smoke in the cockpit at night, since it will displace oxygen in your blood to some extent, and consequently reduce your night vision by an amount comparable to an extra 5,000 ft in altitude. In the long term, a good diet containing foods with Vitamins A and C can improve night vision.

Since bright lights will impair your outside vision at night, it is good airmanship to keep the cockpit lighting at a reasonably low level, but not so low that you cannot see your charts, or find the fuel selector.

There are some occasions, however, when bright cockpit lighting can help preserve your vision. This can occur on an instrument flight, for instance, if flying in the vicinity of electrical storms. Nearby lighting flashes can temporarily degrade your dark adaptation and your vision, particularly if it is in contrast to a dim cockpit. Bright lighting in the cockpit can minimise this effect and, although your external vision will not be as good as with dim cockpit lighting, you will avoid being temporarily blinded by the lightning flashes.

Note that flying near electrical storms is not recommended. They should be avoided by at least 10 miles and, if you are not an instrument-rated pilot in a suitably equipped aeroplane, then perhaps you should stay on the ground at night if there are storms around.

Preparation for Night Flight

Night flying requires careful attention to pre-flight preparation and planning. Unlike daylight hours, when weather conditions in the vicinity of the aerodrome are visible, at night the situation is different. While stars might be clearly visible overhead one minute, the next they may be covered unexpectedly by low cloud, which could have a significant effect on flight in the area.

Study the available **weather reports and forecasts,** paying special attention to any item that could affect visibility and your ability to fly at a safe operating height. Some of the main items to consider are:

☐ **cloud base** and amount;
☐ **weather** – such as rain, snow, fog, mist, etc.;
☐ **temperature/dewpoint** relationship – the closer they are, the more likely fog is to form as temperature drops further;
☐ **wind direction and strength** – from the point of view of runway choice, the possibility of fog being blown in, and the likelihood of windshear due to the diurnal effect (a light surface wind with a strong wind at height as a result of less vertical mixing).

Check any special procedures for night flying at your aerodrome and in the vicinity.

For a cross-country flight, carry the appropriate aeronautical charts, and have them prepared for easy access in the cockpit. The greater the pre-flight preparation of the charts, the lower the in-flight workload.

Note that, if red light is used in the cockpit, red print on charts will be difficult to see. All lines drawn on the chart should preferably be in heavy black, since even white light in the cockpit will probably be dimmed to ensure that good external night vision is retained. If you are instrument-qualified, carry the instrument approach charts for the expected aerodromes of operation, as well as for any other suitable aerodromes nearby just in case unexpected cloud rolls in.

Note on the chart any well-lit landmarks that may be useful, including rotating aerodrome beacons, towns, major roads, railway yards, etc., as well as any radio navigation aids available for use. Be especially aware of significant lit or unlit obstructions.

Carry a reliable torch.

Check personal equipment, including the normal daylight items such as a navigation computer, a plotter (or protractor and scale rule) and pencils. A definite requirement for night flying is a good torch – essential for your external pre-flight checks, and very useful in the cockpit in case of electrical failure.

External Pre-Flight Check

A powerful torch is essential for the external pre-flight check to be completed successfully at night. Not only must the aeroplane be checked, but also the surrounding area should be scanned for obstructions, rough ground and other aircraft. Tie-down ropes and wheel chocks are also more difficult to see (and remove) at night.

While the normal external checks will be made, some additional night items must also be included. These should be incorporated into the check if any night flying at all is to occur, even though the take-off might be made in daylight.

CHECK AIRCRAFT LIGHTS. A check of the aircraft lights is important. A typical technique during the pre-flight check is to position yourself near (or in) the cockpit and:
- ☐ place the master switch ON;
- ☐ check the instrument lighting and dimmers (if fitted);
- ☐ check the cabin lighting;
- ☐ check the taxi light, landing lights and anti-collision beacon by switching them ON, and then OFF again so that they do not drain the battery unnecessarily;
- ☐ switch the navigation lights ON, and leave them ON for the walk-around, since it may be impossible to check them from the cockpit.

Navigation lights must be serviceable for night flight.

During the walk-around:
- ☐ Check all of the lights and their lenses for cleanliness and serviceability;
- ☐ Carefully check the navigation lights (*red*–left, *green*–right, *white*–tail), as navigation lights are essential for night flight. The taxi light is essential for safe taxiing, but the landing lights, while useful, are not essential for flight – good take-offs and landings can be made without them; and

☐ Test any electrical stall warning devices, before returning to the cockpit and placing the master switch back to OFF to minimise electrical load on the battery.

Take great care in the night pre-flight check, focusing the torch on each specific item as it is checked, and also running its beam over the aeroplane as a whole. Ensure that the windscreen is clean and free of dust, dew, frost or ice. If ice or frost is present, check the upper leading edge of the wing (the main lift-producing part of the aeroplane) to ensure that it is also clean. Any ice, frost or other accretion should be removed from the aeroplane (especially from the lift-producing surfaces such as wings and tailplane) prior to flight. Do not forget to remove the pitot cover, otherwise there will be no airspeed reading on the ASI.

Internal Pre-Flight Check

Carry out the internal pre-flight check. Ensure that spare fuses, if required, are available. Place all items that might be needed in flight in a handy position, especially the torch, which should be placed where you can lay your hands on it in complete darkness. While handy, it should still be secure, otherwise it could become a dangerous missile in the cockpit during turbulence.

Cabin lighting should be set at a suitable level. Dim the cabin lights so that external vision is satisfactory, and reflection from the canopy minimised, but do not have them so dim that you cannot see the controls or fuel selector. It is unwise to begin night flying immediately after being in a brightly lit environment. Allow your eyes time to adjust to natural night light.

Start-Up at Night

Make sure that you have the park brakes ON before starting the engine, as movement of the aeroplane will be more difficult to detect than during daylight hours. To avoid draining the battery, unnecessary electrical services should be OFF until after start-up. Ideally, the anti-collision beacon should be turned ON just prior to engine start, to warn any person nearby that the aeroplane is active.

Keep an extremely good lookout before starting the engine – a spinning propeller is deadly, and may be difficult to see at night. With dim cabin lights, opening a window and calling a loud warning that you are about to start the engine, "Clear propeller!", and flashing the taxi lights or landing lights several times, will minimise the risk.

Make sure no one is near the propeller before starting the engine.

Once the engine is running, check outside to make sure that the aeroplane is not moving. The alternator/generator should be checked to ensure that it is functioning correctly, with the ammeter showing positive reading after the start-up. Adjust the engine rpm if necessary to achieve a suitable charging rate. If the anti-collision beacon was OFF for the start-up, it should now be turned ON for added safety. Adjust the cockpit lighting to assist your eyes to adapt to the darkness outside.

Taxiing at Night

The responsibility for all movement of the aeroplane, on the ground and in the air, lies with the pilot. Take advantage of any assistance provided by a marshaller, but remember that you carry the final responsibility. Use the taxi light, but avoid blinding the marshaller or pilots in other aeroplanes, if possible. The taxi light not only assists you to see obstructions and avoid them, it also makes it more obvious to other people that the aircraft is moving, or about to.

Taxi slowly and carefully. Taxiing at night requires additional attention because:

☐ Distance at night is very deceptive – stationary lights may appear to be closer that they really are.

☐ Speed at night is very deceptive, and there is almost always a tendency to taxi too fast. Consciously check taxi speed by looking at the wingtip area where reflected light off surface objects will help you to judge speed, and slow down if necessary.

☐ Other aircraft and any obstacles will be less visible at night. An aeroplane ahead on the taxiway may be showing just a single white tail-light that can be easily lost in the multitude of other lights. So, keep a good lookout.

FOLLOW TAXI GUIDE LINES OR LIGHTS. Taxiway lighting will be either two lines of sideline blue along the taxiway edges, or one line of centreline green. White taxi guide lines may be marked on hard surfaces, and will be visible in the taxi light. Stay in the centre of the taxiway to preserve wingtip clearance from obstacles. The ground reflection of the wingtip navigation lights, especially on a high-wing aeroplane, is useful in judging the clearance between the wingtips and any obstacles at the side of the taxiway.

If there is any doubt about your taxi path, slow down or stop. If you stop, set the park brakes ON. In an extreme situation, say on a flooded or very rough taxiway, it may be advisable to even stop the engine, seek assistance, or check the path ahead on foot. The landing lights may be used to provide a better view ahead, but they will draw more power, and (depending on the aeroplane) their continuous use on the ground may not be advisable.

Pay attention to the welfare of other pilots. Some taxiways run parallel to the runway, so avoid shining your bright lights into the eyes of a pilot taking off or landing, or taxiing, either by switching them off, or positioning the aeroplane conveniently.

Avoid looking into the landing lights of other aircraft yourself, since this could seriously degrade your night vision.

Following start-up and prior to take-off, all of the vital radio-navigation equipment should be checked for correct functioning. This includes VHF-COM, VHF-NAV, DME, ADF/RMI, marker lights and transponder. The altimeter should be checked for the correct subscale setting – check QFE and QNH give a sensible value of airfield elevation between both readings.

During the taxiing run, check the instruments:

TURNING LEFT:
- HI/RMI/compass decreasing;
- ADF/RMI tracking;
- turn coordinator shows left turn;
- balance ball shows skidding right;
- AI steady.

TURNING RIGHT:
- HI/RMI/compass increasing;
- ADF/RMI tracking;
- turn coordinator shows right turn;
- balance ball shows skidding left;
- AI steady.

At the Holding Point

The holding point or holding bay may have special lights or markings. Do not intrude on the runway until you are ready, you have a clearance (if appropriate), and the runway and its approaches are clear of other possibly conflicting aircraft.

Look out for other traffic.

While completing the pre-take-off checks at the holding position, ensure that your taxi and/or landing lights do not blind other pilots. Ensure that the park brakes are ON – an aeroplane can easily move during the power check, and at night there are few visual cues to alert the pilot. During the pre-take-off checks, do not have the cabin lighting so bright that it impairs your night vision. If bright cabin lighting is not desired, then the torch can be used.

Pay special attention to the fuel selection, since the fuel selector may be in a dim part of the cockpit. Ensure that any item required in flight is in a handy position.

Although probably included in the normal daylight pre-take-off check, checking the heading indicator for alignment with the magnetic compass while the aeroplane is stationary is especially important at night, since it will be used for heading guidance, both in the circuit area and on cross-country flights.

A final check of cabin lighting should be made. Ensure that it is adjusted to a suitable minimum, bright enough to see the major items and instruments in the cockpit, but not so bright as to seriously affect your outside vision.

The Night Take-Off

When ready to line up for take-off, make any necessary radio calls, and look carefully for other traffic on the ground and in the air. Clear the approach path to the runway, checking both left and right "Clear left, clear right". Conditions are often calm at night, making either direction on the runway suitable for operations – so ensure that the approach areas at both ends of the runway are clear. The landing lights of an approaching aeroplane are generally quite visible, but often pilots will choose to practise a night landing without using them, in which case the aeroplane will be more difficult to see – unless of course it has strobe lights.

Do not waste runway length when lining up for take-off, especially on a short runway. Line up in the centre of the runway, check that the HI agrees with the runway direction and, with the brakes OFF and the feet well away from the brakes and on the rudder pedals, smoothly apply maximum power.

Directional control during a night take-off is best achieved with reference to the runway edge lighting, using your peripheral vision, since your eyes should be focused well ahead of the aeroplane towards the far end of the runway. Runway centreline markings may also assist. Avoid overcontrolling during the ground run – keeping straight with rudder, and wings level with ailerons.

Transfer your attention to the instruments as soon as you are airborne.

The take-off is the same by night as it is by day. Fly the aeroplane away from the ground at the normal lift-off speed, and adopt the normal climb-out attitude. The big difference is that, at night, visual reference to the ground is quickly lost after lift-off, and any tendency to settle back onto the ground will not be as easily noticed. As soon as the aeroplane is airborne, therefore, transfer your attention to the flight instruments.

Try to be on instruments before losing the last visual references, which typically will be the last set of runway lights, since the first 300–400 ft of the climb-out will probably have to be totally on instruments until you are high enough to regain usable visual references.

Maintain the normal take-off pitch attitude and the wings level on the attitude indicator. Climb power and climb attitude should result in a positive climb away from the ground, reflected in a climb rate on the VSI and a gradually increasing altimeter reading.

The ASI should be checked to ensure that a suitable airspeed is being maintained on the climb-out, with minor adjustments being made on the attitude indicator as necessary, and, once well away from the ground and comfortable in the climb-out, the heading indicator can be checked for heading.

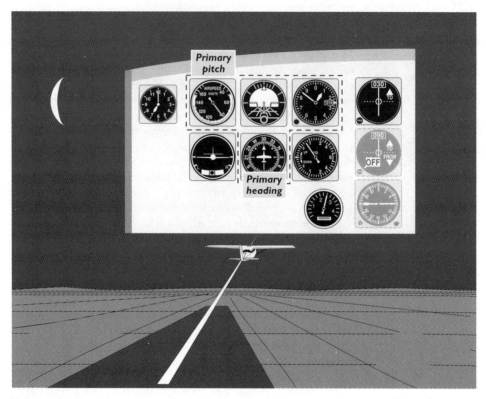

■ *Figure 25-1* **Transfer to instruments after lift-off, and maintain a
positive climb**

In a retractable-undercarriage aeroplane, the gear should not be
raised until a positive climb is indicated on both the altimeter and
the VSI. Flaps should not normally be raised until at least 200 ft
aal, and no turns should be made until a safe height is reached.
Normally, a steady straight climb is maintained until 500 ft aal
before turning onto the crosswind leg.

With little or no natural external horizon visible, the instruments become very important. If glare from the landing lights is
distracting in the cockpit, turn them off when established in the
climb. Mist, haze, smoke or cloud will reflect a lot of light.

If an engine failure occurs during the climb-out, follow the
normal daylight procedures. Lower the nose to the gliding attitude to ensure that a stall does not occur, and use the landing
lights to assist in ground recognition. Maintain control of the
aeroplane. Ideally, if sufficient height is available, re-start the
engine and climb away. Fuel selection may have been the cause (a
very serious error to make!).

If a problem occurs during the take-off ground run prior to lift-off, close the throttle and apply the brakes as necessary, keeping straight with rudder.

The Night Circuit

The circuit pattern at night is usually the same as that by day, except that it is flown mainly by instruments, with reference to the aerodrome lighting to assist in positioning the aeroplane suitably. The normal techniques of attitude flying apply. There is often a tendency to overbank at night, so special attention should be paid to bank angle.

Once the aeroplane makes the first turn, the runway and aerodrome lights will be easily seen and should be referred to frequently. Well-lit landmarks may also be useful for positioning in the circuit.

Allow for drift on the crosswind leg, and level off using normal instrument procedures. Maintain height accurately and carefully scan outside before making any turn. A good lookout for other aircraft must be maintained at all times, and the usual radio procedures followed. Recognising the navigation lights of other aircraft, and responding with an appropriate heading change, will avoid collisions. This is covered in Chapter 1, Volume 2, of *The Air Pilot's Manual*.

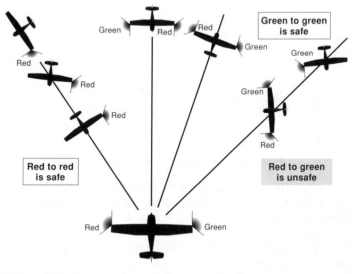

■ *Figure 25-2* **Using navigation lights to avoid collision**

While green to red is not safe, this will be the situation with two aeroplanes flying parallel on downwind. An especially careful lookout will need to be maintained.

Listening to radio transmissions will help you maintain a picture of what else is happening in the circuit.

The turn from downwind onto base leg should be made at the normal position, with reference to the runway lights and any approach lighting. The descent on base leg should be planned so that the turn onto final commences at about 600–700 ft aal, ideally with a 20° bank angle, and certainly no more than 30°.

The Night Approach

A powered approach is preferable at night, rather than a glide approach. In modern training aircraft, the powered approach is generally used by day also. Power gives you more control, a lower rate of descent and, therefore, a less steep slope. The approach to the aiming point should be stable, using any available aids, such as the **runway lighting** and a **VASIS** (visual approach slope indicator system) if available.

Using the runway edge lighting only, correct tracking and slope is achieved when the runway perspective is the same as in daylight. For correct tracking, the runway should appear symmetrical in the windscreen. Guidance on achieving the correct approach slope is obtained from the *apparent* spacing between the runway edge lights. If the aeroplane is getting low on slope, the runway lights will appear to be closer together. If the aeroplane is flying above slope, then the runway lights will appear to be further apart. Also pay attention to the ASI throughout the approach, to ensure that the correct airspeed is being maintained.

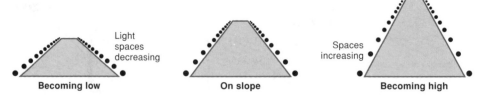

Becoming low — Light spaces decreasing   **On slope**   **Becoming high** — Spaces increasing

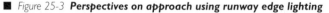

■ *Figure 25-3* **Perspectives on approach using runway edge lighting**

If no VASIS is available, the aiming point during the approach should be a point somewhere between two and four runway edge lights along the runway from the approach threshold.

If there is a VASIS available, however, the aiming point during the approach should be the VASIS. Because it is an approach aid and not a landing aid, the VASIS should be disregarded once below about 200 ft above aerodrome level, and attention placed on the perspective of the runway edge lighting in anticipation of the flare. Following the landing flare and hold-off, the aeroplane will of course touch down some distance beyond the aiming point used during the approach.

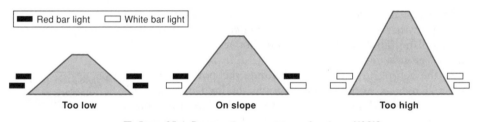

■ Figure 25-4 **Perspectives on approach using a VASIS**

Stay on centreline during the approach.

Any tendency to drift off the extended centreline can be coun-teracted with coordinated turns, and drift can be laid off if a crosswind exists. Be prepared for wind changes as the descent progresses – the difference between the wind at 1,000 ft aal and at ground level is likely to be more pronounced at night than by day. It is common for the wind speed to decrease and the wind direc-tion to back as the aeroplane descends.

Stay on slope during the approach.

Any variations in slope should be corrected with coordinated use of power and attitude. The aiming point should stay, on average, in the same position in the windscreen. Stay on airspeed during the approach. Check airspeed on the ASI, and do not be afraid to use power. Occasionally check the altitude.

Once approaching the threshold, the runway lights near the threshold should start moving down the windscreen, and certain runway features may become visible in the landing lights. The VASIS guidance will become less valuable below about 200 ft and should not be used in the latter stages of the approach, and certainly not in the flare and landing. The VASIS is an approach guide only. It is pilot judgement that counts in the landing.

The Flare, Hold-Off and Landing at Night

Runway edge lighting is the main guide to the flare and hold-off.

The aeroplane should be flown on slope towards the aiming point, where the landing flare will occur. The best guide to flare height and round-out is the runway perspective given by the runway edge lighting. As the aeroplane descends towards the runway, the runway edge lighting that you see in your peripheral vision will appear to rise. The appearance of the ground can sometimes be deceptive at night so, even when using landing lights, use the runway lighting as your main guide in the flare and hold-off, both for depth perception and for tracking guidance. For this reason, your introductory landings may be made without the use of land-ing lights. When you are using landing lights, do not stare straight down the beam, but to one side.

There is a common tendency to flare and hold off a little too high in the first few landings at night, but this tendency can soon be modified with a little practice. The runway perspective on touchdown should resemble that on lift-off, and an appreciation of this is best achieved by looking well ahead towards the far end of the runway. Avoid trying to see the runway under the nose of the aeroplane. This will almost certainly induce a tendency to fly into the ground before rounding out.

As the aeroplane is flared for landing, the power should be gradually reduced as the aeroplane enters the hold-off phase, and the throttle fully closed as the aeroplane settles onto the ground during touchdown. Keep straight during the landing ground run with rudder and, in any crosswind, keep the wings level with aileron.

Reduce power as you enter the hold-off.

Keep on the centreline until the aeroplane has slowed to taxiing speed, using brake if necessary. Taxi clear of the runway, stop the aeroplane, set the brakes to PARK, and complete the after-landing checks.

The Go-Around at Night

The flying technique for a go-around at night is the same as by day, except that it is done primarily by reference to instruments.

Whereas the eyes may be concentrated on the runway lighting during the latter stages of the approach, these lights are no longer necessary when full power is applied and the pitch attitude raised. There will be strong pitch and yaw tendencies due to the power increase that must be controlled with reference to the flight instruments. Hold the desired attitude on the AI, monitor vertical performance on the altimeter, monitor airspeed on the ASI, and hold direction on the HI.

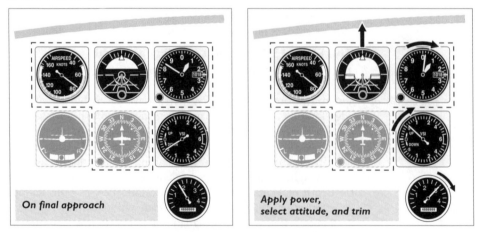

On final approach

Apply power, select attitude, and trim

■ *Figure 25-5* **Go-around at night – hold the desired attitude on the AI**

Do not change configuration (flaps/gear) until established in the go-around, with a positive rate of climb indicated on both the altimeter and the VSI.

Wind Variations with Height

The surface wind at night may differ significantly from the wind at height. The term **surface wind** refers to the wind measured 10 meters (30 feet) above open and level ground – where windsocks and other wind indicators are generally placed. The surface wind is generally weaker than the wind at altitude because of the friction forces existing between the lower layers of the airflow and the earth's surface, which slow it down. The rougher the surface, the greater the slowing down effect. The wind well away from the influence of the surface, typically some thousands of feet above it by day and possible only 500 ft above it by night, is known as the **gradient wind.**

There will be some vertical mixing in the air mass near the earth's surface, depending on a number of things, including heating, which will cause thermal eddies in the lower layers. During a typical day, the earth's surface is heated by the sun. The earth's surface, in turn, heats the air near it, causing the air to rise in turbulent eddies and mix with the upper air. This vertical mixing in the lower levels of the atmosphere brings the effect of the gradient wind closer to the earth's surface.

With vigorous heating (such as over land on a sunny day), the friction layer is deep, and so the stronger upper winds are brought down to lower levels; if the thermal eddying is weak (such as by night or over a cool sea), then the vertical mixing is less, and the friction layer shallower.

At night, therefore, with less heating and less mixing, the effect of a strong gradient wind will not be brought as close to the earth's surface, resulting in a surface wind that is lighter at night than by day. A light wind of 10 kt by day may fall to become practically calm by night, even though the upper winds have not changed.

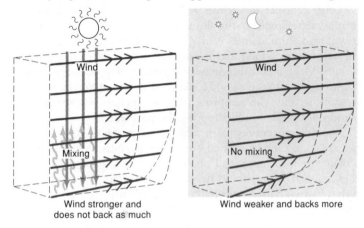

Wind stronger and does not back as much

Wind weaker and backs more

■ Figure 25-6 **The diurnal (daily) variation of wind**

A consequence of a reduced wind speed is a reduced Coriolis effect (see Chapter 19 in Vol. 2 of *The Air Pilot's Manual*), hence the surface wind will *back* compared to the wind at altitude, i.e. the wind direction will move anticlockwise as the aeroplane descends. (The effect is opposite in the southern hemisphere.)

The surface wind will back compared to the wind at altitude.

The difference in wind strength between the surface and at height will generally be more marked at night and, if there is a sudden transition from the lower winds in the shallow friction layer to the undisturbed upper winds at a particular height, say at about 500 ft, then windshear could be experienced as the aeroplane passes through this level.

Expect stronger and sharper wind changes as you climb out by night.

A surface wind of 5 kt at take-off may suddenly become 20 kt at some low level on a clear night (possibly with a significant change in direction as well), yet only 10 kt at 1,000 ft on a clear and sunny day.

Emergencies at Night

Engine Failure

A forced landing at night away from an aerodrome is obviously a more dangerous event than by day, when better vision will allow the easier selection of a suitable field. Moonlight may help at night, but do not count on it! Normal daylight procedures should be followed if the engine fails at night, with the emphasis on keeping the aeroplane at flying speed and restarting the engine.

Maintain flying airspeed after an engine failure.

Flying the aeroplane at a low forward airspeed consistent with retaining full control will help achieve a lower rate of descent, and allow more time for remedial action and for carrying out a forced landing if necessary. A Mayday call should be made promptly to alert the rescue services.

Time available for action will depend on height above the ground, so reference to the altimeter is important. With QNH set, it will read altitude amsl. With QFE set, it will read height above the aerodrome, which may be at a different level to surrounding terrain. Make a commonsense judgement of your height above the ground, and keep a good lookout. If sufficient height and time is available, glide the aeroplane (at a safe speed) back towards the aerodrome, while troubleshooting the problem.

Watch your altitude after an engine failure.

The full procedures for rectifying the problem and restarting the engine should be carried out if time permits. Fuel selection is a major item to consider. If, however, a landing has to be made, then consideration should be given to landing into wind, using only a partial flap setting (rather than full flap) to avoid a steep nose-down gliding attitude with a high descent rate, and to minimise the flare required prior to touchdown. It is preferable to touch down in a fairly flat attitude. Landing lights may be useful during the last few hundred feet, especially in making visual contact with the ground.

Electrical Failure

Electrical failure may cause the loss of instrument lighting, which can be easily compensated for by using the torch (kept in a handy position and with good batteries). A sudden failure of lighting should only deprive you of the instruments for a few seconds but, in this time, make use of visual clues such as the natural horizon.

The natural horizon will generally be of more value when the aeroplane is well above the ground. Close to the ground, shortly after take-off for instance, there may be insufficient ground lighting to provide a horizon and, in any case, the lights could possibly be on a hillside, giving a false horizon, or there could be so few that the aeroplane will quickly fly over them anyway. Scan the flight instruments!

If the electrical failure is only partial, then alternative lighting may be available in the cockpit from another light source or, perhaps, by interchanging bulbs. Panic action is not required – calm and careful consideration is. Do not be distracted from controlling the attitude of the aeroplane!

The attitude indicator, if it is electrical, will gradually run down if its electrical power is removed, but it could remain useful for a brief period. Attention should be paid to the airspeed indicator, however, to ensure that flying speed is maintained. The first step following a failure of any kind is *fly the aeroplane!*

Once flying the aeroplane is under control following engine failure, with a suitable gliding attitude and airspeed achieved, try to rectify the problem, and follow the appropriate emergency procedures or checklists. For an electrical failure, check the switching, monitor the alternator/generator or battery discharge rate, and check circuit breakers and fuses (if convenient) without disturbing your control of the aeroplane. If the electrical failure is only partial, but with a high discharge rate, then off-load the alternator or battery by switching off non-essential services, such as some radios, the landing lights, etc. A landing as soon as reasonably possible should be considered.

RADIO FAILURE. A return to the airfield should be planned, making a radio call if possible, and certainly keeping a good lookout for other aircraft. If it is only a radio failure, then ATC can perhaps be alerted by flying a circuit, descending, and then flying above the landing runway, flashing the landing lights and/ or navigation lights. Without radio, light signals from the ATS personnel on the ground may be used – the main ones being:

☐ **Continuous red** – give way to other aircraft and continue circling.

☐ **Red flashes** – do not land; aerodrome not available for landing.
☐ **Green flashes** – return to the aerodrome; wait for permission to land.
☐ **Continuous green** – you may land.

NAVIGATION LIGHTS FAILURE. If the navigation lights have failed, then the aeroplane should be landed normally as soon as it is safe to do so, unless ATC authorises the continuation of the flight. ATC should be informed of the lack of navigation lights as soon as possible, so that other aircraft can be warned. Loss of the navigation lights will not affect control of the aeroplane in any way – in fact, the pilot generally cannot even see these lights, but it will affect the ability of other aeroplanes to see you and remain clear. A normal circuit and landing should be made.

LANDING LIGHTS FAILURE. If the landing lights have failed, then this is of little importance. They are not required for a pilot to make a normal, safe landing.

Failure of Aerodrome Lighting

Most aerodromes have a standby power supply that will operate within seconds of an aerodrome power failure, but there is a possibility (fairly remote) that a complete power failure could occur. Aircraft in the vicinity of an aerodrome without runway lighting at night should hold at a safe height, and maintain a very good lookout. Radio contact should also be maintained, preferably with ATC on the ground, but if that is not possible, with other aircraft in the circuit or with ATC on an alternative frequency.

If the lighting is not returned to service, then consideration should be given to **diverting** (at a safe height) to a nearby aerodrome where runway lighting is available. A radar service may be available to assist in tracking.

> *Allow a minimum safe altitude of 1,000 ft above the highest obstacle within 5 nm either side of the diversion track (possibly higher if conditions permit).*

Lost

If you become temporarily uncertain of your position, follow the same procedures as you would during daylight hours. Radio navigation aids, if available in the vicinity, should always be taken advantage of – if you know how to use them. If you are really lost, then navigational assistance may be available from ATC, either by radar or with VHF direction-finding using the VHF-COM radio. The choice of alternate aerodromes will be more limited at night, of course, since runway lighting will be required.

Carry enough fuel for a diversion, just in case.

It is always advisable to carry sufficient fuel at night for an unexpected journey to an alternate field.

Night Navigation

Navigating at night follows the same basic principles as navigating by day, except that ground features are more difficult to see, distances are more difficult to estimate, and the likelihood of encountering unexpected cloud or areas of restricted visibility is greater.

GROUND FEATURES. The best ground features to use at night are usually the light patterns of towns, and the beacons of any nearby aerodromes. Cities like London and Manchester are generally too large for distinctive light patterns to be meaningful to a novice night flyer, but small towns, especially if they have areas of darkness around them, are generally good. Busy motorways delineated by a stream of car headlights may also be useful.

On moonlit nights, reflections off the surfaces of lakes and other large bodies of water may make them very visible (especially when viewed against the moon), but this should not be relied on for navigation in case clouds cover the sky unexpectedly.

AERONAUTICAL LIGHT BEACONS, which are installed at various civil and military aerodromes in the UK, are good landmarks. Provided it is during the aerodrome's hours of operation, they can be expected to be on at night and by day in bad visibility. The different types include:

☐ **Identification beacons,** which flash a two-letter Morse code group every 12 seconds (*green* at civil aerodromes and *red* at military aerodromes); and

☐ **Aerodrome beacons,** which give an alternating-colour flash signal instead (usually *white/white* or less commonly *white/green*). They are not normally provided in addition to an identification beacon.

MARINE BEACONS AND LIGHTSHIPS may be useful if you are navigating near the sea by night. They appear on some aeronautical charts with a description of their lighting characteristics.

■ *Figure 26-1* **Marine beacons on an aeronautical chart**

RADIO NAVIGATION AIDS are very useful at night – if you know how to use them correctly. Some aids experience errors at night, such as NDB night effect, which may be greatest during the periods around dawn and dusk. The hours of service should be checked in the AIP to ensure that the aids will indeed be available at the time of your flight. In general, you can expect major en route VORs and NDBs to be operating H24 (24 hours a day), but some aids tied to a particular aerodrome may not be available outside its hours of operation. This could apply to a radar service, a VDF service, an ILS, locator, etc. Better to check first, and be sure.

Aerodrome Availability

Many aerodromes, both civil and military, close at night. It is always advisable to check in the AIP and NOTAMs which aerodromes are available at night and which are not. Call a briefing office if you are unsure. Check not only your planned departure and destination aerodromes, but also those aerodromes which might be useful as alternates in case of a diversion. You must be certain that **runway lighting** will be available for your landing. As well as some aerodromes closing, there are some Danger Areas that are not active at night.

Flight Planning

Good flight planning is especially important at night, since there will be fewer ground features to assist in determining navigation errors, as well as less assistance available from ATSUs in the form of communications, radar or VDF bearings.

WEATHER. The weather takes on special importance at night. All relevant information should be studied carefully, especially the Aerodrome Forecasts for your destination, as well as those for a number of alternates and your aerodrome of departure. Remember that the closeness of the temperature/dewpoint figures provides some clue as to the possibility of mist or fog forming as the temperature falls even further during the night. Fewer observers on duty at night will mean fewer updates of actual weather. Attention should be paid to the possibility of low cloud, mist or fog, and also to the wind strength and direction, at altitude as well as at the surface.

ROUTE SELECTION. A suitable route should be chosen that utilises the best features available at night (the lights of small towns, aerodrome light beacons, operating radio navigation aids, marine beacons, motorways, etc.), even if this route is slightly longer than the direct route. Rugged and/or high terrain is best avoided, and a **safety altitude** to ensure adequate terrain clearance should be calculated. A vertical clearance of 1,000 ft above the highest obstacle within 5 nm of track is required.

FLIGHT LOG. Tracks should be marked on the chart with dark lines, to ensure that they will be clearly seen in a dimly lit cockpit. The flight log should also be filled in with a dark pencil or pen, so that it is easily read in dim lighting. Red lines will not be visible in red lighting, and certain colours on the map may not be as distinguishable by night as by day, which may lead to some difficulties.

Care should be taken in measuring tracks and distances, and then in calculating headings and groundspeeds. Always re-check! Dead-reckoning is very important at night, and a correct flight log is a much better starting point than an incorrect one.

Night flights must operate according to the Instrument Flight Rules (IFR), and so quadrantal cruising levels will apply above 3,000 ft amsl. A safety altitude providing at least 1,000 ft vertical clearance above obstacles within 5 nm of track must be used for all cruising levels, both above and below 3,000 ft amsl.

Calculate an accurate **fuel log,** ensuring that there is sufficient fuel available for a successful diversion and landing, with adequate reserves remaining.

It is recommended that a **flight plan** be submitted for a night cross-country flight, since this increases the protective search and rescue cover.

Fly Accurate Headings and Airspeeds

Altitude and airspeed must be accurate at night.

Distance at night can be deceptive, since there will be fewer ground objects visible for comparison in terms of size and location. The usual tendency at night is to underestimate distance. Height and speed may also be difficult to estimate, so careful attention should be paid to the altimeter and to the airspeed indicator.

Headings and time-keeping must be accurate at night.

The aeroplane should be navigated, according to a predetermined flight log, by flying planned heading and true airspeed. From time to time occasional track corrections and revised ETAs may be required, using reliable pinpoints and radio navigation aids. Accurate heading and time-keeping is essential, and changes should only be made when you are absolutely certain that a change is required.

If you become lost on a night cross-country flight, follow the normal daylight procedures. Use available pinpoints and radio navigation aids to fix your position, or request assistance from an ATSU which may be able to provide a radar fix or a VDF bearing. However, with good flight planning and accurate flying in terms of airspeed and heading, you will always know where you are, even at night.

The IMC Rating

The following extract from CAA Publication CAP 53, *The Private Pilot's Licence and Associated Ratings,* covers the main details of the UK IMC Rating. Further reading in CAP 53 is recommended for such things as *Exemptions,* and Appendices G and H – *The Ground and Flight Training Syllabuses,* and *Flight Test Requirements for the IMC Rating.*

The Instrument Meteorological Conditions Rating

1   **RATING PRIVILEGES**

1.1   An Instrument Meteorological Conditions (IMC) Rating extends the privileges of a PPL(A) holder to allow flight as pilot-in-command (PIC):

    (a)   out of sight of the surface;

    (b)   in a control zone on a special VFR clearance with flight visibility less than 10 km but not less than 3 km;

    (c)   when in IMC outside controlled airspace;

    (d)   during take-off or landing with a flight visibility below cloud of not less than 1800 m.

1.2   The rating confers no privileges for flight in controlled airspace (other than Class D) under circumstances requiring compliance with Instrument Flight Rules (IFR). It is not recognised in other States, and is only of use in UK territorial airspace, and in Channel Islands and Isle of Man airspace.

2   **EXPERIENCE AND TRAINING REQUIREMENTS**

2.1   An applicant for the grant of an IMC Rating must have 25 hours' experience as an aeroplane pilot since the date of application for his PPL(A). The 25 hours must include 10 hours as pilot-in-command (PIC), of which at least 5 hours must be on cross-country flights, and may include the 15 hours' dual instrument instruction specified in paragraph 2.2.

2.2   An applicant must also hold an FRTO licence, and unless exempted under paragraph 6, complete a recognised course of training for the rating before taking the Ground Examination and Flight Test. The course must include 15 hours' training in instrument flying in a suitably equipped dual-control aeroplane, except for up to 2 hours which may be in a simulator recognised by the Authority as being suitable for the training. Not less than 10 of the 15 hours must be flown by sole reference to instruments. These minimum course requirements assume that the applicant has completed the 4 hours of dual instruction in instrument flying specified in the PPL requirements. An applicant, who has not had these 4 hours' training, must satisfy the FTO that he has reached an equivalent standard of ability before starting the course.

2.3   Where an applicant wishes to be tested for the IMC Rating on a multi-engine aeroplane the flying training must ensure that in simulated instrument flight conditions the pilot can maintain stable flight after an engine failure at climb power, then climb at the recommended speed and execute the normal range of flight manoeuvres under asymmetric power.

2.4   A student's ability and experience may be taken into account in deciding how much time should be allotted to each of the following items but the course must cover all of them:

2.4.1 *Basic Stage*

    (a)   Instrument attitude flight.

    (b)   Basic flight manoeuvres.

    (c)   Intermediate flight manoeuvres.

    (d)   Simulated loss of gyroscopic instruments.

    (e)   Simulated loss of pitot/static instruments.

2.4.2 *Applied Stage*

    (a)   Flight planning.

    (b)   Departure and en route techniques.

    (c)   Approach and let-down procedures.

    (d)   Bad weather circuits and landing (a simulator must not be used for this item).

2.5   Instruction on the course may only be given by instructors with rating unrestricted with regard to instrument flying instructions (see Part 2, Chapter 9).

2.6   Ability and experience may be taken into account when deciding on the amount of ground instruction needed by an individual. Normally, however, the course should provide for a minimum of 20 hours covering:

    (a)   Physiological factors.

    (b)   Flight instruments.

    (c)   Aeronautical Information Service.

    (d)   Flight planning.

    (e)   Privileges of the IMC Rating.

2.7   Syllabuses of ground training and flight training are contained in Part 2, Appendices G and H.

3   GROUND EXAMINATIONS

    Unless exempted under paragraph 6, an applicant must pass, in the 12 months before the date of application for the rating, a written examination covering subjects drawn from the IMC Rating course syllabus and the PPL(A) syllabus including questions on the planning and execution of a typical flight under IFR outside controlled airspace.

4   FLIGHT TEST

4.1   Unless exempted under paragraph 6, an applicant for the rating must complete the training requirements before taking a flight test conducted by an examiner authorised by the CAA. The test includes full and limited panel instrument flying, use of radio navigation aids whilst flying by sole reference to the instruments, instrument approach procedures, bad weather circuits and landings. In the case of a multi-engine aeroplane it includes flight with asymmetric power. Detailed contents of the test are in Part 2, Appendix H.

4.2   Initial and revalidation flight tests may be completed in more than one flight but nor more than three and must be completed in a period of 28 days. Failure in any part of the test will require the candidate to take the full test again. Where a candidate chooses not to continue with a test for reasons considered inadequate by the examiner, that test will be regarded as a failure with regard to the items not attempted. There is no limit on the number of cycles of attempts that can be made to pass the flight test.

5   VALIDITY OF IMC RATING

5.1   The IMC Rating C of T is valid for a period of 25 months from the date of the successful flight test.

Night Qualification (JAR-FCL)

If the privileges of the PPL licence are to be exercised at night, at least five additional hours flight time in aeroplanes shall be completed at night. This five additional hours shall comprise three hours of dual instruction including at least one hour cross-country navigation, and five solo take-offs and solo full-stop landings. This qualification will be endorsed on the licence.

NOTE If passengers are to be carried, the JAR–FCL requires that a pilot must have completed at least three take-offs and landings within the preceding 90 days; one of which must be at night if passengers are to be carried at night.

Radio Failure Procedures

The following information on radio failure procedures is extracted from UK AIP ENR 1-6.

3	Radio Failure Procedures For Pilots

3.1   General

3.1.1   In the radio communication failure procedures given below, the expression EAT will mean either an EAT given by the appropriate ATC Unit or the ETA over the holding point, if the pilot has been told 'No delay expected'.

3.1.2   The message 'Delay not determined' will not be considered to be an EAT for the purpose of the radio failure procedures. Pilots whose radio fails after they have received this message, but before an EAT is given, should not attempt to land at their planned destination aerodrome but should fly to another aerodrome, following the procedure given in paragraph 3.3.3.2 (b).

3.2   Failure of Radio Navigation Equipment

3.2.1   If part of an aircraft's radio navigation equipment fails but two-way communication can still be maintained with ATC, the pilot must inform ATC of the failure and report his altitude and approximate position. ATC may, at its discretion, authorize the pilot to continue his flight in or into Controlled Airspace. When radar is available it may, subject to workload, be used to provide navigational assistance to the pilot.

3.2.2   If no authorization to proceed is given by ATC, the pilot should leave, or avoid Controlled Airspace and areas of dense traffic, and either:

    (a)   Go to an area in which he can continue his flight in VMC or (if this is not possible);

    (b)   select a suitable area in which to descend through cloud, fly visually to a suitable aerodrome and land as soon as practicable.

But before doing so, however, he should consult ATC who may be able to give him instructions or advice. He should also take into consideration the latest meteorological information and terrain clearance and should make full use of ground VHF D/F stations. He must at all times keep ATC informed of his intentions.

3.3   Failure of two-way radio Communications Equipment

3.3.1   The basic procedure to be adopted by pilots experiencing two-way radio communications failure is given in paragraph 3.3.2. Other procedures which may be required in certain circumstances because of weather conditions, the last ATC instruction received, etc, are tabulated in paragraph 3.3.3. Similarly, additional procedures are described in paragraph 3.3.4 for departing aircraft flying in Controlled Airspace on certain ATC clearances but which have not reached cruising level.

3.3.2   The basic procedure is:

    (a)   Continue the flight in accordance with the current flight plan to the holding point at the aerodrome of first intended landing. Maintain the last acknowledged cruising levels for the portion of the route for which levels have been assigned and thereafter maintain the cruising levels shown in the flight plan. Operate secondary radar transponder on Mode A, Code 7600, with Mode C;

    (b)   if the aircraft's transmitter is thought to be still functioning, transmit position reports on the appropriate frequency when over the routine reporting points;

    (c)   arrange the flight to arrive over the holding point as closely as possible to the ETA last acknowledged by the appropriate ATC Unit. If no such ETA has been acknowledged, the pilot should use an ETA computed from the last acknowledged position report and flight plan times for the subsequent sections of the flight. Pilots must follow the appropriate inbound route for the Control Zone or Control Area concerned (see AD-2 or ENR 2 Sections);

    (d)   begin to descend over the holding point at the last acknowledged EAT. If no EAT has been acknowledged the descent should be started at the ETA calculated in (c) above. The rate of descent to the lowest level of the holding stack must be not less than 500 ft a minute. It is essential that aircraft should maintain a strict timing; a descent may only be started within the ten minutes immediately following the time that it ought to have begun. If 'Delay not determined' has been given, and no subsequent EAT, do not attempt to land at the destination aerodrome but fly to another aerodrome following the procedure outlined in (e) below;

    (e)   land within 30 minutes of the time descent should have been started (ie the EAT or ETA referred to in (d) above). If unable to land within this time, but able to complete an approach and landing visually, do so. If not able to land within the specified time, nor to approach and land visually, leave the vicinity of the aerodrome and any associated Controlled Airspace at the specified altitude and on the specified route (see AD 2 Sections). If no altitude or route is specified, fly at the last assigned altitude or Minimum Sector Altitude (MSA), whichever is the higher and avoid areas of dense traffic. Then, either:

        (i)   fly to an area in which flight may be continued in VMC and land at a suitable aerodrome there, or (if this is not possible);

        (ii)   select a suitable area in which to descend through cloud, fly visually to a suitable aerodrome and land as soon as practicable.

(continued)

In either case, inform ATC as soon as possible after landing.

(f)   In the event of a missed approach:

   (i)   land at the aerodrome of destination if this can be achieved within 30 minutes of the time descent from the holding point should have started, or (if this is not possible);

   (ii) fly to another aerodrome following the procedure outlined in (e) above.

3.3.3   The procedures to be adopted in certain circumstances are tabulated below.

Table II

Paragraph	Flight Conditions	Details of Circumstances	Procedure to be Adopted
3.3.3.1	VMC	(a) Flight in VMC can be maintained.	Continue flight in VMC, land at the nearest suitable aerodrome and report arrival by the most expeditious means to the appropriate ATC Unit.
		(b) Flight in VMC cannot be maintained.	Adopt the IMC procedure appropriate to the circumstances.

The Air Pilot's **Manual**

Volume 5

Exercises and Answers

About the Exercises

Preparation for these Exercises

The aim of *The Air Pilot's Manual* is, where possible, to treat each topic once, but thoroughly, so, as a PPL holder, you should already have a very sound knowledge of much of what is required for an IMC Rating. It is recommended, however, that you review the following chapters of *The Air Pilot's Manual* (especially if you have any difficulty with the following Exercises):

VOLUME 2. Chapters 1, 2, 3, 4, 23, 25.

VOLUME 3. Chapters 2, 3, 4, 5, 6.

VOLUME 4. Chapters 25, 26, 27.

VOLUME 6. Chapters 2 & 3.

Questions

The questions in these Exercises are arranged in different ways:

☐ Optional answers within questions are in brackets, and divided by an oblique stroke(/).

☐ Options in multiple-choice questions are preceded by (a), (b), (c), etc.

☐ Where questions are divided into parts, these are shown as (i), (ii), (iii), (iv), etc.

References

In developing expertise as an IMC-rated pilot it is important to refer to appropriate chapters of *The Air Pilot's Manual* and also the UK Aeronautical Information Publication (AIP). This vital operational document, published by the CAA, is kept up to date with the CAA's AIP amendment service.

In many cases, you may have to search through the AIP for the required information, but this in itself is a worthwhile exercise since you must become familiar with the document. You should also study the instrument charts that you decide to use, in particular those published by *British Airways/Aerad* or *Jeppesen*.

The answers to a few of our questions have to be obtained from the UK AIP and will require amending from time to time, since the AIP is amended regularly. Use your common sense in such cases.

Finally, please feel free to advise us in writing of any significant changes you may notice – this will help to ensure that our next edition is up to date. Your feedback is always most welcome.

Instrument Flying Techniques

Exercises 1

Instrument Flying Techniques (covers entire Section One)

1 During manoeuvres, to determine the attitude of the aircraft, you should use (the flight instruments and what your eyes tell you/bodily feel and what your balance mechanism tells you).

2 Having settled into a steady banked turn, the balance mechanism will send a message of (level/banked) flight. You should use your ____ to verify the true situation.

3 Immediately after rolling level out of a lengthy, banked turn to the left, the balance mechanism will send a message of (level/right-banked/left-banked) flight. This is known as the ____. You should ____.

4 To minimise balance illusions in instrument flight, you (should/need not) hold your head upright to your body, and use your ____.

5 A strong forward acceleration can cause an illusion of pitching nose (up/down) and tumbling (forwards/backwards). You should ____.

6 A strong deceleration can cause an illusion of pitching nose (up/down) and tumbling (forwards/backwards). You should ____.

7 An illusion of rotation when no rotation is occurring, or vice versa, is known as ____.

8 Vertigo (can/cannot) be caused by accelerations, strong nose-blowing, and sneezing.

9 What pressures are fed to the ASI?

10 What pressures are fed to the VSI and altimeter?

11 What altimeter subscale setting is used when cruising below the transition altitude (usually 3,000 ft amsl in the UK)?

12 What altimeter subscale setting is used when cruising at a flight level above the transition level?

13 What altimeter subscale setting is used when descending from a flight level and approaching an aerodrome at which you plan to land?

14 What altimeter subscale setting is normally used in the UK when on final approach to land?

15 If a missed approach is made following an instrument approach in which the pilot did not become visual, climb instructions may be passed by ATC in the form of an altitude. What altimeter subscale setting would be the most suitable following the commencement of the missed approach?

16 Some attitude indicators are operated electrically, others are operated by ____.

17 Some heading indicators, or direction indicators, are operated electrically, others are operated by ____.

18 If the static vent ices over during descent, the altimeter will:
   (a) continue to read correctly.
   (b) show a constant indication.
   (c) indicate an altitude higher than the actual altitude.

19 If the static vent ices over on the climb, the altimeter will:

(a) continue to read correctly

(b) show a constant indication.

(c) indicate an altitude higher than the actual altitude.

20 If the static vent ices over on the cruise, the ASI will:

(a) show a constant indication, even if the airspeed changes.

(b) read too high if the aeroplane climbs, and too low if it descends.

(c) read too low if the aeroplane climbs, and too high if it descends

(d) continue to read correctly if the aeroplane climbs or descends.

21 If the static vent ices over on the climb, the VSI will:

(a) continue to read correctly.

(b) show a constant positive indication.

(c) indicate zero.

22 If the static vent ices over at any time, a suction-driven attitude indicator will _____.

23 Which flight instruments will be affected by a blocked pitot tube?

24 Pitot pressure equals _____ pressure plus static pressure. The airspeed indicator measures the difference between _____ pressure and _____ pressure and converts this to an indicated airspeed.

25 A blocked pitot tube will mean that the measured (pitot/static) pressure will be incorrect.

26 If a pitot tube is blocked, then during the take-off run the pitot tube will not measure the increase in (dynamic/static) pressure, and the ASI will read (too high/too low/zero).

27 A pitot tube becomes blocked on the cruise, with its measured total pressure remaining constant, then during descent, as the actual static pressure (increases/decreases), the ASI will read (too high/too low/correctly /zero).

28 While cruising at 5,000 ft amsl under ISA conditions, the airspeed indicator shows 100 kt. The true airspeed is approximately:

(a)   100 kt.

(b)   102 kt.

(c)   108 kt.

(d)   120 kt.

29 What is the true airspeed cruising at FL70, OAT −5°C, and IAS 105 kt?

30 While parked at a level aerodrome, elevation 810 ft, the altimeter reads 900 ft, 90 ft too high, with 1015 mb set. What is the Aerodrome QNH and QFE?

31 You are cruising at FL40 in cloud. Regional QNH is 980 mb. What is your vertical distance amsl? Does this provide adequate clearance above an obstacle within 5 nm of track that is 2,560 ft amsl.

32 When turning through north in the northern hemisphere, the magnetic compass will be (sluggish/lively) and will (lag behind/overshoot).

33 Turning errors of the magnetic compass are greatest when turning through _____.

34 In the northern hemisphere, you should (overshoot/undershoot) the desired magnetic heading when turning through north.

35 In the northern hemisphere, you should (overshoot/undershoot) the desired magnetic heading when turning through south.

36 Turning errors of the magnetic compass are (the same/reversed) in the southern hemisphere.

37 Turning errors of the magnetic compass are (greater/smaller/the same) near the equator, compared to when the aircraft is at high latitudes.

38 Acceleration errors of the magnetic compass are greatest on headings of

_____.

39 Name three gyroscopic instruments found in most aircraft.

40 What effect would a low suction pressure have on a vacuum-driven AI?

Radio Navigation Aids

Exercises 9

Radar

1 The process of separating aircraft and positioning them by an ATC radar controller passing headings-to-steer is known as radar ____.

2 If a radar service is not available, then ATC will separate aircraft using procedures based on their estimated positions and known altitudes. This is known as:
(a) non-radar separation.
(b) procedural separation.
(c) standby separation.

3 Primary surveillance radar can detect signals from aircraft, even if they carry no radar equipment. Secondary surveillance radar (SSR) on the ground detects strong responding signals transmitted from aircraft equipped with a ____.

4 An approach to a runway under the guidance of a radar controller who passes tracking and descent advice is known as a ____.

5 What approximate RoD in ft/min is required to achieve a 3° glideslope, which is 300 ft per nm, if the groundspeed of the aeroplane is 60 kt?

6 What approximately RoD in ft/min is required to achieve a 3° glideslope, which is 300 ft per nm, if the groundspeed of the aeroplane is 90 kt?

7 The minimum visibility required for an SRA by an IMC-rated pilot is ____.

8 The decision height for an SRA carried out by an IMC-rated pilot will depend on the obstacle clearance height (plus additions), but in no case may be less than an absolute SRA minimum of ____ ft aal.

9 The approximate range of any VHF signals for an aeroplane at 6,000 ft above the level of a ground station is ____ nm.

10 The approximate range of any VHF signals for an aeroplane at 2,000 ft above the level of a ground station is ____ nm.

11 The approximate range of any VHF signals for an aeroplane at 2,500 ft above the level of a ground station is ____ nm.

12 Where in the UK AIP can you find the special-purpose codes used for secondary surveillance radar?

Exercises 10

DME

1 DME stands for ____.

2 DME measures:
(a) horizontal distance,
(b) vertical distance,
(c) slant distance.

3 The DME is selected on the ____ radio, usually along with a co-located VOR.

4 If an aircraft tracking directly towards a DME ground station is at 37 DME at time 0115, and at 27 DME at time 0120, what is its groundspeed?

5 If an aircraft tracking directly away from a DME ground station is at 22 DME at time 1223, and at 32 DME at time 1230, what is its groundspeed?

6 Tracking abeam a DME ground station, the DME readings change in the following manner as time passes: 25, 21, 17, 15, 14, 15, 17, 21. What was your abeam distance from the DME ground station?

7 A DME can provide a:
 (a) circular position line.
 (b) straight position line.

Exercises 11

The NDB and the ADF

1 NDB stands for ＿＿＿ .

2 The NDB is (a ground-based transmitter/an airborne receiver).

3 NDBs transmit in either the ＿＿＿ or ＿＿＿ frequency bands.

4 ADF stands for ＿＿＿ .

5 The ADF is (a ground-based transmitter/an airborne receiver).

6 A particular NDB may be identified by its ＿＿＿.

7 The Morse code is shown on many aeronautical charts. What is the Morse code ident of the Blackpool NDB, 'BPL'?

8 The three basic steps that a pilot should follow before using a particular NDB or locator beacon for navigation are ＿＿＿.

9 QDM is the (magnetic/true) bearing (from/to) the ground station.

10 QDR is the (magnetic/true) bearing (from/to) the ground station.

11 RBI stands for ＿＿＿ .

12 If an aircraft on heading 250°M has a reading of 030 on its relative bearing indicator, what is:
 (i) the magnetic bearing of the NDB from the aircraft?
 (ii) the magnetic bearing of the aircraft from the NDB?

13 If an aircraft on heading 250°M has a reading of 350 on its relative bearing indicator, calculate:
 (i) the magnetic bearing of the NDB from the aircraft.
 (ii) the magnetic bearing of the aircraft from the NDB.

14 Determine the range of the Chiltern NDB from UK AIP ENR 4-1.

15 An NDB used to locate the aircraft on an instrument approach is called a ＿＿＿.

16 An NDB positioned so that it provides a fix for an aircraft during an instrument approach, and co-located with the outer marker for the approach, may be designated on the instrument approach chart with the letters ＿＿＿.

17 Atmospheric conditions, such as electrical storms or the periods of sunrise and sunset, (may/will not) distort NDB signals, making ADF indications less reliable.

18 Mountains (may/will not) reflect and distort NDB signals, making ADF indications less reliable.

19 The range promulgated in the UK AIP for NDBs is based on a daytime protection ratio between wanted and unwanted signals that limits bearing errors to ±＿＿＿° or less.

20 Write down the Morse code in dots (·) and dashes (–) for all the letters of the alphabet.

Exercises 12

The Relative Bearing Indicator (RBI)

1   An aircraft has a heading of 035°M. Its RBI indicates 040. The magnetic variation in the area is 4°W. Calculate:
    (i)   QDM;
    (ii) QDR;
    (iii) QTE.

2   An aircraft has a heading of 335°M. Its RBI indicates 355. The magnetic variation in the area is 4°W. Calculate:
    (i)   QDM;
    (ii) QDR;
    (iii) QTE.

3   MH 080; RBI 000. Onto what heading should you turn to make a 90° intercept of a track of 040°M to the NDB? What will the RBI indicate at the point of intercept?

4   MH 080; RBI 000. Onto what heading should you turn to make a 60° intercept of a track of 040°M to the NDB? What will the RBI indicate at the point of intercept?

5   MH 070; RBI 010. Which way should you turn to intercept 075°M to the NDB?

6   MH 155, RBI 180. Which way should you turn to intercept a track of 140°M away from the NDB?

7   MH 155, RBI 180. Which way should you turn to intercept a track of 180°M away from the NDB?

8   When tracking towards an NDB, the ADF readings are:
    Time 1: MH 055, RBI 005;
    Time 2: MH 055, RBI 005.
    What track is the aircraft maintaining to the NDB?

9   When tracking towards an NDB, the ADF readings are:

    Time 1: MH 055, RBI 005 and on track;
    Time 2: MH 055, RBI 002.
    Is the aircraft off track to the left or right?

10 To track towards an NDB on a track of 340°M, with an expected crosswind from the right causing 5° of drift, what magnetic heading should you steer, and what do you expect the RBI to indicate?

11 To track away from an NDB on a track of 120°M, with an expected crosswind from the right causing 8° of drift, what magnetic heading should you steer, and what do you expect the RBI to indicate?

12 You wish to track 360°M in nil-wind conditions. What magnetic heading should you steer? What will the RBI indicate as you pass abeam an NDB which is 10 nm to the right of track, i.e. when the NDB is on a bearing of 90° to the track?

13 You wish to track 360°M and you expect 10° of drift caused by a wind from the east. What magnetic heading should you steer? What will the RBI indicate as you pass abeam an NDB which is 10 nm to the right of track?

14 You wish to track 030°M in nil-wind conditions. What magnetic heading should you steer? What will the RBI indicate as you pass abeam an NDB which is 10 nm to the right of track?

15 You are heading 030°M in nil-wind conditions. What is your track? What will the RBI indicate as you pass abeam an NDB which is 10 nm to the left of track?

16 You wish to track 030°M and expect 7° left drift. What magnetic heading should you steer? What will the RBI indicate as you pass abeam an NDB which is 10 nm to the left of track?

17 You are tracking 278°M with 6° of port drift. You can determine your position abeam an NDB which is to the right of track by waiting until the RBI indicates _____.

18 You are tracking 278°M with 6° of port drift. You can determine your position abeam an NDB which is to the left of track by waiting until the RBI indicates _____.

19 You are tracking 278°M with 5° of starboard drift. You can determine your position abeam an NDB which is to the left of track by waiting until the RBI indicates _____.

Exercises 13

The Radio Magnetic Indicator (RMI)

1 An aircraft has a heading of 035°M. Its RMI indicates 075. The magnetic variation in the area is 4°W. Calculate:

(i) QDM;

(ii) QDR;

(c) QTE.

2 An aircraft has a heading of 335°M. Its RMI indicates 330. The magnetic variation in the area is 4°W. Calculate:

(i) QDM;

(ii) QDR;

(iii) QTE.

3 MH 080; RMI 080. Onto what heading should you turn to make a 90° intercept of a track of 040°M to the NDB? What will the RMI indicate at the point of intercept?

4 MH 080; RMI 080. Onto what heading should you turn to make a 60° intercept of a track of 040°M to the NDB? What will the RMI indicate at the point of intercept?

5 MH 070, RMI 080. Which way should you turn to intercept 075°M to the NDB? What will the RMI indicate at the point of intercept?

6 MH 155, RMI 330. Which way should you turn to intercept a track of 140°M away from the NDB? What will the RMI indicate at the point of intercept? What will the tail of the RMI pointer indicate?

7 MH 155, RMI 130. Which way should you turn to intercept a track of 090°M away from the NDB? What will the RMI indicate at the point of intercept? What will the RMI tail indicate?

8 When tracking towards an NDB, the ADF readings are:

Time 1: MH 055, RMI 060;

Time 2: MH 055, RMI 060.

What track is the aircraft maintaining to the NDB?

9 When tracking towards an NDB, the ADF readings are:

Time 1: MH 055, RMI 060 and on track; Time 2: MH 055, RMI 057.

Is the aircraft left or right of track?

10 To track towards an NDB on a track of 340°M, with an expected crosswind from the right causing 5° of drift, what magnetic heading should you steer, and what will you expect the RMI to indicate?

11 To track away from the an NDB on a track of 120°M, with an expected crosswind from the right causing 8° of drift, what magnetic heading should you steer, and what do you expect the RMI to indicate?

12 You wish to track 360°M in nil-wind conditions. What magnetic heading should you steer? What will the RMI indicate as you pass abeam an NDB which is 10 nm to the right of track?

13 You wish to track 360°M and expect 10° of drift caused by a wind from the east. What magnetic heading should you steer? What will the RMI indicate as you pass abeam an NDB which is 10 nm to the right of track?

14 You wish to track 030°M in nil-wind conditions. What magnetic heading should you steer? What will the RMI indicate as you pass abeam an NDB which is 10 nm to the right of track?

15 You are heading 030°M in nil-wind conditions. What is your track? What will the RMI indicate as you pass abeam an NDB which is 10 nm to the left of track?

16 You wish to track 030°M and expect 7° left drift. What magnetic heading should you steer? What will the RMI indicate as you pass abeam an NDB which is 10 nm to the left of track?

17 You are flying on a magnetic track of 239° with 7° of port drift. At a position directly abeam an NDB which is to the left of track, the RMI will read _____.

Exercises 14

The VOR

1 The VOR is a (VHF/LF/MF) radio navigation aid.

2 Many VORs in the UK are coupled with (ILS/DME/NDB/VDF).

3 An aeroplane at 3,000 ft amsl should be able to receive a VOR situated at sea level out to a range of approximately _____ nm.

4 A radial is the (magnetic/true) bearing (to/away from) a VOR ground station.

5 Radial is expressed in the Q-code as _____.

6 You are instructed to track outbound on the 070 radial from a VOR. The more suitable heading is (070/250).

7 You are instructed to track inbound on the 050 radial. The more suitable heading is (050/230).

8 A particular VOR may be identified by its _____.

9 A VOR ground station should transmit to an accuracy of at least ±_____°.

10 VOR stands for _____.

11 The radio set in the cockpit used to select a VOR is the (VHF-COM/ VHF-NAV/ADF).

12 The needle in the VOR cockpit display is known as the CDI (_____).

13 Any one of 360 tracks may be selected in the VOR cockpit display using the OBS (_____), with the selected track displayed on the _____.

14 A 1-dot deviation of the CDI on the VOR cockpit display indicates a displacement of _____° from the selected track.

15 A 2-dot deviation of the CDI on the VOR cockpit display indicates a displacement of _____° from the selected track.

16 A 3-dot deviation of the CDI on the VOR cockpit display indicates a displacement of _____° from the selected track.

17 A 4-dot deviation of the CDI on the VOR cockpit display indicates a displacement of _____° from the selected track.

18 A 5-dot deviation of the CDI on the VOR cockpit display indicates a displacement of _____° from the selected track.

19 If the CDI is centred with 090 selected on the OBI, and the FROM flag showing, what radial is the aircraft on?

20 If the CDI is centred with 090 selected, and the TO flag showing, what radial is the aircraft on?

21 If the CDI is 2 dots right with 090 selected, and the TO flag showing, what radial is the aircraft on?

22 If the CDI is 1dot left with 090 selected on the OBI, and the FROM flag showing, what radial is the aircraft on?

23 Check an aeronautical chart and determine the frequency of the Cranfield VOR (some 40 nm NW of London) and its Morse code ident.

24 What radial from the Cranfield VOR would keep you just to the north of D206?

25 Check an aeronautical chart and determine the frequency of the Newcastle VOR and its Morse code ident.

26 What NEW radial would you track on to the Dean Cross VOR (DCS)?

27 What DCS radial would you be tracking in on from NEW?

28 On the reciprocal track, from DCS to NEW, you would track on the ____ DCS radial and the ____ NEW radial.

29 Specify three means of fixing your position in IMC somewhere along the DCS to NEW track.

30 You depart over DCS at 1427 UTC and pass abeam 'CL' NDB at 1438 UTC. At what time do you estimate NEW?

31 What is the specified designated operational coverage (DOC) of the Dean Cross VOR?

32 You are flying MH 080, with the OBI selected to 080, CDI needle showing 2 dots right, and the FROM flag showing. Your desired track is the 080 radial outbound. Is this track to your left or your right?

33 You are flying MH 300, with the OBI selected to 300, the CDI needle showing 3 dots left, and the TO flag showing. Your desired track is 300°M to the VOR. Is this track out to your left or right?

34 You are flying MH 300, with the OBI selected to 300, the CDI needle showing 3 dots left, and the TO flag showing. If the aircraft is now turned onto the reciprocal heading of MH 120, would the indications in the VOR cockpit display change in any way, assuming the OBI is left unaltered?

35 Specify which of the aircraft illustrated in Figure 1 could have the VOR indications depicted in instruments (i), (ii) and (iii).

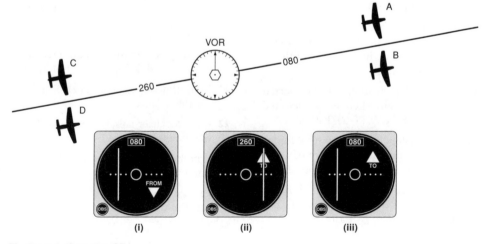

■ *Figure 1* **Question 35**

Exercises 15
The Instrument Landing System (ILS)

1 ILS stands for ____. The ILS is a (precision/non-precision) approach.

2 Name three components of a typical ILS.

3 The ILS is normally selected in the cockpit using the (VHF-COM/VHF-NAV/ADF) radio.

4 In an aircraft fitted with only one VHF-NAV, is it possible to have an ILS and a VOR selected simultaneously?

5 In an aircraft fitted with two VHF-NAVs, is it possible to have an ILS and a VOR selected simultaneously?

6 With the localizer selected, a full-scale deflection of the CDI indicates that the aircraft is ____° or more off the centreline.

7 The localizer track from full-scale deflection left to full-scale deflection right covers an arc of ____°.

8 A 1-dot deflection of the CDI with the localizer selected represents ____°, is which makes the instrument ____ times as sensitive compared to when it is tuned to a VOR.

9 Localizer coverage is ____ nm within ±10° of the front-course line, and ____ nm within 10°–35° of the front-course line.

10 The glideslope is automatically selected when the localizer frequency is selected on the VHF-NAV. (True/False)?

11 A 3° glideslope, which is typical for an ILS, represents a loss of height of approximately ____ ft per nautical mile.

12 At 5 nm from the runway threshold, an aircraft that is on glideslope will be at approximately ____ ft aal.

13 At 2 nm from the runway threshold, an aircraft on glideslope will be at approximately ____ ft aal.

14 To maintain the glideslope at a groundspeed of 60 kt requires a RoD of ____ ft/min.

15 To maintain the glideslope at a groundspeed of 120 kt requires a RoD of ____ ft/min.

16 To maintain the glideslope at a groundspeed of 100 kt requires a RoD of ____ ft/min.

17 There may be false glideslopes:
(a) only above the correct glideslope.
(b) only below the correct glideslope.
(c) both above and below the correct glideslope.

18 The glideslope should always be intercepted from (above/below).

19 As an aeroplane flies in at 1,500 ft aal and intercepts the glideslope from below, the glideslope needle should:
(a) descend from the top of the cockpit indicator.
(b) rise from the bottom of the cockpit indicator.

20 Descent on the glideslope:
(a) should not be commenced unless on track, within half-scale of the localizer.
(b) may be commenced on intercept of the glideslope, even if off track.

21 If the glideslope fails, is it permissible to use the localizer?

22 If the localizer fails, is it permissible to use the glideslope?

23 Can marker beacons be used for homing to a station?

24 Passage over an outer marker is indicated in the cockpit by ____.

25 The localizer usable coverage sector specified in AIC 34/1997 (Pink 141) is ±_____° either side of the nominal course line.

26 The glidepath coverage is _____ nm unless otherwise specified in AIC 34/1997 (Pink 141), and is accurate if the aircraft is within ±_____° left or right of the localizer centreline.

27 The glideslope is nominally _____° to the horizontal. It (may/will never) differ from this.

28 The glideslope, which is nominally 3° to the horizontal, is protected so that it will not give false signals if the aircraft is in the range of _____° to _____° to the horizontal.

Exercises 16
VHF Direction Finding (VDF)

1 VDF stands for _____ .

2 Another abbreviation for VDF is _____.

3 The airborne radio used for VDF is the (ADF/VHF-NAV/VHF-COM).

4 QDM is defined as _____.

5 QDR is defined as _____.

6 A Class B VDF bearing is accurate to ±_____°.

7 When tracking towards a ground station using the QDMs passed by ATC, the pilot (should/should not) allow a wind correction angle to counter any crosswind effect.

8 When tracking towards a ground station, the QDMs gradually increase: QDMs 340,342,345. The aircraft is moving to the (left/right) of track and should turn (left/right).

9 When tracking towards a ground station, the QDMs gradually decrease: QDMs 340, 336, 330. The aircraft is moving to the (left/right) of track and should turn (left/right).

10 When tracking away from a ground station, the QDMs gradually increase: QDMs 360, 006, 010. The aircraft is moving to the (left/right) of track and should turn (left/right).

11 When tracking away from a ground station, the QDMs gradually decrease: QDMs 360, 355, 350. The aircraft is moving to the (left/right) of track and should turn (left/right).

12 The difference between a VDF approach, in which a pilot requests QDMs from an ATSU, and a QGH approach is _____.

Chapter 17
Introduction to RNAV

1 A pseudo-VOR/DME is a (real/phantom) VOR/DME.

2 A pseudo-VOR/DME can be created (anywhere/anywhere within signal coverage).

3 A pseudo-VOR/DME is created by electronically adding a _____ to the position of the real VOR/DME.

4 The CDI, when being used as part of an RNAV system, displays (angular deviation/crosstrack error).

5 The fixes along an off-airways route are known as _____.

6 LORAN-C uses time-difference measurement from widely separated LORAN stations to fix position using (parabolic/hyperbolic/straight/circular) position lines.

7 Approved GPS aircraft systems (may/may not) be used for VFR navigation.

8 Approved GPS aircraft systems (may/may not) be used for IFR navigation.

9 For positional information, at least (one, two, or three) satellites are needed in order to determine aircraft position.

Instrument Procedures

Exercises 18

Preparation for Flight

This topic will be thoroughly tested in the IMC Rating ground examination. Almost all of it is knowledge that you will have gained from your study of navigation and flight planning in *The Air Pilot's Manual,* Volume 3 (especially Chapter 13, *Compiling a Flight Log*), and Volume 2, *Meteorology* section. These Exercises serve merely to test this knowledge. Reference to the UK AIP will also be required – use its indexes to assist you.

Meteorology

1   An Aviation Routine Weather Report is known as a (METAR/RAF); whereas an Aerodrome Forecast is known as a (METAR/TAF).

2   Sketch the symbols used on meteorological charts to indicate the following:
   (i)   a cold front at the surface.
   (ii)   snow.
   (iii) widespread fog.
   (iv) moderate turbulence.
   (v)   hail.
   (vi) freezing precipitation.
   (vii) severe line squall.
   (viii) thunderstorm.
   (ix) rain.
   (x)   drizzle.
   (xi) showers.
   (xii) severe aircraft icing.

3   Temporary variations lasting less than one hour may have this indicated in a forecast by the use of the word ____.

4   The system of providing meteorological information via the public telephone network as well as by AFTN, telex and facsimile equipment is known as ____.

5   The AIRMET service consists of (1/2/3/4) routine Area Forecasts in (plain/coded) language, issued (1/2/3/4) times daily, covering the (UK only/UK and near Continent) with vertical coverage from the surface to (5,000/10,000/15,000/18,000) ft amsl, with winds and temperatures to (5,000/10,000/15,000/18,000/) ft amsl.

6   When are METARs usually issued at those aerodromes providing the service?

7   What is the validity period of a Trend or Landing Forecast?

8   The forecasts that are available continuously via the public telephone network are issued ____ times daily.

9   When the term NOSIG is used in a Trend or Landing Forecast, it means ____ during the ____ hours after the observation time.

10   If you require a special forecast to cover a flight of less than 500 nm, you should give at least ____ hours' notice.

11   If you require a special forecast to cover a flight of more than 500 nm, you should give at least ____ hours' notice.

12   Decode the following meteorological information for Dundee (EGPN):

TAF EGPN 1322 180 15KT 3000 OVC030 BECMG 1518 1000

Can you operate on an IMC Rating throughout the TAF period? Explain.

13 Decode the following meteorological information for Lydd (EGMD):

TAF EGMD 1018 28020KT 6000 SCT014 BECMG 1215 1200

Can you operate on an IMC Rating throughout the TAF period? Explain.

14 Decode the following meteorological information for Oxford (EGTK):

TAF EGTK 1220 350 15G25KT 1500 OVC010 BECMG 151828015KT 2500 BKNO 15

Can you operate on an IMC Rating throughout the TAF period? Explain.

15 Decode:

TAF EGBN 0814 120 15KT 1800 OVC008 BECMG 1012 BKN012

Can you operate on an IMC Rating throughout the TAF period? Explain.

16 Decode:

SAUK 0820 EGNT 12005KT 8000 HZ SCT014 06/05 Q1018

17 Does the following forecast attached to the METAR for Halfpenny Green indicate that the aerodrome is suitable for an IMC-rated pilot to operate? Explain.

METAR EGBO 0940 230 15G25KT 6000 BKN035 12/09 Q 1003 NOSIG

18 Does the following forecast for Aberdeen indicate that the aerodrome is suitable for IMC-rated pilot to operate throughout the period? Explain.

TAF EGPD 0716 280 16KT 8000 HZ BKN010 BKN035 BKN 100 TEMPO 1214 28025G35KT 1000 RA+ OVC 008

19 If you were unable to obtain a forecast for Inverness/Dalcross, which forecast office would you contact, and on what telephone number?

Safety Altitudes

20 For an IMC flight, a vertical clearance of ____ ft is required above the highest obstacle within ____ nm of track.

21 High obstacles close to your planned track are:

(i) 1,237 ft amsl, 3 nm left of track;

(ii) 2,598 ft amsl, 7 nm right of track; and

(iii) 1,610 ft amsl, 4 nm right of track.

What is the lowest required safety altitude?

22 What is the altitude of an aircraft that is cruising at FL55 if the Regional QNH is 1023 mb?

23 What is the altitude of an aircraft that is cruising at FL55 if the Regional QNH is 1003 mb?

24 What is the altitude of an aircraft that is cruising at FL55 if the Regional QNH is 963 mb?

25 Which of the following are suitable quadrantal levels for an aircraft cruising on a track of 137°M? (FL50/FL55/ FL60/FL65/FL70/FL75/FL80).

26 The highest obstacle within 5 nm of track is 1,950 ft. The Regional QNH is 973 mb. Planned track is 085°M. What is the lowest suitable flight level according to the quadrantal rule?

27 The highest obstacle within 5 nm of track is 2,350 ft. The Regional QNH is 953 mb. Planned track is 045°M. What is the lowest suitable flight level according to the quadrantal rule?

Computer Calculations

28 RAS (CAS) is 95 kt. Calculate TAS at FL50, OAT +5°C.

29 RAS (CAS) is 95 kt. Calculate TAS at FL50, OAT −10°C.

30 RAS (CAS) is 95 kt. Calculate TAS at FL80, OAT +5°C.

31 IAS 95 kt, FL50, OAT −8°C, W/V 300/20, track 010. Calculate heading and groundspeed.

32 What time interval is required to cover a distance of 127 nm to the destination at an average groundspeed of 87 kt? If you depart at 0117 UTC, what is your ETA at the destination?

Charts

For these Exercises, refer to your CAA 1:500,000 ICAO Aeronautical Chart for Southern England (Sheet 2171CD). Consider the area between the aerodromes at Bristol (N51 22.9, W002 42.8) and Bournemouth (N50 46.6, W001 50.3).

33 What is the elevation of Bristol aerodrome?

34 What is the frequency of the Bristol NDB, and what is its Morse code identifier?

35 What is the elevation of Bournemouth aerodrome?

36 What is the bearing and distance from Bristol aerodrome to the Bournemouth locator, BIA, which is on the aerodrome? What is a reasonable safety altitude for this leg, and what approximate time interval could you expect for the flight if your expected average groundspeed is 120 knots?

37 There is an NDB at Compton Abbas which you plan to use en route. What is its frequency and Morse code identifier?

38 What aerial activity occurs in the vicinity of Compton Abbas?

39 What Altimeter Setting Regions will you be passing through when flying from Bristol to Bournemouth?

40 Is a full position report required as you cross from one ASR to the next?

41 Are you required to give a full position report as you pass from one FIR (Flight Information Region) to another – say on a flight north, passing from the London FIR into the Scottish FIR?

42 What is the transition altitude at Bristol?

43 What is the FIS frequency that you would use on the flight from Bristol to Bournemouth?

44 What is the large area surrounded by a thick purple-shaded border which is marked on the chart about 10 nm south of Bristol?

45 What is the nature of the airspace around Yeovilton aerodrome?

46 On what frequency would you request a Lower Airspace Radar Service, LARS, in the vicinity of Yeovilton?

47 Within what distance of a participating ATSU is LARS normally available?

48 How could you identify the Yeovilton aerodrome identification beacon, if it is in operation?

49 If, while en route, you decided to penetrate a MATZ, where could you find the appropriate procedures to use, and what would be your initial radio call?

50 What are the radio frequencies for Bristol Tower and Bristol Approach?

51 Who operates Bristol Aerodrome?

52 What is the length of the longest runway at Bristol?

53 Where in the UK AIP would you look to determine the Air Traffic Control rules specific to the Bristol Class D controlled airspace?

54 What is the radio navigation facility situated approximately 22 nm northeast of Bournemouth, and what is its frequency and ident?

55 What is the nature of the airspace surrounding Bournemouth aerodrome?

56 On what VHF–COM frequency would you request permission to enter the Southampton Class D Control Area, if you needed to do so?

57 What details would you specify in your radio call?

58 Where are the loss of communications procedures specified for an aircraft being radar vectored at Bournemouth?

59 About 17 nm SW of Bournemouth is an area labelled P047. What is its significance?

60 About 26 nm SW of Bournemouth is an area labelled D021. What is its significance, and who can assist with crossing information?

61 On what frequency would you listen to a VOLMET covering Bournemouth?

62 A locator beacon, ident BIA, is situated at Bournemouth. What is the range of the locator, and where is it in relation to the aerodrome?

Fuel Calculations

63 You need to uplift 15 US gallons of Avgas. How many litres would you order from the fuel agent?

64 Fuel required at start-up is 43 US gallons. The fuel remaining in your tanks is 13 US gallons. How many litres will you order?

65 Calculate the fuel required for a flight of 100 minutes' duration at an average consumption rate of 9.5 USG per hr, allowing 60 minutes' reserve. What is the margin (in US gallons and in minutes) if there is 48 USG on board?

66 Flight time is 73 minutes. Fuel consumption on the cruise is 7.0 USG/hr, with an additional allowance of 2.5 USG for start-up, take-off and climb to

cruise level. Descent and landing may be calculated at cruise rate.

What is the minimum required fuel on board (FOB) at start-up, allowing 45 minutes' reserve at cruise rate? Give the answer in US gallons and litres.

If the specific gravity is 0.72, what is the weight of the FOB in kg and lb?

67 What total fuel is required to take off for a flight of 63 minutes to a destination for which an alternate aerodrome is required because of poor weather conditions forecast for the time of arrival?

• Flight time to the alternate is 17 minutes.

• Cruise consumption rate is 8 USG/hr.

• Allow 2 USG for climb to cruise altitude.

• Descent and landing may be calculated at cruise rate, although 2 USG should be allowed for an NDB approach at the destination.

• Allow 10.0 USG reserve fuel.

If the fuel on board at take-off is 30.0 USG, how much of this is available for contingencies, calculated at cruise rate?

68 Calculate the fuel required in US gallons for the following flight:

Start-up, taxi, take-off
.... 3 USG
Flight fuel to destination
.... 1 hr 30 mins at 12 USG/hr
Approach and missed approach
.... 3 USG
Alternate fuel
.... 20 mins at 12 USG/hr
Holding
.... 45 mins at 12 USG/hr
Approach and landing
.... 3 USG
Reserve fuel
.... 30 mins at 12 USG/hr

Weight and Balance

69 An aeroplane (may/must not) be flown overloaded.

70 Compared with a correctly loaded aeroplane, an overloaded aeroplane will have (a higher/a lower/the same) stalling speed, (a higher/a lower/the same) acceleration during the take-off run, requiring (a longer/a shorter/the same) take-off distance, (a poorer/a better/the same) rate of climb, (a higher/a lower/the same) maximum operating altitude, (a longer/a shorter/the same) landing distance.

71 An aeroplane that is loaded incorrectly, with the centre of gravity outside limits, (may/will not) be difficult, or even impossible, to control.

72 1 US gallon of Avgas weighs _____ lb.

73 What payload can be carried if the following conditions apply?

Maximum take-off weight authorised
.... 2,200 lb

Pilot weight
.... 180 lb

Aircraft empty weight (including oil and unusable fuel) .... 1,450 lb

Fuel at take-off
.... 25 USG (SG = 0.72)

74 What payload can be carried if the following conditions apply?

Maximum take-off weight authorised
.... 2,550 lb

Pilot weight
.... 180 lb

Aircraft empty weight (including oil and unusable fuel) ...... 1,730 lb

Fuel at take-off
.... 39 USG (SG = 0.72)

IFR

75 Which of the following Instrument Flight Rules apply to a flight by an IMC-rated pilot operating completely outside controlled airspace?

(a) Rule 29: The Minimum Height Rule.

(b) Rule 30: The Quadrantal Rule.

(c) Rule 31: Flight Plan and ATC Clearance.

(d) Rule 32: Position Reports.

76 May a flight plan be submitted for any flight?

77 Must a flight plan be submitted for a flight of 130 nm outside regulated airspace by an IMC-rated pilot in an aeroplane whose maximum total authorised weight is less that 5,700 kg, or is it optional?

78 Must a flight plan be submitted for a flight of 130 nm outside regulated airspace by an IMC-rated pilot in an aeroplane whose maximum total authorised weight exceeds 5,700 kg, or is it optional?

En Route Calculations

79 If 25 nm is covered in 12 minutes, what is the groundspeed? How long will it take to cover a further 15 nm?

80 If the aeroplane is 3 nm left of track after 30 nm, what heading change is required to regain track:

(i) in another 30 nm?

(ii) in 15 nm?

Flight Procedures

81 To within what distance of an approach control unit is a Radar Advisory Service normally limited?

82 Specify the components of a standard position report.

83 Any emergency message or urgency message should be passed on the frequency in use or on the emergency VHF frequency of ____ MHz, and be prefixed by the words ____ or ____.

84 Flight over a congested area should be at an altitude of at least ____ ft above the highest fixed object within ____ metres of the aircraft or at a height at which it can ____ clear in the event of engine failure, whichever is (higher/lower). These low flying regulations are specified in Rule (5/17/21).

85 You are given the following departure clearance, "Turn right on track, not above 2,500 ft QNH until east of the city. "You should fly (at/at or below/at or above) 2,500 ft until east of the city, and not lower than ____.

86 You are given the following departure clearance "Turn left on track, not above 2,000 ft QNH until north of the city." The highest obstacle within 600 metres of the aircraft is 350 ft amsl, and the estimated height needed to glide clear of the small town in case of engine failure is 1,500 ft amsl. You should cross the city at or between the altitudes of ____.

87 When a pilot is using Radar Information Service (RIS) or the Radar Advisory Service (RAS), the responsibility for maintaining adequate terrain clearance rests with the (pilot/radar service controller).

88 RIS controllers will give (traffic information only/traffic information plus advice on collision-avoidance action).

89 RAS controllers will give (traffic information only/traffic information plus advice on collision-avoidance action).

90 While en route, you call the nominated Air Traffic Service Unit to establish if a particular Danger Area is active. You do not get a response. You should assume that the Danger Area is (active/inactive).

91 To cross a Control Zone in Class D airspace around a busy controlled airport, you (should/need not) file a flight plan on the ground or in the air, and then obtain an ____ before entering the airspace. Two-way radio communications with ATC (are/are not) required.

92 If you experience radio failure before entering controlled airspace, you should (continue and land at the controlled aerodrome/remain clear of the controlled airspace and land as soon as possible at a suitable aerodrome).

Visual Illusions

93 Sloping cloud banks by day or town lights on a hillside at night (can/will not) cause visual illusions of a false horizon.

94 The normal approach path to an upwards-sloping runway will appear to be too (steep/shallow), causing a tendency to fly too (high/low) on slope.

95 During a night approach, the apparent gap between the runway edge lights is decreasing. The aeroplane is flying to an aiming point (before/at/beyond) the normal aiming point.

96 Making a 'black-hole approach' at night in clear conditions, with no approach-slope guidance, the runway may appear to be (closer/further away) than it really is, causing a tendency for the pilot to (undershoot/overshoot) the approach.

Exercises 19

Instrument Departures

1 The minimum recommended conditions for take-off by an IMC-rated pilot
in a single-engined aeroplane are:
(i) a cloud ceiling of _____ ft aal; and
(ii) a visibility of _____ metres.

2 SID charts are produced for some busy
aerodromes. SID stands for _____.

3 When climbing to cruise at 3,000 ft
amsl, the altimeter subscale setting
should be on _____.

4 When climbing to cruise above the
transition level, the altimeter subscale
setting should be changed to _____mb.

5 Shortly after departure, you will be
passing near a MATZ with a stub.
Sketch a typical MATZ and stub with
its vertical and horizontal dimensions.

Exercises 20

Holding and Manoeuvring

1 The shape of a typical holding pattern
is a:
(a) circle.
(b) racetrack.
(c) rectangle.
(d) ellipse.

2 A complete one-minute holding
pattern will take _____ minutes if flown
perfectly.

3 In strong head/tailwind conditions, on
the outbound leg of a holding pattern
the timing should be adjusted by _____
second(s) per knot of the estimated
head/tailwind component.

4 With an estimated 15-knot tailwind
component on the outbound leg of a
holding pattern, it is reasonable to
adjust the timing by _____.

5 While tracking guidance is usually
available to you on the inbound leg to
the holding fix, on the outbound leg
there is generally none. In strong crosswind conditions, it is suggested that a
drift correction of _____ be applied on
the outbound leg.

6 If a WCA of 5° to the left is required to
track correctly on the inbound leg of a
holding pattern, then a suitable correction on the outbound leg is _____.

7 Sketch three diagrams of a holding
pattern, showing the three sector
entries.

8 A sector-1 entry is also known as a
_____ entry.

9 A sector-2 entry is also known as a
_____ entry.

10 A sector-3 entry is also known as a
_____ entry.

11 Sketch the pattern of a 45°/180° procedure turn used to reverse direction.

Exercises 21

Instrument Approaches

1 The altimeter setting given to arriving
aircraft will initially be:
(a) standard pressure 1013.2 mb.
(b) Aerodrome QNH.
(c) Aerodrome QFE.
(d) Threshold QFE.

2 The MSA, an abbreviation for ___,
published on *Jeppesen* instrument
approach charts will provide at least
_____ metres, _____ ft, vertical clearance
within _____ nm of the homing facility.
Aerad approach charts show a similar
minimum altitude as _____.

3 The tracks shown on instrument
approach charts are in (°magnetic/
°true).

4 On final approach of an instrument let-down that is closely aligned with the landing runway, it is usual in the UK to have ____ set in the altimeter subscale, so that the altimeter indicates ____.

5 When circling to land on a runway with which the final segment of the instrument approach is not aligned, it is usual in the UK to have ____ set in the altimeter subscale so that the altimeter indicates ____.

6 Name the five possible segments of an instrument approach.

7 A *feeder route* or *terminal route* is an ____ segment.

8 *Crossing heights* and *step-down fixes* shown on an instrument approach chart (are/are not) limiting heights, and (should/need not) be crossed at or above their minimum crossing heights.

9 Descent on the final approach segment of an ILS should not be commenced until the aircraft is within ____ scale deflection of the localizer.

10 Descent on the final approach segment of an NDB or VOR let-down should not be commenced until the aircraft is within ____ of the final approach track.

11 An instrument approach in which both tracking guidance and electronic glideslope guidance is provided is a (precision/non-precision) approach.

12 The term *decision height* applies to a (precision/non-precision) approach.

13 The term *minimum descent height* applies to a (precision/non-precision) approach.

14 The appropriate decision height for an ILS:

(a) will be given to the pilot by ATC.

(b) must be calculated by the pilot.

15 If you do not become visual during a precision approach, then you:

(a) should commence a missed approach at or above your calculated decision height.

(b) should commence a missed approach at or above your calculated minimum descent height.

(c) may track in at your calculated MDH or DH to the aid, from where you should commence a missed approach.

(d) should descend lower in IMC in an attempt to become visual.

16 If you do not become visual during a non-precision approach, then you:

(a) should commence a missed approach at or above your calculated decision height.

(b) should commence a missed approach at or above your calculated minimum descent height.

(c) may track in at your calculated MDH to the MAPt, from where you should commence a missed approach.

(d) may track in at your DH to the MAPt, from where you should commence a missed approach.

(e) should descend lower in IMC in an attempt to become visual.

As an exercise, compare *Aerad* or *Jeppesen* instrument approach charts for the following let-downs with the descriptions and information given in UK AIP, and consider the following questions (to which we will not give answers, since the let-downs will change from time to time). Terms used include: IAF – initial approach fix; IF – intermediate fix; FAF – final approach fix; FAT – final approach track; MAPt – missed approach point.

East Midlands NDB Rwy 09

- What is the date of the chart?
- What radio communications frequencies should be used?
- What is the MSA for an aircraft arriving from the north?
- What is the transition altitude over East Midlands?
- What is the NDB frequency?
- Which radio set is used to select this frequency?
- How would you identify the NDB?
- What is the aerodrome elevation?
- What is the Runway 09 threshold elevation?
- What is your calculated MDH for this approach?
- Why is it MDH, and not DH?
- What visibility do you require to continue the approach to a landing?
- What runway length is available for landing?
- What is your calculated visual manoeuvring OCH if you were to use this approach to become visual for a circling approach onto Rwy 27?
- At or above what height should you be when commencing the outbound leg from the LOM?
- What is the outbound track, and is it stated as °M or °T?
- At or above what minimum height should you be during the procedure turn?
- What is the inbound track?
- What angular deviation from track is considered to be sufficiently on track when inbound before commencing further descent (±5° or ±10°)?

- At or above what height should you remain prior to the locator?
- If not visual at your calculated MDH, may you track in to the aerodrome at this height, or must you immediately commence a missed approach?
- What is the missed approach point for the approach?
- Describe the missed approach.
- What two radio navigation aids can be used for tracking guidance during the missed approach?
- Any climbing instructions passed to you by ATC during the missed approach will be in terms of (altitude/height aal).

Scilly Isles NDB Rwy 28

- What is the date of the chart?
- What is the MSA for an aircraft approaching the Scilly Isles NDB from the northeast?
- For what aeroplane categories is the chart valid?
- What is the frequency of Scillies Approach/Tower?
- What is the transition altitude over the Scilly Isles?
- What is the frequency of the NDB?
- How would you identify it?
- Describe the direct arrival procedure whereby the final approach track is intercepted off the direct track from the VOR LND 242 radial.
- What radio set is tuned to the LND VOR to enable this intercept?
- What radio set is tuned to the STM NDB to enable this intercept?
- At what DME distance from LND should the FAT be intercepted?
- How is the DME selected in the aircraft?
- What is the nominal distance from this point to the runway threshold?

- Is there a DME available at Scilly Isles to assist you?
- Describe the holding pattern.
- What is the inbound track of the race-track procedure?
- What is the minimum height at which the procedure may be commenced?
- How close to the inbound track should the ADF indications be before you commence further descent?
- What is your calculated MDH for this approach? (see our Chapter 19 and UK AIP)
- What is your calculated visual manoeuvring OCH for circling, if necessary? (see UK AIP)
- What is the elevation of the aerodrome?
- What runway length is available for landing?
- At what RoD in ft/min should you descend to achieve a 3° descent gradient if your groundspeed is 90 kt?
- What is the missed approach point (MAPt)?
- Describe the missed approach procedure.
- Are you permitted to use the procedure if your aircraft is not fitted with VOR/DME?

Kirkwall VOR/DME Rwy 27

- What is the date of the chart?
- What radio communications frequencies should be used?
- What is the MSA for an aircraft arriving from the southeast?
- What is the transition altitude over Kirkwall?
- On which navigation facilities is the approach based?
- What is the VOR frequency and which radio set is used to select it?

- Can you make the approach if your DME is unable to receive the KWL DME?
- What is the aerodrome elevation?
- What is Runway 27 threshold elevation?
- What runway length is available for landing?
- What is your calculated MDH for this approach?
- Why is it an MDH rather than a DH?
- What visibility do you require to continue the approach to a landing?
- What is your calculated visual manoeuvring OCH if you were to use this approach to become visual for circling approach onto Rwy 33?
- What is the track for the outbound leg?
- What angular deviation from track is indicated by a two-dot deviation on the CDI? (VHF-NAV tuned to the VOR)
- At what DME distance do you commence the base turn right?
- At or above what minimum height should you be during the base turn?
- What is the final approach track?
- What is the final approach fix?
- How do you determine the IAF when making a direct arrival from the south?
- How do you join the FAT if making a direct arrival from the south?
- What is the minimum height on the DME arc?
- If making the approach without DME, how do you determine the position at which to commence the reversal procedure?
- What percentage is the final approach gradient?
- On this gradient, at what height should you be passing 3 DME on final approach?

- If not visual at your calculated MDH, are you permitted to track in to the aerodrome at this height, or must you immediately commence a missed approach?
- What is the MAPt for the approach?
- Describe the missed approach.
- Any climbing instructions passed to you by ATC during the missed approach will be in terms of (altitude amsl/height aal).

East Midlands ILS Rwy 09

- What is the date of the chart?
- What radio communications frequencies should be used?
- What is the MSA for an aircraft arriving from the south?
- What is the transition altitude over East Midlands?
- What is the localizer frequency?
- Which radio set is used to select this frequency?
- Does the ILS glideslope have to be selected separately, or is it automatically selected with the localizer?
- What is the aerodrome elevation?
- What is the Runway 09 threshold elevation?
- What runway length is available for landing?
- What is your calculated DH for this approach?
- Why is it DH and not MDH?
- What visibility do you require to continue the approach to a landing?
- What is your calculated visual manoeuvring OCH if you were to use this approach to become visual for a circling approach onto Rwy 27?
- What does LOM mean?
- How do you recognise passage of the LOM?

- At or above what height should you be when commencing the outbound leg from the LOM?
- At or above what minimum height should you be during the procedure turn?
- Should the localizer have been intercepted before descent is commenced using the glideslope?
- Before descent on the glideslope can be commenced, what localizer CDI deviation is considered to be sufficiently on track: (full-scale/half-scale/precisely on track)?
- What height at the LOM verifies the accuracy of the glideslope? Is this height amsl (QNH) or aal (QFE)?
- If not visual at your calculated DH, are you permitted to track in to the aerodrome at this height, or must you immediately commence a missed approach?
- What is the MAPt for the approach?
- Describe the missed approach.
- Any climbing instructions passed to you by ATC during the missed approach will be in terms of (altitude amsl/height aal).

Bristol VDF 27

- What is the date of the chart?
- What is the VHF-COM frequency to be used during the approach?
- What is the MSA if the aircraft is approaching Bristol from the northeast?
- What is the transition altitude over Bristol?
- What is the airport elevation?
- What is the commencement height of the VDF/DF procedure?
- What is the track outbound, and what QDM would indicate that you are on track? What QDR would indicate that you are on track?

■ If the QDMs gradually increase on the outbound leg, would you turn left or right to regain track?

■ To what height may you descend on the outbound leg?

■ What QDM would indicate that you are on track when proceeding inbound?

■ If the QDMs gradually increase on the inbound leg, would you turn left or right to regain track?

■ What is your calculated MDH?

■ What is your minimum required visibility to make a landing?

■ What runway length is available for landing?

■ What is the MAPt for the approach?

■ Describe the missed approach procedure.

Edinburgh SRA Rwy 07

■ What is the date of the approach chart?

■ What is the MSA for an aircraft arriving from the southeast?

■ What is the Rwy 07 ILS frequency, to assist with your final approach?

■ How would you identify it?

■ What is the radar termination range (RTR) for the SRA procedure?

■ What is the FAF and what is the minimum height prior to passing it?

■ At what distance and minimum height is the step-down fix?

■ To what locator beacons would you tune to assist in orientation as ATC vectors you towards Runway 07?

■ How would you identify them?

■ What is the MAPt?

■ Describe the missed approach procedure.

■ You break clear of cloud in the final approach area, but suddenly lose radio

contact. What flightpath will you follow until contact is re-established?

■ State the SSR transponder code to squawk if radio contact is not regained?

Exercises 22

Instrument Minima

Take-Off and Landing

1 When planning a take-off in minimum conditions of visibility, a prime consideration, if flying a single-engined aircraft, is to be able to make a safe _____ in the event of engine failure.

2 The recommended minimum conditions for take-off should never be less than _____ ft cloud ceiling or _____ metres visibility.

3 The minimum visibility required for landing for an IMC-rated pilot is _____ .

4 The minimum cloud ceiling required for landing by an IMC-rated pilot descending through cloud for an approach and landing is _____.

5 Should you continue an approach for which the cloud ceiling is reported to be less than your calculated DH or MDH, or the visibility below the value required?

6 Is a visibility of 4,000 given in a METAR sufficient for take-off by an IMC-rated pilot?

7 Is a visibility of 1,500 given in a METAR sufficient for take-off by an IMC-rated pilot?

En Route

8 May an IMC-rated pilot fly in cloud?

9 While cruising in IMC, what is the minimum suitable obstacle clearance?

Approach

10 A precision approach is one in which both tracking and accurate slope guidance is provided. (True/False)?

11 A non-precision approach is one in which both tracking and accurate slope guidance is provided. (True/False)?

12 The minimum height calculated for a precision approach is known as the (decision height/minimum descent height).

13 The minimum height calculated for a non-precision approach is known as the (decision height/minimum descent height).

14 The missed approach following a precision approach in which you do not become visual must be commenced:

(a) as soon as the DA(H) is reached.

(b) at the missed approach point (MAPt) after tracking level to the aid.

15 The missed approach following a non-precision approach in which you do not become visual must be commenced:

(a) as soon as the DA(H) is reached.

(b) at the MAPt, after tracking to the MAPt at or above the MDH.

16 Vertical distance shown on the altimeter when QFE is set is known as (height/altitude).

17 Vertical distance shown on the altimeter when QNH is set is known as (height/altitude).

18 On final approach, it is usual in the UK to have (QFE/QNH/1013 mb) set in the altimeter subscale.

19 The absolute minimum height for a non-precision approach flown by an IMC-rated pilot is ____ ft aal.

20 The absolute minimum height for a precision approach flown by an IMC-rated pilot is ____ ft aal.

21 Obstacle clearance information on instrument approach charts is given in the form of ____.

22 Most training aeroplanes have a nominal threshold speed, V_{AT}, of less than 91 kt and so, for the purposes of obstacle clearance height, fall into Category (A/B/C/D/E).

23 Obstacle clearance information, applicable to Category A aeroplanes, is specified in UK AIP. An IMC-rated pilot must add ____ ft to this, and then take the greater of this value and the absolute minimum of ____ ft aal for a precision approach or ____ ft aal for a non-precision approach, as appropriate.

24 If the published OCH for an ILS is 180 ft, then the system minimum of ____ ft (will/will not) take precedence. To this figure, an IMC-rated pilot (should/should not) add ____ ft as an altimeter position error correction, plus a further ____ ft to obtain a decision height of ____ ft. This (is less than/equals/exceeds) the absolute minimum for an ILS of ____ft, which therefore makes the final decision height ____ ft.

25 If the published OCH for an ILS is 320 ft, then the system minimum of ____ ft (will/will not) take precedence. To this figure, an IMC-rated pilot (should/should not) add ____ ft as an altimeter position error correction, plus a further ____ ft to obtain a minimum descent height of ____ ft. This (is less than/equals/exceeds) the absolute minimum for an ILS of ____ ft, which therefore makes the final minimum descent height ____ ft.

26 If the published OCH for an NDB approach is 600 ft, then the system minimum of _____ ft (will/will not) take precedence. To this figure, an IMC-rated pilot (should/should not) add _____ ft as an altimeter position error correction, plus a further _____ ft to obtain a minimum descent height of _____ ft. This (is less than/equals/exceeds) the absolute mininum for an NDB approach of _____ ft, which therefore makes the final minimum descent height _____. ft.

27 If the published OCH for a VDF approach is 420 ft, then the system minimum of _____ ft (will/will not) take precedence. To this figure, an IMC-rated pilot (should/should not) add _____ ft as an altimeter position error correction, plus a further _____ ft to obtain a mininum desenct height of _____ ft. This (is less than/equals/exceeds) the absolute minimum for a VDF approach of _____ ft, which therefore makes the final minimum descent height _____ ft.

28 (i) What is the published OCH for a Rwy 02 VOR/DME approach at Southampton/Eastleigh, and the recommended minima for an instrument-rated pilot?

(ii) What minima must an IMC-rated pilot use?

(iii) Does the following weather report at Southampton/Eastleigh meet the recommended minima for approach and landing for an IMC-rated pilot?

030 15KT 1400 DZ BKN0600 08/08 Q1015

(iv) What hazards to aviation (if any) would you expect from the weather described in the METAR?

29 What is the published OCH for a Rwy 09 ILS at Jersey, Channel Islands, and what are the recommended minima for an instrument-rated pilot? What minima must an IMC-rated pilot use?

30 During an ILS approach, ATC advises recommended minima of decision height 370 ft and RVR 800 metres. What minima should an IMC-rated pilot use?

31 During an ILS approach, ATC advises recommended minima of decision height 250 ft and RVR 600 metres. What minima should an IMC-rated pilot use?

32 What are the recommended weather minima for an IMC-rated pilot to make a Rwy 13 NDB approach at Plymouth? What are the recommended minima for a Rwy 13 NDB/DME approach?

33 Is it advisable that a pilot be in practice and have flown an instrument approach within the previous few weeks before commencing an instrument approach in poor weather conditions?

34 If you are out of practice, should you increase your personnal minimum height for a particular instrument approach?

35 What instruments would you expect to be affected by the attitude change at the commencement of a missed approach, and for what reasons?

Exercises 23

Visual Manoeuvring

1 For visual manoeuvring (circling) in the vicinity of an aerodrome, a minimum in-flight visibility of not less than _____ metres is recommended.

2 The visual manoeuvring (circling) area for Category A aeroplanes, that circle at less than 100 kt, is _____ nm radius from the runway thresholds.

3 The safety margin for visual manoeuvring in the circling area around an
aerodrome is ____ ft above the highest
obstacle. If the highest obstacle in the
circling area is 370 ft, then the visual
manoeuvring height is ____ ft.

4 If there are no specific obstacles, then
____ ft is allowed for the growth of
trees and foliage, etc., giving the lowest
permissible visual manoeuvring OCH
of ____ ft.

5 What is the visual manoeuvring
(circling) OCH at Guernsey?

6 What is the visual manoeuvring
(circling) OCH at East Midlands?

7 What is the visual manoeuvring
(circling) OCH at Swansea?

8 An IMC-rated pilot can take off or land
if the flight visibility below cloud is
____ metres or greater, and can fly on a
Special VFR clearance in a Control
Zone if the flight visibility is ____ km
or greater.

Appendix 1
The IMC Rating

1 IMC stands for ____.

2 IFR stands for ____.

3 An IMC Rating (is/is not) the same as an IFR Rating, which is also known as an Instrument Rating.

4 An Instrument Meteorological Conditions (IMC) Rating extends the privileges of a Private Pilot's Licence (Aeroplanes) holder to allow flight as pilot-in-command out of sight of the earth's surface.(True/False)?

5 An IMC Rating (extends/does not extend) the privileges of a PPL(A) holder to allow flight as PIC in a Control Zone on a Special VFR clearance with flight visibility less than 8 km but not less than 3 km.

6 An IMC Rating (extends/does not extend) the privileges of a PPL(A) holder to allow flight as PIC when in IMC outside controlled airspace.

7 An IMC Rating (extends/does not extend) the privileges of a PPL(A) holder to allow VFR flight (outside controlled airspace below 3,000 ft amsl) clear of cloud, in sight of the surface, with an in-flight visibility not less than 1,500 m. (Assume an airspeed of 140 kt or less.)

8 An IMC Rating (extends/does not extend) the privileges of a PPL(A) holder to allow flight as PIC during take-off or landing with a flight visibility below cloud of not less than 1,800 m.

9 An IMC Rating (extends/does not extend) the privileges of a PPL(A) holder to allow flight as PIC in controlled airspace under circumstances which require compliance with the Instrument Flight Rules.

10 An IMC Rating allows a pilot to fly in controlled airspace under IFR:
(a) never.
(b) in Entry/Exit Lanes.
(c) below 3,000 ft amsl.
(d) in sight of the surface.

11 An IMC Rating allows a pilot to fly in controlled airspace on an SVFR clearance if the flight visibility is not less than:
(a) 10 nm.
(b) 8 km.
(c) 3 km.
(d) 1,800 m.

12 Is the IMC Rating recognised in the UK?

13 Is the IMC Rating recognised in the Channel Islands?

14 Is the IMC Rating recognised in the Isle of Man?

15 Is the IMC Rating recognised in France?

16 Is the IMC Rating recognised in the USA?

17 Is the IMC Rating recognised anywhere outside the UK, Channel Islands and the Isle of Man?

18 Applicants for an IMC Rating must have _____ hours of experience as an aeroplane pilot since the date of application for their PPL(A).

19 The IMC Rating Certificate of Test, is valid for a period of _____ months from the date of the successful flight test.

20 Your initial flight test for an IMC Rating carried out on May 17th 1995 is successful, and the IMC Rating is issued to you on June 3rd. The last day for which the rating is valid without a further flight test is _____.

21 Your initial flight test for an IMC Rating carried out on December 23rd 1994 is successful, and the IMC Rating is issued to you on January 9th. The last day for which the rating is valid without a further flight test is _____.

22 The minimum flight visibility for take-off and landing for the holder of an IMC Rating is _____ m, below cloud.

Instrument Flying Techniques

Instrument Flying Techniques

1 the flight instruments and what your eyes tell you

2 level, eyes

3 right-banked, the 'leans', use your eyes

4 should, eyes

5 up, backwards, use your eyes

6 down, forwards, use your eyes

7 vertigo

8 can

9 pitot and static pressures

10 static pressure

11 Regional QNH

12 1013.2 mb

13 Aerodrome QNH

14 QFE

15 Aerodrome QNH, causing the altimeter to read *altitude* (UK AIP ENR 1-7)

16 suction

17 suction

18 (b)

19 (b)

20 (c)

21 (c)

22 remain unaffected

23 airspeed indicator only

24 dynamic, pitot, static

25 pitot

26 dynamic, zero

27 increases, too low

28 (c) TAS 108 kt (see Vol. 3, Chapter 2)

29 TAS 115 kt

30 QNH 1012 mb, QFE 985 mb (see Vol. 3, Chapter 6)

31 3,010 ft amsl; no, since 1,000-foot clearance is required

32 sluggish, and lag behind

33 north and south

34 undershoot

35 overshoot

36 reversed

37 smaller near the equator

38 east and west

39 AI, HI and turn coordinator

40 The gyroscope of the AI could run down, causing the AI to become sluggish and erratic.

Radio Navigation Aids

Answers 9

Radar

1   vectoring
2   (b) procedural separation
3   transponder
4   surveillance radar approach
5   300 ft/min
6   450 ft/min
7   1,800 m
8   600 ft aal
9   95 nm
10 55 nm
11 61 nm
12 UK AIP ENR 1-6-9

Answers 10

DME

1   distance-measuring equipment
2   (c) slant distance
3   VHF-NAV
4   10 nm in 5 min = GS 120 kt
5   10 nm in 7 min = GS 86 kt
6   14 nm
7   (a) circular position line

Answers 11

The NDB and the ADF

1   non-directional beacon
2   ground-based transmitter
3   low frequency or medium frequency bands
    (LF/MF)
4   automatic direction finding
5   airborne receiver
6   its Morse code ident
7   *"dah-dit-dit-dit dit-dah-dah-dit dit-dah-dit-dit"*
8   Select the ADF frequency, identify the
    NDB or locator, and check that the needle
    is indeed 'ADFing'.
9   magnetic bearing to the ground station
10 magnetic bearing from the ground station
11 relative bearing indicator

12 (i) QDM 280°M (ii) QDR 100°M
13 (i) QDM 240°M (ii) QDR 060°M
14 25 nm
15 locator
16 LOM (locator outer marker)
17 may
18 may
19 ±5°
20 refer to a CAA 1:500,000 aeronautical
    chart

Answers 12

The Relative Bearing Indicator (RBI)

1   (i) QDM 075, (ii) QDR 255, (iii) QTE 251
2   (i) QDM 330, (ii) QDR 150, (iii) QTE 146
3   right turn onto MH 130, RBI 270
4   right turn onto MH 100, RBI 300
5   right
6   left
7   right
8   060°M
9   right
10 MH 345, RBI 355
11 MH 128, RBI 172
12 MH 360, RBI 090
13 MH 010, RBI 080
14 MH 030, RBI 090
15 030°M, RBI 270
16 MH 037, RBI 263
17 RBI 084
18 RBI 264
19 RBI 275

Answers 13

The Radio Magnetic Indicator (RMI)

1   (i) QDM 075, (ii) QDR 255, (iii) QTE 251
2   (i) QDM 330, (ii) QDR 150, (iii) QTE 146
3   right turn onto MH 130, RMI 040
4   right turn onto MH 100, RMI 040
5   right, RMI 075
6   left, RMI 320, RMI tail on 140

7 left, RMI 270, RMI tail on 090
8 060°M
9 right
10 MH 345, RMI 340
11 MH 128, RMI 300, RMI tail 120
12 MH 360, RMI 090
13 MH 010, RMI 090
14 MH 030, RMI 120
15 030°M, RMI 300
16 MH 037, RMI 300
17 RMI 149

Answers 14

The VOR

1 VHF
2 DME
3 67 nm
4 a radial is a magnetic bearing *from* a VOR ground station
5 QDR
6 MH 070
7 MH 230
8 Morse code ident
9 ±2° accuracy
10 VHF omni-directional radio range
11 VHF-NAV
12 course deviation indicator
13 omni bearing selector, omni bearing indicator
14 2°
15 4°
16 6°
17 8°
18 10° or more
19 090 radial
20 270 radial
21 274 radial (094-TO)
22 092 radial
23 CFD, 116.5 Mhz *"dah-dit-dah-dit dit-dit-dah-dit dah-dit-dit"*
24 CDF 070 radial
25 NEW, 114.25 Mhz, *"dah-dit- dit dit-dah-dah"*
26 258 NEW radial
27 078 DCS radial

28 outbound from DCS on the 078 DCS radial, and inbound to NEW on the 258 NEW radial
29 (i) using the DCS VOR/DME combination to provide a radial and a distance; (ii) using NEW VOR/DME; (iii) using one of the VORs and an abeam position off the Carlisle NDB
30 22 nm in 11 min = GS 120, 38 nm will take 19 min, ETA 1457
31 DOC 60 nm/50,000 ft; 100 nm in the sector 270°–360°T (UK AIP ENR 4-1)
32 desired track is out to the right
33 desired track is out to the left
34 no, the VOR cockpit display is not heading sensitive.
35 (i) aircraft B (ii) aircraft B (iii) aircraft D

Answers 15

The Instrument Landing System (ILS)

1 instrument landing system, precision approach
2 localizer, glideslope, marker beacon(s)
3 VHF-NAV
4 no
5 yes, on different VHF-NAVs
6 2.5°
7 5°
8 0.5°, 4 times
9 25 nm, 17 nm
10 true
11 300 ft/nm
12 1,500 ft aal
13 600 ft aal
14 300 ft/min
15 600 ft/min
16 500 ft/min
17 (a)
18 below
19 (a)
20 (a)
21 yes
22 no
23 No, since they radiate upwards.
24 low-pitched Morse signals *"-dah-dah-dah-dah-dah-"*, accompanied by a flashing blue marker light

25 ±35° (AIC 34/1997 [Pink 141])

26 10 nm (AIC 34/1997 [Pink 141]), ±8°

27 3°, may

28 1.35° to 5.25°

Answers 16
VHF Direction Finding (VDF)

1 VHF direction finding

2 VHF D/F

3 VHF-COM

4 magnetic bearing to the station

5 magnetic bearing from the station

6 ±5°

7 should

8 left of track, turn right

9 right of track, turn left

10 right of track, turn left

11 left of track, turn right

12 In a VDF approach, the pilot initiates his
   own heading corrections based on the
   QDMs given to him, and initiates his own
   descent. In a QGH approach, ATC gives
   the pilot heading and descent instructions.

Chapter 17
Introduction to RNAV

1 phantom

2 anywhere within signal coverage

3 vector

4 crosstrack error

5 waypoints

6 hyperbolic

7 may

8 may

9 three

Instrument Procedures

Preparation for Flight

Meteorology

1 METAR; TAF

2 Refer to Vol. 2, Chapter 25, or to the UK
   AIP GEN 2-3-3 Section.

3 TEMPO

4 AIRMET

5 3, plain, 4 times daily (i.e. every 6 hrs),
   UK and near Continent, 15,000 ft,
   18,000 ft

6 every hour and half-hour (at H and H+30)

7 2 hours from the time of observation

8 four

9 NO SIGnificant change during the two
   hours after the observation time

10 2 hours

11 4 hours

12 Aerodrome Forecast for Dundee, valid for
   the period between 1300 and 2200 UTC;
   wind velocity 180°T at 15 kt, visibility
   3,000 metres, cloud is overcast at 3,000 ft
   aal; becoming, between 1500 and 1800
   UTC, visibility 1000 metres. No, cannot
   operate on an IMC Rating throughout the
   TAF period, but can operate 1300–1500
   UTC, after which the visibility is forecast
   to drop to 1,000 m, which is below the
   IMC-Rating minimum of 1,800 m
   required for take-off and landing at an
   aerodrome outside a Control Zone.

13 Aerodrome Forecast for Lydd, valid from
   1000–1800 UTC, W/V 280°T/20 kt, visibility 6000 metres, scattered cloud (1–4
   OKTAs) at base 1,400 ft aal; becoming,
   between 1200 and 1500 UTC, visibility
   1,200 m. Cannot operate on an IMC
   Rating after 1200 UTC due to visibility
   becoming less than the minimum for an
   IMC Rating (1,800 m) at Lydd (which is
   not in a Control Zone).

14 Aerodrome Forecast for Oxford, valid
   1200–2000 UTC, W/V 350°T/mean

speed 15 kt, with gusts to 25 kt, visibility
1,500 metres, cloud: overcast at base
1,000 ft aal; becoming, between 1500 and
1800 UTC, wind 280°T/15 kt, visibility
2,500 m, broken cloud at base 1,500 ft aal.
Not suitable for IMC-Rated flights until
after 1800 UTC when the visibility
improves from 1,500 m to 2,500 m after
the change which is forecast to arrive
between 1500 and 1800 UTC.

15 Aerodrome Forecast for Nottingham, valid
   0800 to 1400 UTC, W/V 120°T/15 kt,
   visibility 1,800 m, cloud: overcast at base
   800 ft aal; becoming, between 1000 and
   1200 UTC, broken cloud (5–7 OKTAs)
   base 1,200 ft aal. Yes, can operate on an
   IMC Rating throughout the TAF period as
   far as visibility is concerned, but low cloud
   base of 800 ft aal at Nottingham (which has
   no instrument approach) until after 1200
   UTC would require consideration of
   terrain clearance for manoeuvring in the
   circling area – refer to AIP AD 2-10 for
   details of obstacles at Nottingham.

16 SAUK indicates a METAR (surface actual)
   in the UK; observation taken at 0820 UTC
   at Newcastle: W/V 120°T/5 kt, visibility
   8 km, haze, scattered cloud (1–4 OKTAs)
   at base 1,400 ft aal, temperature +6°C,
   dewpoint +5°C, QNH 1018 mb.

17 Yes, the visibility at Halfpenny Green
   (which is outside a Control Zone) exceeds
   the minimum required of 1,800 m, and the
   cloud base at 3,500 ft aal is well above any
   restrictions for an IMC Rating. The gusty
   wind would be a consideration however,
   due to possible crosswind.

18 At Aberdeen, which is in a Control Zone,
   the weather between 1200 and 1400 UTC
   will be unsuitable for an IMC Rating for
   periods less than 60 minutes (TEMPO), as
   the visibility will drop to 2,500 m, which is
   less than the 3 km (3,000 m) required by an
   IMC-rated pilot for a Special VFR clearance in a Control Zone; also, the cloud

base will lower to 800 ft aal, which would require attention to obstacle clearance in the circling area (600 ft clearance required); the gusty and strong winds and heavy rain during the brief periods are also best avoided by light aircraft for flight safety reasons.

19 Glasgow Weather Centre (0141) 221 6116 (UK AIP GEN 3-5-4)

Safety Altitudes

20 1,000 ft within 5 nm

21 2,610 ft on QNH

22 5,800 ft amsl

23 5,200 ft amsl

24 4,000 ft amsl

25 FL55, FL75 (see Vol. 2, Chapter 7)

26 FL50 (safety altitude 2,950 ft amsl, and FL50 on 1013 mb is 3,800 ft amsl when QNH is 973 mb, which is satisfactory since it is above the safety altitude and clears the obstacles by more than 1,000 ft – see Vol. 3, Chapter 6)

27 FL70 (safety altitude 3,350 ft amsl, and FL50 on 1013 mb is 3,200 ft amsl when QNH is 953 mb – not suitable; FL70, however, is 5,200 ft amsl, therefore satisfactory)

Computer Calculations

28 TAS 102 kt

29 TAS 100 kt

30 TAS107 kt

31 TAS 100, heading 360, GS 92

32 ETI 88 min; ETA 0245 UTC

Charts

33 620 ft

34 380 kHz, BRI *"dah-dit-dit-dit dit-dah-dit dit-dit"* (from chart)

35 36 ft

36 138°M, 49 nm; safety altitude 3,000 ft amsl (based on spot height 1995 ft amsl approx. 9 nm south of Bristol – to give 1,000 ft vertical clearance above the highest obstacle within 5 nm of track); ETI 25 minutes

37 349.5 kHz, COM *"dah-dit-dah-dit dah dah dah dah-dah"*

38 hang gliding (chart)

39 Cotswold ASR, Portland ASR (chart)

40 no (UK AIP ENR 1-1-11)

41 yes (UK AIP ENR 1-1-11)

42 3,000 ft aal (UK AIP)

43 London Information on 124.75 MHz (chart)

44 Yeovilton Area of Intense Aerial Activity-AIAA (chart)

45 MATZ (chart)

46 127.35 MHz from Yeovilton (chart)

47 30 nm (UK AIP ENR 1-6)

48 It transmits a two-letter Morse group for VL *"··· − ·−··"* in the colour red. (chart)

49 UK AIP ENR 2-2-2-1; when 15 nm or 5 minutes flying time from the MATZ boundary, whichever is greater, establish radio contact, with the call: "Yeovilton Radar, this is (callsign), request MATZ penetration." When asked to "Go ahead", continue with "callsign and type of aircraft – position – heading – altitude – intentions (destination)."

50 Tower 133.85 MHz; Approach 120.60 MHz (UK AIP AD 2-18)

51 Bristol Airport PLC (UK AIP AD 2-2)

52 Rwy 09/27 is 2,011 metres long (UK AIP AD 2-12, Approach/Landing Charts)

53 UK AIP ENR 1-4-4

54 VOR/DME; 113.35 MHz, SAM (Southampton) *"dit-dit-dit dit-dah dah-dah"*

55 Bournemouth Control Zone (CTR), Class D airspace, from the surface to 2,000 ft amsl, Southampton Control Area (CTS), also Class D, from 2,000 ft amsl to FL55 (chart)

56 120.225 MHz (chart, UK AIP AD 2-18)

57 Call the controlling authority on the appropriate frequency and give details of:
• position;
• level; and
• proposed track

58 UK AIP AD 2 and ENR 1-6, Instrument Approach Charts (Radar Vectoring Area)

59 P047 is a Prohibited Area within which the flight of aircraft is prohibited; it extends from the surface to 1,000 ft amsl for a radius of 2 nm. (chart, UK AIP ENR 5-1)

60 D021 is a Danger Area, from the surface to 1,500 ft amsl, in which naval mortar firing may occur; a Danger Area Crossing Service (DACS) is provided by Plymouth MIL on 124.15 MHz or via London Information on 124.75 MHz (chart).

61 128.60 MHz, London VOLMET-South (UK AIP GEN 3-5-24)

62 Range 20 nm; it is located on the aerodrome (AIP AD 2-19)

Fuel Calculations

63 57 litres

64 30 USG = 114 litres

65

Stage	mins	USG
Route	100	15.8
Reserve	60	9.5
Total	160	25.3
Margin	143	22.7
Total carried	303	48.0

Fuel required is 25.3 USG. With 48 USG on board at start-up, there is 22.7 USG and 143 minutes' margin.

66

Stage	mins	USG
Start, T/O & climb		2.5
Route	73	8.5
Flight fuel	73	11.0
Reserve	45	5.3
Fuel required	118	16.3

Fuel required is 16.3 USG = 62 litres, and this weights 45 kg, which is 99 lb.

67

Stage	mins	USG
Climb	–	2.0
Cruise	63	8.4
NDB let-down	–	2.0
Climb	–	2.0
Diversion	17	2.3
Flight fuel		16.7
Reserves		10.0
Fuel required		26.7

With 30.0 USG on board at take-off, 3.3 USG is available for contingencies, which, at 8 USG/hr, is 24 minutes.

68 46 US gallons

Weight and Balance

69 must not

70 a higher stalling speed, a lower acceleration, a longer take-off distance, a poorer rate of climb, a lower maximum operating altitude, a longer landing distance

71 may

72 6 lb

73 420 lb

74 406 lb

IFR

75 (a) Rule 29: Minimum Height Rule, and (b) Rule 30: Quadrantal Rule (see Vol. 2 of *The Air Pilot's Manual*, Chapter 7)

76 yes

77 optional (UK AIP ENR 1-10)

78 compulsory (UK AIP ENR 1-10)

En Route Calculations

79 125 kt, 7 minutes

80 (i) 12° right using the 1:60 rule; (ii) 18° right

Flight Procedures

81 40 nm of the aerodrome (UK AIP ENR 1-6)

82 "Aircraft callsign, position and time over that position, altitude or flight level, estimate for next position and time over it"

83 121.5 MHz; Mayday for an emergency, Pan-Pan for an urgency message

84 1,500 ft, 600 metres, glide clear, higher, Rule 5

85 at or below, 1,500 ft above the nearest fixed object within 600 metres of the aircraft or the height needed to glide clear in the event of engine failure, whichever is the higher (Rule 5)

86 1,500 ft and 2,000 ft

87 pilot

88 traffic information only

89 traffic information plus advice on collision-avoidance action

90 active

91 should, ATC clearance, are

92 remain clear of the controlled airspace and land as soon as possible at a suitable aerodrome

Visual Illusions

93 can

94 steep, low

95 before

96 closer, undershoot

Instrument Departures

1 (i) ceiling 600 ft, (ii) VIS 1,800 m

2 standard instrument departure

3 Regional QNH

4 1013.2 mb

5 refer to Vol. 2, Chapter 4.

Holding and Manoeuvring

1 (b) racetrack

2 4 minutes

3 1 sec/kt

4 reducing the 60 sec by 15 sec, and flying outbound for 45 seconds

5 3 times the WCA

6 15° right

7 see pages 356 to 357

8 parallel entry

9 teardrop entry

10 direct entry

11 see 360

Instrument Approaches

1 (b) Aerodrome QNH

2 minimum sector altitude, 300 m (1,000 ft) vertical clearance within 25 nm, sector safe altitude

3 °magnetic

4 QFE Threshold, altimeter indicates height above the runway threshold

5 Aerodrome QFE, altimeter indicates height above aerodrome elevation

6 arrival segment; initial approach segment; intermediate approach segment; final approach segment; missed approach segment

7 arrival segment

8 are, should

9 half-scale

10 ±5°

11 precision approach

12 precision approach

13 non-precision approach

14 (b)

15 (a) [option (d) is a recipe for disaster!]

16 (c)

Instrument Minima

Take-Off and Landing

1 a safe forced landing

2 600 ft cloud ceiling, 1,800 m visibility

3 1,800 m

4 at or above your calculated DH for a precision approach or your MDH for a non-precision approach (read the warning in AIP AD 1-1-2)

5 no (AIP AD 1-1-2)

6 yes

7 no

En Route

8 yes

9 1,000 ft above the highest obstacle within 5 nm of track, or above the highest MEF for the proposed route

Approach

10 true

11 false

12 decision height, DH

13 minimum descent height, MDH

14 (a)

15 (b)

16 height

17 altitude

18 QFE

19 600 ft aal (AIP AD 1-1-2)

20 500 ft aal (AIP AD 1-1-2)

21 obstacle clearance height (OCH)

22 Category A

23 Add 200 ft, precision approach 500 ft aal, non-precision approach 600 ft aal

24 ILS system minimum of 200 ft takes precedence, plus PEC 50 ft, plus 200 ft =DH 450 ft, which is less than ILS absolute minimum 500 ft; therefore final DH = 500 ft.

25 OCH 320 ft takes precedence over ILS system minimum of 200 ft, plus PEC 50 ft, plus 200 ft = DH 570 ft, which exceeds the ILS absolute minimum of 500 ft; therefore final DH = 570 ft

26 OCH 600 ft takes precedence over the NDB system minimum of 300 ft (no PEC required as already included for a non-precision approach), plus 200 ft for an IMC-rated pilot = MDH 800 ft, which is greater than the absolute minimum for a non-precision approach of 600 ft; therefore final MDH is 800 ft.

27 OCH 420 ft takes precedence over the VDF system minimum of 300 ft (no PEC required as already included for a non-precision approach), plus 200 ft for an IMC-rated pilot to give MDH 620 ft, which is greater than the absolute minimum for a non-precision approach of 600 ft; therefore final MDH is 620 ft.

28 (i) AIP gives OCH 500 ft for Rwy 02 VOR/DME SAM

(ii) Minima published for an instrument-rated pilot are MDH 500 ft, RVR/MET VIS 1,100 metres; consequently minima for an IMC-rated pilot are (500 + 200) =

MDH 700 ft aal, and minimum visibility of 1,800 m.

(iii) No, on two counts: cloud base 600 ft aal is below MDH 700 ft aal, and visibility 1,400 m is less than the IMC Rating permitted visibility of 1,800 m.

(iv) Hazards include low cloud and poor visibility, and also the possibility of fog/mist and carburettor icing, because OAT +8°C and dewpoint +8°C indicates 100% relative humidity, so very moist air, and any further cooling in the carbutettor could cause icing, especially when low engine power is set, as on approach.

29 OCH 139, DH 250, RVR/VIS 800 m. For an IMC-rated pilot: DH 500 (ILS absolute minimum 500 exceeds 250 + 200 = 450), visibility 1,800 m (AIP AD 1-1-2)

30 DH 570 (370 + 200 exceeds absolute minimum 500 ft),VIS 1,800 m

31 DH 500 (absolute minimum exceeds 250 + 200),VIS 1,800 m

32 Rwy 13 NDB: MDH 1,110 ft,VIS 1,800 m; Rwy 13 NDB/DME: MDH 650 ft,VIS 1,800 m (AIP)

33 yes

34 yes, and it is recommended that as least 100 ft be added to the minimum height for the approach.

35 The pressure instruments (ASI, altimeter and VSI) may show temporary errors due to fluctuations in the pressure readings from the static vent and the pitot tube with the pitch attitude change.

Answers 23

Visual Manoeuvring

1 2,000 m

2 1.68 nm radius from the runway thresholds

3 300 ft safety margin; visual manoeuvring OCH 670 ft aal

4 100 ft; lowest permissible visual manoeuvring OCH 400 ft

5 450 ft aal (AIP)

6 500 ft aal (AIP)

7 520 ft aal (AIP)

8 1,800 m, 3 km

Appendix 1
The IMC Rating

1   Instrument Meteorological Conditions
2   Instrument Flight Rules
3   is not
4   true
5   extends
6   extends
7   extends
8   extends
9   does not extend
10 (a) never
11 (c) 3 km
12 yes
13 yes
14 yes
15 no
16 no
17 no
18 25 hours
19 25 months
20 June 16th, 1997
21 January 22nd, 1997
22 1,800 m

Abbreviations

aal above aerodrome level
ADF automatic direction finder
agl above ground level
AH artifical horizon
AI attitude indicator
AIP Aeronautical Information Publication
ALT altitude
ALTN alternate aerodrome
amsl above mean sea level
ASI airspeed indicator
ASR Altimeter Setting Region; approach surveillance radar
ATC Air Traffic Control
ATIS automatic terminal information service
ATSU Air Traffic Service Unit
BFO beat frequency oscillator
CAP Civil Air Publication
CAS calibrated airspeed
CDI course deviation indicator
CTA Control Area
CTR Control Zone
DA decision altitude; density altitude
DA(H) combination of DA & DH (*Jeppesen* approach charts)
DF direction finding
DG directional gyro
DH decision height; density height
DI direction indicator
DME distance-measuring equipment
DOC designated operational coverage
DR deduced reckoning
EAT expected approach time
EPR engine pressure ratio
EGT exhaust gas temperature
ELEV elevation
FAF final approach fix
FAP final approach point
FAT final approach track
FL flight level
g g-force
GP glidepath
GS glideslope; groundspeed

HAT height above threshold (*Jeppesen* approach charts)
HDG heading
HF high frequency
HI heading indicator
hPa hectopascals
HSI horizontal situation indicator
IAF initial approach fix
IAP instrument approach procedure
IAS indicated airspeed
ICAO International Civil Aviation Organisation
IF intermediate approach fix
IFR Instrument Flight Rules
ILS instrument landing system
IMC Instrument Meteorological Conditions
ISA International Standard Atmosphere
kHz kilohertz
L locator beacon
LARS Lower Airspeed Radar Service
Lctr locator beacon (*Jeppesen* approach charts)
LF low frequency
LITAS low-intensity two-colour approach slope system
LLZ localizer
LOC localizer (*Jeppesen* approach charts)
LOFT line-oriented flight training
LOM locator/outer marker
LOP line of position
°M degrees magnetic
MAP missed approach point (*Aerad* and *Jeppesen* charts); Aeronautical Maps and Charts (section of the AIP)
MAPt missed approach point
MATZ Military Air Traffic Zone
MB magnetic bearing
mb millibars
MDA minimum descent altitude
MDA(H) combination of MDA and MDH (*Jeppesen* approach charts)
MDH minimum descent height
MEF maximum elevation figure

MF medium frequency
MH magnetic heating
MHA minimum holding altitude
MHz megahertz
MLS microwave landing system
MM middle marker
MSA minimum sector altitude (*Jeppesen* approach charts); minimum safe altitude
MSL mean sea level
MTI moving target indicator
NDB non-directional beacon
nm nautical miles
OBI omni bearing indicator
OBS omni bearing selector
OCA obstacle clearance altitude
OCA(H) combination of OCA and OCH (*Jeppesen* approach charts)
OCH obstacle clearance height
OM outer marker
OPS operations
PANS-OPS Procedures for Air Navigation Services – Aircraft Operations
PAPI precision approach path indicator
PAR precision approach radar
PEC position error correction
PL position line
PPI plan position indicator
QDM magnetic bearing to station
QDR magnetic bearing from station
QFE altimeter setting (for aerodrome level)
QGH (approach) an ATC-assisted VDF-type approach
QNE pressure height (1013.2 mb or hPa)
QNH altimeter setting (for height above mean sea level, i.e. altitude)
QTE true bearing from the station
RAS Radar Advisory Service; rectified airspeed
RB relative bearing
RBI relative bearing indicator
RDL radial
RIS Radar Information Service
RMI radio magnetic indicator
RNAV area navigation

RNC radio navigation chart
RoD rate of descent
R/T; RTF radiotelephony
RVR runway visual range
RWY runway
SID standard instrument departure
SRA surveillance radar approach
SSA sector safe altitude (*Aerad* approach charts)
STAR standard terminal arrival route
°T degrees true
TACAN tactical air navigation radio navaid (military)
TAS true airspeed
TCA Terminal Control Area (usually TMA)
TCH threshold crossing height
TDZ touchdown zone
TDZE touchdown zone elevation (*Jeppesen* approach charts)
THR threshold
TMA Terminal Control Area
TTS time to station
UHF ultra-high frequency
UTC coordinated universal time
VASI(S) visual approach slope indicator system
V_{AT} nominal speed at threshold
VDF VHF direction finding
V_{FE} maximum flaps extended speed
VFR Visual Flight Rules
VHF very high frequency
VIS visibility
V_{LE} maximum landing gear (undercarriage) extended speed
VMC Visual Meteorological Conditions
VMH visual manoeuvring height
V_{NE} never-exceed speed
VOR VHF omni range
VORTAC VOR and TACAN combination
VRP visual reference point
VSI vertical speed indicator
WCA wind correction angle
W/V wind velocity

Index

W

Z